Second Edition

INTERVIEWING AND INVESTIGATION

SMART TALK

Denise Kindschi Gosselin

Professor Emerita, Criminal Justice and Sociology
Western New England University

 Pearson

330 Hudson Street, NY NY 10013

Vice President, Portfolio Management: Andrew Gilfillan
Portfolio Manager: Gary Bauer
Editorial Assistant: Lynda Cramer
Field Marketing Manager: Bob Nisbet
Product Marketing Manager: Heather Taylor
**Director, Digital Studio and Content
  Production:** Brian Hyland
Managing Producer: Jennifer Sargunar
Content Producer: Rinki Kaur
Manager, Rights Management: Johanna Burke
Operations Specialist: Deidra Smith
Creative Digital Lead: Mary Siener

Managing Producer, Digital Studio: Autumn Benson
Content Producer, Digital Studio: Maura Barclay
Full-Service Management and Composition: Integra Software
  Services Pvt. Ltd.
Full-Service Project Manager: Kiran Kumar
Cover Designer: Studio Montage
Cover Art (or Cover Photo): Katarzyna Bialasiewicz/123RF,
  Photographee.eu/Shutterstock, Fstop123/E+/Getty Images
Printer/Binder: LSC Communications, Inc.
Cover Printer: Phoenix Color/Hagerstown
Text Font: Times LT Pro

Library of Congress Cataloging-in-Publication Data

Names: Gosselin, Denise Kindschi, 1954- author.
Title: Interviewing and investigation : smart talk / Denise Kindschi
    Gosselin, Professor Emerita of Criminal Justice, Western New England
    University.
Other titles: Smart talk
Description: Second edition. | Upper Saddle River, New Jersey : Pearson
    Education, [2019] | Earlier edition published in 2007 as: Smart talk :
    contemporary interviewing and interrogation.
Identifiers: LCCN 2017045994| ISBN 9780134868196 | ISBN 0134868196
Subjects: LCSH: Interviewing in law enforcement. | Police questioning.
Classification: LCC HV8073 .G67 2018 | DDC 363.25/4--dc23 LC record available at
https://lccn.loc.gov/2017045994

ISBN 10:   0-13-486819-6
ISBN 13: 978-0-13-486819-6

1 17

Dedicated to Cynthia & Jeffrey Schneider, with love and friendship.
Life is a daring adventure to share and enjoy, made even better with family.

BRIEF CONTENTS

CONTENTS

PREFACE

NEW TO THIS EDITION

All chapters have been updated to include the most current methods of interviewing and interrogation.

- To address the changing use of technology, new to chapter 1 is a discussion on cyber informants as a source of investigative interviewing.
- Cutting edge communication styles are included in Chapter 3 with a new section on *Communicating Through Social Media*.
- Continuing with the emphasis on technology, is a new discussion of online interviewing in Chapter 4 as a form of structured interviewing. Acknowledging the changing criminal justice environment for interviewing, added to chapter 4 is a new section on *Group Interviewing*. The addition should stimulate conversations on those situations where single person interviewing is not feasible. The *Scientific Content Analysis* (SCAN) approach to eliciting information is a newly included method to detect deceit through statement analysis.
- New to Chapter 5 are multiple interviewing methods under the category of *Differential Recall Enhancement* (DRE). DRE methods have been assigned significant creditability for interviewing purposes. These include *the Assessment Criteria Indicative of Deception* (ACID), the cognitive load approach, *Strategic Use of Evidence* (SUE) and tactical interviewing.
- New to chapter 6 are *Reality Monitoring* (RM) and *Criteria Based Content Analysis* (CBCA) which have emerged as scientifically valid methods of detecting deceit using the verbal cues in an interview.
- New to this second edition is an entire chapter devoted to *Victim Informed Interviewing*. The new Chapter 7 discusses the *Trauma Informed Victim Approach*, with suggestions on communicating with high-risk victim populations. Students will learn of the crimes involving trafficking in persons. The *Enhanced Cognitive Interview* and *Forensic Experiential Trauma Interview* are compared.
- Improvements in recent years for interviewing children is attributed to an interview protocol known as the *National Institute of Child Health and Human Development* (NICD) method, which is new to chapter 8.
- Chapter 12 has been expanded to include a new discussion on the shortcomings of *Miranda* and Factors in False Confessions.
- Numerous confession-eliciting models are outlined in chapter 13 along with new sections on the *Reid technique*, *PEACE model*, and *HUMINT*.

INSTRUCTOR SUPPLEMENTS

Instructor's Manual with Test Bank. Includes content outlines for classroom discussion, teaching suggestions, and answers to selected end-of-chapter questions from the text. This also contains a Word document version of the test bank.

TestGen. This computerized test generation system gives you maximum flexibility in creating and administering tests on paper, electronically, or online. It provides state-of-the-art features for viewing and editing test bank questions, dragging a selected question into a test you are creating, and printing sleek, formatted tests in a variety of layouts. Select test items from test banks included with TestGen for quick test creation, or write your own questions from scratch. TestGen's random generator provides the option to display different text or calculated number values each time questions are used.

PowerPoint Presentations. Our presentations are clear and straightforward. Photos, illustrations, charts, and tables from the book are included in the presentations when applicable.

To access supplementary materials online, instructors need to request an instructor access code. Go to **www.pearsonhighered.com/irc**, where you can register for an instructor access code. Within 48 hours after registering, you will receive a confirming e-mail, including an instructor access code. Once you have received your code, go to the site and log on for full instructions on downloading the materials you wish to use.

ALTERNATE VERSIONS

eBooks. This text is also available in multiple eBook formats. These are an exciting new choice for students looking to save money. As an alternative to purchasing the printed textbook, students can purchase an electronic version of the same content. With an eTextbook, students can search the text, make notes online, print out reading assignments that incorporate lecture notes, and bookmark important passages for later review. For more information, visit your favorite online eBook reseller or visit www.mypearsonstore.com.

ACKNOWLEDGMENTS

My appreciation to the following reviewers for their helpful comments on the earlier drafts of these chapters:

Dawn Vaughan
Pitt Community College

June Rogers

Jo Ann Grode
Mid-State Technical College
Wisconsin Rapids, Wi

Bruce Delphia
ECPI Technical College
Richmond, VA

Carol Mathews
Century College
White Bear Lake, MN

I owe a special debt of gratitude to my friend and colleague Dawna Komorosky of California State University at Hayward, whose careful reading and suggestions early on contributed significantly to the first edition of the text and the *Instructors Manual*. I thank Patrick J. Faiella of Massasoit Community College, Canton, Massachusetts, who tirelessly read the manuscript and provided insight along with many of the end-of-chapter questions. To my friend and husband, Robert, thank you for your limitless ideas and unwavering support.

Finally, I also thank my friends, colleagues, and students at Western New England University, who encouraged and supported my efforts.

ABOUT THE AUTHOR

A pioneer in law enforcement, the author was the first uniformed female officer in her hometown, Lunenburg, Massachusetts, and the first female campus police officer at the community college she attended. The Massachusetts Senate honored her in 1978 as the first woman appointed constable for the City of Fitchburg. In 2011, Dr. Gosselin was named *Alumna of the Year* at Mt. Wachusett Community College where she now serves as a member on the Board of Trustees.

Denise graduated in the 61st Recruit Training Troop of the Massachusetts State Police in January 1980. During the years that followed she served as a uniformed officer performing route patrol activities, as an instructor at the Massachusetts State Police Academy, and as a detective in major crime investigations. Recognized as a local expert in child abuse investigation, she has spoken on cable television and radio. She appeared on the *America's Most Wanted* television show in connection with a fugitive in a case she was investigating. She has made many presentations at professional meetings with the Department of Social Services, Department of Mental Health, and Office of the District Attorney. She has testified in numerous major crime cases in both criminal and civil hearings.

Dr. Gosselin served as a faculty member and Department Chair in the Criminal Justice and Sociology Department at Western New England University until her retirement as Professor Emerita in 2017. Her other publications include *Heavy Hands: An Introduction to the Crimes of Family Violence*, currently in its sixth edition, and *Crimes and Mental Disorders: The Criminal Justice Response.* Dr. Gosselin has contributed to the *Encyclopedia of Police Science*, the *Encyclopedia of Juvenile Justice*, and the *Encyclopedia of Domestic Violence*, as well as chapters to *Women, Law, & Social Control* and *Policing & Victims.*

Denise is an experienced Criminal Justice Program Reviewer. Her major presentations and invited lectures have been at the 12th United Nations Congress on Crime and Criminal Justice in Salvador, Brazil; the Massachusetts State Police Academy, at West Point Military Academy, Campbell University, NC; and at Gwynedd-Mercy College, PA.

As a life-time member of the *Academy of Criminal Justice Sciences* (ACJS), Denise has served as Region One Trustee 2013–2016 and ACJS Trustee-at-Large 2009–2012. As a member of the *Northeastern Association of Criminal Justice Sciences*, she has served as President, Vice President, and Secretary. Dr. Gosselin is also a member of the European Society of Criminal Justice and is a co-founding member of the Everywoman Everywhere Workgroup, from the Harvard Kennedy School project of the International Commission on Violence Against Women and Girls.

PART I

Laying the Groundwork for Success

This text is about effective communication; it provides the guidelines for gathering information. Chapter 1 stresses the process of communication and the skills required of an interviewer. This chapter defines interviewing and interrogating. Understanding the differences between interviewing and interrogation is critical for choosing the appropriate fact-gathering approach. Interviewing requires a flexible process dictated by the nature of the individual being interviewed. Interrogating requires the use of accusatory persuasion. The chapter also addresses the personal qualities needed by an interviewer: knowledge about the people being interviewed, the case being investigated, and the professionalism that is brought to bear in the process. The development of rapport is critical to successful interviewing and is discussed extensively. An introduction to kinesic communication is also included.

In Chapter 2 the importance of understanding the point of view of the interviewee is recognized and is discussed through social systems theory. A three-phase approach to interviewing is suggested that provides a general framework for the process: preparation, establishing the psychological content, and the actual questioning. Preparation before the interview is as important as the questioning itself. The options for determining when and where the interview should take place are covered. The potential problem of misinformation and its resulting contamination of the interview is outlined. Extensive coverage is given to the types of questions to use in the final phase of interviewing. An important aspect of successful interviewing is knowing which questions illicit the desired responses and which facilitate answers.

Building on the previous chapters, Chapter 3 discusses how to prepare for the questioning. The goals of persuasive interviewing are met by examining the nature of the offense, determining whether a crime was committed, and identifying the perpetrator. Some general approaches to define the nature of the offense and interviewing approaches for victims in specific crime situations are presented. Basic procedures for perpetrator identification are outlined. This chapter also builds on the concept of rapport introduced in Chapter 1. The final section introduces the reader to methods of assessing statement accuracy.

1

Interviewing and Interrogation

Source: Bialasiewicz./123RF.

CHAPTER OBJECTIVES

After completing this chapter, you should be able to:

1. Describe the communication process according to the scheme presented by D. K. Berlo.
2. Define *interview*.
3. List the sources of investigative interviewing.
4. Define *interrogation*.
5. State the purpose of an interview.
6. State the purpose of an interrogation.
7. Describe the qualities of a good interviewer.
8. Explain how rapport affects the quality of the process.

KEY TERMS

Cyber informant	Rapport
Interrogation	Suspect
Interview	Victim
Kinesic	Witness

INTRODUCTION

Crimes are solved when someone decides to talk. The talker's level of cooperation is influenced by the communication skills of the interviewer. Enhancing these skills may improve the quality and quantity of credible information made available during an interview or interrogation. The first lesson in communication involves an acknowledgment that the perceptions of both the interviewee and interviewer will influence the dialogue. Communication includes the exchange of thoughts, messages, or information by speech, signals, writing, or behavior. In this chapter, the processes of communication as envisioned by D. K. Berlo are used to illustrate the complexity of communication. Communication is the core of all interviewing or interrogation. The theory may explain or expand the reasoning for the interviewing and interrogation practices. You will find the theoretical concepts in the introduction of each chapter. Think about the theory presented as you read the rest of the chapter.

Berlo's Source Message Channel Receiver (SMCR) model describes a communication process as an interrelated scheme involving the four most important parts of communication: source, message, channels, and receiver (Berlo, 1960) (Figure 1-1). For an interview to take place between two people, communication must occur back and forth between the individual who initiates the interaction (the source) and the one who

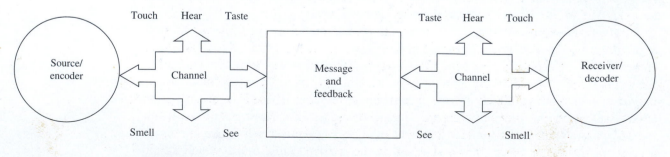

FIGURE 1-1 Berlo's SMCR model.

receives and interprets the meanings (the receiver). The message is made up of content, which is coded (stated) so that it will be received in the way that it is intended. The code is a system of agreed-on communication; it could be the English language, Morse code, sign language, images on motion picture film, and so on.

The substance of the communication is given meaning by an interpretation using the five senses through the channels of seeing, hearing, touching, feeling, and tasting. Interest and prejudice affect the reception, rejection, and filtering of the transmission. The process of meaning is affected by the stimulus. A stimulus is anything that a person can receive through one of his or her senses, anything that can produce a sensation in the human organism. The stimulus reaches the sense organs and is *decoded* by them. One sets about *interpreting* this stimulus while determining what an appropriate *response* might be.

Four factors affect the transmission of the message: communication skills, knowledge level, sociocultural system, and attitudes. The source will make assumptions about the receiver based on these variables; the receiver will do the same regarding the source. The messages back and forth will depend on the opinions formed of the other person according to the senses, which determine how the messages are being received. If the source determines that the receiver is "stupid," he or she will phrase questions based on that opinion; the receiver may sense that "he thinks I am stupid" and form the opinion that the source is arrogant!

Many factors influence the ability to remember and recount experiences or things learned. Among these are the memory, external circumstances, and internal processes. Memory is a fluid progression that incorporates past experiences, beliefs, prejudices, and information gathered through the senses (Sullivan, 2016). External circumstances include things like weather, sight, and proximity to an event. How a person feels and is impacted by an event shapes the perception of the viewer. It is commonly acknowledged that statements from multiple people witnessing the same event are likely to be different even when no one is lying. Hence, a person's perspective is his or her reality. The recall is further influenced by internal processes such as intellectual acuity, mental well-being, and physical wellness. Traumatic events are well known to cause a perceptual narrowing of the senses and memory loss among those experiencing high stress (Sullivan, 2016). Victims, witnesses, suspects, and cyber informants may all experience memory distortion and communicate inaccurate details.

The methods and concepts that are described in this text have broad professional applicability. Individuals who use these skills include all government officials tasked with investigations, including, but not limited to, corrections officers, parole officers, police officers, and probation officers. Interviewing proficiency also benefits individuals in civilian employment such as forensic interviewers, human resources personnel, private investigators, school administrators, social service employees, and social workers. Criminal justice, sociology, and psychology students find ideas for improved communication through the methods used in interviewing. Other professions have similarly high needs for the ability to obtain information through interviews. Interviewing and interrogation are complex tasks that can be learned through education and training. To master the art requires training, which includes meaningful practice opportunities to experience the roles of both the interviewer and the interviewee (Olson, 2016).

Investigative interviewing and interrogation are directed by principles of fairness and constrained by law. Procedures and policies outline the legal limitations, which are rooted in the U.S. Constitution through decisions of the Supreme Court. Unfortunately, their guidance is often conflicting, and states are left to interpret the guidelines for taking statements from public employees and criminal suspects. There is often confusion about the protections and requirements during investigations. Most notably concern the *Miranda* rights, which protect the right of a person against self-incrimination in a criminal matter. A lesser known standard is the *Garrity* Rule, under which public employers may compel their employees to answer questions during an investigation related to the performance of official duties (Woska, 2013). Workplace investigation interviews occur for various reasons, including reports of misconduct, sexual harassment, safety issues, security breaches, student complaints, theft, and other problems.

THE SOURCES OF INVESTIGATIVE INTERVIEWING

An **interview** is a practice of fact finding that elicits information that can lead to conclusions about an event or incident. The core of interviewing is the process of communication. The methods of interviewing are as diverse as its many applications. During an interview, the oral evidence is obtained regarding events that are under investigation. Traditionally, a person is questioned during an interview and assessed by the interviewer for credibility through objective, nonaccusatory conversation. Indirect verbal evidence may also be gathered from social media sources, which contain statements spontaneously made without investigative prompting. The verbal evidence is most valuable during the early stages of an investigation. On the other hand, an interrogation is an exercise in persuasion. If an interviewee is perceived as unwilling to tell the truth, an interview may evolve into an interrogation. The decision to conduct an interrogation may also be at the point when the focus of the investigation moves the individual from witness to suspect.

Before learning about the methods for eliciting information, it is important to understand the categories for verbal communication that may be involved in the process. The four sources of investigative interviewing are victims, witnesses, suspects, and cyber informants. The categories are not mutually exclusive, and they sometimes overlap. For example, there are situations in which the assumed victim turns out to be the perpetrator, or in which the witness may also be a victim. Individuals through social media may make statements regarding culpability. Sometimes the suspect is identified as a victim. Further confusing the process is that the reported incident may not constitute a violation. The investigator determines whether the report does constitute an actionable event.

Victims

A **victim** is the person who is the object of an incident, crime, or other harm. All states have laws to address the needs of victims of crime. Federal crime victims are defined and afforded remedies under the Crime Victims' Rights Act. The Act defines the term "crime victim" as "a person directly and proximately harmed as a result of the commission of a Federal offense or an offense in the District of Columbia" ("The Crime Victims' Rights Act," 2016). Among the ten stated rights, a crime victim has the right to be treated with fairness and with respect for the victim's dignity and privacy. The court appoints a suitable representative in cases where a crime victim is under 18 years of age, incompetent, incapacitated, or deceased. Under no circumstance can the defendant be named as a guardian or representative.

For investigation purposes, it is important to establish if there is a relationship between the victim and the perpetrator. Knowledge of a relationship will direct questioning and affect the interpretation of information. A victim may be unwilling or unable to provide information for use against the perpetrator if there is a relationship; the victim may be hesitant to cooperate if they are intimates. Knowledge of the relationship between the victim and the alleged perpetrator may also shed light on the credibility of the statement should that become an issue.

The amount of cooperation varies from person to person and depends greatly on the type of incident that is under investigation. It may also change during or after the interview. A second interview is not assured; therefore, being thorough is essential. Cooperation is among the many issues of concern. The victim could have substantial injuries that put him or her into a coma or cause death. Investigators must be as thorough as possible when interviewing a victim to gain as much information as possible during the first interview.

BEEN THERE . . . DONE THAT! 1-1

There is a tendency to dismiss victim complaints that sound implausible. For example, a woman once reported to me that someone she knew had offered her a ride home. During the ride, he pulled the car over in a remote area and demanded that she have sex with him. When she refused, he strangled her to unconsciousness. Waking up in the trunk of the car, according to the victim, she sensed he drove for about an hour before stopping and opening up the trunk. He seemed surprised to find her alive. She pleaded with him not to throw her over the bridge, which seemed to be his intent. He carried her to the passenger side of the car instead and then drove her home. She came right to the police department and reported that someone had tried to kill her. Hearing the account, I obtained a warrant to search the interior and trunk of the vehicle. In the trunk was one blonde hair, which was found to be consistent with that of the victim, showing that she had most likely been in that trunk as stated. He was arrested and confessed to crime of kidnapping and assault.

In some cases, the victim may fear that the perpetrator will return for retribution; the victim may feel prejudices against or from the person conducting the interview; the victim may feel tired, angry, or in pain at the time of the interview. It is likely that the person will be under immense stress while being interviewed; stress affects memory and recall (Sullivan, 2016). It is worthwhile to put the interviewee at ease through the establishment of rapport. A second interview may be warranted for taking photographs of bruising that may not appear visible at the initial interview. The victim may be a child or an elder with limited cognitive abilities, a person with an intellectual disability, or someone with something to hide. The victim may be a professor or a student, a prostitute, or a member of the clergy. All of these factors will influence the outcome of the interview.

Witnesses

A **witness** is someone who has knowledge about an incident through personal observation or first-hand experience. Witness information forms the cornerstone of the investigation, yet studies have shown eyewitness reports to be notoriously inaccurate, incomplete, and sometimes unreliable (Milne & Bull, 2016). However, the eyewitness is still of great value to the investigator. The witness can provide valuable information that leads to the perpetrator and ultimately to the offender being held accountable. Since the witness can also give information that is misleading or inaccurate statements must be taken and critically analyzed for their truth, veracity, and relative importance to the case.

Use of techniques to enhance the recall of witnesses is rapidly gaining credibility. Known as cognitive interviewing, this will be explored in depth in Chapter 5. Kinesics and other behavioral approaches to statements are also frequently employed. The traditional interview technique of fact gathering is still valuable for many cases. A frequent complaint from investigators is that they lack the time to sufficiently interview. Case interviewing can be time consuming, and following up the generated leads and corroborating the information is an essential aspect of investigating.

A witness interview is nonaccusatory by the interviewer and may be conducted in a variety of places. The witness may be the person who is making accusations. At the scene of the crime, as many bystanders as possible should be briefly interviewed. One method of handling a large of number of witnesses at a scene is for an investigator to take names and phone numbers first and then interview as time permits. Witnesses may not want to get involved in the situation, and they have a way of disappearing; learning to access the crowd before that can be a challenge.

Witnesses may be reluctant to come forward with information. One reason may be that they simply are unaware that they possess helpful information. Therefore, it is often necessary to seek out witnesses. Many other reasons can contribute to the withholding of information, including not wanting to get involved, the fear that the suspect will retaliate against them for having provided information to the police, a general fear of the suspect, and a relationship to the suspect; it also may come from a distrust of the interviewer. Still others with information will think that the incident is none of their business. Although it is assumed that the witness will be cooperative, that is not always the case. Gentle persuasion may be employed when necessary to encourage witness cooperation.

Witnesses often struggle to provide accurate detail for some reasons. Inconsistencies tend to reduce the value of a statement, but do not necessarily mean that it is fabricated. Children, in particular, may become confused on details of an incident. Receiving similar information from a variety of sources tends to fill in significant voids and can lend credibility to the statement of a child. Perception has a lot to do with differences in reporting. When a manila folder is held up to a group of people, numerous colors will be suggested to describe it. In one study of witnesses who were interviewed about a car chase, those who knew that it had crashed reported the speed of the car to be greater than did those who did not know it had crashed (Abrams, Ramsey, & Mangold, 2015).

Anonymous witness reports should always be regarded with suspicion. In particular, reports from someone who had experienced a personal problem with the accused or is a disgruntled neighbor or when a previous relationship existed are suspect. One should approach these complaints with caution and investigate them thoroughly because it is not unheard of that some complaints get filed in an attempt to get someone in trouble. Conversely, when a relationship goes sour, the reporter may feel free to give information that he or she held back while things were going well. Either way, the investigator would be better off to tread slowly and be thorough.

One cannot anticipate the full effect that stress has on those being interviewed. Some research has suggested that witness accounts are more reliable when the person has been under stress (Abrams et al., 2015), but the opposite effect has also been noted. In highly negative emotional situations, such as witnessing a violent crime, eyewitness accounts are thought to be malleable and subject to influence by the legal system (Smalarz & Wells, 2013). The accuracy of eyewitness evidence has been questioned and reexamined by numerous studies over the years. Often considered unreliable, experts agree that eyewitness identifications are error-prone despite high levels of witness confidence (Wixted, Read, & Lindsay, 2016). Even today, the following principles about witness interviewing represent the characteristics of witnesses (Massachusetts Municipal Police Institute. [1981]. *Police and procedure: Interviewing witnesses.* Unpublished):

1. Witnesses usually see only part of what happens and usually recognize only part of what they see.
2. Witnesses usually remember only part of what they observe and usually describe only part of what they remember.
3. Witnesses who are angry, frightened, or emotionally upset typically perceive only a fraction of what they might observe under normal circumstances.
4. Witnesses often see only what they expect or want to see, and as a result, they provide a distorted version of what happened or an inaccurate physical description of the alleged offender.
5. Witnesses who are involved in violent incidents such as homicides, robberies, rapes, aggravated assaults, and fatal accidents are often unable to provide an adequate description of events or suspects immediately.
6. Witnesses can be affected by some possible physical or emotional factors that may influence the validity of their information.
7. Emotional factors can cause a witness to lie, become uncooperative or forgetful, or give prejudicial information.

BEEN THERE . . . DONE THAT! 1-2

During an investigation into an allegation of sexual assault, the mother of the child victim was interviewed. She gave detailed information on what her daughter had told her. Frequently she cried during the interview. Although her behavior was not unjustified, it was apparent that she had a high stake in the outcome of the case. More than halfway through the interview I discovered that the perpetrator was the woman's father— grandfather to the child victim. The mother confided that he had sexually abused her as a child also, a case that was never reported to the authorities. Among other things, she had suffered genital mutilation at the hands of her father. During an investigation, be aware that additional victims may be discovered through the interviewing process.

8. When interviewing multiple witnesses, it is not unusual to hear different accounts of the same incident or a variety of descriptions for the same offender. Varying accounts are given because every witness sees things differently and relates what he or she saw from different perspectives.

9. An interviewer must recognize all these human limitations and individual differences in witness perception and be aware of the personal motives that can be involved in any particular case.

Suspects

An individual under investigation for having committed a crime or other wrongdoing is considered the **suspect**. For an initial response to the scene of an offense, the responder should remove the suspect immediately if he or she is present. If the suspect is not present at the scene or known to the victim, interviews with the victim or witness should include attempts to identify the perpetrator. Line-ups, composite sketches, and photo identification are among some of the techniques used for identification. Along with a suspect description the interviewer should ask about locations where the suspect may be found. Any utterances made should be documented, including any alibi. Developing a strategy for a later interrogation begins at this stage.

An interview with a suspect should not take place until the interviewer has examined the facts of the case and spoken with the victim. The interviewer should not jump to conclusions during an initial meeting with a person thought to be the offender. It is not uncommon to interview with a suspect before an interrogation. The investigator should not move from interviewing with a suspect to interrogating until fairly certain that the person is guilty. Approaching the suspect should be similar to the procedure with any witness unless it is a dangerous situation that compromises interviewer safety. This means that the approach is respectful, but not solicitous. A suspect may offer information that clears him or her immediately, so one should be open to that possibility. An interview of a suspect takes on immense importance because it is often the only opportunity for a non-adversarial dialogue. Do not narrow the focus of an investigation into the facts of a case suggest with a high level of certainty that a particular person is the one responsible for the situation under investigation. Once an interrogation is started, the ability to freely gather information is over.

Cyber Informants

The use of interactive social media is unprecedented in its value for increased communication and information sharing. The use of electronic devices and computers for talking, texting, e-mailing, tweeting, and posting has changed the way that people

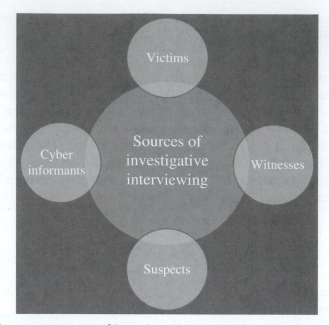

FIGURE 1-2   The newest source of investigative interviewing are cyber informants.

interact with each other. The **cyber informant** is an individual who communicates over the Internet regarding his or her intent to commit crime or involvement in criminal activity, or about their knowledge of others who are involved in wrongdoing. Cyber informants are included as one of the four sources of investigative interviewing since the description of fact finding may be interactive and can elicit verbal evidence (see Figure 1-2). For nvestigators, the goal remains to gather information leading to conclusions regarding a person's involvement or knowledge of wrongdoing. Investigation to verify the creditability of the information is necessary. More than 80 percent of law enforcement professionals use social media for investigative purposes, including identification and evidence collection (LexisNexis Risk Solutions, 2012). Those who do not often lack the knowledge or technical resources.

The primary distinctions between cyber informants and traditional categories of interviewees are that the communication is facilitated by use of the Internet and usually it is self-initiated by the one with information. Incriminating statements are made public through media rather than in response to official questioning. The investigator monitors social media and may follow up on incriminating statements by investigation or contacting persons for a face-to-face interview. An offender may be involved in traditional or online criminal conduct. Categories of online crime that these individuals commit are varied. Cyber bulling, cyber stalking, financial crimes, identify theft, and terrorism are among the concerns. Evidence gleaned from the Internet can be both reliable and creditable if properly evaluated. When information from social media is used as probable cause for search warrants, and it is challenged in court, less than 1 percent has been dismissed, according to a LexisNexis study (2012).

THE NATURE OF INTERROGATION

The words "interview" and "interrogation" are often used incorrectly, particularly in the private sector. There is a tendency not to use the term "interrogation" so that the practice seems less threatening to the public, human resource officers, or union representatives. Despite its negative reputation, an interrogation is a proper word for what is a major step during the investigative process. An **interrogation** is an exercise in persuasion with

BEEN THERE . . . DONE THAT! 1-3

A frantic call came into the station, from a woman claiming that her child had been kidnapped and that she did not know the man who took the infant. Officers *en route* to the scene saw a man walking with an infant in his arms and stopped to speak with him. As it turned out, the "kidnapper" was the father of the child, who had the legal right to have custody of her. His story was that his girlfriend—the mother—was an abusive drunk who was hitting the child. Lacking a car, he had left on foot to protect the infant. At the house, the woman was found to be intoxicated and combative. She admitted to hitting the child and was arrested for assault. In the police cruiser she kept saying that she could not believe that she had been arrested, she was the mother and, after all, she was a woman; she had even made the call to the police! What was this world coming to?

the goal of eliciting truthful information from individuals suspected of wrongdoing. This working definition is specific to gain a deeper understanding of the nature and purpose for conducting an interrogation. In the case of an interrogation, persuasion refers to influencing someone to give information about an act they committed or were substantially involved in.

The interrogation process is a give and take between the suspect and the interrogator, with most of the talking done by the interrogator. This back and forth may last as little as 30 minutes, or it may take hours. It is structured and purposeful. The extent of cooperation is determined early; therefore, the interrogator works within accepted boundaries with the suspect to elicit the information.

The interrogation is different from the interview in many ways. The primary difference between an interview and an interrogation is often in the interviewer's perception. A change from interviewing to interrogation occurs with the change from a nonaccusatory approach to one that is accusatory. An interrogation involves obtaining information from a suspect who is thought to be unwilling to admit to involvement in a crime or appears to have reason to hide the truth. Studies have shown that lying and deception are a normal form of communication (Knapp, McGlone, Griffin, & Earnest, 2016). The interrogator sometimes asserts statements rather than questions.

Concepts about human behavior and communication included in this text as interviewing techniques apply to interrogation practices also. Many professionals may be in a situation of interviewing, yet relatively few will engage in interrogation. Legal interrogation guidelines limit the actions of law enforcement officials. The reason for this narrowed application is that interrogation is restricted to criminal investigations with constitutional requirements that govern state and federal action. The U.S. Supreme Court has defined interrogation as the questioning initiated by law enforcement officers after a person has been taken into custody or otherwise deprived of his or her freedom of action in any significant way (*Miranda v. Arizona*, 1966). The U.S. Constitution and the Bill of Rights protect citizens from actions of government officials and their agents and not from other citizens. Because of this protection, evidence that comes from the interrogation of one citizen by another citizen is not held to the same legal restrictions as an interrogation by a government officer. However, the government may not be able to accept evidence from civilians if extreme interrogation methods such as torture or vigilante action were used to exact information.

The standards that govern interrogation methods can be located in multiple laws and statutes. Evolving standards of justice and acceptable practices guide criminal interrogations. Constitutional law, federal and state statutes along with Anglo-American tradition blend with a current emphasis on the Fifth Amendment right against self-incrimination, the Sixth Amendment guarantee of the right to counsel, and the Fourteenth Amendment guarantee of due process.

Interrogation Controversy

The controversy surrounding interrogation provides sufficient reason for students to study the process, regardless of any direct professional application. Debates over acceptable practices are not new to this generation. Interrogation methods have been controversial at least since the 1600s. Occasional attempts to prohibit torture as an interrogation method are documented in English jurisprudence as early as 1628 (*Bram v. United States*, 1897). The early common law allowed an admission or confession as evidence of guilt, regardless of it being the product of force or duress. Investigations were not done to establish guilt, and law enforcement officers used torture to extract a confession from the accused during an interrogation.

The courts have alternatively used the unreliability of confessions from torture and the requirement for constitutional protections as reasons for rejecting their use against an individual to prove guilt. Psychologists tell us that some people will confess to a crime that they did not commit without outside pressures and that others are susceptible to falsely confess in an interrogation environment (Kassin, 2016). This vulnerability provides a dilemma for officials who are tasked with solving crimes. Interrogation information must be consistent with fact or reality, not false or erroneous, real, genuine, reliable, accurate, narrowly particularized, and highly specific.

Although many veteran investigators felt that interrogations would become a lost art after the *Miranda* decision in 1966, the Supreme Court has recognized the need for criminal justice investigators to conduct interrogations. It is in the best interest of a lawful society to identify correctly individuals whose acts are illegal. When done properly, the interrogation is still a valuable tool for an investigator to consider. Procedural reforms to encourage truth finding during police interrogations have come from concern over false confessions and their role in false convictions (Leo & Cutler, 2016). Among the criminal justice reforms is a requirement in 20 states that interrogations be recorded under certain circumstances (Garrett, 2016).

It is against human nature to implicate oneself in wrongdoing; it is not necessarily in one's best interest. Why would someone confess to having committed an illegal act, knowing that there will be consequences? That individual must be persuaded that it is in his or her best interest to admit to the act. Persuasion can come about through a variety of methods, some of which are described in later chapters.

PURPOSE OF THE INTERROGATION

The process of interrogation is meant to encourage the suspect to provide evidence of guilt or involvement in an event. The interrogator seeks a confession or admission regarding participation or knowledge of wrongdoing. A confession is a statement made by someone who is revealing guilt of the crime with which he or she is charged, excluding the possibility of a reasonable inference to the contrary (*People v. Anderson*, 1965). According to case law, a confession is not limited to words. Confessions may also include the demeanor, conduct, and acts of the person charged with a crime. For example, the court has accepted a situation in which the defendant showed the interrogators how he committed the murder of a young girl by acting out the manner in which he stabbed her (*People v. Baldi*, 1974).

Although the goal is to entice a confession, eliciting an admission is considered a success of the interrogation. An admission is an acknowledgment of criminal conduct that contains only facts from which guilt may or may not be inferred (*People v. Anderson*, 1965). The statement of admission may be a word, act, conduct, or information that in any other way suggests guilt. Contained in an admission is information about the suspect and his or her role or relationship to the crime. An admission may also

BEEN THERE . . . DONE THAT! 1-4

Rapport building is a process of developing a willingness to communicate. It can also be thought of as a getting-to-know-you phase. When interviewing a child or an adult, one should show empathy, concern, or interest to build rapport. Rapport building can be an important phase for interrogations also. In one case I had just arrested a man who had been restrained by four officers to detain him. He was shocked at having been arrested and visibly shaken from the experience. I showed concern and asked if he was all right, making light of the four men having just pounced on him. From the look on his face I detected an immediate reaction of gratitude. Moments later I gave him his rights per *Miranda*, which he waived and agreed to give me a statement. Having sensed his willingness to communicate, I had wasted no time and did the interrogation in the cruiser. On the way to the station, he gave a full confession and a thank-you.

include information about the victim or the place of the offense. The courts do not differentiate between degrees of culpability. For their use as evidence against a person in court, there is no distinction between confessions and admissions.

PERSONAL QUALITIES OF THE INTERVIEWER

The majority of contacts that occur between an investigator and a citizen are face-to-face and typically one-on-one. Effective communication is the most desirable personal quality of an investigator. Often it is assumed that a person who speaks or writes well comes by it naturally. Those who are reluctant to seek help for improvement may be embarrassed about their lack of skill. Some individuals are oblivious to their deficiencies and may need encouragement from a supervisor to improve. Studies have shown that personal characteristics of the interviewer do affect the outcome of an interview (Lafontaine & Cyr, 2016). Excellent oral and written communication are learned skills. It is, therefore, necessary to acquire these skills and then practice them for these shortcomings to be addressed.

How things are said may be more important than what is being said. The way that a person communicates dictates the impression that is given to that person to others. The extent of a persons' professionalism is often judged by their ability to communicate effectively. Those who sit in judgment are fellow professionals, the public, victims, and the perpetrator. The individual alone determines the impression that they give. People frequently state that an interviewer should above all be friendly. I could not disagree more. If the victim or witness wanted to talk to a friend, he or she would go out for coffee, not for an official interview! More appropriately the interviewer must be approachable, understanding, empathetic, patient, and nonjudgmental. In other words, being neutral and nonoffensive without being distant is a personal quality that will benefit the communication process. Interviewees may be looking for help or direction; sometimes they are angry and confused. Confidence is, therefore, a necessary attribute of the interviewer—without arrogance, however. Learning the behaviors needed to be a successful interviewer begins with learning and understanding human nature.

Knowing yourself is the first part of that process. The ability to recognize that each one of us has a perspective that is different carries with it the acknowledgment that you, the investigator, have prejudices and biases about someone or something. Some people cannot stand dumb individuals or those who come across as intellectuals. Others dislike certain physical characteristics or appearances. Some people are disgusted by those who commit criminal acts or who break the law. The successful interviewer learns to put these biases aside in a conscious choice to be professional. Everyone is entitled to his or her opinions, thoughts, and perspectives, but there is no room in the interview for personal preferences. Learning to look past oneself to the case greatly enhances the value of the police interview.

Also, the individual who conducts frequent interviews should have a genuine curiosity. "Curiosity" is a term that refers to an emotional pressure to seek information, to explore, and to learn by observation. Wanting to find out everything possible about a case in this context refers to being open-minded about lifestyles and personal choices that may be different from those of the investigator. A positive attitude by the interviewer has a better chance to surface if interest is allowed to overtake bias. Successful interviewers are commonly inquisitive, observant, and energetic individuals with the ability to put people at ease while eliciting information (Wisconsin Department of Justice, 2011).

A good interviewer is not necessarily an effective interrogator. Because interrogation is only a small part of the communication process, interview skills are of greater value. However, the skills for questioning are an extension of the personal qualities needed for an interviewer, so they are addressed at this point. Training, experience, aptitude, and intelligence are prerequisites. The personal qualities for someone making an interrogation include all of the interview skills along with a high degree of confidence. That trust is achieved internally. The individual must possess self-confidence on his or her ability to face objection and overcome resistance through reason. It is not that different from taking a position on a debating team and arguing for one opinion over another that is being presented. The debate is not a shouting match. It is an intellectual exchange between the position of the interrogator without regard to his or her stake in the outcome. Once the interrogator takes a position, it must be backed up with evidence to strengthen that position. Also, achieving absolute control over personal emotions is paramount for the interrogator. It is natural to feel embarrassment for the suspect when he is caught in a lie or to feel pity for the subject because of the circumstance. Emotions can also drive an interrogator to proceed during an interrogation without regard for the suspect. An interrogation is not an exercise in humiliation, degradation, or torture that is either physical or psychological.

Willing to Develop Rapport

Central to any interview, and in some cases for interrogations, is an exchange called **rapport**. Frequently throughout this book, there will be references to rapport; therefore, the communication concept behind the process is introduced here. Rapport is the communication that results when the interviewee is at ease and comfortable with the interviewer, achieved through mutual respect or understanding. Often described as the most important skill for effective interviewing, rapport describes a connection between the interviewer and the interviewee (Bell, Fahmy, & Gordon, 2016).

The social work interview has long embraced the importance of communication as presented through the theory of David Berlo (Kadushin & Kadushin, 2013). The nature of the communication involves not only what is said and heard—the message encoded, transmitted, received, processed, and decoded—but also the interpersonal context in which the process takes place. The importance of developing rapport in criminal justice interviewing is undisputed (Dreeke, 2012). If the framework of a relationship is positive, then there is a comfortable, trustful, and respectful feeling between the interviewer and the interviewee. The positive relationship, which is another way to describe rapport, lowers barriers and brings a heightened willingness to participate in the interview. Both the interviewer and interviewee are more likely to be receptive to messages being sent after rapport is established. A good relationship is not necessarily a pleasant one, but it is one that is actively used to further the purpose of the interview (Kadushin & Kadushin, 2013).

Knowledgeable

It is thought that investigators have little more than chance to determine deception during interviews and interrogations accurately. The knowledgeable investigator addresses this deficiency. He or she keeps asking questions and continues to learn from each case. The knowledgeable investigator researches the laws pertaining to the offenses that are under investigation before conducting major interviews or interrogations. Gathering specific case facts before questioning is done during each investigation, no matter how many times a similar situation was faced or how routine the situation may appear. Questioning that elicits evaluative facts is believed to improve interview and interrogation results (Levine, 2014).

The knowledgeable interviewer does not make judgments based on past encounters that were similar or by race, gender, or age. Each situation represents the possibility that an unlikely person is at fault. We now know, for example, that intimate violence occurs between individuals of the same sex; that adolescents abuse their parents; and that an older adult woman is just as likely to perpetrate an offense against her husband as the husband is to his wife. Rape is perpetrated against male and female victims, against persons in a courtship or a marriage relationship, and within same-sex relationships. The trained officer knows that the answers must be learned from the circumstances and will come only through listening and watching.

Professional

The interviewer must begin without case bias. Because the goal is to obtain information, the situation must allow the witness or victim to state his or her views of the situation freely. A preconceived notion about what the person may say inhibits conversation. Tolerating ambiguity refers to this skill of reacting positively to new, different, and at times unpredictable situations. Achieving this will call for patience as well as persistence. Both are firm requirements in particular when dealing with people from other societies and places around the world.

The attitude of the interviewer or interrogator strongly affects the extent of witness cooperation. Considered a necessary ingredient of professionalism is the ability to demonstrate cultural respect for age, in the manner of speech, with eye contact, with hand or body gestures, for personal privacy, and so on. Being nonjudgmental requires that the investigator learn to withhold drawing conclusions during the gathering of information while taking into account cultural characteristics that might affect judgment. Also, one must feel comfortable asking uncomfortable questions. Frequently the details of a statement will cause anxiety to the victim or witness. It may necessitate asking personal or probing questions to obtain completeness and accuracy.

COMMUNICATING

Communication is a process that includes sending and receiving both verbal and nonverbal messages. It is estimated that nonverbal communication often conveys a larger share of social information, whereas verbal communication plays a less prominent role (Burgoon, Guerrero, & Floyd, 2016). So much information is conveyed nonverbally that the verbal aspect is negligible. Body language, facial expressions, gestures, personal spacing, and voice characteristics send messages to the recipient.

These communications can be used to facilitate the building of rapport through matching techniques. "Matching" is a subtle form of mimicking the nonverbal and paralanguage behavior of the interviewee (Dotz, Hoobyar, & Sanders, 2013). The purpose is to match the behavior or voice of someone through movement in the same manner as the interviewee, without attracting conscious attention to it. Gaining nonverbal information about an individual through attention to the posture, body position, use of personal space, facial expressions, and eye contact and conveying back the emotional content is a proven technique of communication through matching.

Kinesics

Kinesic communication is a complex form of nonverbal interactions that include body language, facial expressions, and gestures (Burgoon et al., 2016). Dr. Ray L. Birdwhistell is one of the earliest to investigate the relevancy of body motion as nonverbal communication. Credited with having coined the term "kinesics," he argued that communication is the process of socialization to be human (Birdwhistell, 2010). Sometimes a kinesic shift occurs due to special experiences or mental distortion. It can be imitated and predicted. Today's computer software makes use of technology that provides investigators with the means of detecting nonverbal variability to aid in identification. Face and voice recognition, voice inflection, and syntax are examples of the modern use of kinesic principles.

How the body expresses itself to others may be referred to as one's body language. As one of the most effective media, it transmits feelings. The transmission of body language is usually more subconscious than conscious. Observing individuals who are deeply engaged in conversation reveals some similarities between them that they probably aren't consciously aware is happening. For example, two people talking may sit in a similar position, they may make the same types and rhythms of hand gestures, may likely speak in a comparable tonality and tempo, and likely breathe at a similar rate. In some way, the body language of the two will align. Without knowing why individuals who mirror the body language of the other will feel that they understand each other and that the other person "makes sense." The practice of an interviewer matching the body language of the interviewee brings that feeling of making sense to the subject. It can facilitate a willingness to provide information during the interview (Figure 1-3).

FIGURE 1-3   Body language, facial expressions, and gestures are forms of nonverbal communication, which may speak louder than words.

Source: Oliveromg/Shutterstock.

Approval, agreement, acceptance, and continuing attention and understanding are communicated by a head nod from the interviewer (Wainwright & Thompson, 2011). Agreement typically is reported by the largest nods, whereas a slight nod shows feedback on understanding the interviewee. Wainwright and Thompson (2011) suggest that men tend to use head nods more than women and that it may be useful for women to practice and purposefully use head nods more frequently.

A majority of experts agree on the universality of facial expressions. Universally recognized facial expressions include conscious and unconscious movement of the nose, lips, eyebrows, tongue, and eyes (Ekman, 2016). For example, lips may move into a grin to show happiness, grimace for fear, or pout to indicate sadness. When the individual has a lot at stake in a situation and lies about it, emotions such as fear and disgust are shown through facial expressions. Eyebrows frown for anger or concentration and rise for intensity. The most frequent facial expression, according to the pioneering facial recognition work of Paul Ekman (2001), is the lowering or rising of the eyebrows, often to emphasize speech or show disbelief and skepticism. Wide eyes typically indicate surprise or excitement, and narrowed eyes indicate disagreement or a threat. One of the most reliable facial actions is the narrowing of the lips, which signals anger. An interviewer may facilitate rapport by recognizing and addressing what the face reveals.

Gestures are woven inextricably into our social lives, and that vocabulary of gestures can be informative and entertaining, but also threatening (Remland, 2017). Gestures can be menacing; they can indicate warmth or be instructive. Examples are two angry drivers on a freeway, an open-arm welcome, and a police officer giving road directions. Gestures can even be sensuous, such as a Hawaiian hula dancer. Verbal communication, however, transmits words and thoughts. At times understanding the wants and feelings of others is far more important than understanding their words. The crossing of the arms, for example, usually signals a defensive posture. When an interviewer attempts to develop rapport, defensive signals need to be overcome for the interview to proceed effectively.

Conclusions

This chapter described communication as a process according to the scheme elaborated by Berlo. This model provides a framework for consideration of the interrogation and interviewing methods that are described throughout this text. The interrogation and the interview were defined in a way to compare and contrast the goals and methods employed in these approaches to eliciting information. Although they do not constitute an exhaustive list of the personal qualities required for an interviewer, some qualities were given as a guideline to suggest the sort of person who should engage in the investigation process. The different categories of persons who are interviewed and their shifting capabilities are stated. Because the establishment of rapport is such a critical aspect of interviewing, the nonverbal behavioral indicators that may be useful for rapport are covered here. The student can look forward to greater details on interviewing and interrogation methods in later chapters.

Questions for Review

Short-Answer Questions

1. What is Berlo's model of communication?
2. Define interview and describe how it differs from interrogation.
3. What are the sources of investigative interviewing?
4. Explain the qualities of a good interviewer.
5. Describe the term "kinesics."

Fill-in Questions

1. _____ is the process of eliciting a confession from a suspect.
2. _____ is the process of gathering information.
3. The four sources of investigative interviewing are _____, _____, _____, and _____.

4. Successful interviewers are ____ and ____ in order to obtain as much pertinent information possible.

5. ____ is a process that includes sending and receiving both verbal and nonverbal messages.

6. ____ is among the earliest to investigate nonverbal communication, which was coined "kinesics."

7. ____ is a pioneer in his work on facial recognition.

8. One of the most important aspects of interviewing is the development of ____.

Exercises

1. Kinesics is an approach that has been adapted for criminal justice interviewing. Go online and discover additional ways in which kinesics is used.

2. Consider the value of interviewing in everyday life. Come up with a list of ways in which you learn something from someone each day. Describe the category of investigative source and manner of interviewing that takes place in your examples. Explain also the role of rapport in your illustrations.

References

Abrams, D., Ramsey, S., & Mangold, S. (2015). *Children and the law in a nutshell* (5th ed.). St. Paul, MN: West Academic.

Bell, K., Fahmy, E., & Gordon, D. (2016). Quantitative conversations: the importance of developing rapport in standardized interviewing. *Quality & Quantity, 50*(1), 193–212.

Berlo, D. K. (1960). *The process of communication.* New York: Holt, Rinehart, and Winston.

Birdwhistell, R. L. (2010). *Kinesics and context: Essays on body motion communication.* Philadelphia, PA: University of Pennsylvania Press.

Bram v. United States, 168 U.S. 532 (1897).

Burgoon, J., Guerrero, L., & Floyd, K. (2016). *Nonverbal communication.* New York, NY: Routledge.

Dotz, T., Hoobyar, T., & Sanders, S. (2013). *NLP: The essential guide to neuro-linguistic programming.* New York, NY: Harper Collins Publishers.

Dreeke, R. (2012). Mastering rapport and having productive conversations. *FBI law enforcement bulletin* (October).

Ekman, P. (2001). *Telling lies: Clues to deceit in the marketplace, politics, and marriage.* New York: W. W. Norton & Company.

Ekman, P. (2016). What scientists who study emotion agree about. *Perspectives on Psychological Science, 11*(1), 31–34.

Garrett, B. (2016). The myth of the presumption of innocence. *Texas Law Review, 94*(178).

Kadushin, A., & Kadushin, G. (2013). *The social work interview* (5th ed.). New York: Columbia University Press.

Kassin, S. M. (2016). False confessions: From colonial Salem, through Central Park, and into the twenty-first century. In C. Willis-Esqueda & B. H. Bornstein (Eds.), *The Witness Stand and Lawrence S. Wrightsman, Jr.* (pp. 53–74). New York, NY: Springer New York.

Knapp, M., McGlone, M., Griffin, D., & Earnest, W. (2016). *Lying and deception in human interaction.* Dubuque, IA: Kendall Hunt.

Lafontaine, J., & Cyr, M. (2016). A study of the relationship between investigators' personal characteristics and adherence to interview best practices in training. *Psychiatry, Psychology and Law, 23*(5), 782–797.

Leo, R. A., & Cutler, B. L. (2016). False confessions in the twenty-first century. *The Champion Magazine* (May).

Levine, T. R. (2014). Truth-default theory (TDT): A theory of human deception and deception detection. *Journal of Language and Social Psychology, 33*(4), 378–392.

LexisNexis Risk Solutions. (2012). Survey of law enforcement personnel and their use of social media in investigations. Retrieved from www.lexisnexis.com/investigations.

Milne, R., & Bull, R. (2016). Witness interviews and crime investigation. In D. Groome & M. Eysenck (Eds.), *An introduction to applied cognitive psychology* (pp. 175–196). New York, NY: Routledge.

Miranda v. Arizona, 384 U.S. 436 (1966).

Olson, K. (2016). *Essentials of qualitative interviewing.* New York, NY: Routledge.

People v. Anderson, 236 Cal. App. 2d 419 (1965).

People v. Baldi, 80 Misc. 2d 118 (1974).

Remland, M. S. (2017). *Nonverbal communication in everyday life* (4th ed.). Thousand Oaks, CA: Sage Publications.

Smalarz, L., & Wells, G. L. (2013). Eyewitness certainty as a system variable. In B. L. Cutler (Ed.), *Reform of eyewitness identification procedures* (pp. 161–177). Washington, D.C.: American Psychological Association.

Sullivan, J. R. (2016). Navigating the rock and the whirlpool: managing critical incident investigation and Garrity. *Widener Law Journal, 25*(2), 195.

The Crime Victims' Rights Act 18 U.S.C. § 3771, U.S. Department of Justice (2016).

Wainwright, G., & Thompson, R. (2011). *Master body language.* Oxon, UK: Hodder & Stoughton.

Wisconsin Department of Justice. (2011). *Interview and interrogation: A training guide for law enforcement officers.* Wisconsin: Office of the Attorney General.

Wixted, J. T., Read, J. D., & Lindsay, D. S. (2016). The effect of retention interval on the eyewitness identification confidence–accuracy relationship. *Journal of Applied Research in Memory and Cognition, 5*(2), 192–203.

Woska, W. J. (2013). Legal Issues for HR Professionals. *Public Personnel Management, 42*(1), 90–101.

2

The Interview Process

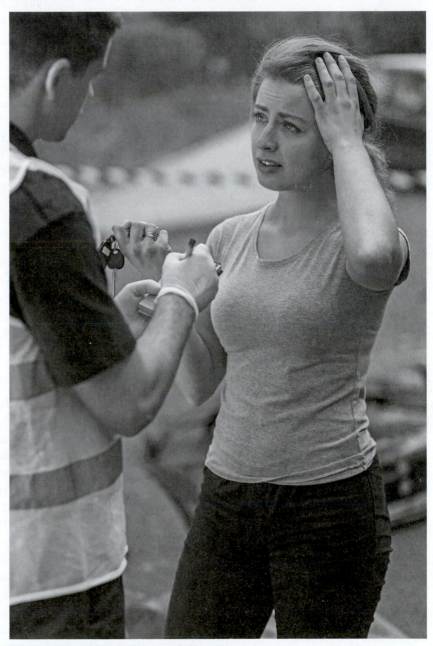

Source: Photographee.eu/Shutterstock.

CHAPTER OBJECTIVES

After completing this chapter, you should be able to:

1. Describe the three phases of the interview process.
2. Change a closed-ended question into the open-ended form.
3. Explain the difference between open and closed questioning.
4. Compare and contrast the methods of approaching the interview.
5. List the ways in which witnesses might make an identification of a suspect.
6. Describe the characteristics of a social systems approach to interviewing.
7. Explain the problem of misinformation and contamination.
8. List ways of minimizing the contamination of witness statements and identification.

KEY TERMS

Postmodernism	Clarifying open-ended question
Contamination	Reinforcing behavior
Leading question	Closed-ended question
Initial open-ended question	Confrontational question

INTRODUCTION

This chapter suggests that the interview process is positioned within the context of a social systems approach. The approach is not a one-two-three method of interviewing. It is a way to conceptualize how interviewing success can be achieved through the approach taken by the interviewer. Investigators should apply the following principles with every contact regardless of the interviewing method is used.

The social systems approach suggests that in response to increased environmental complexity, organizations will cope by increasing internal or external complexity (Schneider, Wickert, & Marti, 2016). What does this mean for the criminal justice interviewer? Criminal justice professionals respond to diverse situations, which require interviewing proficiency. Individuals analyze the resources of the organization and the complexity of issues that are met in the community they serve. Increasing internal complexity means that adequate resources are devoted to specialization within the organization. Interviewing for age appropriate investigations would include persons who are proficient with special populations that are frequently victimized such as older adults or children. Targeted responses for de-escalation of individuals with mental disorders or victimization of persons who do not speak English as a primary language also require unique strategies. Employing persons for communicating through online social media is a growing need for criminal justice. Increasing external complexity is accomplished by forming of collaborative relationships for successful responses to increased social dilemmas (Gosselin, 2017). For example, a department may need to partner with mental health organizations or child protective services if it is not able to adequacy train someone to conduct interviews with special populations.

Another way to look at the social systems approach is to recognize that the interview is a process that does not occur in a vacuum, the system selects only a limited amount of information that is available. The successful interviewer considers the perspectives of the interviewee to maximize the potential of the statement. Valuable perspectives include the viewpoint of the interviewer, the victim(s), the witnesses, and the suspect. To further understand this approach, the theory is broken down into three themes: caring, self-development, and postmodernism (Carter, 2011). These three themes refer to the way that the interviewer conducts the interview process.

The first topic, caring, focuses on interviewing with cultural competence. Ours is a culturally diverse society with widespread global mobility. Interviewing within this caring model requires active listening by the interviewer to assure the accuracy of statements. Interviewers must be qualified to evaluate the differences between trained interpreters and untrained bilinguals. There is a risk of failure to replicate tone or pragmatic force, as well as the factual content when using interpreters (Goodman-Delahunty & Martschuk, 2016). This theme supports the development and expression from the perspective of ethnic minority members who are being asked to provide information. Accepting ethnic perspectives means that during an interview the person who relates the event does so from their unique point of view. The reality is that perspectives are affected by past experiences as well as physical and cognitive limitations. The caring model suggests that the individual who conducts the interview should attempt to go beyond simply hearing the person to include the perspective of the interviewee as part of the interview. The caring model requires sensitivity to meaning that extends beyond the words stated during the interview. For example, is the interviewer experiencing hostility from the interviewee? Caring involves taking the time to ask if the subject has had negative experiences in a similar situation. Assure the interviewee that you are interested in hearing what he or she has to say.

Self-development is the second theme. Self-development of the interviewer encourages him or her to be constantly vigilant and self-aware during the interview process. When conducting an interview, it can be difficult to avoid the pitfalls of having a narrow focus. Time constraints, excessive caseloads, and a desire to bring the investigation to a close are only part of what contributes to this problem. The self-development model suggests the need for openness to redirection and change throughout the entire investigation. It requires a conscious decision to be open and responsive to the interviewee. If one remains flexible during an interview, then objective observations are more readily apparent. Watching for the behavioral indicators of deceit should direct the interview process; sensitivity to proximity allows the interviewer to place himself or herself strategically. Cognizance of nonverbal behavior improves the ability of the interviewer to retain control of the interview. To notice nonverbal behavior the investigator must listen, watch, and be aware of what is going on during the interview. Do not keep asking questions; spend some time listening to what is said—both verbally and physically.

The third theme in this approach, postmodernism, may affect the interviewing success unless it is understood and embraced. **Postmodernism** emphasizes the role of power that will be inherent in any interview conducted by government officials or police officers. What does this mean to the interviewer? It means that when a police officer or other government agent conducts an interview, the individual does not see a person, but a representative of a powerful organization. Many people are in awe of this power, some are fearful of it. An investigator may not be able to change the way an interviewee views the position. However, the interviewer is responsible for how the individual thinks about you as a member of that powerful organization. Make an effort to be respectful of the individuals that are interviewed.

PHASE I: INTERVIEW PREPARATION

One challenge is for the interviewer is to control the events as much as possible, taking the time needed to do a thorough job while at the same time feeling at ease and comfortable with the process. In a perfect world, the following steps would be taken to prepare for an interview: conducting a case review and determining whether there is a prior record. The actual sequence of these steps is not as important as their completeness.

Case Review

The interviewer should not use the case review as a means of determining the outcome. This information should not influence or prejudice the interviewer. The purpose of an interview is to gather as much information as possible to compare and contrast when making a determination on the validity of the case and the creditability of the individuals involved. It identifies potential problems with the case and areas to be explored during an interview. The interviewer must look critically at all case material and determine what part is made up of fact and what statements are conclusions from others. Disregard the judgments and scrutinize the facts. Things may not be what they seem!

The dispatcher or another person who takes the emergency call must collect complete and accurate information from the caller. This information becomes the case that will be reviewed by the responding officer(s). Asking open-ended questions followed by closed-ended questions, the 911 or emergency operator avoids suggestive or leading questions. The information is transmitted to the responding officer(s) and is updated when more information becomes available. The dispatcher becomes the eyes and ears of the responding officer, informing the caller that the police are on the way.

The first responder case review takes place after the initial call for service, typically while an officer is on route to the incident. Just as important as any other case preparation, the first responder must review the specifics of the case such as the number of people involved, their gender, their approximate ages, and their physical descriptions. Find out if a weapon was displayed or used. Request a records check on both the suspect and the victim for outstanding warrants and prior offenses (Figure 2-1). Obtain as much information about the incident as possible, including the location of the alleged perpetrator who is no longer at the scene. From this information determine the level of danger or injury to persons at the scene.

When the interview does not involve an emergency response, obtain and read any prior reports generated regarding the incident. If another police department or social service agency did a preliminary investigation to determine jurisdiction or whether there was a child in need of services, for example, contact that department for any available information. At least speak with the other investigators involved and then to share information about what they did, whom they spoke with, and how and why they came to

FIGURE 2-1   Conduct a background check on the suspect prior to the interview or interrogation.

Source: Courtesy of Denise K. Gosselin.

the conclusion that the case should be handled by another department. This information may be very revealing, but should not influence the interviewer regarding the case or the persons involved.

Determine if other agencies interviewed relative to the incident under investigation. Multiple agency involvements would not be unusual if the victim is a child, an older person, or a person with a disability. Investigative powers are vested in specific state agencies for the protection of each of these special populations. Obtain copies of the statements taken by other organizations. Determine the appropriate avenue to get these documents in the event the statements are not readily available due to confidentiality. It may be necessary to seek the advice of a local district attorney to request that documents be released through a court order. The investigator must assume that prior statements could jeopardize the case, particularly if interviews were not forensically appropriate.

Thoroughly examine the evidence, if any was collected, regarding the incident. The investigator must find out the relevance of any evidence previously gathered and document the identity of the person who collected it along with its initial location at the scene.

Determine Prior Criminal Record

When responding to the site of a crime where the alleged perpetrator is known, have the dispatcher or desk officer run the name of the suspect to determine if a prior record or outstanding warrants exist. In cases of domestic violence crimes, the name of the victim should also be checked for prior offenses and outstanding warrants. To determine the primary aggressor in domestic violence situations, it can be helpful to know if one or the other has a history of committing domestic violence. The existence of a prior record for a similar crime may be useful in making that difficult decision at the scene.

For interviews scheduled after the initial response the existence of a prior record will expose weaknesses of the individual as possible biases that exist. Use that information to determine the best approach and method of interviewing.

Viewing the Scene

Whenever the investigation involves a major crime, the scene should be viewed and personally documented by the interviewer. In cases where the officer was not dispatched to the scene, review any photographs and sketches that were made by the first responder. It is preferable to return as soon as possible after the incident.

Returning to the location of an incident may also be useful after the interview with the victim. Obtain a court order if the site is a home rather than a public place;

BEEN THERE . . . DONE THAT! 2-1

A 10-year-old girl reported that her mother's boyfriend had raped her. She described in detail the assault and how it had happened. Also, she was able to describe the bedroom where it had occurred. The man was arrested and denied the allegations, stating that the child was trying to break up the adults' relationship. The jury might have believed that, but in her statement, she described things that he had used during the rape and where they might be found. The information given by the young girl would not have known unless she had personal knowledge of the suspect. She described where he kept the Vaseline and the rags that he used to clean himself after the incident. The child reported where the suspect hid the magazines which portrayed child sex that he showed her. I obtained a search warrant to get the items, and confirmed their locations in the bedroom. She was more credible than the perpetrator, even though he was an adult. He was tried and convicted of the crime.

remember that there is no exception to the Fourth Amendment requirement for a search warrant even with a murder scene! Obtain a *Mincey* warrant (*Mincey v. Arizona, 1978*) before reentering the scene of a murder. Use this visit to corroborate the statements of the victim with the actual site. If the victim had never been to the place before the incident or if the victim has no reason to have known the particulars about the location yet can describe it, then that scene becomes evidence.

Misinformation

Preparing for an interview includes a conscious effort to reduce witness and victim misinformation. Misinformation refers to internal and external sources of information that produce variation in the answers given by an interviewee. The effect of this phenomenon can be severe and may lead people to report information never actually witnessed. Internal misinformation includes the cognitive and developmental factors associated with the interviewee. Misinformation from external sources includes any information of an event that is acquired by the interviewee after the event occurred. Eliciting reliable information during an interview can be difficult given the unreliability of human memory and the relative perspective of that person.

Internal events, which may distort memory, include factors that are not introduced by the interviewer. For example, field experiments have documented that emotion affects memory. Unknown, however, is whether a police officer should expect a witness to an emotional crime to have a good or bad memory (Wright, Memon, & Dalton, 2013). While internal events are individual specific, some generalizations can be made. Being hungry, tired, sick, or afraid are examples of generalizations, which might be mediated by the police response. Psychological vulnerabilities of a witness represent a potential risk factor for unreliability. Gudjonsson (2006) defines psychological vulnerabilities as psychological characteristics or mental state, which make a witness prone to providing inaccurate information, which may be unreliable or misleading (p. 68). Anticipation may help to evaluate the vulnerabilities of the witness, which may have a bearing on the reliability of their statements. Alcohol and drug abuse, cognitive ability, and age are factors that may influence perception and lead to misinformation.

Experts have argued that there be three sources of mistaken information provided by well-meaning and honest individuals (Gudjonsson, 2010). These are errors in observation, loss of memory with the passage of time, and self-deception. The effect of internal misinformation may be reduced through the use of age- and intellect-appropriate language and methods of questioning. It may be helpful to partner with psychological experts available to assist in specialized interviewing of persons suspected of having psychological vulnerabilities. Young children are considered unreliable due to cognitive development or immaturity, yet resistance to misinformation effects has been noted in children as they age (Paz-Alonso & Goodman, 2016). Research indicates that older adults are more vulnerable to misinformation than young adults. Regardless of being susceptible to misinformation, age alone or age-related dementia does not automatically preclude accurate recollection of events (Wiglesworth & Mosqueda, 2012).

When a person's memory of an event changes due to the introduction of misinformation from external sources, it is called **contamination**. Statement and eyewitness contamination can occur at different stages during an investigation. It can happen to victims, witnesses, and suspects involved in face-to-face encounters or online. Interviewers using suggestive techniques or questioning provide a common source of external change resulting in contamination. Biased instructions and cues can also distort memory (Wells, Steblay, & Dysart, 2012). Participants exposed to misinformation who experience contamination may later misinform about some aspect of the crime. An interviewer may be able to influence the statements of victims, witnesses, and suspects through the type

FIGURE 2-2 Avoid misinformation and be vigilant about the possibility of contaminated evidence. To guard against its effects, corroborate all eyewitness information with physical evidence.

Source: Couperfield/Shutterstock.

of questions asked and the phrasing. Use of the media to correct misinformation and to avoid contamination is now used and is illustrated by the Boston Police Department during the Boston Marathon bombing investigation (Davis, Alves, & Sklansky, 2014).

The effects of external misinformation are reduced by decreasing suggestive influences during questioning. Through leading questions and the tone or pitch of voice that used, the interviewer can distort memories. A **leading question** is one that contains a possible answer. Leading questions or suggestions on what is expected are potential contaminants. An example of misinformation would be the following leading question posed by an interviewer: "Please describe the car, it was red wasn't it?" This leading question suggests that a "red" car was already identified and the interviewer is seeking confirmation. The witness that is contaminated by this information may then report that the car was red, thinking that he or she did, in fact, see a red car.

DETECTING CONTAMINATION.   We cannot know when someone else has contaminated a witness before our contact. Contamination can impede our search for the truth. To minimize the effects of misinformation each person who conducts interviews, either at the scene or later needs to be aware of the possibility and avoid playing a part in this. Second, investigators must attempt to corroborate all information by interviewing additional subjects and collecting physical evidence.

PHASE II: ESTABLISHMENT OF THE PSYCHOLOGICAL CONTENT

The most common situation is the on-the-scene interview, although criminal justice and social service officials conduct interviews in a variety of settings. The investigator who responds to the scene must seek out and identify those who may have knowledge of the event and whose information may contribute to the investigation. Numerous individuals may have to be questioned to obtain the needed information.

Persons who are thought to have information about the case are identified and interviewed. One difficulty for an investigator is that a variety of emotions could interfere with the fact-gathering process. Some of the people will be willing to give information but will be nervous or anxious. Others may not be ready to provide information because they feel intimidated or threatened by questioning from government officials. Some people may not want to give out information due to bias, fear, or concern for retaliation. Make the person as emotionally comfortable as possible.

Whether the questioning takes place at the scene or elsewhere, all interviewees are separated from one another and questioned in private. Keeping the individuals apart will minimize the contamination of information due to overhearing another person give details of the offense and prevent individuals from comparing stories before being interviewed. Separating the individuals also provides the privacy that is needed to assure that an interested person or perpetrator will not hear the statement of another. Some people will only provide information in a private setting.

When Should the Questioning Occur?

The officer should not hesitate to request that witnesses remain at the scene until all of the interviews are completed. Attention must be given to the physical and emotional needs of the witnesses and of the victim(s). If the interviewee is emotionally upset, take the time to calm that excited person, even if it means a delay of the interview until the witness or victim has regained composure. Avoiding the temptation to rush an interview that is at the scene, the officers should create an encouraging atmosphere for the witness to talk freely by selecting a quiet area in which to conduct the interview. Always maintain the privacy of the interviewee to the greatest possible degree. Individuals who are comfortable will likely provide more information. This principle applies to the timing of the interview as well as its setting.

The nature of the offense may dictate the timing of the interviews. When possible, interviewers should retain control over the interviewing timing. Witnesses and victims should be interviewed as soon as possible after the incident under investigation to obtain an identification of the offender. Do this while their memory is still fresh. If the circumstances do not allow for an in-depth interview, such as when an identification of the perpetrator is needed, do not hesitate to inform witnesses that he or she may be contacted for a more thorough interview in the future.

Professionals need to adapt interviewing techniques to support a variety of cultural environments and when interviewing special populations such as children, older adults, and persons with a disability (Harris, 2010). Interviewing should be conducted at a time when they are likely to be most alert and responsive to questioning. Evening or early-morning interviews are not likely to result in quality information from special-population individuals. Before scheduling an interview find out from a caretaker or interested adult when the best interview time for that individual would be.

Where Should the Questioning Occur?

At all times the needs and desires of the interviewee are paramount. Questioning must take place in an area that is free of distractions. Note whether someone appears nervous or reluctant to speak; the individual may prefer a more private place to talk. Selecting the location for an interview relies on the following three considerations:

- Convenience
- The desired effect
- Available resources

CONVENIENCE.   For short interviews or to gather preliminary information, it is often more convenient to interview people at the scene of the crime. The primary benefit to the at-the-scene interview is the freshness of the information. Another benefit is that victim and witness cooperation tends to be highest when the crisis is occurring, and the police officer represents protection. If witnesses are not identified at the scene, there is the risk that they will not be located at a later date.

The downside of conducting a short interview at the site is that people may be reluctant to speak freely to the police in the presence of others. Be aware of this reluctance and offer another meeting place if the witness prefers. Look for an overall nervous appearance, glancing around, or extreme hesitation on the part of the person. Also, an individual may be injured or otherwise unable to give a full and accurate accounting at the scene. Respect the needs of the victims and witnesses to obtain maximum truthful information.

A DESIRED EFFECT.   Another factor in determining the place for an interview arises when there is a calculated determination of a desired effect on the interviewee. For intimidation or control, interviewing at the police station may provide the best choice. An office can be preset with the order of chairs and designed for minimizing distractions. Interviewing someone in their home, with consent, provides a false sense of control to the interviewee that can be used to the advantage of the interviewer. Typically an individual has his or her guard down when in a familiar and comfortable location.

AVAILABLE RESOURCES.   Interview special populations where there are resources available to facilitate communication. The Americans with Disabilities Act (U.S. Department of Justice, 2016) requires accommodations be made for interviewing victims with a disability. Special rooms may be designed for interviewing children and the elderly. Videotaping of interviews is most appropriately conducted in areas designed for this purpose. Documenting the interview through audiotaping or videotaping can free the interviewer to concentrate on the phrasing of questions.

When in the Police Station or an Office

Achieving the greatest control over the environment occurs when the interview takes place in a designated room of the police station or an office. The location should be quiet and free of distractions, preferably within a 10-foot by 12-foot room (Black & Yeschke, 2014). No cell phones, beepers, clocks, or other electronic devices should be in the room unless they are specifically needed for the interview. There should not be any windows and limited wall hangings if any.

Investigators suggest that the chair of the interviewer should be at a 45° angle to the interviewee to avoid presenting a threat at the beginning of the interview (Black & Yeschke, 2014). This practical use of proxemics recognizes the tension that is inherent when the position is changed to face-to-face during an interrogation. The moderate location straddles the social space and personal space where the participants are within 4 feet of each other. This distance allows for questioning that respects personal territory without creating undue stress on the interviewee. Another advantage of this placement is the ease with which the interviewer can lean forward purposefully to cause anxiety in the persuasive interview approach. If there is a third person in the interviewing room, he or she will be sitting out of the direct sight of the individual interviewee. If the placement from Figure 2-3 were used, the third person would sit to the left of the table, which is behind the interviewee.

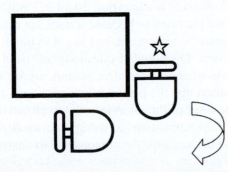

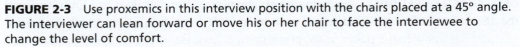

FIGURE 2-3   Use proxemics in this interview position with the chairs placed at a 45° angle. The interviewer can lean forward or move his or her chair to face the interviewee to change the level of comfort.

PHASE III: THE QUESTIONING

Plan to conduct an in-depth interview with the victim as soon as he or she is emotionally and physically able to do so. With the passing of time, an individual may become confused, and statements may lose detail. Avoid asking more than one question at a time, giving the person ample opportunity to provide an answer.

The trained interviewer knows that environmental and personal factors can influence what people hear and see. The lack of sleep, illness, weather, and light conditions are all potential distorters. Determine from the witness if any possible disorders existed at the time of the incident, which might affect his or her ability to provide an accurate statement. Consider the location and distance from the event when questioning witnesses. The ability to accurately observe and interpret things is also affected by pain, hunger, and distress. Emotions such as fear, anger, or worry impair perception. On the other hand, special interests may enable a witness to provide details that seem remarkable, such as a young boy who is interested in cars. What people see can be influenced by smells and sounds. Weave into questioning the five senses of smell, taste, and touch in addition to sight and hearing.

Typically an interview should be one on one. If two interviewers are in the room, one should be the obvious lead and do most of the talking. The second investigator should help by taking notes and assessing the witness's verbal and nonverbal behavior. When a second interviewer is involved, it is preferable for that person to stay off to the side and out of the vision of the interviewee so as not to cause a distraction. At the end of the questioning, the lead can be given to the second interviewer to fill in any gaps that were noted.

The Order of Interviews

The first officer at a scene should attempt to verify the identity of the suspect if he or she is known, as well as his or her location if the suspect is not at the scene. All witnesses should be separated and asked not to discuss the details of the incident with others. The area should be canvassed to identify additional witnesses for questioning.

The type of crime and the availability of personnel to assist with the investigation may dictate the order of the interviews. If there is a victim, he or she should be questioned by the first responder to obtain an identification of the suspect and the nature of any injuries. The suspect may be interviewed at the scene for determining culpability before making an arrest. When no person is in danger and an immediate arrest is not mandated, it may be helpful to conduct a preliminary interview with the suspect. The witnesses are questioned second.

Types of Questions

No specific information or opinion about the case should be offered before the taking of statements. An open-ended question is a question asked in a way that encourages a narrative by giving direction to the interviewee because it does not limit the answer; it is broad and nonspecific. An open-ended question is asked to get as much information as possible about the person or the event. Open-ended questions are used initially and as clarifiers throughout the interview whenever narrative statements are expected. Closed-ended questions limit the information that the person might give, augment information already received, and fill a specific need of the interviewer. A well-balanced interview contains both question types used purposefully. Avoid using emotional or suggestive words. Do not rapid-fire questions at a person; give the person time to answer completely.

OPEN-ENDED QUESTIONS.   An open-ended question is one that does not limit or direct the answer; therefore the phrasing of each open-ended question is important. An **initial**

open-ended question seeks a full-undirected narrative response. A **clarifying open-ended question** seeks to complete or expand on the information already given. To elicit a full response, don't interrupt the account by asking another question. Not interrupting indicates that you are willing to listen to his or her perspective and that you respect what he or she has to say. Interrupting the first narrative gives an impression that what the subject has to say is of little importance. The phrasing of the question can increase or decrease the willingness of the person to respond. Good initial open-ended questions include the following:

- Please tell me what happened to you.
- Would you tell me everything that you know about?
- Please tell me everything that you did this past Saturday.

Initial open-ended questions avoid asking something that involves an imaginative answer or conclusion. Examples of wrong initial open-ended questions include the following:

- Why did he do that to you?
- So what did you do to get her so angry?
- What was your involvement in the Saturday incident?

Encourage the person to continue their narrative through forced silence and reinforcing behaviors. A **reinforcing behavior** does not indicate approval or disapproval of what is said. The behavior to encourage narratives can be verbal or nonverbal. Investigators must be aware that both verbal and nonverbal behavior will influence the statement. Care must be taken to appear objective and nonjudgmental at all times. Suitable reinforcing narrative behaviors include the following:

- Saying "okay" in a matter-of-fact manner
- Saying, "Please continue."
- Saying, "I am listening."

Negative reinforcing behaviors during a narrative include the following:

- Wincing (in response to a painful recollection of the victim)
- Knitting of the brow or tightening of one's lips (as if angry)
- Saying, "You have to be kidding." (as in disbelief)

The nondirected quality of open-ended questions allows the interviewee to say whatever he or she wants without having preconceived expectations of what the interviewer wants to hear, so the questions are necessarily nonleading. Good questions include the following:

- Describe your assailant, please.
- What did the car look like?
- Tell me what you saw (heard, felt, smelled or did).

Bad open-ended questions that limit the answer and suggest an expected response include the following:

- Why don't you start off by telling me what your husband did to you?
- Describe that red car that was used during the incident.
- Did it hurt when he did that to you?

When the person is truthful, the first open-ended narrative should contain segments that are relatively equal in importance. These segments include what happened before the event, the event itself, and what the person did after the event.

During an interview with a rape victim, she appeared to be withholding information. Requests for details of the assault were met with open resistance. At first, I thought she was lying about having been raped. It then became apparent that she was hesitating because the details included things that were extremely difficult for her to talk about. The assailant had done things to her that she did not want to admit had happened. The interview was made easier after I told her why it was necessary for me to know everything, including the things that were embarrassing. She went on to give details, although it was not easy for her to do so. Keep in mind that hesitation may be due to emotional or physical pain, embarrassment or shame.

It may be helpful for the interviewer to encourage a narrative response at some additional point during the questioning or at the end. It can be used to explain events in greater detail, to develop information about subjective feelings, or to wrap things up. Examples of the clarifying open-ended question include the following:

- What did you do?
- What was your first reaction?
- Has anything like this ever happened to you before?
- Is there anything else you think I should know (or that you want to tell me)?

CLOSED-ENDED QUESTIONS.   A **closed-ended question** requires a yes or no or otherwise brief response. They are the most common type of question and are useful for verifying information, filling in gaps of the interview, and obtaining specific factual information. Examples of good closed-ended questions include the following:

- What time did you go to bed on Saturday?
- Do you know the name of the person who did this to you?
- What is your age?

Care must be taken not to lead the witness through suggestive closed-ended questions. For example:

- Was the car a blue Ford?
- Did you go to bed at 10 PM on Saturday?
- Did your father do this to you?

FOLLOW-UP QUESTIONS.   When the narrative is complete, asking follow-up questions probes deeper into the issues presented. Follow-up questions can be of either the open or closed type, and seek to elaborate or to clarify what has already been stated during the interview. Examples of follow-up questions include the following:

- You said that you "had sex"; please tell me what that means, and explain in detail what happened.
- Where exactly did he touch you?
- What time had you gone to bed that night?

DIRECT OR FORCED-CHOICE QUESTIONS.   These closed-ended questions are reserved for when you suspect that the interviewee knows more than he or she is telling you. They are asked in a nonaccusatory tone of voice and without emotion. The purpose of using a direct or forced-choice question would be to obtain information that could later be used to impeachment the credibility of the statement. Examples include

- After you tripped and dropped the baby, was he still breathing?
- What did you trip on?
- Was your boyfriend angry when the baby would not stop crying that night?

CONTROL QUESTIONS.   The person in control of the interview is the one who asks the questions. When you sense that you have lost that control, bring it back with a statement that requires the attention of the suspect. The control question firmly establishes that the interview is not over. Examples of questions used to take back control are as follows:

- I understand that you are upset about this. Please take a deep breath and prepare yourself to answer these questions.
- These issues are difficult, I understand, but I am unable to help you without the details of what happened.
- We are almost finished with the interview, but there are a few things that I am not clear on that need to be answered before we are done.

LEADING QUESTIONS.   Use leading questions when you want to guide the interviewee through a particular line of reasoning in a persuasive interview. By their nature, leading questions suggest an answer and should be avoided except for intentional use. These tend to distort the memory or perception of the interviewee, and the responses seldom reflect the thoughts of the interviewee. The following are examples:

- According to your neighbor …
- As you know …
- Your wife said …

CONFRONTATIONAL QUESTIONS.   A **confrontational question** is a question that is accusatory, typically involving a show of anger or disgust. When confrontational questions are introduced into the interview, you can no longer go back to being friendly and helpful. Be sure that it is time to leave the relationship behind before bridging the interview with the interrogation. The decision to nudge toward an interrogation may begin with this manner of questioning. It is firm, but not necessarily loud. For example:

- John, I have interviewed your son—he tells me that you were the one who touched him. Can you tell me why you did that to him?
- You are good at this, Pete; if I did not know better, I would think these signatures were done by someone else.
- So why did you pick her for your victim?

Determining an Approach

Behavior and personalities can affect your ability to obtain information during an interview. Evaluate each suspect or witness before determining who will conduct the interview. Consider the personality of the interviewee along with his or her obvious likes or dislikes. Do not attempt the interview if there is apparent disdain toward the potential interviewer and another option is available. It may be difficult to overcome hatred and establish rapport, which is a necessary component to a successful interview.

OBLIQUE APPROACH.   This approach is suited for the interview in which the interviewee will tell his or her story without prompting. As an avid listener, ask questions only to clarify points and avoid asking leading questions.

Regardless of the setting that is chosen for the interview, at the scene or a designated place, the voluntariness of the statement is of great importance. If the person is

BEEN THERE . . . DONE THAT! 2-3

Armed with an arrest warrant, my male partner and I picked up a man as he came out of work. The offender snarled at me in a way that a man under arrest should not be doing. It was as if he thought he could intimidate me. So I took the upper hand and passed him on to my partner. On the way to the station, I said two words to the suspect: YOU STINK! It hurt his pride, and he quickly started to explain that he was a working man and had just gotten out without having the chance to shower. Having gotten a reaction, I said it again: YOU STINK! Again he went on that he was not an evil man, just dirty. We arrived at the station, and the two men went into the interrogation room. My partner (quite amused at knowing he was the good guy—again) said, "She is a real bitch, ha?" In their current alliance, the rapport was established. The arrestee said he would answer any questions, as long as I was not in the room. Mission accomplished—a full confession resulted. Never underestimate the value of a good partner!

willing to give information AND the person is not in custody, then *Miranda* warnings are not required.

FORMAL APPROACH.   The formal interview occurs in a controlled environment such as a police station or detective office. A controlled setting is best used to manage an individual who appears overly confident or condescending toward the interviewer. As a home court advantage, the formal setting is usually intimidating enough to free the interviewer to think about more important considerations.

INFORMAL APPROACH.   Taking the informal route takes a lot of confidence! It works well for low-key interrogations that occur in the home of the perpetrator. It requires the willingness to sit and have a conversation along with the ability to persuade the person to invite you in. The informal approach is nonadversarial, and no custody occurs with this approach. By asking questions and encouraging the suspect to talk, you become a gatherer of incriminating evidence that may be used to apply for an arrest warrant, if necessary.

Conclusions

This chapter brought you through the process of interviewing. The three phases represent a progression rather than methods for being a successful interviewer. Each phase should be given equal weight towards the goal of obtaining the truth from witnesses and victims. It should be noted that interviewing is not just about talking. Of equal importance is listening. The process involves knowledge and planning. What is said becomes just as important as how and why it is said. Saying the wrong thing can cause contamination, and failure to ask the right questions can leave the interviewer empty handed. The bottom line is that interviewing is a learned skill.

Questions for Review

Short-Answer Questions

1. What is the social systems approach to interviewing, and what themes are found in modern social systems theory?

2. Phase I of the interview process entails preparation for the interview. What happens during the case review step and what is its purpose?

3. What is contamination and when can it occur?

4. When should the interview take place and where should questioning occur?

5. What is the difference between open-ended and closed-ended questions?

Fill-in Questions

1. The approach to interviewing used in this chapter focuses on caring, self-development, and _____, which emphasizes the role of power that is inherent in any interview.

2. The focus of Phase I is _____.

3. The purpose of _____ is to gather as much information possible to determine the validity of the case.

4. _____ occurs when witnesses or victims give misinformation either through leading questions, when lineups are not conducted properly, or when memories are distorted.

5. Short interviews done at the scene of the crime are usually done out of _____.

6. When interviewers are seeking a full narrative response they will ask _____ questions.

7. _____ are used to verify information.

8. When _____ are introduced into the interview the interviewer can no longer go back to being friendly or helpful.

9. The best approach toward interviewees who are willing to talk is the _____.

10. _____ is the most desirable physical arrangement between the interviewer and the interviewee.

Exercises

1. Find at least one article in the library containing an interview; news articles on controversial issues or political candidates often contain interviews. From the written interviews, identify the type of questioning mostly used, open-ended or closed-ended. Evaluate the article and the quality of responses as well as the type of question that elicited the response. Write a short paper citing the source used and the evaluation.

2. Practice using reinforcing behaviors in conversations with friends. Report if there is a difference in the content or quality of your conversation.

References

Black, I., & Yeschke, C. (2014). *The art of investigative interviewing* (3rd ed.). Boston, MA: Butterworth-Heinemann.

Carter, I. (2011). *Human behavior in the social environment: A social systems approach* (6th ed.). New York: Aldine De Gruyter.

Davis, E., Alves, A., & Sklansky, D. (2014). *Social media and police leadership: Lessons from Boston* (NCJ 244760). Washington, D.C.: National Institute of Justice.

Goodman-Delahunty, J., & Martschuk, N. (2016). Risks and Benefits of Interpreter-Mediated Police Interviews. *Tveganja in koristi vključevanja tolmačev v policijske razgovore, 18*(4), 451–471.

Gosselin, D. K. (2017). *Crime and mental disorders: The criminal justice response*. St. Paul, MN: West Academic Publishing.

Gudjonsson, G. (2006). The psychological vulnerabilities of witnesses and the risk of false accusations and false confessions. In A. Heaton-Armstrong, E. Shepherd, G. Gudjonsson, & D. Wolchover (Eds.), *Witness testimony. Psychological, investigative and evidential perspectives* (pp. 61–75). Oxford: Oxford University Press.

Gudjonsson, G. (2010). Psychological vulnerabilities during police interviews. Why are they important? *Legal & Criminological Psychology, 15*(2), 161–175.

Harris, S. (2010). Toward a better way to interview child victims of sexual abuse. *NIJ Journal, 267*(NCJ 233282).

Mincey v. Arizona, 437 U.S. 385 (1978).

Paz-Alonso, P. M., & Goodman, G. S. (2016). Developmental differences across middle childhood in memory and suggestibility for negative and positive events. *Behavioral Sciences & the Law, 34*(1), 30–54.

Schneider, A., Wickert, C., & Marti, E. (2017). Reducing complexity by creating complexity: A systems theory perspective on how organizations respond to their environments. *Journal of Management Studies, 54*(2), 182–208.

U.S. Department of Justice. (2016). *ADA Amendments Act*. Washington, D.C.: U.S. Department of Justice.

Wells, G. L., Steblay, N. K., & Dysart, J. E. (2012). Eyewitness identification reforms: Are suggestiveness-induced hits and guesses true hits? *Perspectives on Psychological Science, 7*(3), 264–271.

Wiglesworth, A., & Mosqueda, L. (2012). *People with dementia as witnesses to emotional events*: BiblioGov. Available at https://www.ncjrs.gov/pdffiles1/nij/grants/234132.pdf.

Wright, D., Memon, A., & Dalton, G. (2013). Field studies of eyewitness memory. In B. Cutler (Ed.), *Reform of eyewitness identification procedures* (pp. 179–202). Washington, D.C.: American Psychological Association.

Investigative Interviewing

CHAPTER OBJECTIVES

After completing this chapter, you should be able to:

1. Provide six examples of ways to show that a person is actively listening.
2. Name two general categories of factors that interfere with eyewitness accuracy.
3. Explain two components of persuasive interviewing.
4. Describe the role of psychology in three investigative contexts.
5. Explain how testimonial evidence is typically collected.
6. Demonstrate understanding of eyewitness estimator variables though example.
7. List eight system variables that may affect the reliability eyewitness identification.
8. Explain the statement analysis approach.

KEY TERMS

Active listening	Estimator variables
Forensics	Morphostasis
Persuasive interviewing	Telepsychiatry
Testimonial evidence	System variables

INTRODUCTION

This section discusses additional aspects of the broad application of social systems theory to the interviewing process. Do not think of social systems theory as an interviewing method. You will not see it woven throughout the chapter because it stands on its own. This is a broad way to think about interviewing, not a method on conducting an interview. Social systems theory has three general characteristics that assist in framing the persuasive interview. First, it involves a comprehensive approach to interviewing. What this means to the potential interviewer is that there is a bigger picture that looms over each statement and personal contact that takes place. Tying together the pieces presents a greater potential for description and integration of seemingly unrelated events into a single situation. An example is the concept of comprehensive questioning. Comprehensive questioning means getting as much information as possible. Some people would refer to this as "thinking outside of the box." At a car stop with more than one person in the vehicle, does one of them appear upset? Have that person step out of the car away from earshot and ask, "Are you ok?" At the domestic disturbance, speak with the children in the house. When interrogating a sexual offender, ask, "Who did this to you?" For the astute interviewer, looking at the big picture and tying the pieces together brings thoroughness to the process of gathering information.

The concept of continuation is another aspect of social systems theory. This relates to the belief that human behavior is multifaceted yet somewhat predictable. Continuation is also called morphostasis. **Morphostasis** is the understanding that the continuation of a system or family relationship may take priority due to the fear of the anticipated consequences of change. When a family is in danger of being destroyed or radically changed, the individuals may pool their energies. What this means to the potential interviewer is that family members will most likely pull together and forget past differences when faced with something that threatens them. It is a natural response to a perceived threat from the outside. You as the interviewer should expect that family members will work to protect each other in negative situations. Don't expect family members to be totally candid when supplying information about a crime that may have been committed by one of their own. The concept also applies in domestic violence situations in which the victim is unwilling to break apart the family unit. Saying to a domestic violence victim, "When you going to leave this creep?" is counterproductive. A different approach is to say, "If you are going to stay in this relationship, perhaps you should think of safety planning in the event things get out of hand." The first statement creates an enemy. The second recognizes that you do not understand the reasons for staying, but that you are there to help when the victim *is* ready to leave.

A common theoretical language is also suggested by social systems theory. For the interviewer this means that criminal justice professionals will improve their ability to communicate by borrowing from other disciplines to understand the concepts of human behavior. Common language provides the interviewer with *techniques*, which are the devices whose application enables us to accomplish our purposes and carry out our professional responsibilities. When you read this book, note the numerous techniques that are included. Many of the methods for conducting interviews borrow ideas from psychology and sociology. These ideas provide insight into human behavior and how you can use that information to become successful interviewers. Don't shy from theory—it gives you more than you may have thought!

COMMUNICATING THROUGH SOCIAL MEDIA

Gathering or providing information and the use of comprehensive questioning are concepts of investigative communication achieved through interviews. This may occur during traditional face-to-face encounters, using technology, or through social media. Each opportunity for communication has unique characteristics, and yet the means to elicit information often lies in the basics of interviewing techniques. An example of the use of technology for criminal justice investigative communication is seen in video-conferencing. Rising costs of health care associated with mental illness has provided the impetus for increasing use of telepsychiatry for diagnosing and treating inmates with behavioral and addictive disorders (AHRQ, 2009). **Telepsychiatry** refers to the use of videoconferencing for interviews between the psychiatrist and the inmate. In some jurisdictions videoconferencing may be utilized for the interview between an offender and an attorney when the inmate in jail requests legal counsel (Bouffard, 2014).

Social media is the newest avenue, which has been embraced by criminal justice investigators. As a form of community policing, social media is being used to advise

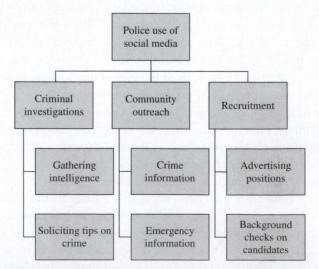

FIGURE 3-1   The police use of social media for communication with the public is evident in all primary functions of law enforcement according to the *Police Social Media Survey* (Adapted from IACP, 2015).

and promote cooperation with the community. The approach has proven to be valuable in high visibility situations during rapidly developing investigations and public safety emergencies. According to the International Association of Chiefs of Police Social Media Survey (2015), more than 96 percent of police agencies in 44 states use social media in some capacity. It appears that the number of law enforcement agencies with social media accounts is growing rapidly. The most frequently used social media platforms are Facebook, Twitter, and YouTube (IACP, 2015). Most commonly, the police departments who responded to the IACP survey use social media for criminal investigations. Departments have learned that members of the public react to the information they receive from social media, making this a valuable avenue for open dialogue (Davis, Alves, & Sklansky, 2014).

The application of science to criminal justice investigations, called **forensics**, involves the collection, preservation, and analysis of evidence. Many forensic specializations are associated with the art and science of obtaining verbal legal evidence through interviews. For example, the direct involvement in criminal investigations commonly includes forensic psychologists (Porter, Rose, & Dilley, 2016). The role of psychology is seen in three investigative contexts, advising police on investigative strategies, evaluating the creditability of suspect statements, and consultations in emergency response during hostage-taking or kidnapping cases. Mental health screening, intervention planning, and determining the competency of criminal offenders illustrates the fastest growing use of psychiatric forensic specialists in diversion and court action (Gosselin, 2017). Forensic specializations are also used for interviewing victims of extreme trauma, individuals suspected of having mental disorders, older adults, and children.

COMPONENTS OF PERSUASIVE INTERVIEWING

An investigator must persuade the person being interviewed to cooperate with an investigation by providing truthful information. Under many circumstances, people are not opposed to giving statements to authorities. Still, there is some amount of encouragement needed in all cases. Usually, the necessary encouragement is subtle, but the range of persuasion is wide. The quality of the information provided during an interview is also linked to the skills of the interviewer. Interviewing skills may involve techniques for memory retrieval in addition to conscious thoughts and observations.

As stated earlier in this text, interviewing skills can be learned—which also suggests that they may not be intuitive. For this reason, I refer to criminal justice and forensic interviewing as persuasive. **Persuasive interviewing** occurs when the interviewer brings a person to the point of communication and the goal of a successful interview results. Persuasive interviewing is not a method but is a broad approach to the process of interviewing. Active listening and rapport development are two important components of any interviewing technique.

Active Listening

Active listening is a skill that makes evident to the person being interviewed that you are attentive to what is being said. It requires the interviewer to mentally relax and draw on his or her self-esteem and confidence. Express a willingness to commiserate and listen by exhibiting patience. It is important not only to listen to what is said, but also to know how it is said. Emotional outbursts and inflections of the voice may give a clue to sensitive areas of the interview. Sudden silence, uncertainty or confusion, or the shifting of conversation to an unrelated subject may indicate that information is being withheld. Nervous bodily reaction or facial reactions may signal that a sensitive area has been reached.

FIGURE 3-2   Active listening is the most important interviewing skill you can learn!

Source: Golden Pixels LLC/Shutterstock.

Understand the subject's frame of reference to figure out what is being said. Listen to the tone, voice inflection, and level of excitement from the interviewee during the interview. Watch for body language and facial expressions to see if they match what is said.

The interviewer must remember what he or she hears. Notes should be taken in a manner that does not interrupt the interviewing process. Some witnesses are reluctant to talk if they notice that the officer is taking down every word they say. Brief notes can be made without deterring or distracting witnesses. In some situations, a room that has recording equipment can be set up in advance of the interview. Alternatively, a microphone can transmit information to another room where a note taker is making a full report.

Active listening may be demonstrated verbally and through nonverbal attentiveness. Examples of ways to show that a person is actively listening include the following:

- Body language—nod your head, look interested, smile, vary your eye contact, lean slightly forward
- Body posture—face squarely or at a 45-degree angle, lean forward, shift as the subject does, be careful not to shift to show displeasure
- Concentrate and listen carefully
- Detachment—be cool and calm without showing emotion
- Do not roll your eyes in response to a statement
- Gestures—keep arms open and palms extended
- Patience—do not rush the interviewee
- Positive silence—silence can indicate acceptance or can be used to signal your control

Rapport Development

Chapter 1 introduced the concept of rapport. Rapport should be considered the first step in any interview. Although it is difficult to describe, rapport is the establishment of two-way communication. The concept represents a working relationship between the interviewer and the subject being interviewed. Whatever the interviewee may be feeling, the interviewer is not responsible for what happened to him or her. However, you are responsible for your reaction to what you are told. The victim may be feeling pain or confusion and may direct anger at the interviewer. During interviews with an angry person try to talk slowly and more softly than normal. Anger on the part of the interviewer is a sign of weakness that indicates a lack of self-control. Avoid showing anger toward a victim. Once it has occurred, the ability to negotiate rapport is gone.

If the interviewee is acting superior to the interviewer, maintain an emotional detachment. The successful interviewer should not take the attitude of the interviewee personally or feel offended. Never apologize for asking questions and refrain from asking questions that are clearly unnecessary. Interviewers should be careful about changing their behavior in response to the interviewee to one of arrogance. To establish a cooperative relationship, the interviewer should:

1. Display a sincere interest
2. Be patient and tactful
3. Be respectful
4. Control personal feelings
5. Provide reassurance
6. Encourage a reluctant witness by asking appropriate questions

THE GOAL OF PERSUASIVE INTERVIEWING

Since the primary goal of persuasive interviewing is to bring the interviewee to the point of truthful communication, it is helpful to view the process of interviewing in stages. Central to preparation is recognizing the reasons for conducting an interview. During the course of an investigation the nature of the offense and determination if a crime was actually committed are paramount. Of added importance is to obtain information that is useful in identifying a suspect. Research suggests that the conscientious person is more persuasive across different modalities when comparing audio, video, and text

BEEN THERE . . . DONE THAT! 3-1

For some reason we tend to think of victims as being nice people and offenders as monsters. When the pattern does not fit it makes it difficult to access the credibility of the victims. The key is active listening—get past the anger and hear what happened. During an interview a woman was yelling at the police and shouting obscenities, and was extremely obnoxious. When I sat her down in a quiet place she explained to me how she had been beaten and raped by two men who had left her without clothes to die in the woods. She had been fortunate to find her way out for help, but thought that the police would not do anything for her because she was a prostitute. After a while she calmed down and gave descriptions of her assailants and recounted that what had happened to her had happened to others on the street. As it turned out I was able to identify five women who had been severely beaten by these two men. Both had extensive violent felony records. They selected prostitutes as their victims because they thought that the women could be intimidated into keeping quiet. The assaults by these men had nothing to do with sex for pay; they were vicious attacks because the perpetrators enjoyed beating and torturing women. They were both arrested, found guilty, and sent back to prison where they belonged.

communications (Mohammadi, Park, Sagae, Vinciarelli, & Morency, 2013). It appears that regardless of the communication mode, the thoroughness of the interviewer may be of greater importance.

The Nature of the Offense

While individuals are each considered to be different from each other, there are some identifiable similarities. That concept comes into play when generalizing about an approach to interviewing based on the nature of the offense. Remain calm and tactful with contradicting or antagonistic witnesses. Remember that witnesses who are angry, frightened, or emotionally upset usually perceive only a fraction of what they might observe under normal circumstances. Emotional factors can cause a witness to lie or to become uncooperative or forgetful. Persuasive interviewing involves modifying an approach to meet the unique challenges of the crime, resulting in a slightly different interviewing approach in order to elicit complete and truthful information.

Being persuasive in your interviewing also requires attention to the nonverbal communication that tell us something about the validity of the message, its urgency, and whether it is being made humorously, seriously, or sarcastically (Kadushin & Kadushin, 2013). Nonverbal behaviors may communicate what interviewees cannot bring themselves to state openly. Feelings and attitudes of which interviewees are only vaguely aware may be clear to the observant interviewer.

Persuasive interviewing also means that the nature of offense will dictate different questioning approaches. The following examples illustrate how the nature of the crime dictates the questioning.

HATE CRIMES. Showing concern for the victim's safety, note and document all injuries. Only one person should conduct the interview, and any other involved person should remain unobtrusive during the questioning (Black & Yeschke, 2014). Be careful not to minimize the crime; display genuine concern for the victim's feelings. Note that it would be difficult for someone not targeted in this way to fully understand the emotional impact it has on the individual. There may be a heightened distrust on the part of the victim toward anyone who resembles the attacker; this obstacle to interviewing is import to anticipate and overcome. Document the financial damages if any and photograph both the victim and the scene. Record spontaneous utterances made by the victim.

Use an open-ended initial question format with follow-up questions. Using closed questions, ask for exact wording of what the suspect said before, during, and after the incident and how often. Ask the victim to describe the suspect with as much detail as possible, including tattoos or clothing.

It is the task of the resourceful police officer to overcome witness reluctance to being involved. Ethnic and racial minorities will likely need to be persuaded to cooperate. Examples of helpful statements include the following:

- It is important to stop this individual (these individuals) from doing this to anyone else in your community.
- There is nothing to stop this from happening to your friends and family; we need your help.
- I know this is difficult for you, but there is something that can done about this.

PARTNER VIOLENCE. There are often strong emotional ties between the victim and the offender in these cases. The victim may even be financially dependent on the assailant. In some cases the perpetrator faces loss of employment if convicted of domestic violence. A victim may therefore be unwilling or unable to provide information that will be used against the partner; hence persuasive interviewing aims to verify and give

BEEN THERE . . . DONE THAT! 3-2

An older gentleman came in with the complaint of his car having been stolen. With great difficulty he explained that he was a professor at a prestigious university with a lot to lose by making the complaint. As it turns out he was being blackmailed by a male prostitute who he had picked up in the city a few nights before. Although he had been a homosexual for years, he was in a marriage of convenience. His reputation in the community was at stake, but he could not bring himself to pay off the demand in order to get his vehicle returned. Without the right environment, this information would not have been forthcoming. Time would have been wasted and likely the theft would not have been solved. A successful "sting" resulted in the arrest and prosecution of the blackmailer.

credibility to the victim without expecting a high level of cooperation. Make sure you get all of the available evidence and victim statements regarding the violence at the scene; do not count on victim cooperation at a later date. Questions that will help to establish the seriousness include the following:

- How often has this happened?
- Have you ever been hospitalized due to these attacks?
- Has he or she ever threatened to kill you?

Some questions will be uncomfortable or feel intrusive to the survivor. Care must be taken to reassure the interviewee that you are a professional who is prepared to listen to what happened. Listen for the description of an assault, indications of force, lack of consent, and signs of premeditation. A responding officer should be concerned with reassuring the victim of his or her immediate safety.

A detailed statement would likely follow after the victim is examined at a medical facility, when appropriate. If the victim directs anger at the police interviewer, it is important to understand that this is misdirected. Patience and compassion are needed to establish the necessary rapport for a more detailed interview at the appropriate time. The hospital examination room should be avoided as a place for that full interview.

Open-ended questions should be asked to allow for the victim to describe the assault in her or his own words. Clarifying questions to establish specific facts should be asked after the victim has completed the narrative. The interviewer should be specifically aware of victim's body language that indicates embarrassment or discomfort. Reassuring the victim that he or she is doing a good job at explaining as well as acknowledging that the questions are embarrassing will help to normalize the conversation.

Was a Crime Committed?

It is not enough for the interviewer to *think* that a crime has been committed. There are constitutional and legal limitations, which define each act that is designated as a crime. These legal points that must be proved by the prosecution in order to sustain a conviction are the parts of the crime called its *elements*. The interviewer must *know* what information is needed to prove that a crime has been committed. To determine the appropriate questions that need to be asked, taking the time to become familiar with the specific elements of the crimes that are being investigated is well worth it. This preparation provides the interviewer the opportunity to mentally prepare the questions that need to be asked in order to prove that the crime was committed. The confidence of knowing what you are looking for in the interview will also help you to be at ease. For example, if the investigation involves an elderly person, the age that defines "elderly" becomes an element that must be verified in addition to the crime elements. All states have laws specific to protecting the elderly against abuse; some statutes contain enhanced penalties. Although federal statutes and most state laws define an elderly person as one who has reached age 65, some states specify age 60 instead. Know before the interview the age that constitutes "elderly" in your state and the crimes that may have enhanced penalties if the interview concerns a crime against an older adult.

Collecting evidence that a crime was committed provides the basis for a successful prosecution. Interviews are an integral part of determining if a crime was committed and if it was, the type of crime. The three primary types of evidence are referred to as real, documentary, or testimonial evidence. **Testimonial evidence** is what the witness says in a court of law; typically this form of evidence is collected through interviews. It is evidence that is required to prove any contested fact. Real or physical evidence is something that may be seen, heard, touched, smelled, or tasted. Documentary evidence are records or receipts that may prove or disprove some fact associated with a crime, such as a credit card receipt or business card. Evidence may prove or disprove the involvement of a person or cast doubt on whether the offense was even committed.

HATE CRIMES.   Traditional offenses committed with an added element of bias constitutes a hate crime. The FBI defines a hate crime as a criminal offense against a person or property motivated in whole or in part by an offender's bias against a race, religion, disability, sexual orientation, ethnicity, gender, or gender identity. Hate itself is not a crime. An overt criminal act must be attempted, threatened, or completed along with the necessary motivation. Bias, bigotry, or prejudice might be indicated through speech or written words from the perpetrator or inferred from the type of crime committed against the victim. The investigator must document that the act committed was associated with bias, not merely that the victim was a member of a group that is known to have been targeted due to bias.

PARTNER VIOLENCE.   For a crime to be one of domestic violence there must be a legally recognized domestic relationship between the victim and the perpetrator. It is important that the interviewer specifically ask if there is a relationship between the offender and the victim in these cases. Frequently acknowledged categories include married and previously married persons; persons who live together as husband and wife; persons who have a child in common; partners of same-sex relationships; parents and their children or grandchildren; siblings; and extended family members through blood or marriage. Some states expand on traditional meanings of domestic through the recognition of persons who live under the same roof, regardless of affiliation. Substantial dating relationships may also meet the definitional standard. If the perpetrator is within one of the domestic categories of relationship to the victim, a special legal category exists. Victimization within a domestic relationship provides additional criminal and civil protections and increased sanctions that are not accessible to persons whose perpetrator is a stranger or someone other than a domestic partner. Siblings, in-laws, and extended family through blood or marriage may also fall under the classification. Without a legally recognized relationship, there is no crime of domestic violence, although the act may constitute a different criminal category.

The primary aggressor in a domestic relationship is the person who is exercising power and control over the other. Identifying the primary aggressor in a domestic relationship is the standard for determining who is at fault when it appears that there is mutual abuse. The standard developed due to the concern that mandatory arrest laws result in the unjust arrest of victims. In states that do not have primary aggressor laws, dual arrests are more than twice as likely to occur (Hirschel & Deveau, 2016). The courts and the legislature discourage the practice of arresting both parties in situations

BEEN THERE . . . DONE THAT! 3-3

Just before Christmas, a call came in at 10 AM from a crying child that daddy was hitting mommy and had pushed her into the Christmas tree. By the time we arrived at the scene the tree was upright, and there was no evidence of domestic abuse. The wife was interviewed apart from her husband and children and refused to give any information. She denied that she had been hit. There were no marks or bruises evident. The husband also denied any battering. There was no probable cause to make an arrest, even though I was sure that the man had hit his wife. The child who had called said she made up the story. No probable cause meant that no arrest could be made.

I next interviewed the three children and asked if they were ok, conducting an assessment on the level of risk for harm to them if we were to leave them. I asked if there were any guns in the house, and the children told me that there was rifle in their bedroom closet! It was fully loaded and did not have a trigger guard attached. Following up these claims led to evidence that the weapon belonged to the husband. Because the failure to secure a weapon in a locked container or with a safety lock is a felony crime, the guns in the house were confiscated and the husband was arrested.

that appear to be mutually combative. Making a primary aggressor determination assists the officer in arresting the person who is responsible for the violence.

Neither the gender nor the size of the individual provides enough information to make that primary aggressor determination. Separating the parties and interviewing them provides the best option. The situation should be examined to find out if violence was used by one person only. Absent evidence of self-defense, it would be a single-arrest situation. If violence was used by both individuals, questions must be asked about prior assaults to find out if one person was acting in self-defense. Without a history of violence, the next step would be to see who is the most fearful and who is in control.

EYEWITNESS IDENTIFICATION EVIDENCE

A primary justification for interviewing is to identify the perpetrator. Obtaining and accurately recording the physical description of a criminal suspect are common components of investigative interviewing. A good physical description can hasten the apprehension of the criminal offender and assist in obtaining a successful conviction. The identification may establish probable cause to support an arrest. An eyewitness identification holds a high amount of creditability in the courtroom. It is, therefore, the responsibility of an investigator to secure the most accurate and complete description possible from those witnesses who had the best opportunity to observe the suspect or who have personal knowledge of his or her identity. The three procedures used by law enforcement officers to identify a perpetrator whose identity is not known are:

- Showups
- Photo lineups
- Live lineups

Despite the high level of credibility afforded witness identification, eyewitness evidence can be inaccurate and lead to the prosecution of innocent persons while the guilty go free. Human visual perception, memory, confidence, and policies governing law enforcement procedures can result in misidentifications with significant consequences. Eyewitness misidentification is thought to be the leading cause of wrongful convictions. Misidentification is an issue in more than 70 percent of more than 300 convictions overturned through DNA testing (The Innocence Project, 2016).

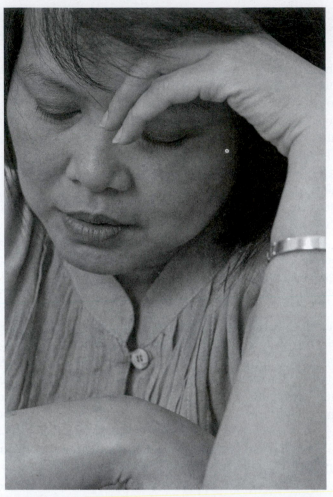

FIGURE 3-3 High levels of stress, witness attention, duration of exposure, environmental viewing conditions, and the characteristics of the eyewitness are among the estimator variables that can affect identification accuracy.

Source: William casey/Shutterstock.

Research suggests two main categories of factors that interfere with eyewitness accuracy; they are referred to as estimator variables and system variables (Batts, DeLone, & Stephens, 2014). **Estimator variables** describe the characteristics of the witness, the alleged perpetrator, and the environmental conditions of the event that cannot be manipulated or adjusted by state actors. Examples of estimator variables are lighting, the presence of a weapon, the degree of stress, distance from the perpetrator, eyesight, and memory. While law enforcement has no control over estimator variables, the National Research Council (2014) recommends that all law enforcement agencies provide their officers and agents with training on vision and memory along with the variables that affect them. **System variables** are the circumstances surrounding the identification procedure itself that are generally within the control of those administering the procedure. Development of best practice policies to control system variables is recommended.

In many of the overturned cases, the eyewitnesses had testified with high levels of confidence that they had identified the correct offender. In reality, little correlation exists between witness confidence and the accuracy of the identification (*State v. Lawson*, 2012). While witnesses who express postidentification high confidence are in fact highly accurate, this group is quite unusual. The Supreme Judicial Court Study Group (2013) research suggests that only a small fraction of witnesses report such high levels

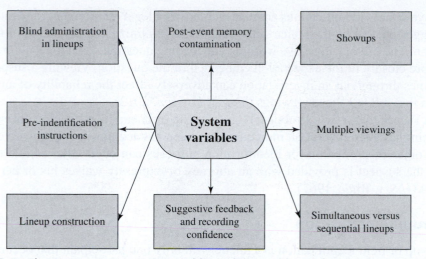

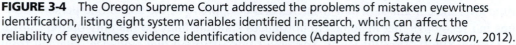

FIGURE 3-4 The Oregon Supreme Court addressed the problems of mistaken eyewitness identification, listing eight system variables identified in research, which can affect the reliability of eyewitness evidence identification evidence (Adapted from *State v. Lawson*, 2012).

of confidence and approximately 10 percent of them make incorrect identifications. Influences affecting the accuracy of the eyewitness identification might occur before the identification or after the identification.

Confirming feedback takes place after an identification and does not affect the actual result. It is not unusual for a witness to want to please the investigator, asking "did I do ok?" The authority should not answer that question! Confidence should be based on the memory of the witness and not on any feedback from the investigator. A simple statement from the authority conducting the identification that the witness "did well" might change the confidence of the person who made the identification as well as their recollections concerning the quality of their opportunity to view a perpetrator and an event. Known as postidentification confirming feedback, this influence tends to falsely inflate the witnesses' confidence in the accuracy of their identification. It can later falsely inflate the witness confidence reflected in the reports they give on factors commonly used by courts and jurors to gauge eyewitness reliability. The danger of confirming feedback lies in its potential to increase the *appearance* of reliability without increasing reliability itself.

Guidance for the development of best practices in eyewitness identification has come from important judicial rulings. The U.S. Supreme Court's 1977 ruling in *Manson v. Brathwaite* provides the foundation for the judicial review of eyewitness identification under the Due Process Clause of the U.S. Constitution. The *Mason v. Brathwaite* test requires judges to evaluate the "reliability" of eyewitness identifications using factors derived from prior rulings and not from empirically validated sources. Several state supreme courts have supplemented the federal standard. In *State v. Lawson*, the Oregon Court reviewed eyewitness identification research and offered a revised procedure that requires the court to decide whether investigators used "suggestive" tactics to get an identification and the extent to which other information supports the identification.

IDENTIFICATION PROCEDURES

The police in the United States investigate millions of crimes each year. The FBI estimated that in 2015 law enforcement agencies nationwide made 10.8 million arrests, excluding traffic violations. Despite investigating a significant number of cases, there is no reliable information on the number of arrests that are based on eyewitness identification.

Eyewitness identifications are made under strict legal requirements and must avoid any suggestiveness by the police with practices to minimize contamination of the identification. The use of suggestive wording and leading questions tend to result in answers that more closely fit the expectation embedded in the question. Viewing a suspect multiple times throughout an investigation can adversely affect the reliability of any identification that follows those viewings (*State v. Lawson*, 2012).

A suspect has a right to counsel for a showup or lineup identification once a formal complaint has been filed or an indictment has been handed down. No showup or lineup or any other confrontation for identification purposes can occur after formal charging unless the suspect is provided with an attorney or expressly waives his or her right to counsel (*U.S. v. Wade*, 1967).

Showup Identification

A showup or field identification is a lineup with only one participant that occurs a short time after the commission of a crime. Courts disapprove of the use of one-person showups but recognize that in some circumstances showups may be the only option (*Stoval v. Denno*, 1967). The Wisconsin Supreme Court affirmed that evidence obtained from a showup in that state would not be admissible except in cases where it was conducted out of necessity (*State v. Dubose*, 2005). Based on a totality-of-circumstances test, the showup would not be necessary under the *Dubose* standard unless the police lacked probable cause to make an arrest or because of other exigent circumstances.

The showup is further limited to circumstances in which a crime has just been committed and a suspect has been apprehended very close in time and place to the offence. Typically, the suspect who has fled the scene is brought back to the witness to see if he or she can make an identification. Its limited use is to prevent an innocent person from being arrested. The suspect has no right to counsel at a showup (*Kirby v. Illinois*, 1972). Policies on the use of showup identification practices vary among the states.

If a showup method of identification is used, it requires careful procedural safeguards. When one or more witnesses interviewed at the scene indicates that they can make an identification of the perpetrator, the investigator must document that description before conducting the field identification showup. If there are one or more witnesses, only one at a time should have access to the suspect. If possible, bring the witness to the place that the suspect is detained. Caution the witness that the perpetrator may not be at the location. Fully document both positive identifications and nonidentification outcomes that occur, the time of the procedure, and its location. The suspect should not be handcuffed or in a jail cell during this form of identification. There is no requirement that the suspect must be given *Miranda* warnings because the evidence is not testimonial or communicative. If multiple witnesses are involved in a case and one has made a positive showup identification alternative methods should be considered for the remaining eyewitness.

Photo and Live Lineups

Composites, photographs, or sketches may be used to help identify persons. Composites images provide a depiction that may be used to develop investigative leads but should not be used as the primary evidence or to establish probable cause for an arrest. Composites are prepared from identikit, artist rendering, or computer-generated images. Do not show a witness a photo or conduct a live lineup before developing a composite; it may influence his or her memory of the suspect and cause contamination.

During an interview, the witness or victim may also indicate a willingness to identify the suspect from a lineup. Typically a police lineup is made up of six people or photographs, one is a suspect and the remaining are fillers. The composition of the lineup must be free from bias, fillers which do not look like the witness's description of

BEEN THERE . . . DONE THAT! 3-4

A photo lineup may or may not result in the identification of the perpetrator during an investigation. Care must be taken to make sure that the victim understands that the perpetrator may not be in the photo array and that he or she must look at all photos before commenting out loud about any of the pictures. In one case the victim told me that she thought the number 3 picture was the man who had assaulted her, then went on to say that she was mistaken—he was number 5. This identification was worthless and therefore discarded. It was later learned that none of the men in the photo array had been the attacker.

the suspect may cause a suspect to stand out. Before viewing either a photo or physical lineup, careful instructions to the witness that the perpetrator may not be in the lineup is imperative. The witness should be instructed that the case is investigated regardless of whether an identification is made and that it is important to clear innocent persons from suspicion as well as identify guilty parties.

The double-blind lineup procedure is considered the best standard by the American Psychology-Law Society and has been adopted by numerous jurisdictions across the United States (Steblay, Wells, & Douglass, 2014). To avoid influencing to the witness identification, the double-blind process requires that the lineup administrator not know which lineup member is the suspect and which are merely fillers. In police lineup identifications, lineup administrators who know the identity of the suspect can consciously or unconsciously suggest that information to the witness. The likelihood of misidentification is significantly decreased when witnesses are instructed prior to an identification procedure that a suspect may or may not be in the lineup or photo array and that it is permissible not to identify anyone.

Experts suggest that people tend to select the individual who looks most like the offender, as compared to the other members of the lineup (Wells, 2006). In *State v. Lawson* (2012) the court recommended the use of a lineup procedure in which the witness is presented with each person or photograph sequentially. The reasoning is that the witness is less able to engage in relative judgment and therefore is less likely to misidentify innocent suspects. In traditional identification procedures, police display several persons or photographs simultaneously to an eyewitness. Witnesses permitted to view all the subjects simultaneously tend to make a "relative judgment" choosing the person or photograph that most closely resembles the perpetrator from among the other subjects as opposed to making an "absolute judgment" comparing each subject to their memory of the perpetrator and deciding whether that subject is the perpetrator. Relative judgments are problematic in lineups that do not include the offender since an innocent person may be selected and confused with recognition memory.

The suspect has no right to counsel that affects his or her photo from being used in a photo lineup (*U.S. v. Ash*, 1973). The array should consist of at least six photos of different people, including only one photo of the suspect. The pictures of nonsuspects should be consistent with unique features such as scars or tattoos but do not need to closely resemble each other in all features. The photos should be viewed one photo at a time. If a witness picks out a suspect during the photo array, insist on showing all of the photographs. Do not use the same pictures in a lineup of a new suspect to the same witness. Document the photo lineup order and the witness responses.

The suspect has no right to counsel at a lineup prior to formal charges being brought against him or her (*U.S. v. Ash*, 1973). One suspect is included with a minimum of five nonsuspects. General resemblances are all that is needed, with the suspect significant features being similar. Avoid using individuals who are so similar as to make identification difficult. Be sure that the suspect does not stand out due to difference by race, ethnicity, age, or height. Document the instructions that are made to the witness and the responses, the time and place of the lineup, and the identities of its participants.

ASSESSING THE ACCURACY OF A STATEMENT

Always consider the possibility of false reporting. The job of the interviewer is to discover the truth if that is possible; therefore, the interviewer should adopt a neutral position to conduct interviews. A full investigation is still necessary even if it is suspected that the person is lying, distorting the facts, or withholding important information. Do not initially accuse the individual of falsely reporting or treat the person as if they were lying. Obtain as much information as possible and follow the leads that are provided. The facts of the case will speak louder than an accusation. It is not necessary to make judgments, and it is unwise to jump to conclusions.

When a claim appears to be exaggerated, consider whether the reporter has any motivations for exaggeration. Look at the repercussions of the act. Is the victim a juvenile, married, or ashamed? Do not judge the reliability of the statement based solely on a moral evaluation of the person providing the information. Reality is stranger than fiction. To dismiss a complaint based on an initial statement because the individual does not fit the profile of a victim exposes the person to further violation and potentially allows a perpetrator to go free. Instead, take the position of corroborating the victim statement to increase its credibility whenever possible.

A witness may provide information that is correct in some ways and incorrect in others. The entire statement does not have to be ignored if it is discovered that part of the statement is inaccurate. It is not unusual for eyewitness accounts to vary on specifics of the situation. One person may remember a vehicle as red, and another report the vehicle as blue. This does not mean that one or the other is lying; just note the inconsistencies for further evaluation. Review the statement for inconsistencies to other statements or known evidence in the case.

Conclusions

This chapter introduced the concept of persuasive interviewing. This is not a method, but a general approach to conducting interviews. The approach brings with it a determination to interview with the goal of obtaining as much accurate information as possible. Investigating different types of crime may require unique interviewing methods. The following chapters will introduce you to a variety of communication options. Consider this chapter as an invitation to develop multiple skills that may involve a face-to-face encounter, using technology or social media. Be flexible and responsive—the reward will be an improved quality of interviews and a development of new skills. Develop and use active listening skills and rapport to enhance the communication within the interview.

The implicit idea is that each phase of the interview process leaves nothing to chance. The interviewer is in control of determining whether a crime was committed. If so, the next step is to learn the identity of the perpetrator. Identifying the offender can be a complicated process of gathering evidence and interviewing multiple individuals. Suspect identification is complicated by the limitations of eyewitness estimator values over which the investigator has no control. System variables of eyewitness identification present challenges for investigators during showups, photo lineups, and live lineups. Avoiding the pitfalls of suggestive feedback and postevent memory contamination require the implementation and strict adherence to policies for conducting these practices. Blind administration of lineups, specific instructions, and lineup construction free of bias are suggested to address system variables during identification. Procedures should involve sequential lineups while avoiding having the eyewitness engage in multiple viewings of lineups. All the information that brings the interviewer to the objective is useful for explaining the crime and justifying the response.

Questions for Review

Short-Answer Questions

1. What are the three general characteristics that assist in framing the persuasive interview according to social systems theory?

2. What is the term that refers to the use of videoconferencing for interviews between the psychiatrist and the inmate?

3. According to the International Association of Chiefs of Police Social Media Survey, what is the estimated percentage of police agencies who use social media in some capacity?

4. What is the type of relationship that must be established by the interviewer in cases of family violence?

5. What are the three procedures used by law enforcement officers to identify a perpetrator whose identify is not known?

Fill-in Questions

1. Two types of lineups that are often used to identify the unknown suspect are _____ and _____.

2. _____ refers to the understanding that the continuation of a system or family relationship may take priority due to the fear of the anticipated consequences of change.

3. Interviews may occur during _____, _____, or through social media.

4. Police use of social media for criminal investigations may involve _____ or for _____.

5. _____ occurs when the interviewer brings a person to the point of communication and the goal of a successful interview results.

6. The skill that makes evident to the person being interviewed that you are attentive to what is being said is referred to as _____.

7. _____ is the establishment of a two-way communication that should be the first step in any interview.

8. When interviewing the victim of a hate crime there may be a _____ on the part of the victim toward anyone who resembles the attacker. This obstacle to interviewing is important to anticipate and overcome.

9. _____ are prepared from identikit, _____, or _____.

10. To avoid influences to the witness identification the _____ procedure is considered the best standard by the American Psychology-Law Society.

Exercises

1. The Innocence Project has done some interesting work on eyewitness misidentification. Go to their website and investigate. Based on what you have learned, write a model policy for conducting photo and live lineups.

2. Take five minutes to have a conversion with someone in the class you do not know and with whom you have never spoken. Ask him or her to explain something that they enjoy doing in their spare time. Listen intently to the conversation using techniques from this chapter. Can you improve your results? Report to the class on how it felt to listen intently.

References

AHRQ. (2009). *Mental health research findings.* [Online.] Retrieved from http://www.ahrq.gov.

Batts, A., DeLone, M., & Stephens, D. (2014). *Policing and wrongful convictions* (NCJ 246328). Washington, D.C.: National Institute of Justice.

Black, I., & Yeschke, C. (2014). *The art of investigative interviewing* (3rd ed.). Boston, MA: Butterworth-Heinemann.

Bouffard, J. (2014). *Montgomery County's Managed Assigned Counsel/Mental Health Program: Final report.* Retrieved from http://www.tidc.texas.gov/media/27762/macmh-2014-final-report-shsu.pdf.

Charman, S. D., & Wells, G. L. (2012). The moderating effect of ecphoric experience on post-identification feedback: A critical test of the cues-based inference conceptualization. *Applied Cognitive Psychology, 26*(2), 243–250.

Davis, E., Alves, A., & Sklansky, D. (2014). *Social media and police leadership: Lessons from Boston* (NCJ 244760). Washington, D.C.: National Institute of Justice.

Gosselin, D. K. (2017). *Crime and mental disorders: The criminal justice response.* St. Paul, MN: West Academic Publishing.

Hirschel, D., & Deveau, L. (2016). The impact of primary aggressor laws on single versus dual arrest in incidents of intimate partner violence. *Violence against Women,* 1077801216657898.

IACP. (2015). International Association of Chiefs of Police 2015 Social Media Results. Retrieved from www.theiacp.org.

Kadushin, A., & Kadushin, G. (2013). *The social work interview.* New York: Columbia University Press.

Kirby v. Illinois, 406 U.S. 682 (1972).

Manson v. Brathwaite, 432 U.S. 98, 114 (1977).

Mohammadi, G., Park, S., Sagae, K., Vinciarelli, A., & Morency, L.-P. (2013). *Who is persuasive?: The role of perceived personality and communication modality in social multimedia.* Paper presented at the 15th ACM on International conference on multimodal interaction, New York, NY.

Porter, S., Rose, K., & Dilley, T. (2016). Enhanced interrogations: The expanding roles of psychology in police investigations in Canada. *Canadian Psychology/ Psychologie canadienne, 57*(1), 35–43.

State v. Dubose, WI 126 (2005).

State v. Lawson, 291 P. 3d 673 (Oregon Supreme Court 2012).

State v. Michaels, 136 N.J. 299, 311–12, 642 A.2d 1372 (1994).

Steblay, N. K., Wells, G. L., & Douglass, A. B. (2014). The eyewitness post identification feedback effect 15 years later: Theoretical and policy implications. *Psychology, Public Policy, and Law, 20*(1), 1–18.

Stoval v. Denno, 388 U.S. 293 (1967).

Supreme Judicial Court Study Group. (2013). *Eyewitness Evidence* (Massachusetts Court system). Retrieved March 2, 2017 from http://www.mass.gov/courts/docs/ sjc/docs/eyewitness-evidence-report-2013.pdf.

The Innocence Project. (2016). *Eyewitness misidentification.* [Online.] Retrieved from https://www.innocenceproject .org/causes/eyewitness-misidentification/

The National Research Council. (2014). *Identifying the culprit: Assessing eyewitness identification.* Washington, D.C.: The National Academies Press.

U.S. v. Ash, 413 U.S. 300 (1973).

U.S. v. Wade, 388 U.S. 218 (1967).

Wells, G. L. (2006). Eyewitness identification: Systemic reforms. *Wisconsin Law Review*, 615 - 1683.

PART II

Methods and Techniques

Checking the crime scene, collecting physical evidence, and case development are three primary activity groups of criminal investigations. Each of these activities also includes interviewing. This section describes some common interviewing methods used in criminal justice and forensic investigation. Chapter 4 discusses unstructured and structured approaches to the criminal justice interview. These may be utilized with the cooperative or uncooperative interviewee. Interviewing techniques, which involve technology, are discussed as they offer viable choices that have joined the face-to-face option. SCAN is a commonly used statement analysis method. The unstructured interviewing approach is based on answering the "five W's and How." The approach is simplistic and without cumbersome procedures. Unstructured interviewing is useful for determining the level of cooperation that can be expected from a witness, gathering emergency and crisis information, and field operations. The structured interview is a three-step method of interviewing. It adds rapport building, narrative descriptions, and ample interviewing opportunity to the unstructured approach and is a valuable tool for interviewers. Conducting interviews online with the use technology as the means of communication is a new phenomenon. The structured interviewing approach emerges as a suitable method for asynchronous textual communication for interviewing. SCAN refers to the *Scientific Content Analysis* method, which involves the use of statement analysis. Each one of these methods is adaptable to the situations in which questioning might occur.

Chapter 5 covers interviewing methods that use memory-jogging techniques to facilitate recall. Forensic hypnosis and cognitive interviewing are the better-known techniques, they are recently joined by *Differential Recall Enhancement* (DRE) methods. The approach used in forensic hypnotic interviewing is different from cognitive interviewing. Forensic hypnosis is frequently employed in therapeutic settings but is rejected in many states for use in court. Evidence gathered from witnesses who have undergone hypnosis may or may not be admissible in a criminal case, although the courts cannot deny the introduction of defendant hypnosis. Cognitive interviewing is a memory-jogging approach that can be mastered by even the novice interviewer. The approach is easily learned and can be adapted to a variety of situations that require information retrieval. Many courts have stated a preference for the cognitive interviewing approach in criminal cases as it has been scientifically tested and found to be a reliable method. The foundation of the cognitive interview is the use of four mnemonics that are the memory-jogging techniques. These should be learned and practiced for use in any interviewing situation. DRE methods that are discussed in chapter 5 are cognitive-based approaches. DRE methods have been assigned significant creditability for interviewing purposes. These include *the Assessment Criteria Indicative of Deception* (ACID), the cognitive load approach, *Strategic Use of Evidence* (SUE) and tactical interviewing.

The principles to detect deception include verbal and nonverbal cues to detect deceit which are covered in chapter 6. Neurolinguistic programing provides the framework to conceptualize the interconnectedness of verbal and nonverbal communication. Verbal cues may be spoken or written. Of these, *Reality Monitoring* (RM) and *Criteria-Based Content Analysis* (CBCA) have emerged as scientifically valid methods of detecting deceit using the verbal cues to detect deceit in an interview.

Behavioral interviewing techniques in Chapter 6 provide tools for investigative interviewing as well. These include the nonverbal indicators such as paralanguage, body language, and proxemics. Techniques based on language consider what a person says and how it is said. Body language refers to posture and gestures. Proxemics is social distance and space. These techniques provide situations for interviewer interpretation. Once learned, the methods are applicable in any interview or interrogation as additional tools when determining truthfulness versus deceit.

4

Unstructured and Structured Interviewing with Online Application and SCAN

Source: Courtesy of Denise K. Gosselin.

CHAPTER OBJECTIVES

After completing this chapter, you should be able to:

1. State the motivations of a side-tracker.
2. Provide two examples when group interviewing might be used.
3. Explain the five W's and How of the unstructured approach.
4. Define *mens rea*.
5. Define *actus reus*.
6. Examine the three steps to the structured approach.
7. Describe the approach to interviewing referred to as SCAN.
8. Using the structure of the statement, classify the three parts to a truthful statement.

KEY TERMS

Actus reus	Asynchronous communication
Extraneous information	Lack of conviction
Mens rea	Side-tracker
Spontaneous corrections	Statement analysis

INTRODUCTION

The chapter starts out by identifying the sources of information and suggested spacing for gathering information. Included in this section are methods of unstructured interviewing, structured interviewing, and scientific content analysis. Unstructured interviewing is a straightforward asking of questions to obtain information about a case. The approach is typically referred to as a "just-the-facts" way to get answers to the issues that describe an incident. It is a neutral process that uses broad questions to elicit information. Questions are rarely formulated, and no technique is involved. The approach is criticized because the question format is usually closed ended and the manner of questioning can be abrupt. Historically it has not encouraged interviewee participation or the free exchange of information, and therefore its use is limited. For these reasons, the unstructured approach does not enjoy a good reputation as an efficient method of interviewing.

The structured interviewing approach uses the best of unstructured questioning methods while applying principles used in cognitive interviewing. While the structured interviewing technique requires more time for preparation, it does allow interviewees the opportunity to establish rapport with the interviewer. Structured interviewing also provides direction in the questioning to facilitate cooperation from the interviewee.

A recent development in the mode of interviewing comes with the use of technology. This innovation overcomes many obstacles and boundaries, which plague face-to-face communication, including time and space. However, the impact of different interview models involving technology has not been thoroughly tested. Researchers suggest that inconsistency may affect outcomes, so caution is warranted when using new technologies for investigative interviewing (Blacksmith, Willford, & Behrend, 2016).

The third approach in this chapter may be the most popular method used in the United States and Europe. Practitioners widely use the SCAN technique for increasing the amount of information from the interviewee.

IDENTIFYING THE SOURCES

Solving a crime depends on the ability of the interviewer to acquire accurate information regarding the details of the event. Information typically comes from multiple people who must be approached to determine their willingness to provide information. The statements must be evaluated for their reliability and applicability to the case. Each interview, regardless of the approach used, must establish the identity of the interviewee. Personal information along with gang affiliations and probation or parole status is often included during the identification stage. Some investigators will document the interviewee by taking a photo. Recording by video or audio means will be discussed in later chapters. Computer apps such as the "Police Field Interview FI Card" are gaining popularity with law enforcement, security agencies, health care, and hospitality investigators for record management and incident reporting (Wave Systems Corporation, 2017). Date, time, and weather are frequently noted as well. The unstructured approach to interviewing provides an adequate way in which to gather identification information and to make preliminary assessments of the interviewee.

Early on in an investigation, it is important to find out which individuals may have information about the case versus those who do not. Sometimes a person will want to

FIGURE 4-1   Identify your sources! Is she the complainant, the victim, or a side-tracker? Is she purposefully attempting to mislead the investigator?

Source: Warren Goldswain/123RF.

give information about a case or claim to be a witness when he or she is not connected with the situation at all. Referred to as a **side-tracker**, this is an individual who is falsely claiming to be a witness or suspect to a crime. The side-tracker may be someone with emotional or mental disorders, seeking publicity, or an individual who has a grudge against someone about whom he or she wants to provide information. It may be the perpetrator who is purposefully attempting to mislead the investigator. If the motive for the giving of information is not clear, try to find out about any relationship the person may have had with the primary individual involved in the investigation. Check all information against the known facts to determine if any of the information is useful before discarding it. A side-tracker can take valuable time away from the focus of an investigation.

The individual who reports a crime or accuses another person of an offense is called the complainant. The complainant may be the victim, someone who saw the crime occur, or one who has information about the situation being investigated. Sometimes the complainant is the perpetrator who is attempting to divert police attention away from his or her actions. If preliminary questions reveal that the complainant may be the perpetrator, then the approach changes from an interview to an interrogation.

If the source of information comes from the victim, keep in mind that stress or shock may influence the individual's memory of an incident (*State v. Lawson*, 2012). Multiple interviews may be needed to obtain an accurate victim statement, but care should be taken to avoid multiple identification procedures. The victim may be overly cooperative or highly emotional at the time of an initial interview. It is probably not necessary to do an in-depth interview under these conditions. Obtain enough information to provide emergency or medical attention and to identify a suspect if an assault was committed.

Ask questions to determine if the complainant is a witness or victim. What did this person see or hear about the incident? When interviewing, always separate the individuals and interview them one at a time and outside of hearing by any other persons. Encourage the person not to discuss the situation with any other witness. A dilemma exists for someone who does not want to tell something that might be hurtful to another.

Group Interviewing

Interviewing a single suspect is the most common approach in crime investigation. Separating suspects occurs as soon as possible to reduce their opportunity for collaboration on responses and to protect or exploit the vulnerable member of a group. In situations where there are multiple individuals to be questioned and only one interviewer available, it may make sense to use group interviewing techniques.

Border and airport security checkpoints are field examples where collective interviewing is a viable option. Another example where group interviewing is used occurs when sham marriages are suspected. Sham marriages used as a way to achieve citizenship are on the increase. According to Vernham et al. (2014), between 4,000 and 10,000 applications to stay in the United Kingdom occur each year based on sham marriages facilitated by organized crime groups. Group interviewing is different from individual interviewing. One example, which uses turn-taking techniques with multiple interviewees, explores cues from suspects communicating and interacting with another (Vernham, Vrij, Mann, Leal, & Hillman, 2014).

GUIDELINES FOR THE UNSTRUCTURED INTERVIEWING APPROACH

The unstructured approach to interviewing is criticized for its excessive simplicity, abruptness, and lack of direction. Other models, such as cognitive interviewing and techniques, which elicit verbal cues to deceit (which are discussed in later chapters), come under fire for extreme complexity, cumbersome techniques, and questions that must be asked in specific and difficult-to-remember order. It is the

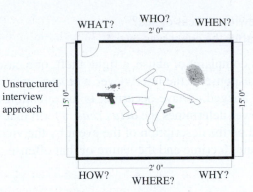

FIGURE 4-2   There is no required order for the guidelines to be used during the unstructured interview. Instead, think of the five W's and How as a checklist to make sure that as much information has been gathered as possible.

responsibility of the interviewer to determine which approach works best for the case under investigation.

Questioning that follows these simple guidelines takes advantage of the immediate cooperation from an interviewee. The six guidelines to unstructured interviewing involve questions that answer who, what, when, where, why, and how—the five W's and How. A primary purpose of the unstructured approach is to gather only the information that is necessary for the investigation. This method is used most often in field situations during which time for conducting interviews may be scarce. It can be followed up with more directed interviewing as time permits in the future. The majority of information gained through unstructured interviewing is helpful for any investigation. The difference between unstructured methods of interviewing and other approaches is the way the questions are asked. The unstructured method approach is often abrupt and straight to the point. Rather than encouraging narrative responses, this interviewing approach tends to limits answers. There is no order required during questioning and no suggested steps for conducting the interview.

One reason to use the unstructured interview approach is to determine the level of cooperation that can be expected from a witness. A potential witness may be called on the phone to determine if a full interview might be helpful to the investigation. An additional use of the unstructured interviewing approach is to obtain emergency response information and general details of the event at the scene of the crime.

People should be addressed in a manner that is most likely going to encourage their cooperation. Understand the reasons why a person may or may not want to provide information. Avoid antagonizing the person being interviewed because they are less likely to provide information if they sense conflict or anger.

What?

Questions should not be asked in a way that leads the person being interviewed to give a particular answer, nor should they be accusatory. Individuals seeking to please the interviewer may inadvertently provide information that is false rather than gives no information at all. Instruct the interviewee that although you depend on their cooperation, you understand that they will not have all the answers.

In obtaining complete information about an incident, the interviewer should search for what happened before the incident, what occurred during the incident, and what happened after the incident. An initial determination of *What* covers the following circumstances:

- What offense was committed?
- What happened?
- What weapon was used?
- What was said?

- What did the eyewitness hear or see?
- What happened after the event was over?

Is the situation a complaint of abuse, a fight, theft, or a case of stolen or damaged property? The initial response of the interviewer will vary greatly based on the general knowledge of what is alleged to have occurred. Is the situation even a violation of the law? Here the interviewer determines the *actus reus*, a term that widely known to mean the "guilty act." Based on the description of the event by the victim or witnesses, determine if the act constitutes a crime and the nature of that offense.

Who?

Find out the names and descriptions of all people involved. If this is a primary response, ask the dispatcher for the name of the complainant when in route to the scene. Determine when possible if the complainant or suspect will likely still be at the site at the time of arrival and request both be instructed to wait there. If the call originated from a neighbor or witness, obtain names, addresses, and telephone number through dispatch or within the case file. If an anonymous reporter is involved in reporting, attempt to identify that individual through caller ID or witnesses. Relevant questions to be asked include the following:

- Who is the victim?
- Who is the perpetrator?
- Who are the witnesses?

Are there likely to be a group of individuals to be reckoned with, or is the situation between two persons? Whether there is a small group of people or a few individuals make a difference on who should be questioned about the case. The number of people present also will affect the way that the officer will approach persons at the scene. If the dispatcher has the names of persons at the scene, ask for a records check to determine if either party has been involved in prior offenses, has an outstanding warrant against them, or is the subject of a current restraining order. In particular, when the response is to a disturbance, determine if either party has a current firearms license. Find out if there are any children in the home.

Who are the people in relation to each other? Is there a relationship between the victim and the perpetrator? Are they friends or acquaintances? Could they be related to someone? The existence of any relationship opens the possibility of motives to give inaccurate information because of trying to protect someone or having a grudge against someone. Ask people about their prior law enforcement contact. Have they been arrested before? Have they been a victim or witness in a previously reported crime? Are they related to a law enforcement person? These questions on the relationship of the individual to those involved can help in establishing rapport and for assessing the credibility of the individual.

When?

Find out if the incident is still ongoing. Is the complaint about the recently discovered missing property or is this an old complaint? The response will be different from that to an offense involving a recently discovered theft of property and an allegation of violence. Has the complainant made similar allegations about this person in the past? Is this a situation of reoccurring abuse? Is there an order of protection or restraining order that is in effect? Has this type of offense ever occurred against the victim in the past? Possible questions include the following:

- When did this incident occur?
- When was the event reported?
- When did injuries occur?

BEEN THERE ... DONE THAT! 4-1

On a warm day, in the middle of summer, the body of a missing 15-year-old girl was located in the river. Her hands were tied behind her back with a dirty white sock. The autopsy confirmed that she had died of drowning, so she was likely bound and thrown into the river while she was still alive. Why did this occur? It was puzzling because she was still dressed, including her underwear. Early in the investigation, the motive of sexual assault was dismissed because of her being fully clothed. I noted that she was wearing a sanitary pad at the time of her death.

Two males were identified as suspects and interrogated. They were both under the age of 20 years. When asked how they knew the victim, each one responded that she was a friend. She got into their car to go for a ride because she knew them. Together the three of them went to a secluded spot on the river where kids often go for underage drinking. It still did not make sense. Why would they kill a friend?

During the questioning I asked if they had had sex with her, knowing that they had not. Immediately one man drew his lips tight as if in anger! They wanted to have sex with her, but she had said "NO." She had before; they did not understand why she would not do it then. They fought with her to remove her clothing; she struggled and yelled. In anger, one man had taken off his socks and tied her hands. Partially pulling down her underwear, they noted that she was having her period. One of the young men had been arrested for rape in a neighboring state but had received a suspended sentence. He became concerned that she would tell someone. He convinced his accomplice that they had to keep her from telling anyone. To cover up the attempted rape, they threw her into the river, still struggling and screaming. The tragedy still did not make sense to me, but the "why" had been answered.

Where?

Did the offense occur at the place where the witness or victim is currently? This information may help to determine if the offender is likely to be near the crime scene or not. Of equal importance is whether evidence of the crime may be at a different location than the victim, which would require the preservation of that scene. Consider exploring the following issues:

- Where was the location of the incident?
- Where did the event begin and where did it end?
- Where were the witnesses located in relation to the offense?
- Where is the best place to conduct the interview?

In addition to knowing the place where the event happened, questions should be asked to determine why it happened at that location. In a purse-snatching example, the event may have occurred on the street with a burnt-out light. The location may indicate that the perpetrator was familiar with the area rather than it being a random attack. If the event was in a home, whose home is it? Was the person a guest or an intruder? Were there indications of forced entry?

When doing the initial assessment for victim cooperation using the unstructured approach, it is useful to consider the place where the interview should occur. If interviewing takes place in an open area, care should be taken to keep the interviewee outside of sight and earshot of other individuals.

Why?

The motivation for an event may not be readily observable and could be related to the value structure or relationship of the person to the situation. To determine why something happens might involve some value judgments on the part of the interviewer. Be careful to properly phrase information that is a judgment rather than a fact in any report that contains it.

Why did this occur?

Interviewing should establish the *mens rea* of the case. **Mens rea** refers to the state of mind of the perpetrator, not the victim. *Mens rea* is the guilty-mind requirement or the knowledge of a wrongful purpose. This condition is not the same as intent; it is present when a person should have known better, even if he or she did not intend the consequences. Determining that the individual did not intend the consequences does not mean that he or she is not legally responsible for what happened. There are four levels of *mens rea*:

1. Purposefulness—The act is intentional and is done for a reason or goal. An example is when a person kills another for monetary gains, such as life insurance or an inheritance.
2. Knowing—If a person engages in activity that he or she should know will have dire consequences, then responsibility for that act exists. Walking into a crowded room swinging a baseball bat would be likely to hurt someone. Even if the person did not intend to hurt anyone, it is a likely consequence of his or her actions.
3. Reckless behavior—A person may engage in activity that is reckless, that is, increases the risk of harm. Driving at high speeds and driving under the influence of alcohol are examples.
4. Neglect—This situation may occur though the failure to do something. When a legal duty to care for a child or an older adult is established, the failure to provide the care results in criminal culpability if harm results. Criminal neglect is an extreme failure, for example, when a child dies because the parent did not provide food.

How?

The how of a crime is concerned with the event and everything leading up to it. How did the offender gain access to the victim, to the money stolen, or to the area to cause damage? Once access was gained, what was the way he or she committed the act? What instruments or tools were used in the commission of the act? What evidence would there be to support information that is being provided in the interview?

- How did it happen?
- How was the victim approached?
- How did the perpetrator gain access?
- How often has a similar event occurred?

Of importance is the sequence of events of when things happened during the incident. Knowing the exact sequence of events can render the event plausible or not.

BEEN THERE . . . DONE THAT! 4-2

A mother left her two children alone in the apartment so that she could get some dope. She locked the children in their bedroom when she left because she did not think she would be gone long. The two young boys started to play with matches and their bed caught on fire. They could not get out of the room; they died there. Their death was a tragic accident—their mother did not mean them any harm. Was she responsible? She lacked the *mens rea* because she did not intend that her actions would cause the deaths of her children. She had a duty to care for these children, but a few years earlier the state had repealed its law on criminal neglect. The mother could not be charged with having committed any crime. In part, due to this case, a new law was passed that defined acts of neglect that would be considered illegal. If this same scenario happens again, the mother could be arrested and charged with a crime, but the law was not retroactive.

FIGURE 4-3   Look at the picture as if it were a real situation that you are investigating. Can you answer: Who? What? When? Where? Why? How?

Source: Stuart Jenner/Shutterstock.

Now that each component of the unstructured interview method has been outlined look at Figure 4-3 and see how the unstructured method of questioning would help in determining what happened.

WHAT IS STRUCTURED INTERVIEWING?

The structured interviewing approach builds on the unstructured interview by adding three components. They are rapport building, narrative description, and an ample interviewee response opportunity. Many of the positive aspects of the cognitive approach to interviewing are also incorporated into structured interviewing, such as active listening, use of open questions, and appropriate nonverbal behavior (Schiek & Ullrich, 2016).

STEPS FOR STRUCTURED INTERVIEWING

Among the most serious issues in criminal justice is the growing threat of cybercrime (Wexler, 2014). Additionally, cyberbullying and cybervictimization are a phenomenon that impacts almost all modern societies. Some are suggesting the formation of Internet behavior rules, global legislation and communication security policies where no such policy exists (Stylios, Thanou, Androulidakis, & Zaitseva, 2016). Investigative strategies are lagging far behind. In a world where cybercrime has no specific reference in law, its targets range from governments and multinational corporations to individuals (Jónasson & Gunnlaugsson, 2016). An urgent need exists for the application of digital forensics and modern interviewing techniques to these crime scenarios (Fianyi, 2016). The structured interviewing method appears to have application in some situations.

The structured interview is a common face-to-face interview method. It is also well suited for use in online asynchronous interviews (Schiek & Ullrich, 2016). **Asynchronous communication** uses technology as a means of communication, which contains pauses of varying lengths between statements, in a relationship that takes place online and at a distance using electronic screen-based text. Structured interviewing is carefully planned and followed to maximize the amount of useful information that is gathered. Video conferencing and synchronous text chats are likely selected in everyday life to compensate for the physical absence of people and to make up for the distance inherent in those methods of communication. In contrast, e-mails, blogs, forums, provides distance from the communication partner. Schiek & Ullrich (2016) suggest that asynchronous communication allows opportunities to relay deeply personal and emotional experiences, which might not be stated if they were in a face-to-face situation with an interviewer. The absence of an immediate other and the time lag in interaction seem to enable specific actions by individuals.

Step One: Build Rapport

Establish rapport. The ability to establish rapport is considered to be more important than any technique for increasing truthful information. Attempt to create rapport so that the interviewee is at ease and is willing to give information. Remember from earlier chapters that the purpose of rapport is to establish a two-way communication between the interviewer and the interviewee. It is a relationship of trust that encourages conversation by paying attention and actively listening to the interviewee. It is important to convey a perception of caring about what is being said.

Building trust for the online approach requires that the interviewer make the interests and needs of the interviewee central in the communication. The anonymity of an online technique may give license to the interviewee to provide more personal information than in the face-to-face approach. Some researchers suggest that the absence of physical presence of an interviewer may be liberating, particularly when sensitive issues are discussed (Bampton, Cowton, & Downes, 2013). Greater attention to inquiry techniques, which demonstrate active listening and recognition of the statements, is the needed. Researchers argue that this is accomplished, in part, through nondirective text questioning to stimulate a free flow of large amounts of information (Schiek & Ullrich, 2016).

Step Two: Encourage Participation

Encourage the individual to participate actively and to report information rather than just respond to the questions that are asked. Do not volunteer information about the case or the suspect when conducting an interview. Ask open-ended questions frequently and do not interrupt the person who is making a statement. Record the statements accurately and completely. If it is practicable, take notes during the interview. As soon as possible after the interview, write the full statement down using the witness's own words.

FIGURE 4-4 The structured interview involves the rapport building step and the encouragement of interviewee participation.

Source: Studio 8/Pearson Education Ltd.

BEEN THERE . . . DONE THAT! 4-3

Sketchy details of a kidnapping and an attempt to commit murder were the reasons why I was called out in the middle of the night. While in route to the scene I thought about the absurdity of this alleged crime. A woman reported that while she was hitchhiking in her rural home town, she was picked up and given a ride by a man whom she knew. She said that she was strangled to unconsciousness by him and later woke up in the trunk of his car. Furthermore, I was told, when the car stopped and the trunk was opened, she found that they were parked on the side of a bridge with a long drop to the river below. She reported that he was going to throw her in the river but that she pleaded with him and he took her home instead!

The report sounded like a lie, yet I knew that it was important to find out more information. When I interviewed the victim, I was looking for more signs of dishonesty. What convinced me that she was telling the truth was that she recounted waking up in the car and described in detail that the driver had stopped at a gas station—she heard the gas going into the tank and smelled it. She described how frightening it had been in the small, dark place without any way to get out. In detail, she described the roads as being bumpy or smooth so that she had an idea where they were at the point he opened the trunk. The entire statement was woven together with how experiences that involved her senses and her emotions. It made sense that she described sequentially the experience and feelings she had while locked in the trunk.

The next day I called for the forensic specialists to look inside the trunk for evidence of her being there. They found one long blonde hair belonging to her; it verified that she was telling the truth.

To obtain information on an incident, ask nonleading and open questions that allow for a free narrative account. The interviewer should specifically request the free narrative. Ask the subject to describe, in as much detail as possible, everything that he or she remembers about the event. To avoid contaminating the statement, avoid introducing any new information or details about the event. Avoid interrupting the account or asking for clarification of the details at this stage. For example:

1. "Can you tell me about the car?" This opened-ended question gives the person an unlimited range of answers without leading him or her to what you might be expecting to hear.
2. "Can you tell me anything about the color, make, or model of the car?" This question is an also opened-ended without limiting the answer to any particular aspect of the car. It does not imply that the person should remember any particular aspect of the car. It is not leading the witness or suggestive because it does not suggest any color, make, or model of vehicle.

Specific probing questions are next used to elaborate on the details that were provided by the interviewee during the free narrative account. Open-ended questions are preferred. The interviewer may incorporate the five W's and How in this step.

Limiting the number of questions is a technique to encourage participation in the online interview. Researchers suggest that e-mail etiquette requires the body of the message to be visible without scrolling, keeping within this limit maintains the online conversation format vs. a written communication (Bampton et al., 2013). During an asynchronous interview, the time lag can be moments, days, or longer. For better or worse, this gives the interviewee time to think about their response.

Step Three: Review the Statement

In the final step of the structured interview, the subject is asked to recount the entire scene or event again to bring new recollections into the account. When it is completed, allow the witness to read this statement and make corrections to it. Do not write a statement as if it were the words of the witness unless it is. For example, a four-year-old would not use the word "intercourse"! Be careful not to substitute your words for someone else's without specifying that the statement is a paraphrase of the witness's statement.

This last step in the structured interview is made easier in the online interview since the text can be reviewed for inconsistencies and probed for obvious incongruities. The messages may be scrutinized using any content analysis format that is preferred by the interviewer.

SCIENTIFIC CONTENT ANALYSIS (SCAN)

Content analysis, the reading of textual data to identify preselected criteria, is a traditional technique used in research (Webb & Wang, 2013). To conduct content analysis interviewers first request a written statement. The account is then reviewed for criteria to differentiate truth from fabrication within the report. In the *Scientific Content Analysis (SCAN)* procedure, the interviewee is asked to write a detailed description of his or her activities during a critical period under investigation (Vrij, 2015). This updated content analysis approach was developed by a former polygraph examiner, Avinoam Sapir. SCAN is widely used in countries around the world as well as Federal agencies and the Military (Sapir, 2017). The criteria used for analysis in SCAN are based on the idea that accounts of experience will contain language characteristics, which are absent from reports that are fabricated. Sometimes SCAN is called **statement analysis**, which is the word-by-word examination of the written account.

SCAN is used to gauge the credibility and reliability of a statement for law enforcement, private corporations, and social services use according to its developer (Sapir, 2017). As few as 8 and as many as 28 distinct criteria have been identified as being used during statement analysis (Bogaard, Meijer, Vrij, Broers, & Merckelbach, 2014). Often the criteria include logical structure, quality of details, use of superfluous details, and lack of memory. The approach recognizes that both structure and content of a report will vary between persons who are deceptive and those who are not. Examine also the

---

BEEN THERE . . . DONE THAT! 4-4

The phone rang. It was 2 AM. A kidnapping and rape had just been reported, and I was being dispatched to investigate. Arriving at the scene, I found it strange that the victim had been driven so far off of the main road. It was as if the offender knew where he was going, yet the report I had received stated that the woman was kidnapped from a neighboring state. How did the perpetrator know to come off the road at this particular exit and travel 15 minutes to this location, which was secluded? In the interview with the victim she was very calm and matter of fact about her abduction, claiming that a man was hiding under a horse blanket in the passenger front seat who had risen up to abduct her. The description of the hiding place did not seem possible given the size of the area and the proximity to the driver. There were also verbal clues that indicated that her situation was questionable. She referred to the kidnapper with a "we" statement over and over. When pressed for specifics about the assault, she used equivocating terms with a lack of detail. There were attempts to absolve her of responsibility when she stated that she could not have possibly known that he was hiding under the blanket. Her statement was hard to understand because it started in the middle of the incident, continued from the beginning, and then jumped to the end. It made little sense, and I found myself asking her repeatedly to explain things to me—they lacked any chronological order.

The investigation continued after the initial interview with the victim. Even the identification was so unclear that it was meaningless. Finally, I called the police department where she lived and found that the victim was well known to them. She had made a similar kidnapping complaint a year earlier to that department and a third police department before that. There was no evidence of a kidnapping; it was a false report. The victim was making a plea for help, however. In a situation like this it is appropriate to make referrals for intervention.

individual parts of speech that are used in the statement, particularly pronouns, nouns, and verbs, and establish the norm for each. If a change from the norm becomes apparent, seek the reason for that difference. Word choices are purposeful, even when they are selected subconsciously. According to Vrij (2015), there are 12 criteria (described below) which are often taught in SCAN seminars.

✓ **Change in language.** Refers to a change in the term used to describe something or someone within a statement.

  Example: The typical statement would not describe an object using different terms unless there was a change in the reality of the interviewee. A couch remains a couch throughout the account. Emotion has the greatest impact on language change. For a subject speaking freely, a change in language is triggered by something, and it is a change in reality. Here the interviewee is talking about his mother after he stabbed her to death the woman was no longer his mother but was the devil. "I loved my mother. I did not mean to hurt her; the devil was stabbed."

✓ **Denial of allegations.** Whether the interviewee directly denies the allegation in the statement.

  Example: "My story has never changed; I never hurt the boy, I love him." It is not unusual for an offender to refer to his or her statement as a *story*. The verb *hurt* in this example minimizes the crime, which was perpetrated against the young boy. By minimizing the offense, the offender is also playing down his role in causing any harm to the child. Using the verb *love* suggests a positive experience rather than the heinous crime that occurred. Here the perpetrator uses the phrase *the child* rather than the name. Distancing himself, this offender objectifies the victim, suggesting that the statement may be false.

✓ **Emotions.** The position during the statement when emotions occur is important. If emotions such as anger, disgust, fear, or joy occur just before the climax of the story the person may be lying. If the display occurs throughout or after the climax of the story, there is a greater likelihood that the interviewee is truthful.

  Example: People generally do not choose the emotion they experience, when they feel it—it is expressed. On the other hand, liars go to great lengths to control or disguise their behaviors to present an emotionally cool appearance (Fitch, 2014). Well placed emotional outbursts may be contrived to suggest what they should be feeling rather than being real.

✓ **Extraneous information.** Comments that are irrelevant or unnecessary are extraneous. It refers to situations in which the interviewee provides information that does not answer the question and or is presented out of order.

  Example: When a truthful person with nothing to hide is asked, "What happened," he or she will provide the events in chronological order. Subjects will avoid revealing information by asking questions in response to interviewers. The extra information is given to avoid talking directly about the event rather than denying the allegation or lying about it outright. Extraneous phrasing associated with deception includes "I believe," "I think," Kind of," and "To the best of my knowledge." Although the subject may provide truthful extraneous information, it could be used as an alternative to specific details about the incident. Guilty or involved persons will use this tactic to justify their actions.

✓ **First person singular past tense.** When someone uses memory to recall past events, it is normal to use the first person, singular past tense. It becomes significant if an individual being interviewed varies the verb tense during the statement because the event occurred in the past. Any change in the tense of the verb should provide a signal to the interviewer that deception may exist.

  Example: "I saw the shooting. I am so scared that I run away as fast as I can." Here the sentence starts in the past tense and moves to the present tense, which indicates a lack of commitment to being the witness; it is suggestive of greater involvement than the interviewee has admitted. Change of tense from the past to the present tense may signal deception. Using the past tense when referring to missing persons is also considered a deviation of the norm.

✓ **Lack of conviction.** Refers to words that are used to label or change the meaning of something; these are equivocating terms.

Example: Does the interviewee use the phrases "sort of," "kind of," "I guess," "little bit," and "hopefully"? The interviewer should always look more closely at a statement in which a person consistently says "I don't recall" or "I do not remember." Other qualifying terms such as "I think" or "I believe" are used to minimize the statements conviction. A victim's use of terms that minimize the event such as "kind of surprised" or "sort of hurt" suggests a deviation from the expected norm.

✓ **Missing information.** The inclusion of words that indicate that some information has been left out.

Example: When the interviewee leaves out information using terms such as "sometime after," "finally," "later on," and "shortly thereafter" there is a suggestion of deceit. It might be that the information left out was an important conversation, a phone call, or a meeting with someone. It could be anything, and it signals that something of significance has taken place to cause the subject to "pause" in his progression of his account and this pause. This deliberate move to conceal information suggests that subject is working from memory, which also makes the rest of the statement highly reliable.

✓ **Objective and subjective time.** How different time periods are covered in a statement.

Example: Objective time is the duration of events described in a statement. Subjective time is the amount of words spent to describe what happened during that time. In a truthful statement, the description of events is expected to be roughly equivalent to three lines per hour. If an inordinate amount of space is devoted to one part of the day versus another, then it may be an effort to avoid describing other events. This would look like someone going into much detail about a mundane period: "At 6a, I got up, turned off my alarm clock, brushed my teeth, and hit the shower. I ate some pop tarts and left the house at 6:50 AM. The traffic was really bad, and I had to make some stops and get gas. At the gas station, I saw a guy I knew and talked for a while about my car. The brakes have been making noise lately, and he works there part time and said he could fit me in next week but I don't know how much money it is going to cost."

Missing time within the statement changes the balance and suggests something has been left out. The interviewer should attempt to determine what was missing and whether the information was either not relevant or was perceived as not being important to the subject.

✓ **Pronouns.** Common pronouns are I, me, you, he she, we, they, and it. Truthful people provide statements using the pronoun "I," which is first person singular. Deviating from the use of first person singular during an interview is a signal of possible deception. An overuse of the pronoun "we" indicates a lack of commitment to the statement and unwillingness to take responsibility for something.

Example: We all met at school and went to class. We left when the bell rang for lunch and drove around. Possessive pronouns such as my, our, your, his, her, and their suggest a relationship between a person or object and the interviewee. Changing the relationship is a deviation from the norm and suggests a distancing from that person or object.

Example: My grandchild and I were walking in the woods. She needed to go to the bathroom, so the child was helped with taking down the underwear. The child was never touched in a bad way.

✓ **Social introduction.** The failure to introduce someone in the statement is suggestive of a weak relationship and is interpreted as the writer attempting to hide something. Using the adjectives of "that" and "those" to reference a person or object suggests distancing. Referring to a person though spatial adjectives is a deviation of the norm, particularly when a relationship should exist.

Example: Calling someone "the ex" is not good, but reference to "the mother of my child" is bad and can be seen where the subject may want to murder her. When reading this in a statement it will indicate a lot about the relationship and is cause for concern if the person being referenced is the victim.

✓ **Spontaneous corrections**. Presence of corrections in the statement, such as crossing out what has been written. Interviewees are explicitly instructed not to cross anything out in the SCAN method (Vrij, 2015).

Example: A failure to follow this instruction is believed to indicate deceit.

✓ **Structure of the statement.** This refers to the before—during—after balance of the statement.

Example: A truthful statement will contain three parts: prior to the incident, the incident itself, and the events after the incident. The statement should be examined for balance; if any part is missing, it is most likely false. It is more likely that the statement is true when it contains equal amounts of information in all three parts. A person who is attempting to justify his or her actions will give information that does not answer the questions or will include more than is necessary to explain what happened. An extremely large "before" section compared to the "after" section is an indication of a lack of emotion and may be a false or incomplete accounting of what happened.

Despite its widespread use, research has not supported claims of SCAN's diagnostic accuracy, however. Several studies suggest that the SCAN criteria could not differentiate between true and fabricated accounts (Bogaard, Meijer, Vrij, & Merckelbach, 2016). In a recent study, Bogaard et al. (2016) concluded that despite the research problems associated with SCAN, its appeal might be that practitioners can adapt the SCAN criteria to their own needs. The approach is praised as having the potential to increase the amount of information related during the interview. It is typically a stand-alone statement analysis, but could also be valuable when used with any form of interviewing method as an assessment of the information recorded in a statement.

Application of the statement analysis technique is time consuming and can be tedious if the statement is complex. Its use is sometimes limited due to a lack of understanding and training in the entire approach. The basic components of statement content analysis form the foundation for SCAN.

Conclusions

This chapter covered the primary methods of interviewing used by investigative interviewers. Each approach has its pros and cons. Unstructured interviewing is best used in situations in which the intent is to get right to the point. As suggested earlier, this approach can be used to make a preliminary assessment of the value of the witness, identifying the individual for future, more in-depth interviewing. It is comprehensive, but it is often used in a haphazard way that diminishes its value.

The structured interview offers a humanistic approach to obtaining information. This approach is more comprehensive and focused than the unstructured

method. The added value of using a structured interview is that there are no difficult steps to memorize, it is fairly easy to use, and it has a decent response rate. The reason the structured interview is so widely used is its lack of complexity. The structured interview approach is being used for online interviewing and data gathering.

The statement analysis approach is seen in the SCAN approach. This contains many useful tools to assist the interviewer in looking for verbal clues to deception and indications that further investigation may be needed. The method is complex and may be difficult to use.

Questions for Review

Short-Answer Questions

1. What does unstructured interviewing hope to attain?

2. Why is it important to determine the role the complainant may have played in the commission of a crime?

3. What are the six guidelines of the unstructured interview? Explain.

4. In a structured interview should the person being interviewed be encouraged to be an active part of the discussion? If so, why? If not, why not?

5. What types of interviews can benefit from statement analysis?

Fill-in Questions

1. A person who is falsely claiming involvement as a witness or suspect to a crime is referred to as a ____.

2. ____ refer to the presence of corrections in the statement, such as crossing out what has been written.

3. In situations where there are multiple individuals to be questioned and only one interviewer available, it may make sense to use ____ interviewing techniques.

4. ____ refers to irrelevant or unnecessary statements, and should be looked for. It refers to situations in which the interviewee provides information that does not answer the question and or is presented out of order.

5. In addition to knowing ____ the event happened, questions should be asked to determine why it might have happened at that place.

6. The ____ interviewing approach builds on the unstructured interview by adding the following components: rapport building, narrative description, and an ample interviewee response opportunity.

7. The three steps of the structured interviewing are: ____, encouraging participation, and reviewing the statement.

8. Sometimes SCAN is called ____, which is a word-by-word examination of the written statement.

9. The ____ approach recognizes that both structure and content of a report will vary between persons who are deceptive and those who are not.

10. ____ refers to words that are used to label or change the meaning of something; these are equivocating terms.

Exercises

1. Pair off with a classmate for about 10–15 minutes. Interview your partner about the last TV show he or she watched. Use the unstructured interviewing approach, and only the five W's and How. Verbally or in writing report what you learned about the program.

2. Pair off with a classmate for about 10–15 minutes. Using the structural interviewing approach, interview your partner about the last TV show he or she watched. Verbally or in writing report what you learned about the program.

References

Bampton, R., Cowton, C., & Downes, Y. (2013). The e-interview in qualitative research. Retrieved March 16, 2017 from IGI Global http://eprints.hud.ac.uk/17259/

Blacksmith, N., Willford, J. C., & Behrend, T. S. (2016). Technology in the employment interview: A meta-analysis and future research agenda. *Personnel Assessment and Decisions, 2*(1), 2.

Bogaard, G., Meijer, E. H., Vrij, A., Broers, N. J., & Merckelbach, H. (2014). SCAN is largely driven by 12 criteria: Results from sexual abuse statements. *Psychology, Crime & Law, 20*(5), 430–449.

Bogaard, G., Meijer, E. H., Vrij, A., & Merckelbach, H. (2016). Strong, but wrong: Lay people's and police officers' beliefs about verbal and nonverbal cues to deception. *PLoS ONE, 11*(6), e0156615.

Fianyi, I. (2016). Curbing cyber-crime and Enhancing e-commerce security with Digital Forensics. *arXiv preprint arXiv:1610.08369.*

Fitch, B. (2014). The truth about lying: What investigators need to know. Retrieved April 12, 2017 from FBI.gov https://leb.fbi.gov/2014/june/the-truth-about-lying-what-investigators-need-to-know.

Jónasson, J. O., & Gunnlaugsson, H. (2016). *How widespread is cybercrime: Types and volume of public victimization in Iceland.* Paper presented at the NSfK's 58. Research Seminar.

Sapir, A. (2017). Past participants of the SCAN course. Retrieved from http://www.lsiscan.com/id29.htm.

Schiek, D., & Ullrich, C. (2016). Techniques for obtaining qualitative data in written online inquires. Retrieved 2017 from http://revistas.ua.pt//index.php/ilcj/index.

State v. Lawson, 291 P. 3d 673 (Oregon Supreme Court 2012).

Stylios, I. C., Thanou, O., Androulidakis, I., & Zaitseva, E. (2016). *Communication security & cyberbullying: A review of the legal issues.* Paper presented at the Proceedings of the SouthEast European Design Automation, Computer Engineering, Computer Networks and Social Media Conference, Kastoria, Greece.

Vernham, Z., Vrij, A., Mann, S., Leal, S., & Hillman, J. (2014). Collective interviewing: Eliciting cues to deceit using a turn-taking approach. *Psychology, Public Policy, and Law, 20*(3), 309–324.

Vrij, A. (2015). Verbal lie detection tools: Statement Validity Analysis, Reality Monitoring and Scientific Content Analysis. In P. A. Granhag, A. Vrij, & B. Verschuere (Eds.), *Detecting deception: Current challenges and cognitive approaches*. Malden, MA: Wiley Blackwell.

Wave Systems Corporation. (2017). Police Field Interview FI. Retrieved from http://www.wavesystems.com/

Webb, L., & Wang, Y. (2013). Techniques for analyzing blogs and micro-blogs. In N. Sappleton (Ed.), *Advancing research methods with new technologies* (pp. 206–227). Hershey, PA: IGI Global.

Wexler, C. (2014). *Cybercrime: A new critical issue*. Critical Issues in Policing Series. Washington, D.C.: Police Executive Research Forum.

5

Memory Enhanced and Retrieval Interviewing

Source: Marcin Balcerzak/Shutterstock.

CHAPTER OBJECTIVES

After completing this chapter, you should be able to:

1. Compare and contrast the four phases of forensic hypnosis.
2. Analyze the limitations of forensic hypnosis evidence for court use.
3. State the three tests for admissibility of scientific evidence.
4. Describe the four steps of the cognitive interviewing method.
5. Apply the four mnemonic principles.
6. List and explain the four approaches included in the *Differential Recall Enhancement* (DRE) category.
7. Define the concept known as a lie scrip.
8. Restate the behaviors known as verbal leakage.

KEY TERMS

Cognitive interviewing method	*Daubert* test
Forensic hypnosis	*Frye* test
Lie scrip	Memory hardening
Mnemonics	Verbal leakage

INTRODUCTION

Memory has been subjected to scientific investigation for over a century. Researchers tell us that most of what we now know about enhanced memory retrieval come from attempts by some of the most well-respected experimental psychologists of the nineteenth century to understand the effects of hypnosis (Mazzoni, Laurence, & Heap, 2014). Interest in investigative hypnosis waned at the beginning of the twentieth century but continued to have use in therapeutic settings. Renewed interest in hypnosis came from the criminal justice community as police officers were clamoring for new investigative techniques. From the 1950s through the 1990s the reliability of memories retried through hypnosis has been argued and researched across America (Winter, 2013). While laypersons and psychotherapists reveal high rates of endorsement regarding hypnosis as a vehicle to enhance memory, most courts no longer hold the technique to be scientifically reliable (Mazzoni et al., 2014). The use of hypnosis in criminal justice investigations remains a controversial approach. This chapter will start with a review and current state of forensic hypnosis as an interviewing method.

The gold standard for interviewing and interrogation now rests with cognitive interviewing. The cognitive interviewing approach jogs the memory by a process that is entirely controlled by the person being interviewed. Originally designed for use with compliant witnesses and victims, a version of cognitive interviewing with suspects is available as well. The National Institute of Justice recommends cognitive interviewing for criminal justice use. Deception scholars have devised several methods in recent years, which are based on the cognitive interviewing concepts of memory enhancement and retrieval with the addition of deceit detection. As a group, these are called *Differential Recall Enhancement* (DRE) methods. DRE techniques being used to detect deceit that are covered in this chapter include the Assessment Criteria Indicative of Deception (ACID), the cognitive load approach, Strategic Use of Evidence (SUE), and tactical interviewing.

The memory enhanced and retrieval approaches to interviewing share the same goal, which is to increase the amount of information that an interviewee can remember.

They use memory-jogging techniques to obtain information but differ in the methods they use to jog the memory. The memory enhanced and retrieval interviewing approach, in general, seeks to promote memory through a process of heightened awareness brought about by the interviewer. Recent additions to the approach come from the deception scholars' attempts to provide avenues of evaluating statement reliability.

WHAT IS HYPNOSIS?

Forensic hypnosis is an investigative memory retrieval technique used to enhance recall in legally relevant situations. Hypnosis is a state of increased receptivity to suggestion characterized by an altered state of consciousness. During the hypnotic session, a person allows himself or herself to become more suggestible. Results differ according to individual responses (American Psychotherapy and Medical Hypnosis Association [APMHA], 2017). Individuals do not lose control, and some describe the experience as a heightened awareness (APMHA, 2017). Persons under hypnosis are aware of what is going on; they do not become zombies. Hypnosis in criminal investigations is typically used to

1. Enhance an accused defendant's memory about events occurring around the time of the crime.
2. Help an eyewitness to a crime to provide details about the behavior or physical appearance of the perpetrator.
3. Assist in generating leads for investigators through recall of salient details.

Advocates of hypnosis in criminal investigation cite numerous cases in which police investigators successfully solved crimes using hypnosis as a tool (Wagstaff, 2009). The goal of forensic hypnosis is memory enhancement and retrieval for use in a specific civil or criminal case. Strong arguments have been made that forensic hypnosis sessions should be conducted by police officers who are skilled in relevant interviewing techniques and have sophisticated legal knowledge. Others suggest that clinicians are the most appropriate forensic hypnotists.

FORENSIC HYPNOSIS INTERVIEWING METHODS

The public's perception of hypnosis is quite favorable. Research shows that a significant percentage of people continue to believe in the positive use of forensic hypnosis (Mazzoni et al., 2014). In contrast, the legal and medical communities have long taken positions against the accuracy of facts recalled under hypnosis in hotly contested debates regarding its reliability. During the 1970s and 1980s, severe attacks were made against the use of forensic hypnosis. During the 1990s, professional organizations called for limiting or banning its use. The American Medical Association recommends that the use of hypnosis be restricted to the investigative processes and its results not be used as evidence in court. The American Psychological Association and the Canadian Psychiatric Association recommend against the use of hypnosis for memory retrieval (Lynn, Boycheva, Deming, Lilienfeld, & Hallquist, 2009). Nonetheless, hundreds of cases presented in court do include testimony enhanced through hypnosis.

Guidelines for the Use of Forensic Hypnosis

The hypnotic forensic approach begins with preparation. There are four phases: the induction phase, the narrative phase, the closure phase, and the recall phase. The evidence established before the session must be documented to differentiate between pre- and post-hypnotic information. The hypnotist should arrange for a quiet room free of distractions. Only the

A child had been abducted and there were no leads to locating the child or identifying the kidnapper. In desperation, a hypnotist was called to conduct interviews of the family members. No useful information came from the interviews, but the procedure did cause a lot of discussion among the detectives. In the state of Massachusetts, information obtained after a person has been hypnotized is not acceptable as evidence in court. Sometimes it is worth taking the chance that evidence will not be admissible in court if the process might save a life. The decision is one that should be debated. Some states do allow hypnotically refreshed memory. What is the status of hypnotic evidence in your state?

hypnotist and the subject are allowed in the room, unless the hypnotist determines that it is necessary to include others. There should be a two-way mirror for session viewing by persons involved in the investigation such as legal representation and police investigators. Ideally, there should be a form of communication from the viewers to the hypnotist, such as via a small ear receiver. All conversations between the hypnotist and the subject should be videotaped before, during, and after the session. The documentation includes the place, date, and time of the session. Before beginning, the hypnotist makes an independent assessment of the subject's suitability for hypnosis and willingness to proceed.

CHALLENGES TO HYPNOTIC MEMORY RETRIEVAL

As with any approach to interviewing, there are challenges to the use of the hypnotic forensic technique. Situations of abuse, particularly child abuse, should be approached with extra caution. There are indications that events may be altered, deleted, and created by events that occur during and after the time of encoding, during the period of storage, and during any attempts at retrieval (Wagstaff, 2009). In other words, the memory of abuse may be influenced by abuse that occurs after the initial event or at any time, including the hypnotic session.

Forensic hypnosis is not recommended for use on a defendant or person suspected of being involved in the crime under investigation. People can and do lie while under

FIGURE 5-1 The first phase of hypnosis is the induction phase. Eye fixation is a common approach.

Source: Courtesy of Denise K. Gosselin.

hypnosis. Confabulation is the unconscious filling in gaps in memory with fabricated facts and experiences. It can occur when the person hypnotized creates memory perceptions in an unconscious effort to please the hypnotist. The results of a hypnotic session with a suspect are of questionable value.

Memory Hardening and Suggestibility

Opponents to the use of forensic hypnosis believe that hypnotism causes **memory hardening**. The phenomenon gives the subject increased confidence regarding the facts remembered during hypnosis, regardless of whether the supposed facts are true or false (Baltman & Lynn, 2016).

Posthypnotic suggestion can become permanent if it is repeated many times or over several sessions. Also, the effect of hypnosis varies among individuals; some people may be hypersensitive to these techniques. Critics argue that a person undergoing hypnosis experiences an increased susceptibility to suggestion and a loss of critical judgment regarding cues planted by the hypnotist (Baltman & Lynn, 2016).

HYPNOSIS EVIDENCE IN COURT

Every defendant has the Constitutional right to use hypnotically refreshed memory in their defense during a criminal trial. This rule was determined through the case of *Rock v. Arkansas* (1987), which challenged an Arkansas *per se* rule excluding a criminal defendant's hypnotic memories. The U.S. Supreme Court found that denying a defendant the use of refreshed testimony, as a defense, violates the Fifth, Sixth, and Fourteenth Amendments. Further, the Court conceded that despite the unreliability that hypnosis

FIGURE 5-2 Defendants have a constitutional right to submit testimony achieved through hypnosis, witnesses or victims do not have this right.

Source: RF Corbis Value/Alamy Stock Photo.

may introduce, procedural safeguards and the recording of the interrogations before, during, and after hypnosis might reduce the possibility of bias.

The U.S. Department of Justice (DOJ) maintains that the use of forensic hypnosis with prosecution witnesses should not be used, except in limited cases where there is a clear need for additional information and following specific guidelines. Subject to serious objections, the Federal courts have adopted a "case-by-case approach" in determining the admissibility of hypnotic memory retrieval of witnesses and victims in court (DOJ, 2017). Only a psychologist or psychiatrist trained in forensic hypnosis should be allowed to hypnotize a witness, and the witness must give written consent to be placed under hypnosis. Interrogations involving suspects should be videotaped and a transcript prepared for examination.

The majority of state courts do not allow a victim or witness post-hypnotic memories as evidence in court. Research over the last 30 years has found that memories recovered during hypnosis are less likely or no more likely to be accurate than recollections reported when hypnosis is not used. Hypnotically elicited witness testimony is barred in 27 states, only four states have adopted a *per se* admissible rule, and 13 have held that admissibility should be determined on a case-by-case basis (Baltman & Lynn, 2016).

Scientific evidence must meet certain tests to be admitted by the courts. According to the **Frye test**, the scientific method must have gained general acceptance in the medical and psychological communities as a reliable method to be acceptable *(Frye v. United States, 1923)*. The *Frye* rule was first articulated in a criminal case that attempted to introduce evidence from a polygraph test. Forensic hypnosis is used in both medical and legal settings but is not generally accepted as reliable. Those states that determine scientific reliability based on use of the *Frye* rule generally exclude the use of hypnotic memories. A more recent test of the reliability of scientific evidence is articulated in *Daubert v. Merrell Dow Pharmaceuticals* (1993). The four-part **Daubert test**, which has become the federal standard concerning the admissibility of scientific evidence, has replaced *Frye* in some states. It asks

1. Whether the type of evidence can and has been tested by scientific methods.
2. Whether the underlying theory or technique has been subjected to peer review and published in the professional literature.
3. How reliable the results are regarding potential error rate.
4. Whether there is general acceptance of the technique (the *Frye* test).

Some courts may allow information gathered before the witnesses being subjected to hypnosis if it can be shown that the evidence was indeed provided before the hypnosis, whereas others ban its use in criminal proceedings altogether.

A few states specifically allow hypnotically refreshed recall as evidence in court. Among these are Texas and Nevada. Hypnotically refreshed recall has been admissible in Texas in both criminal and civil cases under the rules established in *Zani v. State* (1989). Texas mandates minimum training standards, testing, and certification of police officers who use investigative hypnosis. The Nevada legislature declared that hypnotically refreshed testimony is admissible in both civil and criminal cases (Nevada Revised Statutes, 2015). Nevada specifically named police officers trained in forensic hypnosis as among the persons whose interview may qualify as admissible in court. It is suggested that all information be independently verified when possible and its use limited to witness and victim statements.

WHAT IS COGNITIVE INTERVIEWING?

The **cognitive interviewing method** (CI) is a family of memory-jogging and retrieval tools for evaluating survey questions and questionnaires and conducting interviews. The approaches to cognitive interviewing are as diverse as the individuals who apply them. During the last decade, many institutions from around the world have come to rely on cognitive methods. Federal statistical agencies that use this approach include researchers from the National Crime Victimization Survey (NCVS) and the U.S. Bureau of Justice Statistics (Lee, Bradburn, Poland, Brownstein, & Krishnamurty, 2013). Cognitive methods are used for reducing substance abuse among probationers (Willison, Biegeler, & Kim, 2014) and for police interviewing (Shaw, 2015).

Cognitive interviewing is an approach for increasing the amount of information recalled by a witness without increasing the level of confabulation. It is deceptively simple and might not seem to be particularly useful or different. However, the methods for jogging memory used along with several specific techniques provide a potent and efficient means of eliciting a complete and accurate picture of the events recalled. The most important thing about cognitive interviewing is that when it is done properly, it works. Caution is warranted, however. It may be possible to alter the memory of an interviewee if misinformation about an event is introduced (Shaw, 2015).

Although cognitive interviewing has been compared to hypnosis, its original authors maintain that there are major differences between the two (Geiselman & Fisher, 1985). For example, there is no hypnotic induction in cognitive interviewing. Evidence indicates that it is a successful memory retrieval tool. Although cognitive interviewing involves memory-jogging and recovery techniques, there is no induction phase, and the interviewee is a full participant in the process.

Research results have indicated that cognitive interviewing is an effective approach for use with either complainants or suspects (Westera, Kebbell, & Milne, 2016). With relatively little training, the results from a cognitive interview may increase the gain in information. In trials in which individuals were reinterviewed after a standard interview, they reported new facts with the cognitive approach.

Both specific and general memory-jogging guidance techniques are combined to form the cognitive interview technique. Because memory is composed of a collection of several elements, the more elements a memory retrieval aid has in common with the memory of the event, the more effective the aid is. The general idea is that memory is accessible through several access routes, so that information that is not accessible though one retrieval cue may be reached through another. For an interview to be successful, the details of the crime need to be recalled and communicated to the interviewer. The cognitive interview technique has been adapted for use with children as well as with adults.

COGNITIVE INTERVIEWING TECHNIQUES

The approach stresses using a secluded, quiet place free of distractions for the interview as well as urging subjects to speak slowly. Cognitive interviewing encourages the witness to do the talking while the interviewer listens. It attempts to avoid some of the mistakes commonly associated with police interviewing such as interrupting the narrative and rushing the account. Witnesses must feel comfortable in taking the time to think and reflect on what happened. They should feel free to say anything, knowing that there is sufficient time to speak and that the interviewer will not make judgments on the statements. Specific questions are for clarification. The interviewer holds these back until the narrative is fully stated. It is common knowledge that cases are solved when someone talks about what happened! Cognitive interviewing is designed to get the interviewee talking. A major challenge is not to interrupt.

Mnemonics

Mnemonics are the four cognitive interviewing principles used for remembering information that is otherwise difficult to recall. The principles of memory involved in the cognitive interview use of mnemonics are encoding and retrieval (Holliday et al., 2012).

Encoding is a process that the brain goes through when something happens. The information received is filtered and stored. Mnemonics are merely ways to find the information. Think of the brain as a filing cabinet. There are many drawers; within the drawers are file hangers. Typically, the files are labeled by category or alphabetically, but that depends on who is doing the filing! If you cannot find a file, then it is necessary to think about how you categorized the information. Was the order by the case number, incident type, perpetrator, or victim? Was the date or the location used as a method to file the information? This is similar to the process used for mnemonics.

Recall through mnemonics requires the use of imagination, association, and location. Use of imagination does not suggest fantasy, but imagery. The description of an event will be more realistic and complete if an individual verbalizes how he or she felt or reacted at the time of a crime. The association aspect of cognitive interviewing allows the individual to remember one thought to move to another. The interviewer asks, for example, whether there was a familiar smell, shape, or feeling during the incident. The third principle in the attempt to promote recall has to do with the location of the incident. The interviewee pictures the place where the incident occurred in order to describe in detail everything about the place.

Mnemonics are not complicated; they are simply ways to jog the memory to find information that is not easily accessible. The foundation of the cognitive interview is the use of the following four mnemonics as memory-jogging techniques (Geiselman & Fisher, 1985):

- Mentally reconstruct the context of the event.
- Report every detail, regardless of apparent importance.
- Recall the events in a variety of orders, moving backward and forward in time.
- Change perspectives and recall events from different points of view.

These four principles are tools to use within the interview process. Explained to the witness before the interview begins, they allow the witness to approach memory recall and retrieval from several different avenues. The first two methods attempt to increase the overlap of elements between the stored memory and retrieval cues. The goal is to encourage witnesses to construct a new description of the event. The last two methods encourage using many retrieval paths.

BEEN THERE . . . DONE THAT! 5-2

On a back country road in the middle of the afternoon, a female jogger sprinted effortlessly. It was a warm and sunny summer day. The woman being interviewed said that her mind was blank as she enjoyed her run until a truck stopped in front of her and a man came toward her. Grabbing her, the man pushed her into the tall corn stalks along the side of the road. She struggled while he lay on top of her and fought until she got free. Once free, she ran like she was in a marathon in the other direction and went into the first house to call the police.

During the interview, it was apparent that details were missing that would enhance the case. By use of imagery I asked her to tell me every detail, no matter how small. She changed the order of the attack and reconstructed the context of the event. She was able to describe the smell of the field and the sound of a car going by. He did not rape her; he struggled to get her pants down. His pants were unzipped and part way down his hips when she escaped. From this information, I knew that there was at least one other witness who had seen the truck parked on the side of the road. A check with the local police department confirmed that someone had called them with information on that suspicious truck. We now had a plate number and were able to locate the driver. The driver was located and interrogated. His clothing was taken, and evidence of his being in a corn field was evident. His pants and underclothes were taken and sent to the lab. Pre-ejaculatory fluid in his shorts confirmed his sexual intentions. He was convicted of an assault and attempted rape.

Reconstruction Technique

For reconstruction, the investigator assists the witness to recreate the incident scene. Instructing the interviewee to think about the circumstances that surrounded the incident, the investigator suggests that he or she think about the room where the incident occurred, the location of furniture, vehicles, weather, lighting, any nearby people, objects, or smells. The individual interviewed is to think about how he or she felt at the time and his or her reaction to the incident. The purpose of this line of inquiry is to return the witness deeply to the scene of the crime. Visualizing a situation strongly through imagery helps an individual to remember. Reconstruction is accomplished by asking witnesses to relive the events mentally before, during, and after the crime.

The interviewer instructs the witness that reconstruction includes talking about the time of day, day, month, and year of the event. In other words, the witness reconstructs the scene according to when it happened. What was the weather? How did he or she know? Was it light or dark? This line of thinking will open up thoughts particularly when multiple events or assaults occurred, and they need to be separated into single occurrences that are otherwise blurred over time. Reconstruction also includes talking about the location of the incident in relation to other houses, furniture, equipment, or any other tangible item that can be described.

Reporting-Everything Technique

For the reporting phase, the investigator explains that some people hold back information because they are not quite sure that the information is important. The witness should not edit anything, even things that may not seem important. Providing this permission to recount everything may cause the witness to remember something otherwise forgotten. Throughout the interview, the interviewee should be reminded to talk about everything he or she remembers. One should continue to encourage his or her participation.

Changing the Order of Events

This aspect includes an instruction to recall the events in a different order. Typically, a witness is asked to begin at the beginning, which may cause him or her to fill in gaps so that the story sounds logical. Sticking to an expected order may lead to an account that may not be completely accurate. The instruction for this technique may ask that the beginning point be the thing that impressed the witness (frightened him or her, or made him or her aware that something was going on). The witness is asked to try starting from a point that he or she remembers most vividly and either go backward or forward from that point.

Changing the Perspective

In the fourth phase of this process, the witness is instructed to recall the incident from different perspectives or adopt the perspective of others who were present. Depending on the circumstances of the event, the investigator may also instruct the witness to place himself or herself in the role of someone else in the incident and think about what he or she must have seen.

Additional Memory-Jogging Techniques

1. **Appearance.**   What type of clothing was the witness or perpetrator wearing at the time of the event? Was there anything unusual about the physical appearance of the individual involved? What was it that seemed unusual? Did the perpetrator remind the witness of anyone, and why? The characteristics that are familiar to an individual may cue him or her to think of someone else. The behavior, speech, or physical appearance may be one of many characteristics that lead the witness to remember the

individual in more detail than previously thought. As a description of physical appearance evolves, the investigator should take note of the mention of detail that goes beyond a typical description. Examples include a hat, haircut, condition of the hair or skin, jewelry, or tattoos. Keep in mind that individuals have preferences in underclothing that may not change, for example, the kind of underwear or t-shirt worn.

2. **Conversation.**   In what place did conversation occur, if any? What was said and by whom? Was something happening that prompted the statements? Were there particular words that seemed to be significant? Was there a way that the person spoke that was peculiar?

3. **Names.**   If a name was spoken, does the witness remember it? The interviewee should be instructed to think about the number of syllables or letter of that name.

4. **Senses.**   Was there a smell associated with the event? What did the person, place, or surroundings smell like?

5. **Speech.**   Did anyone involved have a speech impediment or speak with an accent? Was the conversation loud or soft, high-pitched or deliberate?

STEPS OF THE COGNITIVE INTERVIEW METHOD

As basic skills for effective cognitive interviewing, the interviewer is expected to have developed the skills for establishing rapport, listening actively, and avoiding interrupting. Additional competence is required for encouraging intense concentration and the use of imagery. Asking open-ended and compatible questions assist in obtaining detailed descriptions and recreating the original context of the event.

The order of the cognitive interview is important; the steps must take place one after the other to be effective.

Step One: Meet and Greet

In the first step, the interviewer explains to the interviewee that there will be seven steps in the interview process. The first step describes cognitive interviewing and what to expect during the interview. The person is told that full cooperation is expected and that no information or details should be left out, regardless of whether they appear important or not. Most of the interview will consist of the interviewee doing the talking. Instructions will come on how to jog memory along with techniques proven to improve the interview process.

The interviewer asks questions in a standard approach but instructs the interviewee to think aloud, express his or her opinion, and say if he or she has any difficulty in answering questions. In other words, the investigator gives the control of the interview to the person being interviewed. Police officers and other interviewers are used to asking the questions. In this approach, they are listeners and encourage the witness to do the talking.

- Control anxiety and develop a rapport with the interviewee. This may be done by helping the subject to feel more comfortable through the development of rapport. Nervousness and anxiety are sometimes evident through laughing, yawning, sweating, shaking, or crying. Be concerned about the subject's comfort and ask about it. Avoid comments that may be judgmental or are confrontational.
- Encourage active participation by outlining what you expect from the interviewee. Explain that you are not going to ask all the questions but are depending on him or her to explain what happened.
- Ask the witness to reveal every detail regardless of whether he or she thinks that the information is valuable. Note that this is one of the mnemonic memory-jogging techniques.
- Give the interviewee permission to say that he or she does not know the answer to a question.

Step Two: Narrative Phases

This step involves three parts: free recall, guided recall of the event, and clarification. First, the interviewee is asked to supply a narrative report of the incident in his or her own words. Active listening requires that the interviewer avoid interrupting or asking for details during this phase. Paying particular attention to the narration, the interviewer notes the perspective of the statement. For example, where does the subject alter the level of description, alter his or her voice to mimic the assailant's speech, or deflect his or her gaze away from the interviewer?

Next, comes the part where the interviewer assists the interviewee in the recall. Talking about the need for concentration, instructions may include questions such as "How did you feel?", "What did you hear?", and "What happened?" The investigator asks for the witness to think about what happened as perceived through their senses; what did the interviewee see, hear, smell, or touch? The interviewee is reminded to talk about everything he or she remembers, even if it seems unimportant. Reconstruction techniques are employed in this directed segment of the interview. Context reinstatement is used to help the interviewee to go back to the place or context in which the event occurred. This is done by asking open-ended questions designed to stimulate stored memories. The interviewer should not attempt to fill in gaps or interrupt even if questions arise or something needs clarification.

At this point in the narrative-gathering process, the interviewer may have a list of questions concerning missing or unclear information. Taking care not to verbally pounce on the interviewee, the interviewer reminds him or her to share all information by reporting everything. Now is the time for extensive note taking and asking questions. One should avoid closed-ended questions that will limit the response of the interviewee.

Step Three: Extensive Recall through Mnemonics

The interviewee should be encouraged to retrieve more information through memory-enhancing techniques. The interviewer should explain that the strategies for obtaining more information are being used not because the statement was faulty, but that these techniques have been shown to increase memory retrieval. Primary techniques that provide more information include the reconstruction technique, recalling events from a different order, and changing the perspective.

The reconstruction technique involves talking to the interviewee about concentration and asking that he or she think about the sound environment, the rooms, the

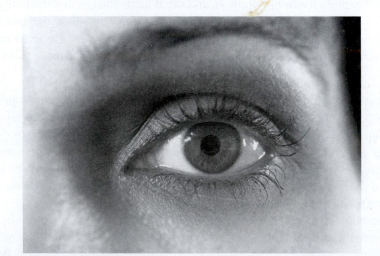

FIGURE 5-3 Aiding in recall through the use of mnemonics is an important part of cognitive interviewing.

Source: RF Corbis Value/Alamy Stock Photo.

furniture, the weather, lighting, or people. What was the witness feeling or hearing at the time of the event?

Recalling events from a different order, also called "switching the temporal order," is another mnemonic used during this stage. The interviewee is instructed to recall the incident backward. Prompting takes place by asking, "What is the last thing you remember? What before that? What happened before that?"

Changing perspectives is also helpful during this stage of the interview. The purpose is to see the event through the eyes of another, but it should be made clear to the interviewee that he or she must only report facts that were witnessed and not to fabricate or guess. Additional memory-jogging techniques that were described earlier in the chapter may be helpful at this time.

Step Four: Summary and Closure

This may be the last chance to get information from this individual. Ask if there is anyone that he or she recommends you speak with or anything else you should know. Briefly, summarize the information that the interviewee has provided.

Closure occurs by reestablishing the personal connection with the interviewee. Always end on a positive note with appreciation for the time and effort put into the interview. Update the contact information and encourage the interviewee to call with any new information.

CHALLENGES TO MEMORY RETRIEVAL

Everyday memory-encoding problems such as challenging lighting conditions or distance to the event and distractions will negatively affect the way that recall occurs. An individual's emotions and the process of scripting cause interference with memory retrieval. Memories do change over time, and the new memories may or may not reflect the reality more accurately.

Contamination

One of the most common sources of eyewitness error occurs when witnesses' memories become contaminated by information that they acquired since they witnessed the event. Sometimes referred to as "misinformation," the source of contamination is typically someone involved in the case who shares his or her bias early on in the investigation.

Leading, misleading, and forced questions can confuse a witness and produce contaminated information. For example, "Did you hear her scream?" implies that someone did scream. The interviewee is now led to believe that someone screamed, misled if that did not occur, and forced to state that he or she did not miss something. The answer will probably be "Yes, I heard her scream," even if it did not occur. An investigator may not know whether the question he or she is asking is misleading; open-ended questioning avoids this problem. In the same situation the witness may be asked, "Did you hear anything?" or "What did you hear?" One should avoid mentioning any new information that has not been previously given.

WHAT IS DIFFERENTIAL RECALL ENHANCEMENT?

A promising new approach to interviewing is called "Differential Recall Enhancement" (DRE), which involves the use of techniques to detect deception by increasing recall for honest interviewees while making deceptive individuals more apparent (Colwell, Hiscock-Anisman, & Fede, 2013). The foundation of the deception detection approach is attributing behaviors to deceivers that distinguish them from truth-tellers. It is based

BEEN THERE . . . DONE THAT! 5-3

Memory can be changed by contamination, high emotion, and scripting. Recall of an event is different than playing back a movie with all of the details of what happened. Memory is more delicate and can be influenced by what a person thinks he or she should have done and by guilt for what he or she may have done. I once interviewed a woman named Stella whose child was in the hospital with apparent shaken-baby syndrome. The baby was not expected to live due to massive injuries to the brain. Stella told me that the baby woke up crying in the middle of the night and woke up her live-in boyfriend. The boyfriend was furious and yelled at her to do something to stop the crying of the baby. There were two rooms in the apartment, the bedroom where two children slept with their mother and boyfriend and the kitchen. Stella got up from the bed and carried the baby into the kitchen. On the way she tripped over a toy that was left on the floor and dropped the baby. It was a horrible accident. At my request, Stella drew a picture of the kitchen and indicated where she had tripped and where the baby had landed after the fall.

I served a search warrant on the apartment to collect the toy and document the accident. What I found was surprising. There were no toys at all in the apartment, not one—nothing to trip over. Looking at the drawing that Stella had provided of the place where the baby had landed indicated that it was not where the trip had occurred, but that the baby had landed to the left of where Stella had "tripped." To the right was a stove with a small dent. If the baby had been thrown to the right against the stove, he would have landed to the left and forward of where Stella indicated that he had fallen. Was this faulty memory or a lie? You decide.

on the belief that individuals who are attempting to lie are more concerned with appearing to be truthful than those who are not being deceptive.

The perspective recognizes that people who are telling the truth are not concerned with minor inconsistencies or changes to their statement since honesty is not at issue. To tell convincing lies, a deceptive person is likely to develop a **lie scrip**, which is a created narrative to explain events that become the basis for responding rather than memory (Dando, Bull, Ormerod, & Sandham, 2015). The lie scrip is rehearsed to avoid making mistakes or giving the wrong impression when asked questions. Techniques being used to expose the lie scrip make deceptive responding more difficult and apparent. The DRE approaches include the ACID, the cognitive load approach, SUE, and tactical interviewing.

The four deception detection methods of the DRE approach rely on psychological differences between the truth-tellers and liars, attempting to expose and highlight the variances. It is not easy to make veracity judgments of guilt or innocence! Studies have consistently found that criminal justice professionals are no better at making these judgments than chance when relying on verbal or nonverbal cues to detect deception (Dando et al., 2015). The methods categorized as DRE approaches attempt to better the odds of accuracy using verbal deceit detection and memory research results. Each model is somewhat different, yet all have been tested empirically and found to increase validity in clinical trials.

Assessment Criteria Indicative of Deception (ACID)

ACID is a way to assess statement creditability by examining the quality and spontaneity of the account. It uses the mnemonics approach of the Cognitive interview described earlier in this chapter, elements of reality interviewing, and examines the type–token ratio of the statement. It is thought that truth-tellers provide more words and unique details than deceptive respondents. According to researchers, the training program for police officers emphasizes interviewing by assessing the verbal content and decision-making process involved in the statement (Colwell, James-Kangal, Hiscok-Anisman, & Phelan, 2015). The ACID approach is complex and may not have general applicability among interviewers, however.

Investigators must learn to rely on verbal cues of deception and ignore visual cues. To avoid reliance on visual cues and reduce the cumbersome practice of verbatim transcripts, audio recordings are relied on for assessment purposes. The reality interview component of ACID involves the use of three forced-choice modules spaced among the mnemonics (Colwell et al., 2015). These are questions that require a yes or no response and are unexpected. For example, "Was a crime committed?", "Were there any weapons?", and "Could you have been wrong about this?"

The type–token ratio is the ratio of the number of different unique spoken or written words (types) to the total number of spoken or written words (tokens). For example, if a text is 1,000 words long, it is said to have 1,000 tokens. There may be only, say, 400 different words (types) in the text because many of them may be repeated. The ratio between types and tokens in this example is 400/1,000, or 40 percent. Statement fabrication is associated with higher type–token ratios as compared to truthful statements. The deception that is highly motivated has been associated with a shorter response length, a slower rate of speech, and more speech errors. These behaviors, collectively known as **verbal leakage**, are the unconscious verbal responses that indicate deception (Hartwig & Bond, 2014). Follow-up questions are used to probe suspected deception have been helpful in uncovering purposeful deceit by nonskilled liars.

According to a recent study conducted by Colwell et al. (2015), untrained police officers are highly unlikely to have the skills to determine when someone is being honest or lying to them. In an experiment of training in ACID, a group of officers performed significantly better in detecting deceit than they had before the training. The trained officers in the Colwell study fared significantly better than a group of police officers who were never trained (89% correct versus 54% correct). The research suggests that relying on verbal cues to deception is more reliable and valid compared to nonverbal cues.

Cognitive Load Approach

The cognitive load approach was conceived in 2006 by Sporer and Schwandt (Sporer, 2016). These authors theorize that liars need to plan what they are saying, attempt not to contradict themselves, observe the reaction of the interviewer, and control their behavior and speech so that they appear credible. They assume that while it is cognitively demanding for liars to provide statements, accomplished liars may change only a minor but important detail rather than the entire story to ease the difficulty of lying. Liars can appear to be at ease when they have practiced their account or during those times when the truth forms the basis of a statement. Distinguishing the truthful individuals from the liars can be very difficult during an interview for these reasons.

We know that an increased cognitive demand is required for a person to lie convincingly. Research observations have documented the effects of an increased cognitive demand, which is associated with lying. Examples include increased pulse, decreased blinking, and decreased hand and finger movements among liars versus truth-tellers (Vrij, 2014). The psychological changes may be subtle and difficult to detect, however, particularly during criminal interviews. The cognitive load approach was devised to place additional cognitive demands on interviewees to make it more difficult for liars to be as good as those who are telling the truth.

Liars should think harder and may look more nervous than honest interviewees. This occurs over time during the interview when there is an increase in the cognitive load. The investigative interviewer should be looking for subtle behavioral changes to the interviewee that are indicative of deceit. Ways to increase an individual's cognitive

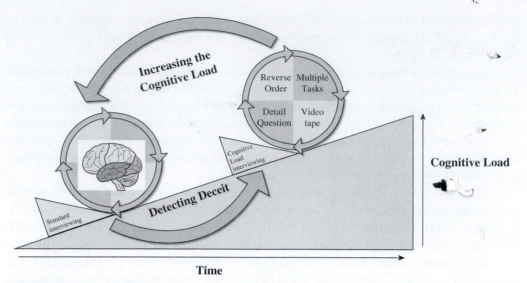

FIGURE 5-4 Four techniques have been used to increase the cognitive load to detect deceit (Sporer, 2016).

load include requiring the suspect during an interview to reverse order, by asking unanticipated questions, interviewing while multitasking, and videotaping (Sporer, 2016).

✓ **Reverse Order.** Note that this step is also referred to as "changing the order of events" during the cognitive interviewing technique. This step is believed to increase the cognitive load because it is counter to the normal forward order, making it more difficult to fabricate a reconstruction of events.

✓ **Multiple Tasks.** Carrying out two tasks at the same time is cognitively more difficult than doing only one task. An example of multiple tasking would be to ask the interviewee to recall their story while driving a car or cooking a meal. Liars would find it more difficult than truth-tellers due to the cognitive demand of presenting a plausible lie.

✓ **Detail Question.** The detail question approach requires that the investigative interviewer ask questions that are unanticipated by the suspect and therefore requires more thought. Liars could refuse to answer questions but fear it would create suspicion. It is always easier to answer questions that are planned and rehearsed versus fabricating an answer to unexpected questions.

✓ **Videotape.** Videotaping an interview increases the stress of an interviewee. When a suspect is videotaped, the process itself may increase the cognitive load disproportionally for the liar versus the truth-teller.

Strategic Use of Evidence (SUE)

The Strategic Use of Evidence (SUE) technique was developed to plan, structure, conduct, and evaluate interviews in criminal and intelligence gathering contexts (Hartwig & Bond, 2014). According to the researchers, the approach is based on the psychology of self-regulation. This is a concept explaining that people control their behavior to achieve desired goals. The goal of persons being interviewed is to convince the interviewer that their statement is true.

The SUE technique suggests that there is a difference in the way that dishonest and honest persons will reach this goal. For suspects in interview settings, the cognitive control strategies may be complex. The liar will need to offer information in place of the truth to appear credible, making decisions about what to avoid, deny, and admit during the interview. Liars typically plan their statements to reach the goal of appearing

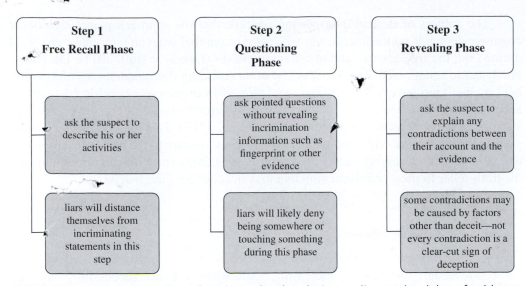

Step 1 Free Recall Phase	Step 2 Questioning Phase	Step 3 Revealing Phase
ask the suspect to describe his or her activities	ask pointed questions without revealing incrimination information such as fingerprint or other evidence	ask the suspect to explain any contradictions between their account and the evidence
liars will distance themselves from incriminating statements in this step	liars will likely deny being somewhere or touching something during this phase	some contradictions may be caused by factors other than deceit—not every contradiction is a clear-cut sign of deception

FIGURE 5-5 The Strategic Use of Evidence (SUE) technique relies on the delay of evidence disclosure.

truthful. The honest person will simply believe that if they tell the truth, the interviewer will believe them.

Typically, free recall prompts during questioning lead to omissions in liars' statements and specific questions lead to blatant signs of dishonesty in the form of contradictions with the facts. The verbal denial cues are more pronounced and more noticeable than the omission cues. In a study conducted by Hartwig and Bond (2014) subjects were sent into a store where they viewed a briefcase containing a wallet. Those who were truthful during the interview admitted to having been in the store and seeing the briefcase and wallet. Those who had been instructed to lie avoided mentioning the store or having seen either the briefcase or wallet.

A major difference between the SUE technique and typical police interviews is the withholding of information about known evidence until the end of the interview (Bull, 2013). The delay prevents a story from being fabricated at the beginning of the interview and encourages an open mind, providing the liar with false comfort. Studies have suggested that use of the technique increased accurate deception detection in more than 85% from a 56% accuracy rate without SUE (Vrij, Granhag, & Porter, 2010).

Tactical Interviewing

There are three common timings during which information or evidence is presented to the suspect during an interview. As you see in the SUE approach, evidence production is withheld until late in the interview. Another common method is that information indicative of guilt be revealed early in the interview to overwhelm the suspect and influence the guilty person to confess (Inbau, Reid, Buckley, & Jayne, 2013). A third timing has been referred to as a "drip" approach; it is the gradual revelation of information throughout the fact-finding interview (Dando et al., 2015).

The gradual revelation of information is the timing used during tactical interviewing, as part of a strategy to avoid bringing bias into the interview. Keeping an open mind about the importance of information or evidence that is held by the interviewers requires that no weight be given to any information that the interviewers have about the event. This means that the interviewers use a non-accusatory approach that allows a free recall from the suspects followed by a gradual presentation separately of each "piece" of potentially incriminating information (Bull, 2013). Information dispersed throughout the questioning phase of the interview is not limited to potentially incriminating evidence.

The authors of tactical interviewing concede that the approach places significant cognitive demands on the interviewer who must remember what an interviewee has said during both the free account and questioning phases (Dando & Bull, 2011). Interviews are dynamic situations that evolve quickly, often revealing discrepancies to information held by the interviewers. The gradual revelation of information is considered superior, according to researchers, since it allows for investigators to make inferences on the consistency of the statements throughout (Dando et al., 2015). This method challenges the suspect during the interview and requires the suspect to adapt to the numerous questions and tasks that are necessary during the various stages. It also provides an opportunity for the truth-teller to provide information that may account for their behavior.

Conclusions

Forensic hypnosis remains a controversial evidence-gathering technique. Numerous court cases have provided guidance on its use and standards for admissibility as evidence. Hypnotically refreshed evidence should be utilized as a tool in the investigation and not as the sole source of information. Corroboration is necessary to support the information gathered through hypnosis. Despite the controversy, hypnosis seems to be making a small comeback in recent years as a positive and reliable information-gathering tool.

Cognitive interviewing is the most respected form of criminal justice interviewing. Proper use of the memory-jogging techniques along with the overall atmosphere of cooperation has been shown to improve interviewing results. The use of cognitive interviewing increases the information recalled by a witness without increasing confabulation. It has successfully survived a court challenge. Cognitive techniques can easily be incorporated into any interviewing method that the investigator chooses to use, and this flexibility increases its potential use. It also works well for interviewing children.

The four approaches included in the *Differential, Recall Enhancement* (DRE) category have been empirically tested and found to have creditability for forensic purposes. The common thread among these approaches is that they are cognitive-based approaches using memory-jogging techniques. All are assumed to be appropriate fact-gathering approaches which assume that the interviewee may be either truthful or deceptive. Each approach relies on verbal, rather than behavioral, cues for detecting deceit.

Questions for Review

Short-Answer Questions

1. What are some of the arguments against the use of hypnosis during court testimony?
2. What are the four phases of forensic hypnosis?
3. What is memory hardening?
4. What are the four steps of the cognitive interviewing method?
5. Explain the term "scripting."

Fill-in Questions

1. _____ refers to an investigative memory retrieval technique used to enhance recall in legally relevant situations.
2. Persons under hypnosis are _____ of what is going on; those in the state of hypnosis do not become zombies.
3. The American Psychological Association recommends _____ the use of hypnosis for memory retrieval.
4. The phenomenon which gives the subject increased confidence regarding the facts remembered during hypnosis, regardless of whether the supposed facts are true or false is called _____.
5. Every defendant has the _____ _____ to use hypnotically refreshed memory in their defense during a criminal trial.
6. The _____ interviewing method is a family of memory-jogging and retrieval tools for evaluating survey questions and questionnaires and conducting interviews.
7. _____ is the term that describes the four cognitive interviewing principles used for remembering information that is otherwise difficult to recall.
8. One of the most common sources of eyewitness error occurs when witnesses' memories become _____ by information that they acquired since they witnessed the event.

9. In order to tell convincing lies, a deceptive person is likely to develop a ____ ____, which is a created narrative to explain events that become the basis for responding rather than memory.

10. The methods categorized as ____ approaches attempt to better the odds of accuracy using verbal deceit detection and memory research results.

Exercises

1. Think about something that happened to you. This incident will be the basis for the practice interview; it can be a positive or negative experience. The interview will be concerned with obtaining information about that experience. Form interview teams of two students each. Practice the cognitive interview steps in these following exercises.

   i. Practice step one of the cognitive method, meet and greet; 5-minute exercise.

   ii. Practice step two of the cognitive method, narrative phases; 20-minute exercise.

   iii. Practice step three of the cognitive method, extensive recall through mnemonics; 25-minute exercise.

   iv. Practice step four of the cognitive method, summary, and closure; 10-minute exercise.

2. To illustrate enhancing recall through mnemonics, pair off for this brief 15-minute exercise. Identify one student as the interviewer and one as the interviewee. Have the interviewer ask the interviewee, "What was the last program you watched on TV?" The interviewer should then use step three of the cognitive interview method, extensive recall through mnemonics. Asking for recall from a different order and changing the perspective, the interviewer should attempt to obtain more information about the particular TV program.

References

Adams, S. (2004). Statement analysis: Beyond the words. *FBI Law Enforcement Bulletin, 73*(4), 22–23.

American Psychotherapy and Medical Hypnosis Association. (2017). Definition of the process of hypnosis and trance states. [Online.] Available: http://apmha.com.

Baltman, J., & Lynn, S. J. (2016). Hypnosis, memory, and expectation. In S. Trusz & P. Bąbel (Eds.), *Interpersonal and intrapersonal expectancies* (pp. 47–51). New York, NY: Routledge.

Bull, R. (2013). *Developments in the interviewing/interrogation of suspects to produce discourse: Some contributions from psychological research.* Paper presented at the Proceedings of the 2nd International Conference on Law, Language and Discourse: Multiculturalism, Multimodality and Multidimensionality.

Colwell, K., Hiscock-Anisman, C., & Fede, J. (2013). Assessment Criteria Indicative of Deception (ACID): An example of the new paradigm of Differential Recall Enhancement. In B. Cooper, D. Griesel, & M. Ternes (Eds.), *Applied issues in eyewitness memory, credibility assessment, and investigative interviewing* (pp. 259–291). New York, NY: Springer.

Colwell, K., James-Kangal, N., Hiscok-Anisman, C., & Phelan, V. (2015). Should police use ACID? Training and credibility assessment using transcripts versus recordings. *Journal of Forensic Psychiatry & Psychology, 15*, 226–247.

Dando, C., & Bull, R. (2011). Maximizing opportunities to detect verbal deception: Training police officers to interview tactically. *Journal of Investigative Psychology and Offender Profiling, 8*(2), 189–202.

Dando, C., Bull, R., Ormerod, T., & Sandham, A. (2015). Helping to sort the liars from the truth-tellers: The gradual revelation of information during investigative interviews. *Legal and Criminological Psychology, 20*(1), 114–128.

Daubert v. Merrell Dow Pharmaceuticals, 113 S.Ct 2786 (1993).

DOJ. (2017). *United States Attorneys' Manual* Vol. CRM 287–294. *Criminal Resource Manual.* Retrieved from https://www.justice.gov/usam/criminal-resource-manual-287-use-hypnosis-purpose

Frye v. United States, 23 Fed. 1013 (1923).

Geiselman, R. E., & Fisher, R. P. (1985). *Interviewing victims and witnesses of crime* (Report No. NCJ 99061). Washington, D.C.: National Institute of Justice.

Hartwig, M., & Bond, C. (2014). Lie detection from multiple cues: A meta-analysis. *Applied Cognitive Psychology, [Online].* doi:10.1002/acp.3052

Holliday, R. E., Humphries, J. E., Milne, R., Memon, A., Houlder, L., Lyons, A., & Bull, R. (2012). Reducing misinformation effects in older adults with cognitive interview mnemonics. *Psychology and Aging, 27*(4), 1191.

Inbau, F., Reid, J., Buckley, J., & Jayne, B. (2013). *Essentials of the Reid technique: Criminal interrogation and confessions* (2nd ed.). Sudbury, MA: Jones and Bartlett Publishers.

Lee, L., Bradburn, N., Poland, S., Brownstein, H., & Krishnamurty, P. (2013). *Methodological research to support the redesign of the National Crime Victimization Survey: Enhanced contextual priming as a memory aid.* Washington, D.C.: Bureau of Justice Statistics.

Lynn, S. J., Boycheva, E., Deming, A., Lilienfeld, S. O., & Hallquist, M. N. (2009). Forensic hypnosis. In J. Skeem, K. Douglas, & S. Lilienfeld (Eds.), *Psychological science in the courtroom: Consensus and controversy* (p. 80). New York, NY: Guilford Press.

Mazzoni, G., Laurence, J.-R., & Heap, M. (2014). Hypnosis and memory: Two hundred years of adventures and still going! *Psychology of Consciousness: Theory, Research, and Practice, 1*(2), 153.

Nevada Revised Statutes. (2015). Testimony of witness who previously underwent hypnosis to recall subject matter of testimony. Vol. Title 4 *Witness and Evidence,* Chapter 48, Section 039.

Rock v. Arkansas, 483 U.S. 44 (1987).

Shaw, J. (2015). Remembering crimes that never happened. *The Police Chief, 82*(June), 16–17.

Sporer, S. L. (2016). Deception and cognitive load: Expanding our horizon with a working memory model. *Frontiers in Psychology, 7*(420).

Vrij, A. (2014). Interviewing to detect deception. *European Psychologist, 19*(3), 184–194.

Vrij, A., & Fisher, R. P. (2016). Which lie detection tools are ready for use in the criminal justice system? *Journal of Applied Research in Memory and Cognition, 5*(3), 302–307.

Vrij, A., Granhag, P. A., & Porter, S. (2010). Pitfalls and opportunities in nonverbal and verbal lie detection. *Psychological Science in the Public Interest, 11*(3), 89–121.

Wagstaff, G. F. (2009). Is there a future for investigative hypnosis? *Journal of Investigative Psychology & Offender Profiling, 6*(1), 43

Westera, N. J., Kebbell, M. R., & Milne, B. (2016). Want a better criminal justice response to rape? Improve police interviews with complainants and suspects. *Violence Against Women, 22*(14), 1748–1769.

Willison, J., Biegeler, S., & Kim, K. (2014). *Evaluation of the Allegheny County jail collaborative reentry programs.* Washington, D.C.: Urban Institute.

Winter, A. (2013). The rise and fall of forensic hypnosis. *Studies in History and Philosophy of Science Part C: Studies in History and Philosophy of Biological and Biomedical Sciences, 44*(1), 26–35.

Zani v. State, 767 S.W.2d 825 (Court of Appeals of Texas, Texarkana 1989).

Principles to Detect Deception

Source: Joseasreyes/123rf.

CHAPTER OBJECTIVES

After completing this chapter, you should be able to:

1. Summarize the three principles used to detect deception.
2. Describe five considerations to avoid the danger of disbelieving the truth.
3. Define neurolinguistic programming.
4. Evaluate uses for *mirroring* and *shifting*.
5. Give an example of the use of *modeling*.
6. Compare the two methods which focus on verbal indicators to detect deceit.
7. Discuss the use of *priming*.
8. Explain three categories of nonverbal indicators of deceit.

KEY TERMS

Emblems	Shifting
Modeling	Mirroring
Neurolinguistic programming	Priming
Paralanguage	Undeutsch hypothesis

INTRODUCTION

Examples of detecting deception can be found since ancient times and throughout history. Verbal and nonverbal indicators of deceit during interviews are based on theories of communication and learning, which influence unintended communications. It is thought that verbal and nonverbal cues, known as behavioral anomalies, could be observed by the astute interviewer. Message exchanges unconsciously guide the communication of meaning between individuals. Knowledge of learning processes and their application to verbal and behavioral responses are useful for persons conducting interviews and interrogations. Acknowledging that individuals will vary in their responses due to differential encoding, this chapter will provide a broader understanding of human interactions. Brain development begins in utero; incomplete at the time of birth, it continues to mature. Experiences during childhood affect intellectual function and some aspects of normal language skills. Due to the influence of experience on the processes of learning, no two people will think or respond exactly alike.

The techniques described in this chapter are tools to use in framing the direction of the investigative interview. Finding one or two indicators of deception does not always mean that a person is lying. Considerations of the speech, behavior, and physiological changes that occur during an interview are three parts of the deception-detecting process. There are verbal and nonverbal cues mistaken for deceit that might reflect the personality, culture, and gender of the person being interviewed or interrogated, which can cause biases. Bias can originate from the interviewer and the number of details he or she provides and with the interviewer who perceives and interprets cues as truthful or deceitful. Interviewers must be wary of indicators that cannot be corroborated by evidence. There is no magic bullet to determine if someone is lying! Cases that center on indicators of deceit must be fully investigated and statements corroborated with evidence.

Both verbal and nonverbal behavioral indicators are covered in this chapter. A common thread to these is the belief that human communication is affected by learning, which in turn affects verbal, nonverbal, and physiological indicators that can be observed and interpreted. Sometimes these techniques are referred to as "arousal based" lie detection. The verbal cues included here have been scientifically tested and found to improve the reliability of statements regardless of which method is being used. Nonverbal indicators, including posturing, sensory verbal communication, and eye movement, are among the phenomena presented. The intent is for the interviewer to recognize unintended communications, also called "neurocommunications," which allow interpretation by the interviewer.

WHY DO INVESTIGATORS CARE ABOUT DECEIT?

Lying and deception are normal behaviors. These have always been part of the human experience. It is well acknowledged that people lie for a variety of reasons in their public and private lives. Deception is so common that it has attracted the attention of scholars who wonder about the frequency and reasons why people lie. It appears that lying is a part of everyday life, and people generally lie once a day; seasoned liars lie more frequently (Remland, 2017). We lie to protect ourselves, to avoid tension and conflict, to avoid responsibility, and to minimize hurt feelings. Most people are not very good at detecting deception, and professionals in the field generally do no better than chance (Vrij, Meissner, & Kassin, 2015). Efforts to improve these odds form the basis for this chapter of study.

Lying behaviors are common in various settings. Age seems to matter. Research suggests that children may lie as early as age 3, but skilled lie-telling develops around age 8 (Remland, 2017). Lying into adulthood is thought to involve sequences of behaviors, the continuation of childhood behavior. Some people lie, well, just because they never learned that it is bad (Fryling, 2016). Some forms of lying are socially acceptable, such as lying about online availability or how a loved one looks. Some forms of lying involve behaviors, which cause harm to others. Accidental lying is an exception, as it involves self-gratification. It can be deliberate falsification, appropriate, or even accidental. It is no wonder that investigative interviewers whose goal is to discover the truth are consumed with trying to tell the difference between the truth and the lie. The problem is, how?

Catching liars typically involves the three principles to detect deception: observing behaviors, listening to speech content, and noting any physiological responses. The major problem in using behavioral anomalies to detect deceit is that many cues that investigative interviewers have come to rely on have not been verified as true indicators of deceit. For example, looking up to the left and twitching of the left eyebrow are not true indicators of lying (Matsumoto, Skinner, & Hwang, 2014). Some behavioral anomalies have been validated by research while others have not. Mere observation of a behavioral change is not sufficient to claim it as an indicator of deceit. After making observations of an interviewee and noting speech errors, hesitation, lack of confidence, or indicators of stress may suggest *some* cause; these do not conclusively indicate deception (Navarro, 2012). Research has suggested that the combination of verbal and nonverbal behavioral indicators provide an improved source for gauging truthfulness (Matsumoto, Hwang, Skinner, & Frank, 2011).

Detecting Deceit

It is universally accepted that there is no one sign of deceit—no gesture, facial expression, or muscle twitch that in and of itself means that a person is lying. There are only clues that the person is poorly prepared and clues of emotions that don't fit the person's line. Knowing that people suspected of being liars are judged by their words and their behaviors, a deceptive person will closely monitor what he or she says and his or her actions.

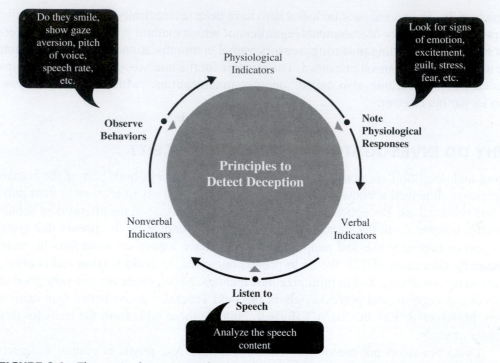

FIGURE 6-1 There are three general principles to detect deception: Verbal Indicators, Nonverbal Indicators, and Psychological Changes. All must be observed and evaluated by the investigative interviewer.

When attempting to detect deceit, the greatest danger is in disbelieving the truth; this occurs when a person trying to catch a liar mistakenly judges a truthful person to be lying. The following considerations are suggested to avoid this danger:

1. Remember that the absence of a sign of deceit is not evidence of truth.
2. Comparisons must be made between the suspect's usual behavior and that when under suspicion.
3. Consider the possibility that a sign of emotion is not a clue to deceit but a clue to how a truthful person feels about being suspected of lying.
4. Discount the sign of an emotion as a clue to deceit if the suspect's personality makes the suspect likely to have such a feeling even if he or she were being truthful.
5. Realize that the polygraph only measures the arousal of emotion, not which emotion is felt. Studies indicate that it is better than chance that a person feeling strong emotion at being suspected may fail the polygraph although he or she is being truthful.

NEUROLINGUISTIC PROGRAMMING

The term **neurolinguistic programming** (NLP) refers to the interconnectedness and process of primary forms of human communication, verbal (and written) and nonverbal (behavior). Developed during the 1970s by John Grinder and Richard Bandler, it involves the psychology of how individuals think, communicate, and decipher information (Dilts, Bandler, & Bandler, 1980). NLP is the study of what's actually going on when we think and the framework to analyze human communication (Dotz, Hoobyar, & Sanders, 2013).

"Neuro" refers to the brain and the neural network that feeds into the brain. Neurons, or nerve cells, are the working units used by the nervous system to send, receive, and store signals that add up to information. Neurolinguistics include the idea that behavior originates from the five senses: seeing, hearing, smelling, tasting, and touching. Incorporated into the theory are psychological reactions to ideas and events. "Linguistics" refers to the way that we communicate both verbally and nonverbally. The "programming" part of the term relates to the unique way that human beings manipulate the signals and convert them into useful information. Based on prior experience, the brain directs the programming process into thinking patterns and behaviors that become part of our life experiences and emotions.

The principles of NLP suggest that when a person does something that is unhealthy or even criminal, they do it because in that person's mind the behavior is necessary (Dotz, Hoobyar, & Sanders, 2013). A second presupposition, according to Dotz and colleagues, is that every behavior has a positive intention. The learning modes in the NLP model involve visual, auditory, and kinesthetic (tactile) senses. People will usually speak in the same sensory mode by which they learn. To aid in the building of rapport, the interviewer will mirror the same sensory language used by the subject.

Mirroring

Mirroring occurs when the interviewer uses the same sensory language as the interviewee to establish common ground on which the subject feels comfortable. It is a legitimate way to speak the same language as the subject to improve rapport. Another use of the information regarding sensory communication is for the purpose of shifting. **Shifting** occurs when the interviewer uses the same sensory language to ask the subject questions and to move that person into the area under investigation through comfortable and familiar language. This occurs when the interviewer has determined the preferred sense of communication and uses the terms provided by the subject to move to the preferred topic for discussion. Involving the senses in descriptions by victims and witnesses tends to increase their credibility in many cases, particularly for sexual assault complaints, for children, and when interviewing developmentally challenged adults.

In attempting to shift the interview from one sense of relating to another, one incorporates new terms into the questions. For example, consider a victim who states, "It was awful, I can still feel his hands on me." A response calculated to shift the conversation to the visual mode is, "When you felt his hands on you, what did you see? Did he wear any rings? Were there any tattoos on his fingers?" To move the conversation into the auditory type of thought, the interviewer might ask, "When you felt his hands on you, what did you hear? Did he say anything while he was touching you?" Another use of sensory analysis includes exploration of other kinesthetic areas such as smell or taste. An example is, "When he was touching you, what did he smell like?"

The vast majority of the population are visual learners who are affected by charts, graphs, and pictures. They think in visual terms; when asked a question, a picture of thoughts goes through their minds. The language of these learners will, therefore, be visually constructed. People who communicate through the sense of sight will use phrases such as "Do I have to draw you a *picture*"? I do not *see* why I am here. You are *looking* at the wrong guy!" The interviewer should mimic the subject with appropriate verbal cues such as "I *see* what you mean, *picture* this, *look* at it this way." Common gestures noted in visual persons include movement of the hands and arms near the neck level when they are talking. They become quick and animated, with a quick, shallow method of breathing. These traits should help in identifying the visual person.

A small portion of individuals, notably musicians, singers, and orators, are auditory learners. Individuals who rely primarily on the sense of hearing will tend to speak moderately and rhythmically. Auditory thinkers hear the thoughts as they are being processed and in turn are affected by what they hear. To reach these auditory individuals, the interviewer's language should use similar auditory expressions: "I *hear* what you're saying, *listen* to this, and *tell* me what you mean." When such a person is asked to explain something, the interviewer might notice the person's hands or arms move below the shoulder while pointing to the ear. The way to persuade an auditory thinker is to moderate your vocal rate and breathe deeply.

A small percentage of people are emotional thinkers, who have a kinesthetic thought process. Facts and charts are not impressive to these people; they may be athletes or have heightened spiritual awareness. Their language will contain "feeling terms," which the interviewer should also use. These include phrases like "I *feel* your pain; I know what you are *going through*, how do you *feel*?" Note whether their gaze is frequently down and their breathing is slow and deep during an interview. Slow down and be particularly calm to communicate with this type of person!

Modeling

A major strategy in the NLP method is **modeling**, which refers to learning to reflect individual behavior (Ekman & Friesen, 1969). Also called "pacing" or "matching," it is a form of imitation that indicates to the subject (subconsciously) that you are alike. Used during an interview, modeling suggests harmony and agreement between the interviewee and the subject. When two people adopt similar sitting positions, the nonverbal statement is "We are alike." Numerous possibilities exist concerning what might be matched with a subject in either posture or gesture. Notice whether the individual presents with stiff-fingered palms and an extended, rigid thumb, which is a control gesture warning people to remain at a distance. It also signals, "I will not give up my position." The interviewer would want to match this gesture to relay the same emotional position.

Modeling is an approach that is also used to establish rapport. Matching posture and gesture must be done in a subtle way that does not appear to mimic the person, or it will have the opposite effect. When the person changes body position, wait an appropriate period and change yours to match. Don't assume that you must be exactly like the individual to use modeling. Establish yourself as the authority through your status, clothing, and other symbols to achieve a meaningful figure worth modeling to maximize your influence on the subject.

WHAT ARE VERBAL INDICATORS OF DECEIT?

Verbal communication is the encoding of messages into words that are written or spoken. Verbal indicators of deceit are discovered by an analysis of the content of the statement. An analysis is possible by the investigator who can listen intently and simultaneously look for nonverbal indicators and changes in physiological responses of the interviewee during the interview. Although cognitively demanding, this can be achieved by the skilled investigator. To analyze the speech content, an audio recording is helpful. A transcript of the interview may be needed for in-depth evaluation. Investigators may also rely on their notes during the interview or a written statement provided by the interviewee.

Research suggests that verbal indicators of deception may be more accurate than nonverbal indicators, although the latter is more widely covered in law enforcement training manuals (Logue, Book, Frosina, Huizinga, & Amos, 2015). It is important to listen not only to what is said during an interview but also to how it is said. Emotional outbursts and inflections of the voice may give a clue to sensitive areas of the interview. Research has found that greater accuracy in classifying both truthful and deceitful statements can be achieved through the investigative interview by obtaining a high-familiarity with the case before the interview (Reinhard, Sporer, Scharmach, & Marksteiner, 2011). It is the high-familiarity condition that is associated with more use of verbal content cues versus nonverbal cues, according to Reinhard and colleagues (2011). Therefore, to increase success at detecting verbal indicators, the first step of an investigation should always be in becoming familiar with the case under investigation.

One method to detect verbal indicators of deceit is in statement content analysis, such as the *Scientific Content Analysis* (SCAN) method covered in Chapter 4. Greater use of minimizing and editing adverbs and changes in nouns and verbs are associated with lying (Matsumoto et al., 2011). Examine the individual parts of speech that are used in the statement, particularly pronouns, nouns, and verbs, and establish the norm for each. If a change from the norm becomes apparent, seek the reason for that difference. Word choices are purposeful, even when they are selected subconsciously. *Reality Monitoring* (RM) and the *Criteria-Based Content Analysis* (CBCA) are two examples of methods which focus on verbal indicators.

REALITY MONITORING (RM)

An individual's memory of an incident can be attributed to an actual event or imagination. Research on evaluating whether a memory originated from a real experience or an imagined event is called *Reality Monitoring* (RM). RM to assess truthfulness or detect deceit has become a recent focus of scholars but has been a part of investigative interviewing practice for many years. According to research, memories of experienced events should be clear and sharp, while imagined events are vague and less tangible (Virj, 2015). Memories from real experiences should have more sensory, contextual, and affective information than memories that originate from imagination (Bogaard, Meijer, Vrij, & Merckelbach, 2016). To improve deception detection, RM is frequently paired up for use with the Cognitive Interview (CI) for witnesses and the Cognitive Interview for Suspects (CIS).

Exact criteria for RM have not yet been established. Aldert Vrij (2014) proposed eight criteria to consider in RM: clarity, perceptual (i.e., sensory) information, spatial information, temporal information, affect, constructability of the story, realism, and cognitive operations. Events that are experienced, rather than imagined, will contain

FIGURE 6-2   *Reality Monitoring* is used to evaluate reality when the interviewee accesses memories based on the human senses with recall that is clear and sharp.

Source: ostill/Shutterstock.

sensory cues, the person's physical and emotional state, and typically are stated in chronological order (Logue et al., 2015). Common categories that are assessed in RM include the following:

- **Sensatory cues.**   This is information that involves the senses smell, taste, touch (feel), visual details (seeing), auditory details (hearing).
- **Physical and emotional state.**   Includes contextual information such as the where the event took place and how objects and people were positioned in relation to the victim or to each other.
- **Emotional state.**   Having an experience involves affective information, the details about how it felt and how the act influenced the feelings of the person who experienced it as well as his or her response to the information.
- **Order of event.**   The temporal details are the time order and duration of the act. How it occurred would be in chronological order.

Researchers have concluded after significant research that RM is helpful in detecting truthful from deceitful individuals. Vrij (2014) reports that from 12 studies that tested the accuracy of RM the average rate for identifying honest persons is about 71 to 72 percent and the accuracy for detecting deceitful persons is between 62 to 66 percent. In a recent study, researchers found that combing the RM criteria with CIS provided an accurate classification as truthful or deceptive in over 86 percent of the statements (Logue et al., 2015).

Priming

Weaving RM into any interviewing technique is simple and effective. It can be prompted by questioning or achieved through priming. **Priming** is when the interviewer exposes the interviewee to a verbal stimulus to enhance their ability to recall, which occurs as a nonconscious process of memory (Dawson, Hartwig, & Brimbal, 2015). Primed interviewees may reveal twice as much information as those who were not.

Cognitive priming is a method to gain better information from an interviewee by using a subliminal stimulus as preparation for questioning (Chalfoun & Frasson, 2012). Research on the applicability of priming has led to a recommendation for the redesign of the National Victimization Survey. Authors found that among both higher and lower education level, crime recall may be enhanced through priming (Lee, Bradburn, Poland, Brownstein, & Krishnamurty, 2013). Preparatory statements used during the study were included on safety, trust, and the places people go. The researchers concluded that this added depth to understanding the experiences of victims and nonvictims. Examples of priming statements used in the study (Lee et al., 2013) included the following:

BEEN THERE . . . DONE THAT! 6-1

Historically, child allegations of sexual abuse are viewed with skepticism. During an interview with a six-year-old, she told me that he had put IT in her mouth. I asked, "What did IT taste like?" She shuddered and exclaimed, "Ugh, white stuff came out, and it tasted like spinach." The spontaneous description accomplished two things: First, it verified a key element of the crime of rape, oral penetration had occurred. Second, the manner in which the child screwed up her face and described the taste of the ejaculation gave strong evidence that this was not a situation of coaching or witnessing sex. The child was describing an experience based on her senses; it was real not imagined. When the defense attorney saw the videotaped interview, a plea bargain was struck that sent the perpetrator to prison.

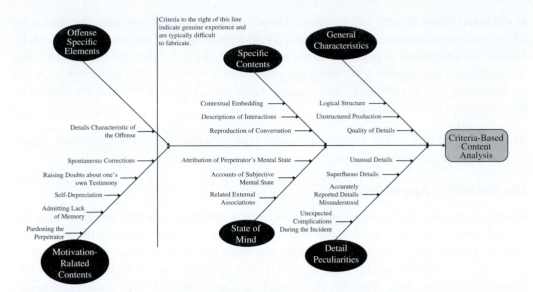

FIGURE 6-3 There are 19 CBCA criteria used by investigative interviewers to evaluate the validity of the statement content (Adapted from Amado et al., 2015; Steller & Kohnken, 1989; Vrij, 2015).

✓ "I am going to ask you some questions about crimes that may have happened to you .... Before we talk about these crimes, let's think about your feelings of safety at home, the places you go, and your trust in the people you meet."

✓ "Crimes can be committed by people we know well, by acquaintances, or by strangers.... Please tell me how much you agree or disagree with each statement." "I trust strangers." "I trust people in my neighborhood." "I trust people I work or go to school with." "I trust people in my family."

CRITERIA-BASED CONTENT ANALYSIS (CBCA)

The *Criteria-Based Content Analysis* (CBCA) was developed for use in evaluating statements from children in sexual abuse cases. We now know that CBCA provides accurate results with adults and in other types of investigations as well. While numerous techniques to evaluate lie detection have surfaced over the years, systems of content analysis are the most frequently admitted into the courts as scientific evidence.

The courts in Germany, Holland, Spain, Sweden, and several states in the United States admit these categorical systems as scientific evidence (Amado, Arce, & Fariña, 2015). The foundation for categorical content systems is the **Undeutsch hypothesis**, which states that the memory of an experienced real-life event differs in content and quality from a fabricated or imaged event (Amado et al., 2015). Researchers have combined all categorical systems into a deceit detection method known as *Criteria Based Content Analysis* (CBCA). CBCA interviewing is done in three distinct parts:

1. A semi-structured interview, consisting of a free narrative phase
2. Content analysis on CBCA criteria
3. Evaluation of CBCA outcomes using the Validity Checklist

The CBCA criteria composed of 19 categories that are expected to be more present in true compared to the untrue statement (Amado et al., 2015; Steller & Kohnken, 1989; Vrij, 2015). Scientific evidence exists that liars typically tell a less coherent story and are less likely to make spontaneous corrections to their story (Bogaard et al., 2016). Liars, for example, are less likely to admit forgetting details.

STATEMENT COHERENCE. A statement should make sense by not violating the rules of nature or contradicting itself. This step is an examination of the general characteristics of the statement, requiring that the statement is logical. Does the statement make sense when it is complete? Are there questions that are unanswered that must be asked to determine if it is complete? Did the statement contradict itself? Does the statement contradict the laws of nature?

STATEMENT DETAIL. The statement should explain where the event happened, when, who was there, and what occurred.

Verifiability Approach

Research has shown that an impressive 70 percent accuracy rate can be obtained using *Reality Monitoring* and the *Criteria-Based Content Analysis* as veracity tools (Nahari, Vrij, & Fisher, 2014). Nahari and colleagues warn that in time, liars may learn about these successful tools and prepare themselves to counteract them. Apparently, liars that are coached about these methods are difficult to detect! What can be done? The verifiability approach, they suggest, may actually enable rather than hinder lie detection when liars have knowledge about the approach.

The verifiability approach consists of a pre-interview during which the investigator notifies the interviewees about his or her intention to check their statement for verifiable details. This presents a dilemma for liars, but not for truth tellers. Liars are often unable to provide significant, verifiable details, but the truth tellers should stand out as they can do that task. In an experiment to test the theory, truthful interviewees were found to provide on average twice as many verifiable details than liars (Nahari et al., 2014).

WHAT ARE NONVERBAL INDICATORS?

Nonverbal communication is the encoding of messages through the observable nuances of paralanguage, body language, and proxemics. Sometimes referred to as "behavioral interviewing," it is the application of communication theory and the study of patterns of behavior to guide the interview process, which is deceit detection through nonverbal indicators. Detection involves taking signals from the interviewee, regardless of whether these involve subconscious behavior responses or verbal patterns.

Sudden silence, uncertainty or confusion, or the shifting of conversation to an unrelated subject may indicate that individual is uncomfortable with the subject being discussed. Nervous bodily reactions or facial characteristics may also signal that a sensitive area has been reached. By noting these things, an interviewer will know what

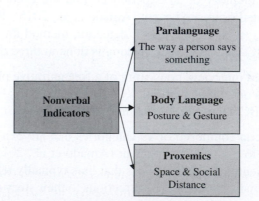

FIGURE 6-4 Nonverbal indicators are patterns of behavior that can be observed for additional cues to evaluate truthfulness or deceit.

portions of the statement may require further probing or clarification. Taken together with verbal indicators of deceit these may provide reliable indicators.

Significant research suggests that to deceive, individuals practice impression management by controlling their nonverbal cues (Riggio, 2014). Nonverbally skilled persons are evaluated more positively than others if they control facial expressions of emotion. It appears as though certain people can deceive successfully and avoid detection through nonverbal control of cues. Due to the multifaceted nature of accurate deception detection, research has not been able to establish conclusive connections between specific nonverbal cues and deceit detection.

Nonverbal indicators were once thought to stand alone as indicators of deceit. However, research has shown that gaze aversion and fidgety feet (or hands) are not scientifically validated indicators of deceit (Matsumoto et al., 2011). Likewise, body posture has been tested and found to be only weakly associated with deception. However, when nonverbal indicators emerge during an investigative interview, along with the actual words spoken, differentiating between lying and truth telling might be determined with high levels of accuracy.

Culture and Gender Considerations

Nonverbal communication is considered to be culture constrained. Researchers point out that although facial recognition appears to be universal, the way that feelings and emotions are expressed through facial expression is dictated by socio-psychological rather than political states (Lee et al., 2014). Interpretations are therefore most accurate from a similar cultural background which is not constrained by geographical boundaries. Demographic changes and the growth of ethnic minority populations in the United States suggest that behavioral indicators must be used with caution.

The complexity of cultural influences is suggested by a comparison of Arabic and American conversations. Research has shown that Arabs sit closer to one another, touch one another, make more eye contact with one another and speak more loudly than Americans (Taylor, Larner, Conchie, & Zee, 2015). Americans tend to misinterpret this conversational style as confrontational. Similarly, Japanese are inclined to smile for social correctness and less likely than Americans to display true feelings of pleasure by smiling (Taylor et al., 2015). The difficulty for investigators is that they may miss cues or make false assumptions based on behaviors if there is a lack of confidence to make these critical judgments. More work is needed for investigative interviewers to be able to make appropriate inferences from a person's behavior.

Nonverbal communications are also affected by gender. Interpretation and use of facial expressions can be different. Men appear to use different nonverbal communication styles when speaking to other men than when speaking to women. Women are more non-verbally expressive than men in ways that spontaneously express emotions on their faces (Riggio, 2014). Women smile more spontaneously than men.

Because of variances due to personal characteristics, culture, and gender (to name a few), a critical aspect of behavioral interviewing is the establishment of a baseline through conversational speech. To determine the normal communication modes of the individual, making an assessment during the investigative interview must begin with observation before starting the interview itself.

PARALANGUAGE

Paralanguage, or the vocal part of speech and its nuances, is communication that goes beyond the specific spoken words. Language is only one of the ways that messages are sent; paralanguage includes the person's tone, pitch, and reflection, all of which express emotions. It includes pitch, amplitude, rate, and voice quality of speech. Paralanguage

FIGURE 6-5   Some individuals may attempt to cover up their emotions through fake facial expressions.

Source: Image copyright Xalanx/Fotolia. Used under NAPPA subscription.

reminds us that people convey their feelings not only in *what* they say but also in *how* they say it. Active emotions such as anger and fear may be expressed by a fast rate of speech, loud volume, high pitch, and tone.

Passive emotions usually are relayed by a slower rate of speech, lower volume, and lower pitch. In the interview setting, attention to pronunciation may provide valuable information on the emotional state of the person being interviewed. Assigning meaning to the nuances of speech is difficult but may provide cues on how the interviewer might respond to someone who exhibits these. If pitch suggests anger, for example, it would be beneficial to explore why the person is angry. Yes, it could be deceit. Research has demonstrated a somewhat reliable trend for detecting deceit for higher pitch (Logue et al., 2015). Still, it might also indicate that a witness or victim feels powerless due to recent victimization. Reassurance from the interviewer should improve the rapport and facilitate the conversation. Voice characteristics can provide important clues to the truthfulness of the person speaking. Changes in speech may be notable during the interview.

BODY LANGUAGE

Because of the different neural networks involved in emotion and conscious reasoning responses, emotions seem to shortcut the circuits for reasoning. Once believed to be psychologically based, scientific discoveries have shown that emotions are physiologically based. Emotions appear to occur spontaneously. Facial expressions, however, may fake emotion or attempt to cover it. Whereas the expression of emotion can be suppressed, the feeling cannot. Studies suggest that some emotions elicit observable responses. If noted, these emotional behavior states can be observed and evaluated in the context of the situation. The limitation is that honest individuals can experience the same emotions as liars, particularly if they are afraid of not being believed (Vrij, Granhag, & Porter, 2010). Those of potential value to the interviewer include facial expression and body posture.

The complexity of lie detection through observable behaviors is that some people are natural and proficient liars (Vrij et al., 2010). Individuals who lie often are well skilled in masking their behaviors to avoid appearing guilty of lying. Some people will exhibit characteristics that are mistaken for lying when they are not. Emotions, facial expressions, body posture, and even eye movements may be indicative what the person is feeling and have nothing to do with lying. Experts suggest that the existence of small differences between liars and truth tellers make it difficult to determine lie detection in verbal or nonverbal cues alone (Vrij et al., 2010). This means that investigators may want to know more about verbal and nonverbal cues as tools to understand interviewees, but they should not be relied on as the sole source for determining deception.

Ekman and Friesen (1969) classified body language into five categories: emblems, illustrators, affect displays, regulators, and adaptors. Of these categories, emblems are most frequently referred to within the context of interviewing and interrogation. **Emblems** are nonverbal gestures that have a verbal counterpart. By themselves, emblems have little meaning, but they are widely understood within a given culture (Jensen & Emanuelsson, 2016). Examples of these deliberate and often unconscious slips of body movements include the following:

- Giving a person the "finger" means "fuck you."
- Shrugging indicates "I do not know" or "What difference does it make?"
- A head nod means "Yes."
- A head shake means "No."

Clues that an emblem may be a leakage of information that the individual did not intend includes an incomplete gesture, such as only one shoulder raised, and presenting an emblem out of a normal position, such as two hands slightly tilted outward on a table. Look for a slight nod of "yes" while a person is saying "no."

Facial Expression

Extensive research has suggested that liars are extremely difficult to detect by facial expression alone, despite the belief that facial expressions of emotion are accepted as universal (Elaad, 2015). A recent exception to the use of facial configurations for lie detection is the finding that micro-expressions may relate to specific emotions strongly felt by the individual being interviewed, according to Elaad (2015). These spontaneous emotional expressions appear only for a short period before they fade away. Micro-expressions are brought about automatically in the muscles of the face by feelings of strong emotions. Trained observers may notice them and run a video in slow motion may reveal micro-expressions.

Facial expressions may include movements to emphasize speech, so the interviewer should note movements that are not typical of the individual. A baseline should be formed by observing conversational speech. A lie catcher should never rely on one clue to deceit; there must be many. The liar who succeeds in deceiving himself or herself into believing that the lie is true is not likely to exhibit signs of deceit. Facial cuues should be confirmed by cues from voice, words, or body.

People may attempt to conceal emotion with facial expressions. The smile is the most common cover or mask, noted when there is not a full expression across the face. A smile that indicates pleasure may be concealed by pressing the lips together and pushing the chin muscles up.

Some dangers exist for the interviewer who relies solely on expressive characteristics to determine innocence or guilt. These are tools that should be used in conjunction with other interviewing techniques for the optimum results. Failure to recognize that an innocent person may feel guilty about something else or afraid of being disbelieved and may leak emotion is one hazard to be aware of. Most guilty people will not avert their gaze because they know that everyone expects experts to be able to detect deception in this way. Psychopaths and natural liars have an extraordinary ability to inhibit facial signs of their true feelings.

BEEN THERE... DONE THAT! 6-2

Susan was a very religious woman whose brother was a Catholic priest. She knew and respected many of the local priests and was very involved with the ministry. Frequently she volunteered at the church and got to know Father Tom. She reported that he had come to her home while her husband was at work and had forced her to have sex against her will.

I interviewed Father Tom, who denied that he had raped his parishioner. He had difficulty looking at me while he answered my questions; during most of the interview his head was down, and his eyes were averted. He was fidgety and appeared very nervous. Verbally, he hedged frequently. Continuing the investigation, I learned that Father Tom was promoted within the week and transferred to Rome. Was he guilty? Rome is one of the few places in the world where it is impossible to extradite a suspect.

Body Posture

Behavior indicators include well-known body positions that make a statement about the individual or send signals about the way they think of themselves. Authority stances are among the most common. Someone who stands with hands on hips and feet spread apart is showing defiance or aggression. This is also seen when someone is making a power play. Take on the same stance, and you are telling the individual you represent that same power. Then modify your stance; for example, if confronted with someone who has his or her arms crossed, uncross your arms to see if he or she will follow your behavioral lead. If he or she does, you have achieved control over the situation! Truthful people tend to lean forward, indicating they are listening. Deceitful people tend to move away. Posturing has long been taught by interviewing experts.

Generally Truthful Body Postures

- Open and relaxed posture
- Frontally aligned
- Upright in the chair
- Smooth changes in body positions

Generally Deceptive Body Postures

- Rigid posture
- Head and body slump
- Rapid, abrupt changes of posture
- Slouching in a chair
- Head and body slump (toilet position)

Personal Gestures Indicative of Stress

- Rubbing of hands
- Picking a nose or earlobes
- Hair twirling
- Licking of lips or difficulty swallowing
- Nail biting
- Profuse sweating

Actors are taught that there are two body postures: rising/approaching and sinking/withdrawing. Rising energy is reflected in a lift of the body, ebbing energy in a drooping body. Upward movement is associated with life: a growing plant, a young child, a person of vigor. Downward movement is related to death, sickness, weariness, and discouragement. This fundamental rising/sinking action is usually motivated by our inner feelings and emotions. Excellent posture suggests power, such as the stance taken by a military individual. Exhibiting respect and attention, such a person will stand with heels together, and toes pointed out at a slight angle.

Male aggression is communicated when the individual stands with feet wide apart. Typically, people who walk rapidly and swing their arms freely tend to be goal oriented. People who habitually walk with their hands in their pockets tend to be critical and secretive. When people feel depressed, they shuffle along with their hands in their pockets and seldom look where they are going, making it difficult for them to be goal oriented. Stooped or bowed shoulders usually mean something negative. One could be afraid, submissive, guilty, or self-conscious. Raised shoulders denote fear or tension. Squared shoulders suggest strength or responsibility.

Eye-Tracking

Observing the eyes provides another way to access the information needed to make an appropriate response. Rapport and control can also be established through the unconscious or subconscious movement of the eyes.

Everyone processes in all three learning modes and develops a preference or dominant pattern of response. Before identifying the eye pattern in response to questioning, a baseline must be established to find out the dominant response for that particular individual. Watching the direction of the subject's eyes in response to visual, auditory, or kinesthetic terms during a rapport-building phase in which nonthreatening, nonobtrusive, and nonoffensive questions are asked establishes the norm for that individual. When the eyes are defocused or staring straight ahead, it typically indicates recalled or remembered images.

PROXEMICS

Proxemics is the study of our use of space and how differences in that use make us feel more relaxed or more anxious. Researcher Edward Hall coined the term during the 1950s (Salzmann, Stanlaw, & Adachi, 2012). Hall identified four body distances—*intimate* (0 to 18 inches), *personal-casual* (1.5 to 4 feet), *social-consultive* (4 to 10 feet), and *public* (10 feet and beyond)—as key points in human spacing behavior. Hall noted that different cultures set distinctive norms for closeness in, for example, speaking, business, and courting and that standing too close or too far away can lead to misunderstandings. Comfortable communication with someone who is not an intimate should take place outside of the intimate distance, or greater than 18 inches.

Changing the distance between two people can convey a desire for intimacy, declare a lack of interest, or increase/decrease domination. Violation of personal space can nonverbally convey a message; for example, officers are encouraged to use the strategy of sitting close and crowding a suspect during an interrogation to gain the psychological advantage. When our bubble of space has been invaded, we feel uncomfortable, and tension and fear result. Most people will get up and leave rather than deal with the uncomfortable feeling of someone invading their space. Care should be taken that the interviewer does not violate individual space during the rapport establishment phase. If there are signals that the person is uncomfortable, the interviewer should back off until he or she notices that the subject is willing to proceed.

PHYSIOLOGICAL RESPONSE TESTING

Physiological variations that occur during an interview or interrogation may also give clues to the truth of a statement. Most people associate lying with "shifty eyes" and fidgeting behavior. Referred to as "manipulators," these are poor indicators and are unreliable when attempting to detect deceit. These movements may indicate discomfort or relaxation and vary according to the stakes involved. Liars will consciously control these behaviors because of their known interpretations. Lip biting and lip sucking are other manipulative behaviors easily constructed to feign concern or hide other emotions. Instead, look for physiological changes that people cannot easily control. Changes in skin color, voice tone, and breathing rate are examples. A variable breathing rate is associated with increased anxiety levels. Stress also causes a dry mouth, which may result in the repeated clearing of the throat or cracking of the voice. A liar will raise irrelevant issues, such as remarking about a relative who gets him into trouble or that the police are always picking on him. Technology is being used to measure physiological reaction.

There is little evidence that technology can accurately determine guilt from innocence; however, these are frequently used as screening and interview tools. The FAST (Future Attribute Screening Technology) program of the U.S. Department of Homeland Security has engaged in research to develop technologies that will assist security officers in screening persons to identify potential security risks. Since 2008 researchers are verifying and validating five sensor types that can detect physiological cues to deception (Burns, 2008):

1. A remote cardiovascular and respiratory sensor to measure heart rate and respiration, which allows for the calculation of heart rate, heart rate variability, respiration rate, and respiratory sinus arrhythmia.
2. A remote eye tracker, which is a device that uses a camera and processing software to track the position and gaze of the eyes (and, in some instances, the entire head) of a subject. Most eye trackers will also provide a measurement of the pupil diameter.
3. Thermal cameras that provide detailed information on the changes in the thermal properties of the skin in the face will help assess electrodermal activity and measure respiration and eye movements.
4. A high-resolution video that allows for highly detailed images of the face and body to be taken so that image analysis can determine facial features and expressions and body movements, and an audio system for analyzing human voice for pitch change.
5. Other sensor types such as pheromones detectors are also under consideration.

Polygraph Exam

The polygraph, commonly known as the "lie detector," entered the American courtroom almost 90 years ago. It is the most widely used type of psychophysiological deception detection test. During the traditional polygraph exam, most operators use Comparison Question Test (CQT) format (Honts & Reavy, 2015). The CQT uses direct accusatory questions such as "Did you kill your wife?" A more recent test, the Concealed Information Test (CIT), is a polygraph technique designed to detect a person's guilty knowledge of the crime (McConnell & Weber, 2014).

Critics of the polygraph claim that there is a lack of scientific evidence and theoretical foundation to support its use for determining criminal guilt. American courts agree. In *Frye v. United States* (1923), the D.C. Circuit Court excluded expert testimony about the findings from a polygraph. The court noted that the "systolic blood pressure deception test," the polygraph, had "not yet gained such standing and scientific recognition among physiological and psychological authorities as would justify the courts in admitting expert testimony. . . ." Since that time, the majority of courts have banned results of polygraph testing in criminal proceedings (*United States v. Scheffer*, 1998).

Renewed Interest in scientific validation on the reliability of polygraph testing is recently evidenced in the United States, Canada, Latin America, Europe, and

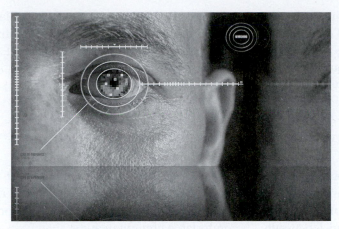

FIGURE 6-6 Eye-tracking technology is among the advances in measuring physiological variations between truth tellers and those with malintent.

Source: Tlorna/Shutterstock.

South Africa (Honts & Reavy, 2015). Meanwhile, polygraph use continues in many areas outside of the courtroom within military and criminal justice contexts. Many police departments require a polygraph as a pre-employment screening test and use it as an investigative tool. Community corrections officers may use polygraph exams to monitor compliance with conditions of supervision and as a part of presentence investigations.

Voice Stress Analysis

Early attempts to measure psychological responses came in the development of voice stress analysis (VSA) systems. Over the last three decades, law enforcement has come to accept that a relationship between speech, deception, and psychological stress does exist. Numerous commercial devices have emerged that claim to measure the acoustic correlates to stress and deception in speech. However, studies that examine the accuracy of measuring psychological responses to stress through voice analysis have been disappointing. Still, no effective assessment technologies to detect deception through voice analysis has yet to be developed (Harnsberger, Hollien, Martin, & Hollien, 2009). Instruments such as the Psychological Stress Evaluator (PSE) and the Computer Voice Stress Analyzer (CVSA) have been found to produce detection rates that are no different from chance at detecting deceit (Elaad, 2015). Due to the lack of reliability, the use of VSA instruments as an indicator of deception is not recommended for investigative interviewing.

Despite its limited value for lie detection, VSA is commonly used as an investigative tool. NITV Federal Services, makers of the CVSA II, maintain that hundreds of cases have been solved by police and military officers who use the CVSA II during investigations (NITV, 2015). The firm claims that the use of computer-assisted VSA as an interview tool has been upheld in at least four states and supported for use with offenders under the supervision of U.S. Probation in the Northern District of New York. Ohio, New York, New Jersey, and Wisconsin are among the state courts that allow the use of the CVSA results.

Eye-Tracking

Also referred to as "gaze-based biometrics," eye-tracking has been used by the military for decades (Cantoni, Musci, Nugrahaningsih, & Porta, 2016). The advancement in eye-tracking technology for criminal justice contexts involves cameras that document pupil size, eye fixation, and blinking rates. The approach to lie detection is a promising noninvasive test using infrared technology. According to Elaad (2015), the premise behind eye-tracking is the assumption that the additional cognitive load associated with lying is linked with pupil dilation, longer fixation on a target, and decreased blinking. Although pupil dilation is also related to arousal and emotion states the pupil size increases with deception.

Conclusions

Communication is both verbal and nonverbal, influenced by the way that we learn through our senses. Lie detection has come to rely on these modes of expression to develop baseline expectations to distinguish between truth tellers and liars. Researchers are actively developing technology to detect and measure physiological cues to deceit. Because most of the stimuli to the brain occur on an unconscious level, attempts to persuade through the subconscious often occur. Interviewers can gain insight into a person by identifying the person's primary learning mode and using that information to mirror and model. Shifting is a method of playing back to the individual the mode in which he or she feels most comfortable communicating.

Behavioral interviewing is not an interviewing model but a rich source of techniques that incorporates verbal, nonverbal, and physiological communications awareness. During an interview or interrogation, the investigator should be acutely aware of the cognitive indicators that may indicate deceit through behaviors.

Questions for Review

Short-Answer Questions

1. Explain the three principles used to detect deception.
2. What are some considerations to avoid the danger in disbelieving the truth?
3. Explain two methods which focus on verbal indicators to detect deceit.
4. How would you describe the *Criteria-Based Content Analysis* (CBCA) method?
5. What are the three categories of nonverbal indicators of deceit?

7. Paralanguage, body language, and ____ are nonverbal indicators which can be observed for cues to evaluate truthfulness or deceit.
8. Nonverbal indicators are influenced by culture and ____.
9. The study of our use of space and how differences in that space make us feel more relaxed or more anxious is called ____.
10. ____ variations that occur during the course of an interview or interrogation may also give clues to the truth of a statement.

Fill-in Questions

1. The term ____ refers to the interconnectedness of primary forms of human communication: thinking, speaking, and patterns of behavior.
2. Verbal indicators, ____, and physiological indicators are the principles to detect deception.
3. ____ occurs when the interviewer uses the same sensory language as the interviewee to establish common ground on which the subject feels comfortable.
4. A major strategy in the NLP method is ____, which refers to learning to reflect individual behavior.
5. ____ ____ and the Criteria-Based Content Analysis are two examples of methods which focus on verbal indicators.
6. The ____ approach consists of a preinterview during which the investigator notifies the interviewees about their intention to check their statement for verifiable details.

Exercises

1. Test the principles of proxemics. Find someone on campus in the library or at the lunchroom who is sitting alone. Sit at the personal-casual distance (1.5 to 4 feet) next to this person. Observe what he or she does. Next, sit facing someone else who is alone, without talking to them. Observe what the person does. Was the reaction different when the individual was male or female? Report your findings in a written report to the instructor.
2. Practice mirroring. Pair up with a member of the class for this 10-minute exercise. Sitting across from and facing one another, one of the students to describes what he or she did since getting up that day. During this "interview" the listening partner should match the interviewee's posture and gesture in a subtle way that does not appear to mimic him or her.

References

Amado, B. G., Arce, R., & Fariña, F. (2015). Undeutsch hypothesis and criteria based content analysis: A meta-analytic review. *The European Journal of Psychology Applied to Legal Context, 7*(1), 3–12.

Birdwhistell, R. (1970). *Kinesics and context: Essays on body motion communication.* Philadelphia: University of Pennsylvania Press.

Bogaard, G., Meijer, E. H., Vrij, A., & Merckelbach, H. (2016). Strong, but wrong: Lay people's and police officers' beliefs about verbal and nonverbal cues to deception. *PLoS ONE, 11*(6), e0156615.

Burns, R. (2008). *Future Attribute Screening Technology (FAST) project.* Washington, D.C.: Homeland Security.

Cantoni, V., Musci, M., Nugrahaningsih, N., & Porta, M. (2016). Gaze-based biometrics: An introduction to forensic applications. *Pattern Recognition Letters.* Retrieved from https://doi.org/10.1016/j.patrec.2016.12.006

Chalfoun, P., & Frasson, C. (2012). Cognitive priming: Assessing the use of non-conscious perception to enhance learner's reasoning ability. In S. A. Cerri, W. J. Clancey, G. Papadourakis, & K. Panourgia (Eds.), *Intelligent tutoring systems: 11th International Conference, ITS 2012, Chania, Crete, Greece, June 14–18, 2012. Proceedings* (pp. 84–89). Berlin, Heidelberg: Springer Berlin Heidelberg.

Dawson, E., Hartwig, M., & Brimbal, L. (2015). Interviewing to elicit information: Using priming to promote disclosure. *Law and Human Behavior, 39*(5), 443–450.

Dilts, R., Bandler, L. C., & Bandler, R. (1980). *Neuro-linguistic programming.* Capitola, CA: META Publications.

Dotz, T., Hoobyar, T., & Sanders, S. (2013). *NLP: The essential guide to neuro-linguistic programming.* New York, NY: Harper Collins Publishers.

Ekman, P., & Friesen, W. (1969). The repertoire of non-verbal behaviour: Categories, origins, usage and codings. *Semiotics, 1*, 49–98.

Elaad, E. (2015). Covert detection of deception. In P. A. Granhag, A. Vrij, & B. Verschuere (Eds.), *Detecting deception: Current challenges and cognitive approaches* (pp. 220–244). Malden, MA: Wiley Blackwell.

Frye v. United States, 23 Fed. 1013 (1923).

Fryling, M. (2016). A developmental-behavioral analysis of lying. *International Journal of Psychology and Psychological Therapy, 16*(1), 13–22.

Harnsberger, J. D., Hollien, H., Martin, C. A., & Hollien, K. A. (2009). Stress and deception in speech: Evaluating layered voice analysis. *Journal of Forensic Sciences, 54*(3), 642–650.

Honts, C. R., & Reavy, R. (2015). The comparison question polygraph test: A contrast of methods and scoring. *Physiology & Behavior, 143*, 15–26.

Jensen, M., & Emanuelsson, L. M. (2016). Integrated communication systems and kinesic code-switching in interpersonal interaction. *Journal of Studies in Social Sciences, 14*(2).

Lee, L., Bradburn, N., Poland, S., Brownstein, H., & Krishnamurty, P. (2013). *Methodological research to support the redesign of the National Crime Victimization Survey: Enhanced contextual priming as a memory aid.* Washington, D.C.: Bureau of Justice Statistics.

Lee, M., Matsumoto, D., Kobayashi, M., Krupp, D., Maniatis, E., & Roberts, W. (2014). Cultural influences on nonverbal behavior in applied settings. In R. Feldman (Ed.), *Applications of nonverbal behavioral theories and research* (pp. 200–218). New York, NY: Psychology Press.

Logue, M., Book, A. S., Frosina, P., Huizinga, T., & Amos, S. (2015). Using reality monitoring to improve deception detection in the context of the cognitive interview for suspects. *Law and Human Behavior, 39*(4), 360–367.

Matsumoto, D., Hwang, H. S., Skinner, L., & Frank, M. (2011). Evaluating truthfulness and detecting deception. *FBI Law Enforcement Bulletin* (June).

Matsumoto, D., Skinner, L., & Hwang, H. (2014). Reading people: Behavioral anomalies and investigative interviewing. *FBI Law Enforcement Bulletin* (March).

McConnell, B., & Weber, T. (2014). The concealed information test: An alternative to the traditional polygraph. *FBI Law Enforcement Bulletin* (August).

Nahari, G., Vrij, A., & Fisher, R. (2014). The verifiability approach: Counter measures facilitate its ability to discriminate between truths and lies. *Applied Cognitive Psychology, 28*, 122–128.

Navarro, J. (2012). Detecting deception. *FBI Law Enforcement Bulletin* (August).

Remland, M. (2017). *Nonverbal communication in everyday life* (4th ed.). Thousand Oaks, CA: SAGE Publications.

Reinhard, M.-A., Sporer, S. L., Scharmach, M., & Marksteiner, T. (2011). Listening, not watching: situational familiarity and the ability to detect deception. *Journal of Personality and Social Psychology, 101*(3), 467.

Riggio, R. (2014). Social interaction skills and nonverbal behavior. In R. Feldman (Ed.), *Applications of nonverbal behavioral theories and research* (pp. 11–33). New York, NY: Psychology Press.

Salzmann, Z., Stanlaw, J., & Adachi, N. (2012). *Language, culture, and society: An introduction to linguistic anthropology.* Boulder, CO: Westview Press.

Steller, M., & Kohnken, G. (1989). Criteria-based content analysis. In D. Raskin (Ed.), *Psychological methods in criminal investigation and evidence* (pp. 217–245). New York, NY: Springer-Verlag.

Taylor, P., Larner, S., Conchie, S., & Zee, S. v. d. (2015). Cross-cultural deception detection. In P. A. Granhag, A. Vrij, & B. Verschuere (Eds.), *Detecting deception: Current challenges and cognitive approaches* (pp. 76–103). Chichester, West Sussex UK: Wiley Blackwell.

United States v. Scheffer, 523 U.S. 303 (1998).

Vrij, A., Granhag, P. A., & Porter, S. (2010). Pitfalls and opportunities in nonverbal and verbal lie detection. *Psychological Science in the Public Interest, 11*(3), 89–121.

Vrij, A. (2015). Verbal lie detection tools: Statement validity analysis, reality monitoring and scientific content analysis. In P. A. Granhag, A. Vrij, & B. Verschuere (Eds.), *Detecting deception: Current challenges and cognitive approaches*. Malden, MA: Wiley Blackwell.

Vrij, A., Meissner, C. A., & Kassin, S. M. (2015). Problems in expert deception detection and the risk of false confessions: No proof to the contrary in Levine et al. (2014). *Psychology, Crime & Law, 21*(9), 901–909.

Walters, S. (2017). *Principles of Kinesic interview and interrogation* (3rd ed.). New York, NY: CRC Press.

Willingham, D. T., Hughes, E. M., & Dobolyi, D. G. (2015). The scientific status of learning styles theories. *Teaching of Psychology, 42*(3), 266–271.

PART III

Interviewing Special Populations

The next four chapters discuss interviewing and interrogation approaches for special populations. Professionals frequently are involved in circumstances that require interviews with individuals who are at high risk of trauma, children, the elderly, and persons with disabilities. This section prepares you for some of the unusual circumstances that you might encounter in situations with these populations.

This section opens with a chapter devoted to interviewing victims of trauma. Chapter 7 introduces the concept of the trauma-informed victim approach. This recent addition to interviewing methods is primarily used by social service and service providers, forensic nurses, therapists and other trauma interventionalists as a public health approach. Specialized law enforcement agencies, which investigate human trafficking and cases involving trauma, will find this especially useful. The approach is victim sensitive and trauma informed, the concepts can be incorporated into numerous interviewing techniques.

Chapter 8 covers interviewing children. Different models for child interviewing are provided along with child-adapted versions of cognitive interviewing and forensic interviewing. These can be practiced for increased understanding and proficiency. It is important when interviewing children to take account of developmental considerations according to the child's age. Knowledge of the developmental stages can assist the interviewer to avoid the limitations inherent in child interviews.

As the elderly population increases in America, the criminal justice community must grow to meet the needs of that population. A greater understanding of the complexities of interviewing older adults is addressed in Chapter 9. The types of crimes and approaches to interviews are among the topics discussed. Although physical limitations due to aging can be expected, these can be anticipated by the interviewer. In most cases, the limitations can successfully be overcome.

Interviewing persons with disabilities is the topic of Chapter 9. It addresses the legal requirements of the Americans with Disabilities Act as it pertains to criminal justice personnel. Reasonable accommodations must be made for persons having a disability. Also, the courts are increasingly holding criminal justice professionals accountable for their actions when confronted with individuals who have a disability. This responsibility translates into a need for increased awareness on the part of the police and court and corrections personnel. People with mental retardation, mental illness, and personality disorders are overly represented in the jails and prisons in the United States.

Trauma-Informed Victim Approach

Source: Chepko Danil Vitalevich/Shutterstock.

CHAPTER OBJECTIVES

After completing this chapter, you should be able to:

1. Describe the three *E*s of the trauma-informed victim approach.
2. Illustrate the SCRIPT approach.
3. Explain the trauma-informed victim approach.
4. List three categories of high-risk populations.
5. Discuss the crimes of human trafficking.
6. Assess the utility of the *Trafficking Victim Identification Tool.*
7. Summarize the concept behind the FETI interviewing technique.
8. Compare and contrast the CI technique with the FETI technique.

KEY TERMS

Confidentiality

Psychophysiological technique

Trafficking in persons

Trauma-informed victim approach

High-risk victim population

Sham marriage

Trauma

Victim-centered approach

INTRODUCTION

Trauma occurs as a result of violence, abuse, neglect, loss, disaster, war, and other emotionally harmful experiences. Trauma spans the boundaries of age, gender, socioeconomic status, race, ethnicity, geography, or sexual orientation. In other words, trauma may affect any one, at anytime, anywhere. Increasingly there is a trend to address trauma as a multipronged issue requiring a public health approach. Over the last five years, social service providers are being asked to provide treatment within a framework of trauma-informed care.

The trauma-informed victim approach is not a method itself or a specific interviewing protocol. Rather it is a multidisciplinary response framework for interventions with victims of trauma. It is not unusual for victims to deny victimization, to bond with the abuser(s), or to experience *Post Traumatic Stress Disorder* (PTSD). A multidisciplinary response is a major component involving a victim sensitive style. The approach may involve responses for children or adults that are at high risk for abuse.

The team approach in place for most jurisdictions include members of law enforcement agencies, prosecutors, mental health and health care professionals, child protective services, and religious leaders. Crimes involving offenders who are known to the victim make up a significant percentage of violence against women and human trafficking crimes. Cases of intimate partner violence are addressed by domestic violence response teams (DVRTs) and coordinated community response teams (CCRs); sexual assault response teams (SARTs) offer specialized sexual assault intervention services; and human trafficking response teams (HTRTs) are similar to DVRTs and SARTs, but often with the additional recognition that prevention through curbing demand is also a critical component of the response. These multidisciplinary teams operate on the belief that highly traumatic events are often characterized by emotional or physical pain, shock, and denial.

This chapter includes commonly recommended investigative interview approaches within the trauma-informed victim approach, the *Enhanced Cognitive Interview* (ECI) and the *Forensic Experiential Trauma Interview* (FETI). Both interview protocols involve memory enhancement and retrieval methods to increase the amount of recall.

The *Cognitive Interview* is a well-respected technique, which was discussed in Chapter 5. FETI has gained acceptance among the therapeutic community, social services, and for specialized law enforcement investigations involving high-risk populations.

Using a victim-centered approach is not limited to these interviewing methods; integrate the overall philosophy of concern with any investigative interview. Remember that the interviewer must be well-trained and comfortable when using a specific interviewing method to be successful. Providing services for the high-risk population is a critical response component. A method for agency identification of those in need, which is included in this chapter is the *Trafficking Victim Identification Tool* (TVIT).

THE TRAUMA-INFORMED VICTIM APPROACH

SAMHSA suggests a framework for the behavioral health sectors than could be adapted to child welfare, education, criminal and juvenile justice, primary health care, the military and other settings where there is a potential to ease or exacerbate a person's ability to cope with trauma (see Figure 7-1).

> **Trauma** is defined as resulting from an event, series of events, or set of circumstances that is experienced by an individual as physically or emotionally harmful or life threatening and that has lasting adverse effects on the individual's functioning and mental, physical, social, emotion, or spiritual well-being (SAMHSA, 2014, pg. 7).

The **trauma-informed victim approach** acknowledges the physiological effect of trauma on some survivors, the influence that it can have on their ability to recall facts and details, and the limits and possibilities of obtaining information from such witnesses. It is acknowledged that individuals exposed to trauma experience changes to the prefrontal cortex of the brain, which can render them less capable of providing accurate details of experienced traumatic events. To assure that their needs are being met, the goal of the model is in establishing trust between the individual experiencing trauma and the

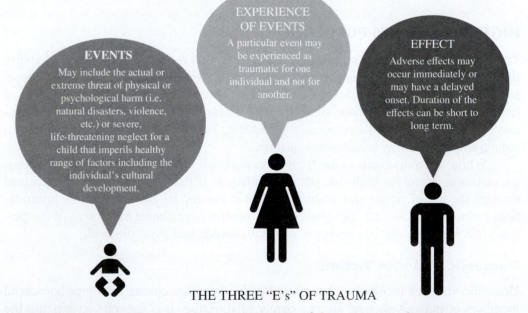

EVENTS

May include the actual or extreme threat of physical or psychological harm (i.e. natural disasters, violence, etc.) or severe, life-threatening neglect for a child that imperils healthy range of factors including the individual's cultural development.

EXPERIENCE OF EVENTS

A particular event may be experienced as traumatic for one individual and not for another.

EFFECT

Adverse effects may occur immediately or may have a delayed onset. Duration of the effects can be short to long term.

THE THREE "E's" OF TRAUMA

FIGURE 7-1 Survivors have highlighted the impact of these three *Es* of trauma.

Source: Adapted from SAMHSA (2014).

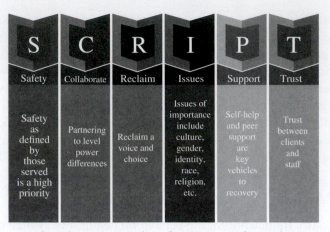

FIGURE 7-2 To remember the six principles of a trauma-informed approach, follow the SCRIPT.

person obtaining information. Inconsistent statements are considered the norm for this population; therefore, judgments of creditability are not made based on responses alone. Cases that involve criminal prosecution require evidentiary information in addition to the interview. Realistic expectations on the part of the service provider or interviewer can reduce frustration and reduce dismissal due to questions of credibility.

The foundations of a trauma-informed victim approach center on six fundamental principles, which are represented in Figure 7-2 as the SCRIPT. Ensuring a trauma-informed victim approach requires that interviewers primarily set a high priority on the safety of the victim. Since the population and needs of the victim are diverse, collaboration with agencies and organizations to give decision-making power to the client is essential. "Reclaim" refers to an empowerment of the people served, which is achieved by their voice and in making their own choices for recovery. The organization must actively move past all of the "issues" of bias grounded on difference or minority statuses. Support comes from within, and among those who are involved in the healing process, self-help and peer support is promoted. Last, but not least, is the issue of trust. Without trust between the staff and clients, there is no intervention, it is an essential element of the approach.

HIGH-RISK VICTIM POPULATIONS

The term **high-risk victim population** is a concept that reflects a chance or probability that a group or individual is particularly vulnerable to danger, exploitation or abuse. Indicators of high risk include exposure to trauma such as natural disaster, low level of education, family dysfunction, abuse, mental illness, and substance abuse. Many factors can increase a person's vulnerability, including transnationally organized crime elements, and a person's socioeconomic profile.

While the individuals come from diverse racial, ethnic, and gender populations, the common thread for high-risk victim populations is that they have been traumatized through the use of power and control. Control is exerted by abuse, coercion, intimidation, isolation, and threats. The abusers exert control over almost every area of the person's life. Violence can be emotional, physical, sexual, and psychological.

Domestic Violence Victims

Domestic violence involves violent or aggressive behavior among family or household members or individuals who are in a dating relationship. It is the relationship, not the age, that defines who is victimized through domestic violence when trauma is inflicted. Crimes against children and older adults are covered in-depth in following chapters.

BEEN THERE . . . DONE THAT! 7-1

Put yourself in a position of extreme trauma and think about how you would act. Then expect something very different in reality. I found that what I thought was an appropriate response was typically not what happened when responding to a scene. Those who are traumatized may feel angry, fearful, disappointed, or in shock when something violent happens. At homicide scenes, it was not unusual to find family members in disbelief—sometimes targeting the police as if they were to blame. Being exposed to violence takes its toll on everyone involved. The *trauma-informed approach* gets that; do you?

Intimate partner violence (IPV) occurs among heterosexual or same-sex couples and does not require sexual intimacy (Breiding, Basile, Smith, & Mahendra, 2015). IPV victimization includes sexual violence, stalking, physical violence, psychological aggression, and control of reproductive sexual health. Considering all types of IPV trauma, an estimated one in three men or women are victimized by an intimate partner during their lifetime in the United States (Smith et al., 2017). In the 12 months before taking the *National Intimate Partner and Sexual Violence Survey,* an estimated 2.7 percent of women and 2.0 percent of men reported having experienced severe physical violence by an intimate partner (Black et al., 2011).

Refugees and Migrants

According to the *Global Report on Trafficking in Persons* (2016), the world is experiencing the largest movement of refugees and migrants since World War II. An estimated 40 percent increase of international migrants across the world has been documented since 2000. Typical hosting areas such as Australia, Europe, and North America have tightened their immigration laws in recent years in response to the high influx of asylum seekers (Schock, Rosner, & Knaevelsrud, 2015). Within these large groups of migrating persons are vulnerable children, women, and men who can easily be exploited.

Secreted among the traumatized are deceptive refugees seeking international protection from the prosecution of crimes they have committed in their country of origin. Increasing numbers of asylum seekers has put tremendous pressure on immigration authorities to determine who needs international protection and who does not (Veldhuizen, Horselenberg, Landstrom, Granhag, & Koppen, 2016). The determination frequently rests on the interview with the asylum seeker, with questions asked to assess credibility. The assessment for asylum has grave consequences for all parties involved. An incorrect determination potentially could result in the return of an individual to a place where they face persecution, torture or even death (Veldhuizen et al., 2016).

Refugees that are attempting to escape war are easily targeted by traffickers who use their desperation to deceive them into exploitation. These individuals are particularly vulnerable to becoming victims of trafficking. Human trafficking patterns often resemble migration flows, according to the UNDOC (2016).

Sexual Assault Victims

Research has shown that in the United States as many as 60 percent of sexual assault victims never report the crime to the police (Holderness, Moen, & Hull, 2014). Efforts to improve the reporting options led to the development of the *You Have Options Program.* This is a victim-center and offender-focused program requiring that a victim of sexual

FIGURE 7-3   Trafficking in persons is for exploitation, achieved by coercion, deception, or abuse.

Source: Sasa Prudkov/Shutterstock.

assault be offered three options for reporting: Information Only, Partial Investigation, and Complete Investigation. Reporting may be done in person with the police or online, anonymous or not. The victim has total control over the extent of information provided, and when probable cause to make an arrest exists, the victim must give consent. The approach is far from mainstream, however. Only six police departments are listed on the website as participating in the program (Currie, nd).

Human Rights Watch suggests that the initial contact by the first responder to a sexual assault should be brief but compassionate. The officer should address safety or medical concerns, collect just enough to establish the elements of the crime, and identify the potential suspect(s) and security evidence. Research suggests that the Forensic Experiential Trauma Interview is useful when interviewing victims of sexual assault (Lisak, 2016).

CRIMES INVOLVING TRAFFICKING IN PERSONS

The majority of trafficking victims is believed to be of women and children. Sexual exploitation and forced labor are the most well-known forms of trafficking. Additional victimization occurs against persons who are made to act as beggars, become part of sham marriages, commit benefit fraud, engage in pornography, comply with organ removal, and more. A significant increase in the trafficking of men is the most recent trend noted by the United Nations, the majority of which are for forced labor.

Worldwide, children make up about 28 percent of detected victims and men are 21 percent (UNODC, 2016). Similarly, in the United States, only slightly more than half of trafficked victims are women (Gozdziak & Lowell, 2016). Surprisingly, the majority of persons (75%) are trafficked for labor, 18 percent for sexual exploitation, and 7 percent for both.

Crimes involving trafficking in human beings often overlap. Modern slavery, for example, involves individuals exploited for labor as well as women forced into sham marriages. UNDOC (2016) defines **trafficking in persons** as a crime that includes three elements:

1. The act of recruiting, transporting, transferring, harboring, or receiving a person;
2. by means of coercion, deception, or abuse of vulnerability;
3. for the purpose of exploitation.

Sexual Exploitation

Sexual exploitation is accomplished through a variety of criminal conduct. Women and girls tend to be trafficked for marriages and sexual slavery (UNDOC, 2016). Rape of women and children forced production of pornography, and sexual enslavement are some examples. The actual scope of commercial sexual exploitation of minors in America is difficult to quantify, yet is recognized as a problem of grave concern (National Research Council, 2013).

Children with a history of abuse, runaways, and throwaways (children refused permission to return home) are at risk for commercial sexual exploitation. Children between the ages of 11 and 14 often become victims and 70 percent of women involved in prostitution began before age 18 (Kotria, 2010). Concern over the revictimization by the juvenile justice system led to a 3.5-month effort of screening boys and girls ages 9–19 in Washington Clark County Court for risk factors (Salisbury, Dabney, & Russell, 2015). Within the 535 children screened, six girls were confirmed to be victims of commercial sexual exploitation and successfully diverted from juvenile detention with an additional 47 youths having reported risk factors for abuse. A concerted commitment for the juvenile justice system to address the complex challenge of identifying victims of commercial sexual exploitation is suggested by Salisbury and colleagues.

Forced Labor/Slavery

The numbers of victims who are trafficked for forced labor has increased over the past 10 years. About four in ten victims found between 2012 and 2014 were trafficked for forced labor and 63 percent were men (UNDOC, 2016). Men and boys are typically exploited in forced labor in the mining sector, in the fishing industry, as porters, as soldiers and as slaves. Women and girls are typically abducted for domestic work. Trafficking for forced labor is reported nearly everywhere.

Sham Marriages

Sham marriages or sham civil partnerships are marriages of convenience contracted for immigration advantage by a couple who are not in a genuine relationship (Home Office, 2013). Officials in the United Kingdom report that sham relationships pose a significant threat to immigration control, with an estimated 4,000–10,000 sham marriage applications being received each year. Women and girls tend to be trafficked to be used for marriages and sexual slavery, according to UNDOC (2016). In South-East Asia and affluent countries this frequently involves forced marriages or unions without the consent of the woman (or girl).

Organ Removal

In the past 20 years, the global organ shortage has led to the development of transplant tourism: the practice of traveling outside one's own country to obtain organ transplantation. Transplant tourism is estimated to account for 10 percent of organ transplants performed in 2007, often involving organ trade or trafficking (Tsai et al., 2017). Patients desperate to survive are willing to pay for organs that are unavailable due to high demand in their own country.

According to the UNDOC (2016), at least 10 countries have reported trafficking of human beings for the removal of organs, primarily in North Africa and the Middle East. Experts suggest that human trafficking for organ removal is a highly complex crime to detect and prosecute, compounded by a general lack of awareness of the offence among criminal justice practitioners (Holmes et al., 2016).

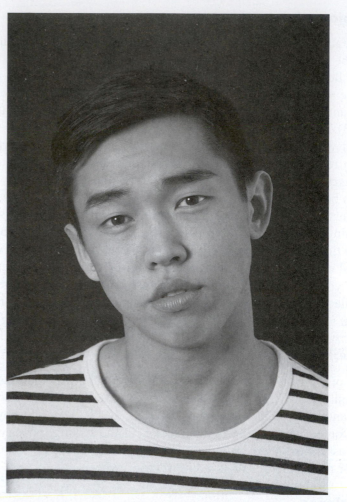

FIGURE 7-4   Boys and men can be victims of trafficking for forced labor or sexual exploitation.

Source: Vladimir Wrangel/Shutterstock.

Trafficking in organs is a three-pronged crime. There are cases where victims are forced or tricked into giving up an organ; cases where they agree to sell an organ and are cheated out of the money promised, and when vulnerable persons are treated for a sickness (which may or may not exist) and organs are removed without their knowledge. Commonly traded body parts are kidneys and liver, although any organ that can be removed and used can be traded. The U.N. Protocol to Prevent, Suppress and Punish Trafficking in Persons includes "organ removal" and its sale as an end purpose of trafficking. The World Health Organization (WHO) Guiding Principles on Human Organ Transplantation (1991) state that commercialization of human organs is a "violation of human rights and human dignity."

TRAFFICKING VICTIM IDENTIFICATION TOOL

Identifying victims of human trafficking to provide services and protection is a daunting task for professionals. In response, the Vera Institute has developed the TVIT as an aid for interviewing suspected victims of trafficking. The Institute recommends that interviewers first establish trust and rapport before asking difficult questions that center on traumatic experiences of the interviewee. Victim privacy should be paramount to the interviewers. Within the context of interviewing, **privacy** is the victim's

BEEN THERE . . . DONE THAT! 7-2

In response to the call of a person barricaded in her home with a weapon, the SWAT team was dispatched along with local and state police. What followed was a surreal stand-off where a woman in her forties held her female partner captive in the house. A hostage negotiator revealed over the course of hours that the distraught women had been told by her live-in girlfriend that the relationship was over. The time when a domestic relationship is terminated, or one person believes it is over, is a very dangerous period for the victim of intimate partner violence. In this case, the perpetrator gave up her gun and the victim was released unharmed. It is imperative that response officials have training and develop expertise on responding to a scene of violence. What approach to interviewing the victim do you think might be appropriate in this case?

right to control disclosure of his or her story and personal information. A victim should not be compelled to disclose abuse. Maintaining privacy may directly reduce the chances of revictimization. Interviewers should be sensitive to the special needs of trafficking victims. The TVIT is recommended to be used by interviewers who are familiar with the **victim-centered approach**, which places equal value on the well-being of victim with that of the criminal investigation. Trafficking victims have often been held in servitude through threats of harm or fear of deportation by police and immigration authorities. The TVIT is a way to establish a safe environment where the victims feel protected.

Step 1: Prepare for the Interview

Before conducting an interview is the realization that trafficking victims have often been held by threats of harm and fear arrest or deportation by police and immigration authorities. An important component of the TVIT is in maintaining victim confidentiality. **Confidentiality** is a more limited a concept than privacy as it describes the laws, rules, and regulations that prohibit certain professionals from disclosing information that can be used to identify the individuals they serve. Maintaining confidentiality is imperative for working with individuals and families when they try to escape captivity.

The TVIT survey may not be appropriate for use by mandatory reporters, which will include police officers in numerous states, since maintaining confidence is a complex issue (Vera Institute of Justice, 2014). The TVIT is a questionnaire intended for use during a regular intake process to assist in deciding whether or not a client is a victim of human trafficking. This tool may be used by any social service agency that regularly has contact with the public to provide services. Be respectful of the person's cultural background and religious observances.

- Find a safe and comfortable location for the interview. Interview in private without distractions. Do not include any person who accompanied the individual as it may be someone working for the trafficker.
- Employ competent, trustworthy interpreters if the victim's first language is not English.
- Be honest about the purpose of the screening and the role of the interview process.
- Screeners should be familiar with common signs of trauma since trafficking victims may exhibit effects of psychological and physical abuse, traumatic experiences, chronic substance abuse, or violent physical and psychological assaults.
- Avoid retraumatizing the victim by asking that individuals recount or repeat details of the crime.

Step 2: Interview Using the TVIT

Determining if someone is a victim of trafficking involves an assessment on the totality of the circumstances based on responses to the needs for safety, housing, legal assistance, social services, or employment. The survey itself comes in a long or shorter version of 5–10 pages. Components of the TVIT screening involve the collection of information on

- the background and demographics of the interviewee, including the county of birth
- their migration status
- working or living conditions
- safety
- economic situation.

Step 3: Postassessment

The screener completes a written assessment after the client interview that includes any nonverbal indicators of past victimization, indicators that responses may have been inaccurate, and service referrals that are indicated. Before using the identification toolkit, the screener views agency guidelines on how to proceed in cases of suspected trafficking. Available community resources and referral options should also be explored, so that accurate information is provided at this stage.

THE ENHANCED COGNITIVE INTERVIEW

The *Enhanced Cognitive Interview* (ECI) was developed by Fisher and Geiselman (Fisher, 1995) to improve on their original *Cognitive Interview Method*. The ECI is a tool kit to be used in total or alongside other interview approaches. The ECI is the most well-researched forensic interview approach and has consistently been found to increase the amount of correct information recalled (Paulo, Albuquerque, Saraiva, & Bull, 2015). Consistent with the trauma-informed approach, the interviewee drives the process in the ECI while the interviewer acts as a facilitator. Controlling the victim's level of anxiety and providing a safe interview process is important. The interviewer must resist the temptation to interrupt the free flow of information provided during the interview.

The ECI added rapport building to the CI and kept the four original mnemonics of the *Cognitive Interview*. The mnemonics to facilitate memory recall are (1) mentally reinstate the context of the event; (2) report every detail, even if it seems trivial or irrelevant; (3) report the event in different temporal orders, moving back and forth in time; and (4) describe the event from various points of view. In an ECI interview, it is expressly stated that all information is valuable and all memories can be shared. The seven phases of the ECI are as follows (Fisher, 1995):

PHASE 1: MEET AND GREET
- Establish rapport

PHASE 2: FACILITATING COMMUNICATION AND RECALL
- Focused retrieval and concentrate hard
- Report everything
- Transfer control

PHASE 3: FREE REPORT: MAXIMIZING COGNITIVE PROCESSING
- Context reinstatement
- Open-ended questions

PHASE 4: QUESTIONING AND PROMOTING RETRIEVAL
- Report everything
- Interviewee-compatible questioning

- OK to say "I do not know" or "I do not understand."
- Activate and probe an image
- Open and appropriate closed questions

PHASE 5: EXTENSIVE RETRIEVAL
- Varied and extensive retrieval
- Change the temporal order
- Change perspectives and spotlighting
- Focus on all senses

PHASE 6: SUMMARY
- Briefly summarize the information provided
- Encourage victim to interrupt with new information

PHASE 7: CLOSURE
- Reestablish your connection—say thank you!
- Remind her to call if she thinks of any new information

THE FORENSIC EXPERIENTIAL TRAUMA INTERVIEW (FETI)

The *Forensic Experiential Trauma Interview* (FETI) is a method that accepts the premise of trauma-informed interviewing. Implicit is that traumatic victimization may cause physiological changes to the survivor's memory that can disadvantage the fact-gathering process. Based on neuroscience, the approach was developed in 2009 by Russell Strand as a procedure to investigate sexual assaults reported in the military (Cronk, 2013). The interview method trains investigators to allow a free recall in any order to encourage communication of the experienced events. The information-gathering process of FETI is termed as **psychophysiological technique**, which refers to an interview method that relates to physiological psychology involving mental and physical human processes. The powerful technique triggers memories by involving the sights, smells, sounds, tastes, and feelings of the victim for a better understanding of what happened.

Note that several of the components used in FETI mirror interviewing techniques described in previous chapters. This overlap suggests a growing trend toward interviewing techniques, which elevate the victim status to more than a mere witness, as previously has been the case. There is an increased movement toward appreciating the information, which is shared during an interview on traumatic experiences.

The FETI technique involves the use of principles employed in critical incident stress debriefing and defusing (Lisak & Markel, 2016). It draws from principles and techniques developed for forensic child interviews as well as from neurobiology of memory and psychological trauma. The technique provides an opportunity for the victim to describe the experience of the sexual assault or another traumatic event, physically and emotionally. FETI has been adapted for use by Sexual Assault Nurse Examiners, medical personnel, and other first responders in addition to law enforcement, attorneys, and forensic interviewers (Malone & Strand, 2015). There are eight components to the FETI interview, according to Strand (nd):

1. **Recognize the victim's trauma and/or pain**
   This first step involves the demonstration of genuine empathy, patience, and understanding toward victims of violence or trauma. It is the responsibility of the interviewer to build trust through a nonjudgmental manner and approach with the interviewee.

2. **Ask the victim/witness what they can remember**
   The reason for asking if the interviewee is able to remember signifies an understanding that not all victims can recall all significant information about what has

FIGURE 7-5   The foundation of the FETI interviewing technique rests on understanding the effects of trauma.

Source: Justin Hoffmann/Pearson Education.

happened to them. This open-ended prompt uses active listening skills to the words of the victim. It allows the interviewer to gather a significantly more information through dialogue as compared to a question-answer approach.

3. **Ask the victim/witness about their thought process during their experience**
   Avoid asking the interviewee "why" questions. A victim of trauma will have difficulty with the answer since it requires a judgment on the actions of another person toward them. It may re-victimize an interviewee who will self-blame for the abusive situation that was experienced. Do ask what the victim was thinking at the time, a tactic that will likely expose physiological evidence of the crime(s).

4. **Ask about tactile memories that involve the senses**
   As humans, we associate memories, both good and bad, with our senses of hearing, sight, smell, sound, and feeling. Using sensory information may help the victim to disclose additional information, which in turn can increase creditability to the statement as a real experience.

5. **Ask the interviewee how this experience affected them**
   This is the stage of the interview where the victim is encouraged to talk about the effects of the experience both physically and emotionally. The investigative interviewer should document the physiological reactions to trauma, which often accompany the context of the abuse. Fear, anger, shock, sadness, or loss may be among the emotions that are related relative to a traumatic experience.

6. **Ask the victim what was the most difficult part of the experience**

   While this question may seem duplicitous, it provides an additional opportunity for the interviewer to ask what was most important to the victim. The perspective of the victim is not necessarily the same as the interviewer, so this step may provide additional insight to the experience.

7. **The interviewer should ask if there is anything that the interviewee cannot forget about their experience**

   Firmly giving control of the interview to the victim, this question allows for an additional flow of information from their perspective. Do not be surprised to hear more sensory information that will further assist in establishing the credibility of the interviewee with psychophysiological evidence.

8. **The interviewer should clarify other information and details (e.g., who, what, where, when, and how)**

   When the interviewee has exhausted their recollection of events, and after the psychophysiological component of the interview, clarifying questions might be asked. This component serves to provide another avenue for disclosure while accessing additional portions of the brain.

Comparing the ECI and FETI

The Enhanced Cognitive Interview (ECI) was developed years before FETI and is used extensively by law enforcement officers. The ECI is based on cognitive psychology and includes principles to enhance recall. Numerous studies have concluded that the cognitive interview increases the amount of accurate information reported by witnesses (Vredeveldt et al., 2015).

According to Malone & Strand (2015), the FETI is often criticized for being too similar to the cognitive interviewing approach and lacking scientific validations as well. The authors maintain that FETI is a natural progression in the development of scientifically based interview methods, which will continue to grow and change as new science is developed. The ECI and FETI are similar in that they include open-ended and non-leading questions in addition to rapport building and avoidance of victim blaming. Each is meant to enhance victim memory of experienced events. These qualities are included in many approaches to interviewing, which place emphasis on victims, however.

Proponents of FETI suggest that the Reverse Order (RO) element of the CI could contribute to inconsistencies in memories due to the trauma-induced alterations of the brain, which reduces the encoding and consolidation of the time-sequencing of events (Malone & Strand, 2015). Further, that those errors and inconsistencies produced by the CI could cause victims to lose creditability with investigators, prosecutors and leave them more vulnerable to attacks from defense attorneys. The potential harm as suggested by Malone & Strand (2015) is that victims may fail in the legal system.

THE VICTIM AS A WITNESS

The relationship of the victim to the process of the American justice system has always been complex. Traditionally, victims were without differential treatment or consideration, compared to other witnesses. The recent crime victims' rights movement began more than 30 years ago with the Supreme Court decision in *Linda R.S. v. Richard D.* (1972). The prevailing view that a crime victim cannot compel criminal prosecution was noted in dicta with recommendations by the Court for overcoming the situation. Statutes creating legal rights for victims emerged over the years since.

The recent movement, which calls for a victim-centered approach for survivors, extends the public sense of justice. Central to this new line of thought are needed changes in interviewing methods and procedures, which put the victim first. Law enforcement and prosecutors are expected to understand and account for trauma and its impact on victims when working with high-risk victim populations.

Researchers suggest that the interview process can exacerbate symptoms of PTSD among the populations of highly traumatized persons (Schock et al., 2015). Typical behaviors that are believed to be indicators of deceit may, in fact, be effects of accumulated trauma along with the stress of the interviews. Failing memory, inability to focus, difficulty in providing consistent statements indicate victim trauma, along with the high stress of the process. Greater investment in time and patience by law enforcement and prosecutors is needed in cases that involve trauma victims.

Empowering the Victim

Utilizing trauma-informed approaches first requires an understanding that victims of high-risk trauma may act differently than others. Strong reactions should not be taken personally. If the individual appears to shut down or disconnect, it may be a sign that the survivor is overwhelmed. You might encounter someone who seems spacey, jumpy, angry, or weepy. Make sure that the victim is hearing and understanding the information that is being provided. Focus on the facts and do not mirror their emotion. Providing opportunities for empowerment and control include offering choice about meeting times or where to sit in a room.

CRIME PERPETRATED BY VICTIMS

It is important to note that the picture of commercial sex trafficking may not be as simple as the victim portrayal might suggest. A study on the migration of women from China to the United States to engage in commercial sex found that prostitution is a multifaceted trade (Finckenauer & Chin, 2011). The Finckenauer study involved 350 face-to-face interviews with women who participate in commercial sex, sex ring operators, law enforcement officials, NGOs, and other informants. By these efforts, the researchers uncovered evidence in stark contrast to the current trafficking paradigm.

Most of the women interviewed in the Finckenauer study reported that they did not view prostitution as inherently evil but saw it as an opportunity for them to make the kind of money that they could never make in any other profession. The people who helped them were not viewed as evil, violence against them was rare, and it was not used as a means to control them. The women sometimes developed intimate relationships with their customers that lasted for months or years. Contrary to the portrayal of foreign prostitutes as being helpless, child-like, and passive—the opposite was found. The vast majority of women reported that they made a choice to leave their country for illegal employment of commercial sex and their earnings were not withheld by the individuals who brought them to the United States.

Domestic violence is also being defined as a multifaceted phenomenon that occurs within four contexts. Contrary to public opinion, the most common type of intimate partner violence is initiated by women as often as men and rarely accompanied by violence. Domestic violence perpetrated by a victim in retaliation for past violence is illegal behavior. Mental disorders may also play a role when violence within a relationship occurs. All of this does not change the reality that domestic violence can be considered battering, which is accompanied by violence or a threat of harm and a pattern of coercive control.

There are no simple answers to understanding trauma victims or victimization. No single brush can paint a picture of all individuals whom the justice system will encounter. Different individuals will act differently in the same situation! Many people who experience trauma emerge strong and successful. Be careful about overgeneralizing on any group of persons.

Conclusions

This chapter introduced the concept of the trauma-informed victim approach. This is a framework for interventions with victims that have experienced trauma. This approach recognizes that there is a physiological effect of trauma on some survivors that can limit obtaining information from those persons. Exposure to traumatic events can render them as less capable of providing accurate details of events. Realistic expectations can reduce frustration and dismissal from authorities that question their credibility.

Understanding the dynamics of trauma first requires exposure to categories of persons that are recognized as high-risk victim populations. Domestic violence victims, refugees and migrants, and sexual assault victims are recognized within the high-risk population. The TVIT is an innovative victim-centered approach to provide privacy and confidentiality for traumatized victims.

There are multiple types of crimes classified as forms of human trafficking. Men, women, and children are all victimized in countries all over the world. No single country is immune from the industry. Sexual exploitation and forced labor are frequently cited as the most common forms of trafficking. Recent trends see an increase in the numbers of individuals who are trafficked for forced labor. Sham marriages may be compelled to avoid immigration problems, or they may involve the buying of a bride who is forced to submit to the union without consent. Organ removal is an area of trafficking that is not well known but is a developing problem around the world. The life-saving practice of organ transplantation has caused a shortage of kidneys and livers in developed countries. Trafficking has emerged to meet the needs of desperate people who are unable to obtain organs by taking from those who are desperate to sell.

Two common interviewing methods that are consistent with the trauma-informed victim approach are the Enhanced Cognitive Interview and the Forensic Experiential Trauma Interview. These two approaches are similar in that they include open-ended and non-leading questions in addition to rapport building and avoid victim blaming. Each is meant to enhance memory of events.

Questions for Review

Short Answer Questions

1. What is the trauma-informed approach and why is it used?
2. Explain the six fundamental principles of the trauma-informed victim approach.
3. What are the three elements of the crime of trafficking in persons according to the *Global Report on Trafficking in Persons*?
4. Describe the *Enhanced Cognitive Interview*.
5. Explain the *Forensic Experiential Trauma Interview*.

Fill-in Questions and Answers

1. _____ is defined as resulting from an event, series of events, or set of circumstances that is experienced by an individual as physically or emotionally harmful or life threatening and that has lasting adverse effects on the individual's functioning and mental, physical, social, emotion, or spiritual well-being.
2. The three *E*s of trauma are events, experience of events, and _____.
3. Action that involves violent or aggressive behavior among family or household members or individuals who are in a dating relationship is called _____.
4. Indicators of high-risk include exposure to _____ such as natural disaster, low level of education, family dysfunction, abuse, mental illness, and substance abuse.
5. An estimated _____ increase of international migrants across the world has been documented since the year 2000.
6. Research has shown that in the United States as many as 60 percent of _____ victims never report the crime to the police.
7. Traveling outside one's own country to obtain organ transplantation is called transplant _____.
8. Within the context of interviewing, _____ is the victim's right to control disclosure of his or her story and personal information
9. The _____ is the most well-researched forensic interview approach, and has consistently been found to increase the amount of correct information recalled
10. Traumatic victimization may cause _____ changes to the survivor's memory that can disadvantage the fact-gathering process.

Exercises

1. Ask participants to take a moment and write down three ways that they would build trust and cooperation with a victim of trauma. Discuss your answers in class.
2. Break up into pairs. One person is designated as the interviewer and the other an interviewee. Use techniques to encourage the victim to tell his or her story in an uninterrupted narrative. Switch roles. Discuss in class what you found to be the most difficult part of this exercise.

References

Battered Women's Justice Project. (nd). *Offender intervention*. Retrieved from http://www.bwjp.org/our-work/topics/offender-intervention.html

Black, M., Basile, K., Breiding, M., Smith, S., Walters, M., Merrick, M., … Stevens, M. (2011). *The National Intimate Partner and Sexual Violence Survey (NISVS): 2010 Summary Report*. Atlanta, Georgia: CDC.

Cronk, T. (2013). *New Approach Helps Sexual Assault Victims Recall Details*. Retrieved from http://archive.defense.gov/news/newsarticle.aspx?id=119738

Currie, C. (nd). *You Have Options Program: Sexual Assault Reporting*. Retrieved from https://www.reportingoptions.org/

Finckenauer, J. O., & Chin, K.-l. (2011). *Researching and rethinking sex trafficking: The movement of Chinese women to Asia and the United States for commercial sex*. Washington, D.C.: National Institute of Justice.

Fisher, R. P. (1995). Interviewing Victims and Witnesses of Crime. *Psychology, Public Policy, and Law, 1*(4), 732.

Gozdziak, E., & Lowell, L. (2016). *After rescue: Evaluation of strategies to stabilize and integrate adult survivors of human trafficking to the United States* (NIJ 249672). Washington, D.C.: National Institute of Justice.

Holderness, T., Moen, S., & Hull, C. (2014). You Have Options: Improving law enforcement's response to sexual assault. *The Police Chief, 81*(December).

Holmes, P., Rijken, C., D'orsi, S., Esser, L., Hol, F., Gallagher, A., … McCarthy, S. (2016). Establishing trafficking in human beings for the purpose of organ removal and improving cross-border collaboration in criminal cases: recommendations. *Transplantation Direct, 2*(2):e56.

Home Office. (2013). *Sham marriages and civil partnerships: Background information and proposed referral and investigation scheme*. Retrieved from https://www.gov.uk/government/uploads/system/uploads/attachment_data/file/256257/Sham_Marriage_and_Civil_Partnerships.pdf

Kotria, K. (2010). Domestic minor sex trafficking in the United States. *Social Work*, 55.

Kristiansson, V., & Whitman-Barr, C. (2015). Integrating a trauma-informed response in violence against women and human trafficking prosecutions. *Strategies: The Prosecutors' Newsletter on Violence Against Women*, February (13).

Linda R.S. v. Richard D., 410 U.S. 614 (1972).

Lisak, D., & Markel, D. (2016). Using science to increase effectiveness of sexual assault investigations. *The Police Chief, 83*, 22–25.

Malone, R., & Strand, R. (2015). *Forensic Experiential Trauma Interview (FETI)*. Washington D.C.: U.S. Army Criminal Investigation Command.

National Research Council. (2013). *Confronting Commercial Sexual Exploitation and Sex Trafficking of Minors in the United States: A Guide for Providers of Victim and Support Services.*

Paulo, R. M., Albuquerque, P. B., & Bull, R. (2016). Improving the Enhanced Cognitive Interview with a new interview strategy: Category Clustering Recall. *Applied Cognitive Psychology, 30*(5), 775–784.

Paulo, R. M., Albuquerque, P. B., Saraiva, M., & Bull, R. (2015). The Enhanced Cognitive Interview: Testing appropriateness perception, memory capacity and error estimate relation with report quality. *Applied Cognitive Psychology, 29*(4), 536–543.

SAMHSA. (2014). *SAMHSA's Concept of Trauma and Guidance for a Trauma-Informed Approach*. (HHS Publication No. (SMA) 14-4884). Rockville, MD: Substance Abuse and Mental Health Services Administration.

Schock, K., Rosner, R., & Knaevelsrud, C. (2015). Impact of asylum interviews on the mental health of traumatized asylum seekers. *European Journal of Psychotraumatology 6*(1), 26286.

Smith, S., Chen, J., Basile, K., Gilbert, L., Merrick, M., Patel, N., … Jain, A. (2017). *The National Intimate Partner and Sexual Violence Survey (NISVS): 2010-2012 State Report*. Atlanta, GA: National Center for Injury Prevention and Control, Centers for Disease Control and Prevention.

Strand, R. (2017). The Forensic Experiential Trauma Interview (FETI). *Minnesota Coalition Against Sexual Assault*. Retrieved from http://www.mncasa.org/assets/PDFs/FETI%20-%20Public%20Description.pdf

Tsai, D. F.-C., Huang, S.-W., Holm, S., Lin, Y.-P., Chang, Y.-K., & Hsu, C.-C. (2017). The outcomes and controversies of transplant tourism—Lessons of an 11-year retrospective cohort study from Taiwan. *PLoS ONE, 12*(6), e0178569.

UN. (2000). *Protocol to Prevent, Suppress and Punish Trafficking in Persons Especially Women and Children*. Retrieved from http://www.ohchr.org/EN/ProfessionalInterest/Pages/ProtocolTraffickingInPersons.aspx

UNODC. (2016). *Global Report on Trafficking in Persons 2016*. New York, NY: United Nations Publication, Sales No. E.16.IV.6.

Veldhuizen, T. v., Horselenberg, R., Landstrom, S., Granhag, P., & Koppen, P. (2016). Interviewing asylum seekers: A vignette study on the questions asked to assess credibility of claims about origin and persecution. *Journal of Investigative Psychology and Offender Profiling, 14*(1), 3–22.

Vera Institute of Justice. (2014). *Screening for Human Trafficking: Guidelines for Administering the Trafficking Victim Identification Tool (TVIT)*. (NCJ #246713). New York, NY: National Institute of Justice.

Vredeveldt, A., Tredoux, C. G., Nortje, A., Kempen, K., Puljević, C., & Labuschagne, G. N. (2015). A field evaluation of the Eye-Closure Interview with witnesses of serious crimes. *Law and Human Behavior, 39*(2), 189–197.

8

Interviewing Children

Source: Marina Dyakonova/Shutterstock.

CHAPTER OBJECTIVES

After completing this chapter, you should be able to:

1. Summarize the four child development stages.
2. Describe questions used for making a risk assessment.
3. List the four components of the preliminary considerations checklist.
4. Define the forensic interview.
5. Explain the five phases used in forensic interviewing.
6. State the three phases of the Developmental Narrative Elaboration Interview.
7. Describe when the NICHD protocol is used.
8. Recognize the cognitive child interviewing method.

KEY TERMS

Child development stages

Credibility

Forensic interview

NICHD protocol

Preliminary considerations checklist

Cognitive child interviewing

DNE interview

Risk assessment

INTRODUCTION

Interviewing children can provide unique challenges and opportunities for crime investigators. It is helpful to understand child mental development from the subjective experiences of a child for a variety of reasons. Communicating with children through interviews is highly dependent on their developmental level. As criminal justice professionals, we are concerned with the violence perpetrated by children and against children and in the effects of their being witnesses to domestic violence. Child eyewitness testimony is potentially important to decision making in a range of criminal and civil matters (Thomas D. Lyon, Scurich, Choi, Handmaker, & Blank, 2012). In addition to the theoretical reasons for exploring methods of effective interviewing is the practical and pressing concern of forensically documenting abuses against children (Wolfman, Brown, & Jose, 2016).

Both the identification and recognition of child abuse and the impact of violence are also of consequence to the investigator. Insight into the reactions of the victim may provide a more detailed and accurate portrayal of a harmful situation to the child. The investigator has a unique opportunity to document the full extent of injury, both physical

BEEN THERE . . . DONE THAT! 8-1

A multidisciplinary task force was established in my county to jointly investigate major crimes committed against children. We came from many different professions. I was the police officer; there was a medical doctor, a prosecuting attorney, a social worker, a clinician, and a victim–witness advocate. After an interview in a particular case the team recommended that I arrest the alleged perpetrator. Even though I also believed that the child had been sexually abused, there was a lack of sufficient probable cause. It was a heated discussion, without compromise. Now what—leave the child unprotected from further abuse? The suggestion was made that we offer the suspect a pretrial diversion. In exchange for him admitting guilt and going to counseling as well as staying away from the victim, we would not prosecute. He agreed. It was a win–win for everyone. Never compromise your reputation by effecting an arrest that lacks probable cause—it will come back to haunt you.

and psychological, if those signs and symptoms present themselves. The likelihood of successful prosecution is enhanced with increased documentation and evidence of harm.

The role of criminal justice investigator differs from and may conflict with that of investigators from social service agencies. Criminal investigators must determine *what* happened rather than an emotional belief that *something* happened (Benneworth-Gray, 2014). The determination of whether a crime has been committed and the development of admissible evidence are central to the criminal justice perspective. To be effective, interviewers and investigators must be in control of their feelings about abuse and have the ability to react dispassionately.

During the investigation of suspected child abuse, the most likely source of information will come from the victim. Second-hand disclosure regarding the maltreatment of a child should never be considered reliable without corroboration. Verifying as much of the information as possible is necessary. Reliability issues compounded with the suggestibility of children and limited memory development heighten the urgency of finding methods to improve child testimony.

CHILD DEVELOPMENT STAGES

Child development stages refer to the process of human development measured from infancy to adolescents, characterized by milestones of child development. The ability of a child witness or victim to accurately report experiences is limited by the child's developmental stage. Because all children do not mature at the same rate, one should be careful about overgeneralization. Poverty, culture, exposure to violence, and a variety of other variables affect cognitive development. The investigator can go into the interview with a rough idea of what might be expected from the interviewee. This knowledge is most helpful before the interview begins. Use it to determine where to conduct the questioning, who should be present, and how to structure the questions.

Age-Related Limitations on Reporting

The child is expected to be preverbal during *infancy*, and direct questioning is unlikely to be productive. Documenting connected terms or crying that indicates an injury or expresses pain is worthwhile for the investigator to include in the report of suspected child abuse. During *early childhood*, the ability to verbalize is increased, particularly through play. The best approach for eliciting information from a child under the age of 6 years is within a play therapy framework. *Middle childhood* brings an improvement in the ability to answer questions and to describe events. *Adolescence* is a time of self-consciousness, self-doubt, or overconfidence, and moodiness. Exact dates are still a problem, but seasons associated with clothing and events occurring around holidays help to establish the timing of supposed assaults.

INFANCY: THE FIRST 2 YEARS.   An infant's language consists of utterances, crying, and gestures. A high level of anxiety is reached when immediate needs are not met, such as hunger and relief of pain. The earliest documentation regarding an infant victim refers to the recognition of pain or discomfort. In addition to the medical report of injury, the investigator should note verbal expressions that indicate pain while the child is being examined by a physician in addition to the reports given by the caretaker. Vocabulary is established slowly through single and then connected words. By the time the child is 24 months of age, he or she is likely to be using expressive terms such as "me want," "man bad," and "hit you." Behavioral indicators of abuse are more likely the "language" during infancy.

The investigator should obtain interviews with all caretakers, regardless of their status as a suspect. A parent who says that the infant does not cry excessively or appear in pain may later become a suspect if the child is found to have extensive internal injury, for example. Early documentation of suspected infant abuse is critical. Physical examination by a medical professional is required to provide evidence of a crime; a team approach is most beneficial for cases involving an infant victim.

EARLY CHILDHOOD: AGES 2–6 YEARS.   These years are collectively referred to as the preschool stage. During early childhood, there is an expectation that the child will verbally communicate, particularly through play. This child will have an active imagination that is grounded in reality; fantasies are about things similar to what the child has experienced but are not necessarily what happened to them. It is necessary to clarify what the child heard, saw, or felt to determine the origin of his or her experiences regarding the topic of the interview. Such children cannot concentrate on any one thing for more than a few minutes, although their attention span increases as they grow older. Interviewers need to assess the attention span and structure the interview to accommodate the needs of the child. For example, a child can be encouraged to color between questions.

An intense single experience or a repeatedly rehearsed situation may be retained in a child's long-term memory. Time and space are concepts that the young child has difficulties expressing. The extent of recall is dependent on the level of the child's social interactions. By age 5, most children can recall and recount things that occurred in the past. Extended questioning should not be expected; this does not mean that the interview will be short. The opposite is true; the structure needs to involve purposely provided natural breaks. The interview will require significant time with lots of concentration on the part of the interviewer. Only in rare instances should a child of this age be interviewed for longer than 0.5 hour.

As young children mature, they will push their physical limits by running, leaping, and climbing. Unsupervised or neglected children are susceptible to injury caused by falling.

MIDDLE CHILDHOOD: AGES 7–12 YEARS.   During their middle years, children's mental processes develop at a faster rate than in the earlier stages. Their language is well developed and their understanding of time and space concepts improves. These children can be more specific in explaining when and where they had the experiences that you want to document. Having a strong need for trust, a victimized child at this age may require additional attention and support to compensate for the violation that occurred toward them.

Play remains their primary expression, supplemented with emotion language. This age group should be capable of explaining what they felt as a result of their experiences. During an interview, follow-up questions such as, "What did that feel like?," "What did it taste like?," and "How did that make you feel?" are quite appropriate in response to their descriptions. Their cognitive development becomes more sophisticated, including increased reasoning capacity and the ability to distinguish fiction from reality. "How do you know" and "What is he like?" can stimulate expressive responses. Their perception of others may be categorized as "good" or "bad," and they will be able to tell why.

ADOLESCENTS: AGES 13–18 YEARS.   During the teenage years adolescents move from concrete toward abstract thinking. This age group is anxious about peer acceptance and concerned with self-identity. It is usual that the teenager establishes independence through conflicts with peer and family. Teenagers are generally known to be the most difficult age group to interview. It is important to build a trusting relationship, be respectful, and listen carefully. During the interview, use body language to suggest acceptance and understanding. Give encouragements often and ask for clarifications as needed.

FIELD ASSESSMENT

In cases where a police officer is responding to a complaint of child abuse or neglect, an assessment is made to determine whether criminal action should be investigated. This assessment includes a field interview with the child. The majority of calls will not be acted on independently by the police officer; he or she may act as the first responder who then makes a report to the social services. In making an assessment in the field, the child should be interviewed at the scene, with documentation of the name, address, and age of the child in addition to his or her demeanor. The names and addresses of the caretaker and the family situation are also documented.

After explaining the reason for the visit to the caretaker, the police officers should ask to see the child. If the child is old enough to understand, he or she should be told why the police are there and what they will be doing. Depending on the allegations and the child's age, the investigators will need to visually examine the child for signs of obvious trauma. Investigators should document any injuries noted and, if possible, photograph areas of injury or questionable physical findings.

The child should be interviewed outside the presence of the caregiver. If the child has sustained life-threatening or severe injuries, the priority is securing emergency medical attention. The U.S. Department of Health and Human Services (ACF, 2014) suggests that the following information should be determined from the interview:

- The child's developmental level
- The child's explanation of any injuries
- Who the child perceives as his or her caretakers
- How the child is disciplined
- How other children in the home are disciplined
- How often the victim and/or siblings have been injured in the past
- What type of weapon or implement was used and where it is now
- If the child bled after the assault, where the clothing is now, or any other item that might have been stained
- Who else saw the incident
- Who the child told of the incident

INITIAL CONSIDERATIONS FOR CHILD INTERVIEWS

As this chapter progresses, differences will emerge regarding interview techniques with children. That is because the purpose and scope of the interview with a child may change at any point during the interview process. A child who is being questioned primarily for having been victimized may also have begun perpetrating. The child may have been victimized by more than one person and through different forms of abuse. Children who have been victimized may also have witnessed other victimizations; they may have information from the perpetrator of others who have been abused. These variables will in turn affect the choice of the person to conduct the questioning.

Step 1: Risk Assessment

Before beginning any investigation that involves interviewing a child, a determination must be made on whether that child is safe. Assessing the present and future risk of harm to a child is more than just an indication about the investigator's level of caring, it is a legal requirement called **risk assessment**. All 50 states, the District of Columbia, American Samoa, Guam, the Northern Mariana Islands, Puerto Rico, and the U.S. Virgin Islands have legislation that requires certain individuals to report when a child is at risk due to suspected child abuse and neglect (Child Welfare Information Gateway, 2016).

FIGURE 8-1   An assessment is conducted prior to interviewing to determine if a child is at risk for abuse or neglect.

Source: Lucian Coman/Shutterstock.

The standard of proof necessary to make this assessment is mere suspicion alone. Some questions that are helpful in making a risk assessment include the following:

1. Is there any reason to believe that this child has been abused, neglected, or witnessed abuse toward a parent or sibling in his or her home?
2. Has the child received a suspicious injury or threat of injury?
3. Has another child in the home been abused or neglected?
4. Are there weapons or ammunition that is accessible to this child? Note that some states make it illegal to have unsecured weapons or ammunition in the home.
5. Does the primary caretaker abuse alcohol or drugs?
6. Is the child depressed or suffering from lack of medical attention?

If the answer to any of the questions above is "yes," then a report of suspected abuse must be filed with the appropriate receiving agency for that state. Child protection services, departments of social services, and police departments are examples of agencies that are designated by law as obligated to receive these reports.

If the child divulges during an interview that abuse has occurred from a caretaker, the interviewer must determine whether the child is likely to be punished for having made the report about a family member or intimate of a parent. This would be a high-risk situation that requires immediate intervention. A local child protection agency should be called regarding this case before the child is released to the caretaker. Police officers in every state have temporary or emergency removal powers for the purposes of protecting children. Removal of the victim to a safe living environment is an option that should be exercised only if a nonoffending parent or guardian is unwilling or unable to protect the child from the suspect.

Step 2: Preliminary Considerations

Step 2 consists of using a checklist that will assist the interviewer in determining the type of interview that will be needed. There are four components to the **preliminary considerations checklist**: determine the reason for questioning, determine the purpose of questioning, identify the population, and identify the interviewer.

1. *Determine the reason for questioning*
   - Has the child been victimized? (Requires lengthy interview)
   - Has the child been witness to a crime? (Requires short interview)
   - Is the child suspected of having committed a crime? (Requires interrogation)
2. *Determine the purpose of the questioning*
   - Abuse determination: What is the best model to meet your needs?
   - Risk assessment: Is this child at risk for future victimization?
   - Obtaining evidence: Will the child be able to give verbal or written evidence?
3. *Identify the population*
   - Age: What are the expectations and limitations of this child?
   - Gender: What are the gender-related expectations and limitations of this child?
   - Special needs: Are special accommodations necessary to conduct the questioning?
   - Cultural background and ethnicity: Can certain outcomes be predicted or avoided?
   - Current or recent traumatizing events: What do you know about this person?
4. *Identify the interviewer*
   - Age: Can he or she interact with the target?
   - Gender: Would this make a difference with regard to target response?
   - Ethnicity: Will the interviewer have credibility with the target?
   - Specialization: What sort of special knowledge of interview or interrogation techniques should the interviewer have?
   - Experience of the interviewer: What is the skill level with the target population?
   - Approach: What attitude is required according to the purpose of questioning?
   - Confidence: Is he or she comfortable with the target?

Step 3: Remaining Neutral

Approaching each interview without bias is essential. The purpose of the interview is to determine the truth; this is done based on facts and evidence. The kind of evidence that is sought includes the interview with the child, corroborating physical evidence, and testimonial evidence such as statements taken from persons with knowledge about the case.

To obtain testimony for legal evidence the investigator cannot rely on second-hand information garnered from another agency. Statements that were taken by another police agency should not be used without the present investigator having had an active role in the interview process to protect the victim as well as the rights of the accused. As with any criminal investigation, certain criteria must be satisfied for the matter to be considered a criminal offense. Resist the temptation to run out and make an arrest without reviewing the statement to determine if probable cause has been adequately established through the following information *for every allegation*. Here are some questions to which the interviewer must have answers to proceed with the criminal process:

1. What, if any, crime has occurred?

    All criteria for the commission of the crime must be satisfied. For example, if the allegation is the rape of a child, penetration must have occurred. What is the evidence of penetration? Penetration may be perpetrated by any object into any orifice. Determine the genitalia that was penetrated and the object that was used. It may be a body part or a physical object inserted into the child. Depending on the age of the victim, force may also be an element of the crime. Force may involve any amount of coercion, which may even be satisfied by a "command." Identify what level of force was used, if any. For a young child, this is not an issue.

2. Who had committed the crime?

    It may be difficult for a young child to adequately identify the perpetrator. A person cannot be accused of a crime without having been identified. If the child only knows the first name of the individual (and this is not unusual), it is necessary to follow up with a question on where he or she knows John or where the abuse occurred. With a younger child, the information might be obtained from the guardian. For example, if "John" was responsible, how does the child know him? Where did it happen? If the offense occurred in "John's house," find out whether John is the grandfather, the uncle, or a babysitter. It is not appropriate to suggest that a child has been abused, but once the statement is made that abuse did occur, direct questions to clarify what has already been stated are permissible. Keep asking questions until you are satisfied that the alleged perpetrator's identity is firmly established.

3. Where did the crime occur?

    Expect that the description of the place will be age appropriate. "In the woods," "In the house," and "At school" are examples of what you might hear. Build on what the child says if clarification is needed. If the place of victimization was at day care, find out the times and dates that the child was enrolled in and attended day care. If the abuse occurred at the house of a relative, see whether the person cared for the child regularly or on a sporadic basis.

4. When did the crime occur?

    Many children will not be able to state the exact date that they were victimized. Their concept of time is different from that of adults, and the abuse may have occurred over an extended period. To clarify the specific instances of abuse, ask questions to help the child to narrow down within a time frame. For example, ask, "What were you wearing?" The answer may indicate the season. Determine the last time that the alleged perpetrator had access to the child. Children older than the age of 6 years are more likely to be able to accurately define the period in relation to an important event in their life such as a holiday or birthday; ask, "Was it before your birthday or after?" If you know that the alleged perpetrator had frequent access to the child, ask whether "it" happened the last time they were together.

5. Against whom was the crime perpetrated?

    Clarify with the child whether he or she was the victim or might have seen something happen to someone else. If there is any question in your mind, be direct; ask, "Did this happen to you?"

6. How was the crime perpetrated?

    This part of the questioning can be most difficult for the interviewer. He or she must be comfortable asking for specific clarification on how the crime was perpetrated. It can be helpful for the interviewer to feign misunderstanding; ask the child to help understand what happened. Here are a few examples (depending on the crime being investigated): "You told me that a stick was there; what happened with the stick? Can you show me on the doll (or picture) where the stick was put? Did it touch you outside or did it go inside? What did that feel like?" When asking questions for clarification interviewer neutrality is important. Do not act surprised, angry, happy, or thankful. It is appropriate to thank the child for clearing up the misunderstanding.

WHAT IS THE FORENSIC APPROACH TO CHILD INTERVIEWING?

The forensic approach to child interviewing is used when primary victimization is suspected. Based on the multidisciplinary model, it involves multiple individuals with different expertise working together to gather information and collect evidence. The approach is legal oriented with an effort toward maintaining the integrity of the case to meet possible future court challenges. All interviews and collection of evidence must be done by individuals who are trained and familiar with the legal standards of the state where the offense is alleged to have occurred. The interviewer may be a police officer, a child psychologist, a certified forensic interviewer, or any member of the team who is qualified to conduct the questioning of the victim based on the preliminary considerations. Collaboration with mandated reporting agencies means that members of the forensic team are consulted and have full participation in the process.

There is a recent trend toward the use of a certified forensic interviewer who can establish a nonbiased position as neither an advocate for the child nor an employee of the court. This method is meant to reduce the number of interviews that may ultimately contaminate the child's testimony through repetitive questioning. It involves a standardized procedure that documents the affect or nonverbal report of the child as well as the verbal account. Often this is accomplished by videotaping the victim during

FIGURE 8-2 When asked to draw a picture of the person who "touched her in a place she did not like" a 4-year-old girl drew this picture. It was used as evidence of her sexual assault.

Source: Courtesy of Denise K. Gosselin.

the interview. There is no legal requirement that children be informed that they are being interviewed. The decision on giving this information to the child is a matter of organization policy. The permission of a parent or guardian should be obtained before videotaping a child.

Forensic interviewing uses a structured or semi-structured approach for a child interview that is designed to minimize future court challenges through strict adherence to legal principles. The interview requires planning and precision. A detailed history of abuse or suspected current abuse is obtained before the interview. An interview room is specifically designed for the comfort of the designated age group to be interviewed. Direct questioning is necessary to elicit details of assault, but care is taken not to be suggestive in the form of questioning. The *Office of Juvenile Justice and Delinquency Prevention* furthers the following definition to promote consensus within the field (Newlin et al., 2015):

> A **forensic interview** of a child is a developmentally sensitive and legally sound method of gathering factual information regarding allegations of abuse or exposure to violence. This interview is conducted by a competently trained, neutral professional utilizing research and practice-informed techniques as part of a larger investigative process.

FORENSIC INTERVIEWING TECHNIQUES

Following 20 years of research, professionals have gained significant insight into how to maximize children's potential to relate information. The process is commonly referred to as forensic interviewing. Interviewing children takes time and can be a difficult process. There is no single model of forensic interviewing that has been endorsed as the gold standard, despite widespread acceptance that professionals should have forensic interview training (Newlin et al., 2015).

The purpose of the interview will determine how complex it will be. Young children are easily distracted and often reluctant to disclose abuse. When they feel attached to the abuser they may fear the consequences, including what the interviewer might do to them as a result. To avoid this problem, the interviewer should not show approval or disapproval at anything the child says. The emotions of the interviewer must be held in check. Signs of disgust, disbelief, or even approval are not appropriate because they may influence the child.

Phase I: Caretaker Instructions

Before meeting with the child, instructions should be given to the caretaker. The caretaker should be advised not to answer any questions about the interview from the child. No attempt should be made by the caretaker to gain further information from the child about the event. Warn the caretaker not to discuss case specifics because others may also be involved who have not yet been identified.

Explain to the caretaker that a bathroom break needs to be provided for the child just before the interview.

If it does not compromise the investigation, attempt to put the caretaker at ease by telling him or her about the process at this stage. Include the fact that you will need to talk to the child alone.

Immediately before the interview have the guardian sign a prepared form of release to conduct and document the interview. This is important because the process may result in information that implicates the caretaker or those whom the caretaker wants to protect. When an interrogation of a juvenile is the focus, additional legal requirements must be met.

Phase II: Evaluation

Using the *common preliminary considerations checklist*, conduct an evaluation of the upcoming interview. From this exercise, the interviewer will know the approximate length and approach that will be needed.

Determine the appropriate place to conduct the interview. For all interviews, the room should be quiet and free of distractions. There should not be any electronic devices, such as phone, cell phone, beeper, pager, clock, or radio, in the room that will make noise. For a child interview, no chairs are necessary if there are comfortable places to sit on the floor. This puts the interviewer at a more even level with the child and is less threatening. Audio or video recording devices should not be visible to the child because he or she may "ham it up" for a camera. For an interrogation, there should be a table for writing and a visible recording device if one is to be used.

Preparation for the interview includes the reading of any statements that may have brought the child to the attention of the police. Any information regarding past or present allegations of abuse should be researched. A background check of the alleged perpetrator should be made before the interview with the supposed victim.

Phase III: Preparing the Child

Interviewers are often frustrated by inaccurate and unreliable statements taken from young children. This is, in part, due to developmental limitations on children's ability to communicate when they do not understand the questions. The interviewer is not made aware of the situation because children will merely provide an answer that is false rather than communicate that they do not understand.

Children being prepared for the interview should (1) practice identifying instances of noncomprehension, (2) practice responding with verbalizations that indicate their lack of understanding (after being taught by someone using explicit feedback, modeling, and praise), and (3) increase their awareness of the negative consequences of responding to questions not fully understood (e.g., misordering in a restaurant and receiving the wrong food, missing out on a favorite activity). After the preparation phase, the child should be given adequate time for some food, beverage, and, of course, a bathroom break.

Phase IV: Establishing Rapport

The interviewer should meet and greet the child in a relaxed and comfortable manner. Rather than asking for his name, say, "Hi, you must be Bill," and state your first name. Tell the child that you have been expecting him, and then ask the guardian if it is all right for Bill to take a walk with you. This simple act reassures the child that you are someone to whom he is able (given permission) to go with and to talk to. Make this introduction appropriate to the age of the child. If this is a young child, kneel down to the child's level at the beginning of the meeting. The interview should be conducted without the presence of the guardian unless his or her presence is absolutely necessary.

Take whatever time necessary to ensure that the child is relaxed and does not feel threatened. The interview room should afford flexibility for the child to move around, but should not be large enough to allow "escape." Crayons and paper should be available to occupy the child and allow him or her to talk unguarded. Talk about the child's likes such as colors, activities, games, movies—get to know the child. Let the child know a bit about you. This is the time to access the developmental level of the child and his or her ability to communicate. For very young children it might be sufficient to say that you are someone who talks to kids about things on their minds. Older children may want to know more about your role as a police officer, social worker, and so on. This is the stage in which you determine the sexual terminology of the child if the interview concerns sexual abuse. Use appropriate tools to aid in this vocabulary development. You may want to ask questions to determine the child's level of sophistication, such as "Can you write?", "Do you know your alphabet?", "Do you read?" With an interrogation, the child must be told if you are a police officer.

Phase V: Conducting the Interview

At this point, the interviewer is ready to find out what happened. Establish that the child knows the difference between the truth and a lie and that the child is willing to tell you if he or she does not understand questions. Ask "Do you know what a lie is?" Ask for an example. "Do you know what telling the truth is?" Ask for an example. "If I said your name was Bill, is that a lie or the truth?" "If I say that this crayon is red, is that the truth or a lie?" Give the child license by saying that you also will ask when you don't understand something.

Don't use "cop talk." Use language that is appropriate to the child's age and developmental level. Words like incident, occur, penetration, prior, ejaculation, and perpetrator can be confusing to a child. Look for signs that the child does not understand you. Avoid using language that sounds accusatory, such as "Why?" Don't say, "Why did you do that?," "Why did you go to that house?," or "Why did he touch you?" Never threaten or try to force a reluctant child to talk. If gentle coaxing is insufficient to overcome the child's unwillingness, stop the interview.

Do not lead the child by offering a possible place for the event or name for the perpetrator. Start the conversation by asking what happened, or "I need for you to tell me what happened to you." Ask simple and direct questions for clarification. Be as open-ended as possible to solicit narratives. Don't ask questions that can foreclose possible additional information by being answered with a simple "yes" or "no." Determine whether threats were made against the child if he or she told what happened. Close the interview by thanking the child for his or her cooperation. Do not try to exact promises about testifying.

WHAT IS THE DNE INTERVIEW?

The **Developmental Narrative Elaboration Interview** (DNE) is a forensic semistructured approach to interviewing children aged 4–12, developed by Saywitz and Camparo (2013). The three-phase approach provides general guidelines for interviewing as well as flexibility on the goal. For example, statements may be prompted about the identities of the participants, locations of abuse, threats, force, and physical sensations when the children's memory is at question. Gathering information that will assist in decisions on the best interest of the child may provide the focus for the DNE interview also.

The preliminary phase typically involves introductions and rapport building, but may also include strategies for enhanced memory retrieval and reducing suggestion. The core interview phase involves the prompting for a narrative of events that the child experienced or witnessed. Cued elaborations in this second phase may include the use of simple line drawings. A closure phase provides the opportunity for the interviewer to answer questions and prepare the child for what might happen next. If the child has become upset during the interview, it is essential that these be addressed at the end of the interview.

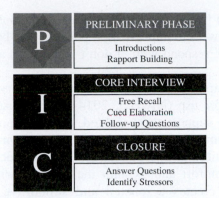

FIGURE 8-3 The DNE protocol is an evidence-based method consisting of three phases in a semistructured approach.

Source: Adapted from Saywitz, K. J., & Camparo, L. B. (2014). Interviewing children: A primer. The Sage handbook of child research, 371–390.

WHAT IS THE NICHD INVESTIGATIVE PROTOCOL?

The investigative interview protocol was developed by the *Eunice Kennedy Shriver* National Institute of Child Health and Human Development. The **National Institute of Child Health and Human Development** (NICHD) protocol is a forensic interviewing method consisting of three phases to child interviewing when sexual abuse is suspected. The protocol can be used by social workers, medical doctors, psychologists, prosecutors, and police officers. This is an evidence-based investigative method that involves a structured approach using open-ended questions designed to increase the amount of

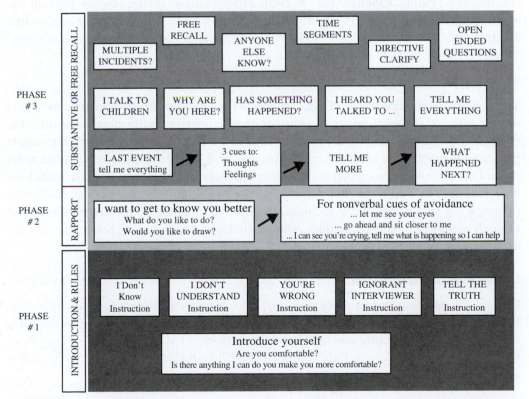

FIGURE 8-4 The NICHD Protocol revision seeks to support reluctant children to elicit disclosures of sexual abuse. Here is an overview of the key features, illustrated in the three phases.

Source: Adapted from NICHD Protocol: International Evidence-Based Investigative Interviewing of Children. Retrieved from http://nichdprotocol.com.

information elicited from free recall memory (Brown & Lamb, 2015). Instructions are provided to child interviewees to improve their performative by giving them permission to correct the interviewer, respond with "I don't know," and assure them about disclosure (Lyon, 2014).

Widely accepted around the world, 20 translated versions of the NICHD protocol are available for use (NICHD, 2014). The revised protocol is designed to enhance rapport and support to suspected victims who might be unwilling to report (Hershkowitz, Lamb, & Katz, 2014). The NICHD protocol has three phases: introductory, rapport building, and substantive or free recall. The introduction is designed to promote comfort and explain the tasks. During the rapport-building phase, the interviewer creates a relaxed and supportive environment that may include talking about events unrelated to the suspected abuse. A series of nonsuggestive prompts are used during the presubstantive and substantive phases of the interview. Only after exhaustive open-ended questioning should the interviewers ask more direct questions.

WHAT IS THE COGNITIVE APPROACH TO INTERVIEWING CHILDREN?

The cognitive interviewing method for children is a memory-jogging and retrieval tool that was developed in the hope of improving the completeness and accuracy of eyewitness accounts, which has been modified for interviewing children. Studies have determined that cognitive interviewing increases the amount of correct information elicited from eyewitnesses without increasing the proportion of incorrect information (Paulo, Albuquerque, & Bull, 2016). However, it does not prevent the child from reporting false information after having been subjected to a misleading suggestion.

COGNITIVE INTERVIEWING TECHNIQUES

The cognitive approach is useful when interviewing younger children because they tend to give less complete information, although their cognitive ability is not that different from older children (Thomas D. Lyon et al., 2012). The method is deceptively simple but requires practice for one to become proficient in it. It stresses using a secluded, quiet place free of distractions along with urging subjects to speak slowly. It is useful for questioning both victims and witnesses. Most of this approach incorporates traditional interviewing techniques, but it includes an improved method of recalling information through memory-jogging techniques rather than direct questioning. This method is only used with a willing participant.

Caretaker Instructions

Prepare the guardian, parent, or caretaker in the same way as for any forensic interview. Request that the person does not ask the child about the reported abuse. Put the caretaker at ease by answering any questions that would not jeopardize the investigation. Obtain the necessary release forms from the guardian, parent, or caretaker to interview with the child.

Practice Interview

A cognitive practice interview is optional but recommended. If a practice interview is used, the interviewer should be different from the person who conducts the practice session. Giving the child experience with being interviewed serves to clarify the methods that will be used in the actual interview and encourages the child to use recall techniques. The child is introduced to a scenario that will be used to practice for the actual interview through a short video or the introduction of a person who has a short conversation with the child and leaves the room. Tell the child that he or she will now practice for the interview that will happen another time with the "detective" or "Mary" or "the social worker." Research indicates that children who were given a practice interview on an unrelated event before the actual interview gave the most complete reports about the event (Newlin et al., 2015).

Establishing Rapport: Cognitive Interview Step 1

The new interviewer must establish rapport and prepare the child before questioning. Instruct the child that this is the interview he or she has been waiting for to talk about what happened. Rapport development here is the same as with the forensic interviewing approach. Consideration must be given to assuring that the child is relaxed and comfortable before the interview. Positive and open-ended questions promote expanded conversation, such as asking the child about his or her favorite TV show.

The interviewer prepares the child for future questions with the following instructions:

1. There may be some questions that you do not know the answers to. That's okay. Nobody can remember everything. If you don't know the answer to a question, then tell me "I don't know," but do not guess or make anything up. It is very important to tell me only what you really remember, only what really happened.
2. If you do not want to answer some of the questions, you don't have to. That's ok. Tell me "I don't want to answer that question."
3. If you do not know what something I ask you means, tell me "I don't know what you mean." Tell me to say it in new words.
4. I may ask you some questions more than one time. Sometimes I forget that I already asked you that question. You don't have to change your answer. Just tell me what you remember the best you can.

BEEN THERE . . . DONE THAT! 8-3

Leading questions are dangerous in interviewing because they may provide misinformation to the person being interviewed. It can happen very subtly that a victim or witness is given misinformation without specifically stating the answer; they come to believe a response is expected. If they don't know the answer, they make one up. Once a victim or witness has misinformation there is a chance that he or she will repeat it with increased emphasis. One day I took a 6-year-old boy through the station as a way to establish rapport. He went over to my desk and was allowed to sit in my chair. We lingered for a few moments, making easy conversation. We then started walking through the office back to the room where the interview was to occur. This child knew exactly why he was there and started talking about being abused before we made it past all of the desks in the office.

My mistake was to not insulating him from distractions that would cause misinformation. Walking past the rows of detectives sitting at their desks, he caught a glimpse of the shiney gold badge worn by the sergeant. At that exact time I asked, "What did he (the man who sexually abused him) look like?" Without hesitation the child pointed to the sergeant with the shiney gold badge and loudly exclaimed, "He looked like him!" As I ran the child out of the room, I heard something like, "get that _____ kid out of here!" I would not recommend starting an interview while walking by other people.

Reconstruction and Reporting Everything: Cognitive Interview Step 2

Two mnemonic techniques are used in Step 2. The child is asked to **reconstruct the circumstances** surrounding the incident by being coaxed to give a narrative account of what happened. The interviewer should listen intently and not interrupt. Notes should be taken sparingly; it would best if the interview were being videotaped or audiotaped. Someone listening to the interview but outside of the view of the child can take more complete notes.

In instructing the child to reconstruct the circumstances of the incident, one should include sample directions such as the following: "Picture the time when [the scenario] was happening as if it was happening right now. Tell me what it was like. Tell me out loud. Were there any smells? Was it dark? Was it light? Was there anyone else there? Who? What things were there? How were you feeling?" The description includes not only the appearance of the scene and the people present or nearby but also the child's thoughts and feelings at the time of the scenario.

The next part is to ask the child to start at the beginning and say from the beginning, to the middle, to the end, everything that he or she remembers even little parts he or she doesn't think are very important. Ask the child to **report everything** that happened. Do not interrupt while the child is talking. Prompt by asking what happened only when needed. Clarify at this point by asking an open-ended question whenever possible. Do not ask more than one question at a time. Speak in a relaxed tone. When clarifying details that the child has provided, use a positive questioning approach.

Praise the child's effort, not the content of the responses. For example, the interviewer should say, "I understand what you are saying" or "You are doing a great job in explaining to me." Do not say, "Thanks for telling me what Uncle Joe did to you."

Changing the Order and Perspective: Cognitive Interview Step 3

The third step in the child version of cognitive interviewing consists in using two additional memory-jogging techniques to enhance the narrative account. Studies have suggested that changing the perspective and changing the order mnemonics may be problematic for younger children (Saywitz & Camparo, 2014). Any or all of these techniques may be used in the interview depending on the information that is being sought.

- **Change the order.**   Ask the child to recall what happened in backward order, from the end to the beginning. Prepare the child for that technique before asking. After each response, ask the child, "What happened right before that?"
- **Change the perspective.**   Ask the child to recount the incident from a new perspective. This is done by instructing the child to say what he or she would have seen through the eyes of an inanimate object, such as a stuffed animal that was present. Avoid asking the child to recount the story from the perspective of the supposed perpetrator.

Additional memory-jogging techniques may be useful when seeking to clarify specific information that has been provided by the child. Examples include the following:

- **Alphabet search.**   To help the child to remember names or places, ask the child to go through the alphabet to help recall the information.
- **Speech characteristics.**   Probe for speech traits if the offender was not identified. Ask if the voice reminded the child of anyone or was unusual in any way.
- **Conversation.**   Ask how the child felt about what was said. Were there any unusual phrases or words used by the perpetrator?

BEEN THERE . . . DONE THAT! 8-4

Early in a career of interviewing children, I learned from trial and error what items should be kept out of the interview room. One particular child grew increasingly anxious as he began to divulge being sexually molested. As I pressed him with follow-up questions about specifics he became avoidant. Everything that could be picked up became a focus for him. Gently I would take the toys away and ask for him to explain things to me. Exasperated, he picked up a bottle of glue and poured it into my hair! That was quickly followed by a toy hurled in my direction. We did talk some more, but afterward, everything sharp and sticky was removed from the room! Don't expect children to enjoy the process any more than you would if you were asked to talk about your negative experiences. Your goal is to make a potentially uncomfortable situation as comfortable as possible through your attitude and kind nature. The articles in the child-interviewing room should be selected carefully. Do not include toys or otherwise distracting items, and leave out the glue.

In the most recent version of the cognitive method, the two methods incorporated into the child interview are **reconstruct the circumstances** and **report everything.** The approaches of thinking out loud and giving a narrative account add to the completeness of the child's report.

THE CHILD AS REPORTER

The only people who should be present in the interview room are the child being interviewed and the person designated to conduct the interview. The interviewer cannot know beforehand whether that influence will be positive or negative. Supporting parents or friends may act to encourage the child to divulge, and a disapproving parent (or one the child perceives to be disapproving) will have the opposite effect.

The nature of the relationship between the child and the interviewer is one of the most important components of a successful interview. A child who feels respected and secure will communicate more openly and honestly than one who feels threatened by the process (Schetky, 2014). Research suggests that children who have promised to tell the truth prior to the substantive phase of the interview are less likely to make false statements (Newlin et al., 2015).

Accuracy

A child's account of events may be incomplete. This does not mean that the child isn't telling the truth. Children tend to block out unpleasant events, and the interview may produce information regarding a prior incident intermingled with present events. Before beginning the interviewer should know any history that might exist of prior victimization so that clarifications can be made during the interview. If leading questions are asked, the responses may be distorted. Inaccurate responses also occur if the child does not fully understand the question but does not acknowledge that comprehension is an issue. Interviewers can increase the probability of accurate responses using age-appropriate language and confirming throughout the interview that the child understands.

Memory and Fantasy

When a child is being interviewed, it is difficult to determine with certainty, on the basis of the child's memory alone, whether the child is recounting something suggested, coached, or actually witnessed. Children under the age of 4 may confuse fact with fantasy (Schetky, 2014). It is possible that the best results for a pristine memory recall can be obtained by learning to keep quiet and allowing the child to take over in the

BEEN THERE . . . DONE THAT! 8-5

The interviewer needs to speak the language of the child. To allow children to get comfortable with anatomical dolls and to supply me with vocabulary to use during the interview, I would point to the eye, the nose, the chest, and so on of the doll. Each time I would ask, "What is this called?" Sometimes it is hard to keep from laughing; no positive or negative response should be given. Be prepared for anything. Wingy, dingy, Fred, flop, friend, mine, po, pet, and ping are among the many responses I have heard.

first open free-recall attempt. Although adult memory is not always accurate, we do not question adult recollections to the same extent as we question the memory of children. Always investigate for corroborating evidence in cases of child abuse. To minimize fantasy during a child interview, avoid using terms such as *pretend* or *imagine*.

THE CHILD AS VICTIM

There are numerous considerations when interviewing a child who is suspected of being a victim of abuse. The interview may uncover both direct and indirect forms of ill-treatment. An injury or a pattern of injuries that is nonaccidental characterizes direct child abuse. It is damage to a child for which no explanation is reasonable or fitting to the injuries that the child has sustained. Such abuse may take the form of emotional and psychological maltreatment, physical injury abuse, and sexual assault. Another form of direct maltreatment is considered passive: the action or inaction of a legally recognized caretaker who fails to fulfill his or her responsibility to a dependent child. These neglectful categories of abuse are becoming more familiar to criminal justice and social service agencies as they struggle to enforce an increasing number of child protection statutes. Examples of passive maltreatment are neglect, which may be physical or emotional; educational neglect; inadequate care in such areas as food, clothing, and shelter; lack of supervision; denial or the lack of medical care; nonsupport of a minor child; and parental kidnapping.

Two noted categories of secondary abuse are witnessing domestic violence and witnessing the homicide of a parent. Secondary abuse occurs as the consequence of residing in a violent home. Violence toward an intimate partner causes a variety of psychological problems for children and places them at greater risk for delinquency and adult criminality. Research has suggested that children subjected to repeated rates of violence have higher rates of trauma-related neurological symptoms, psychological symptoms, and developmental difficulties (Dudley, 2015). Although we cannot predict which children will become victims of abuse, those who reside in violent homes are at greater risk. When responding to calls of domestic abuse, an officer should interview all children living in the home. This type of interview is short. Questions should not be asked within sight of either parent. The initial question is, "Are you ok?" Watching for the response, the officer/interviewer will determine if he or she needs to sit down and talk in depth about the situation.

Victims can be found throughout society with no regard to age or gender. This does not mean that all children are victimized, but boys and girls of all ages can be victims. A child is defined as a person under the age of 18 years, except in those states that specify a younger age. Always interview the children in a home when responding to domestic violence.

Tools for Interviewing Children

The goal of the interview is for the child to describe his or her experience verbally. Of controversy is whether tools such as paper, markers, anatomically detailed drawings, or dolls may be used during the interview to assist in making descriptions. Interviewer comfort and multidisciplinary team preference may influence the use of tools during the

FIGURE 8-5   Here is an example of anatomically correct dolls used for interviews with children.

Source: Courtesy of Denise K. Gosselin.

interview (Newlin et al., 2015). The use of drawing may be helpful when interviewing any child younger than the age of 12 years and in some cases older children.

Anatomically correct dolls are a helpful tool for a variety of reasons. First, they help to establish the child's vocabulary so that you can use language that is understood by both of you. Dolls can also be utilized by the child to demonstrate what occurred. Caution should be exercised in using dolls in interviews with extremely young children with poorer cognitive and verbal abilities since they are at the greatest risk of being influenced by the use of recognition-based prompts (National Children's Advocacy Center, 2015).

Paper and crayons are essential tools to have available in all interview rooms. Use crayons to build rapport. Ask the child what his or her favorite color is; allow the child to use one crayon that he or she has chosen. This simple act gives some control to the child, acknowledges something of value to him or her, and establishes whether they know colors. Then the rest of the crayons may be put aside so that they do not become a distraction. Do not have glue, scissors, or toys available in the interview room that will provide an opportunity to avoid distressing topics. Drawings may be used to facilitate expression about what has happened to the child.

BOLSTERING CREDIBILITY THROUGH EVIDENCE

Credibility refers to the believability of the witness or victim. It is a major factor that must be established during an interview. Research has shown that child credibility is directly related to court outcomes (Johnson & Shelley, 2014). Higher credibility is positively associated with guilty verdicts. As a credibility assessment, the interviewer must consider whether the child can comprehend what is being said. How well is her or his observation of things? Can the person see well enough to describe events as he or she observed them? Does nonverbal behavior indicate possible deception? For states that do not have a predetermined age required to testify, credibility is established as part of the process of determining competency. Gathering physical evidence is a way to enhance the credibility of a child.

What should the interviewer search to bolster credibility? Anything. If a child describes being physically assaulted with any object, the investigator should seize that object. If the place is anywhere other than the child's residence, it might be photographed inside for comparison with the child's description of the area. When the victim reports sexual molestation, the subject of the search includes any area where tissues, towels, magazines, lubricants, or photos are kept by the alleged perpetrator.

If the child is severely injured or has died, the place of death must be searched to determine, if possible, whether the explanations for the injury are consistent with the environment.

There is no substitute for physical evidence to support the child's statement. When interviewing a child, any object that is involved with the crime that might later be seized with a legally obtained search warrant. Clarify during the interview the exact location and description of any possible evidence. Obtaining physical evidence for use in prosecution is helpful when the victim is an adult. For abuses against children, this is a critical part of the case. Merely presenting the word of a child against the word of an adult makes prosecutions more difficult. Seek a search warrant if the place of the event is exactly known and the alleged perpetrator has positively been identified.

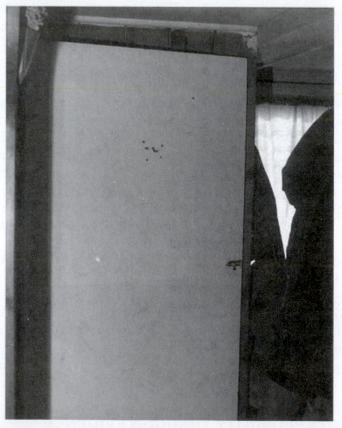

FIGURE 8-6 This is a picture of the door where Tim was made to stand while being shot at. Notice the bullet holes and the place where the Mickey Mouse picture had hung. Read on for the rest of the story!

Source: Courtesy of Denise K. Gosselin.

BEEN THERE . . . DONE THAT! 8-6

Nine-year-old Tim reported that mommy's boyfriend made him stand in front of Mickey Mouse while he shot Mickey. Tim stated that he thought he was *dead* when the bullets went so close to his head. When Virgil put the gun down Tim ran into the bedroom and jumped onto the bed. Virgil came after him and tried to break his head open with the end of the gun, but it hit the wall instead. A search warrant was obtained for Virgil's one-bedroom house. The wall next to the bed evidenced a hole that was consistent with the butt of a rifle. Small ammunitions and a handgun were retrieved in addition to a shotgun. As the search continued, a poster of Mickey Mouse was located between the mattresses. There were small holes that perfectly matched the ones found on the hall door. One hole was measured as being 1 inch higher than the height of Tim. The door was seized along with the other evidence. At trial, Tim's mother testified that Tim was a liar and had fabricated the assault. Nothing spoke louder than the poster of Mickey Mouse and the door riddled with bullet holes. The jury gasped when Tim was instructed by the prosecution to stand in front of Mickey Mouse, and they saw that the bullet holes aligned with his little body. Virgil was convicted.

DETERMINING COMPETENCY

During the investigation of suspected child abuse, the most likely source of information will come from the victim. Standing alone, eyewitness testimony is considered the least reliable form of evidence. Reliability issues compounded with the suggestibility of children and limited memory development heighten the need for methods to

FIGURE 8-7 Note the bullet holes on Mickey's face! This was the poster that was found during the search of the home where the assault in Been There ... Done That! 8-6 occurred. The poster was hidden under a mattress.

Source: Courtesy of Denise K. Gosselin.

improve child testimony. Studies have confirmed that children do have the ability to communicate reliability when questioned properly (Johnson, McWilliams, Goodman, Shelley, & Piper, 2016).

Competency is a preliminary question of law that a judge must decide before a witness is permitted to testify. One aspect of the determination hinges on whether the child can recall events, separate fact from fantasy, and maintain those memories independently without being influenced by others. There is no federal standard for determining competency. The 1974 Federal Rules of Evidence, which have been widely adopted by the states, abolished the competency rule for trial in federal courts. Rule 601 states, in part: Every person is competent to be a witness except as otherwise provided in this regulation. The dominant view of competency is that it is a matter to be decided on a case by case basis (Schetky, 2014).

Conclusions

This chapter began with a description of child development stages. Knowledge of the development stages is an essential foundation for conducting interviews with young children. Although all children do not develop in the same way, knowledge of child development can assist the interviewer to determine the best individual to conduct the interview. The chapter also provided some insight into the role of the criminal justice investigator in interviewing children during the field assessment.

Discussed is the risk assessment process, a requirement for professionals who are mandated to report situations when a child is suspected to be in danger of abuse or neglect. To help with the determination of the type of interview to conduct the preliminary considerations checklist is included. Remaining neutral is essential to interviewing without bias.

Forensic interviewing for children is outlined as an approach that is sensitive to child development and complies with legal requirements. While no one forensic interviewing method is universally accepted, some are emerging scientifically valid protocols. Forensic interviewing as an approach includes the establishment of rapport, open-ended questions, and prompting for a narrative. Among the methods that are scientifically validated are the Developmental Narrative Elaboration Interview (DNE) and the National Institute of Child Health and Human Development (NICHD protocol).

The cognitive child interviewing method is the most researched and accepted approach to investigative interviewing of children, modified from the adult version studied earlier in this text. The technique includes a three-step approach. Only recently has the "change the order" been viewed as problematic for younger children. Using this method as a tool-kit is one way to overcome challenges to its use with a particular population, however. The cognitive approach has been shown to provide more accurate information than other formats, but it is a lengthier method.

Issues specific to obtaining reliable and credible statements from children, given their suggestibility and immature cognitive development, is a topic of value. Investigative interviewing involves viewing the population through the lens of "the child as a reporter" and "the child as a victim." Recognizing that there is a difference between the reporter and victim can alert the interviewer to considerations, which need to be addressed during an investigation. Each perspective may include challenges to successful child interviewing. Interviewers may elect to use anatomically correct dolls or drawings as tools to facilitate communication.

Finally, the investigator must conduct interviews with an eye toward an assessment of the credibility of the child statement and therefore their competency of that child to testify in court. Credibility concerns the believability of the child statement. The way the interview is conducted influences the credibility of the statement. Competency speaks to the whether the child can testify in a way that involves an independent recall that is factual, and independent of outside influences.

Questions For Review

Short-Answer Questions

1. Do you think it is beneficial for investigative interviews to have knowledge of the four child development stages? Why or why not?

2. How would the interviewer use the preliminary considerations checklist?

3. What is the gold standard regarding the forensic interview?

4. How is the DNE different from the NICHD protocol?

5. Briefly, explain the cognitive child interviewing method.

Fill-in Questions

1. The determination of whether a crime has been committed and the development of admissible ____ are central to the criminal justice perspective.

2. ____ refer to the process of human development measured from infancy to adolescents, characterized by milestones of child development.

3. The 1974 Federal Rules of Evidence, which have been widely adopted by the states, abolished the ____ rule for trial in federal courts.

4. Assessing the present and future risk of harm to a child is more than just an indication about the investigator's level of caring, it is a legal requirement called ____.

5. The purpose of the interview is to determine the ____; this is done based on facts and evidence.

6. The ____ approach to child interviewing is used when primary victimization is suspected.

7. Immediately ____ to the interview have the guardian sign a prepared form of release to conduct and document the interview.

8. The interviewer should meet and greet the child in a ____ and comfortable manner.

9. The ____ is a forensic semistructured approach to interviewing children aged 4–12, developed by Saywitz and Camparo.

10. Widely accepted around the world, 20 translated versions of the ____ protocol are available for use.

Exercises

Practice your cognitive interviewing techniques. Divide into pairs. One student will be the interviewer and the other will be the interviewee.

1. The interviewer is to find out as much detail as possible about the interviewee's last experience in taking an exam. Instruct the interviewee on the **report everything** approach. Take 5 minutes for this mnemonic exercise.

2. The interviewers are asked to recall what they learned about their partner's last exam. Take 5 minutes for this discussion.

References

ACF. (2014). *Child and Family Services reviews case-related interview guides and instructions.* Washington, D.C.: U.S. Department of Health & Human Services.

Benneworth-Gray, K. (2014). "Are you going to tell me the truth today?" Invoking obligations of honesty in police–suspect interviews. *International Journal of Speech, Language & the Law, 21*(2), 251–277.

Brown, D. A., & Lamb, M. E. (2015). Can children be useful witnesses? It depends how they are questioned. *Child Development Perspectives, 9*(4), 250–255.

Brubacher, S. P., Poole, D. A., & Dickinson, J. J. (2015). The use of ground rules in investigative interviews with children: A synthesis and call for research. *Developmental Review, 36*, 15–33.

Child Welfare Information Gateway. (2016). *Mandatory reporters of child abuse and neglect.* Washington, D.C.: U.S. Department of Health and Human Services Retrieved from https://www.childwelfare .gov/pubPDFs/manda.pdf/manda/.

Dudley, R. (2015). *Childhood trauma and its effects: Implications for police.* (NCJ 248686). Washington, D.C.: National Institute of Justice.

Hershkowitz, I., Lamb, M. E., & Katz, C. (2014). Allegation rates in forensic child abuse investigations: Comparing the revised and standard NICHD protocols. *Psychology, Public Policy, and Law, 20*(3), 336.

Johnson, J., McWilliams, K., Goodman, G., Shelley, A., & Piper, B. (2016). Basic principles of interviewing the child eyewitness. In W. O'Donohue & M. Fanetti (Eds.), *Forensic interviews regarding child sexual abuse* (pp. 179–195). Switzerland: Springer.

Johnson, J. L., & Shelley, A. E. (2014). Effects of child interview tactics on prospective jurors' decisions. *Behavioral Sciences & the Law, 32*(6), 846–866.

Lyon, T. D. (2014). Interviewing children. *Annual Review of Law and Social Science, 10*, 73–89.

Lyon, T. D., Scurich, N., Choi, K., Handmaker, S., & Blank, R. (2012). "How did you feel?": Increasing child sexual abuse witnesses' production of evaluative information. *Law and Human Behavior, 36*(5), 448–457.

National Children's Advocacy Center. (2015). *Position paper on the use of human figure drawings in forensic interviews.* Huntsville, AL: Author.

Newlin, C., Steele, L., Chamberlin, A., Anderson, J., Kenniston, J., Russell, A., … Vaughan-Eden, V. (2015). *Child forensic interviewing: Best practices.* (NCJ 248749). Washington, D.C.: Office of Juvenile Justice and Delinquency Prevention.

NICHD. (2014). NICHD Protocol: *International Evidence-Based Investigative Interviewing of Child*ren. Retrieved from http://nichdprotocol.com/

Paulo, R. M., Albuquerque, P. B., & Bull, R. (2016). Improving the Enhanced Cognitive Interview With a New Interview Strategy: Category Clustering Recall. *Applied Cognitive Psychology, 30*(5), 775–784.

Saywitz, K. J., & Camparo, L. B. (2013). *Evidence-based child forensic interviewing: The developmental narrative elaboration interview.* New York, NY: Oxford University Press.

Saywitz, K., & Camparo, L. (2014). Interviewing children: A primer. In G. Melton, A. Ben-Arieh, J. Cashmore, G. Goodman, & N. Worley (Eds.), *The Sage handbook of child research* (pp. 371–390). Washington, DC: Sage.

Schetky, D. (2014). The child as witness. In D. Schetky & A. Green (Eds.), *Child sexual abuse: A handbook for health care and legal professionals* (pp. 166–180). New York, NY: Routledge.

Wolfman, M., Brown, D., & Jose, P. (2016). Talking past each other: Interviewer and child verbal exchanges in forensic interviews. *Law and Human Behavior, 40*(2), 107–117.

9

Interviewing Older Adults

Source: Courtesy of Denise K. Gosselin.

CHAPTER OBJECTIVES

After completing this chapter, you should be able to:

1. Explain the scope of elder abuse.
2. Define elder abuse.
3. Summarize five common categories of elder abuse.
4. Describe financial abuse.
5. Report the significance of the pre-interview.
6. Relate the concept of a multidisciplinary approach to elder crime.
7. Explain the five steps for conducting an interview with the older adult.
8. Relate the concept of a multidisciplinary approach to elder crime.

KEY TERMS

Conversation-observing
  evaluation
Elder abuse
Financial abuse

Mandatory reporting
Multidisciplinary teams
Polyvictimization
Source confusion

INTRODUCTION

Elder abuse is a serious problem in the United States. These crimes are highly underreported, so it is difficult to tell exactly how much occurs. There is a lack of data, but past research suggests that an estimated 1 in 10 older adults reports emotional, physical, sexual abuse, or other victimization each year. Compounding the problem of occurrence is that many older adults are afraid or unable to report to the police or other professionals. They may not know who to report to; they may be unable to report due to illness or isolation. It is also difficult to report to a stranger that they are being abused by a family member or caretaker whom they care about or depend on for care.

There is a growing awareness among professionals that older adults are targeted in significant numbers through scams by greedy individuals who prey on their frailty, vulnerability, or loneliness. Criminals sometimes identify their victims by old age and graying hair. Financial crimes are on the rise among this population whose numbers have swelled.

These cases present many challenges to the criminal justice community. Listening to the complaints of older citizens is time-consuming and often arduous. In the past, these crimes were largely handled by social services rather than law enforcement. Policy makers and researchers are now recognizing that the prevalence and financial costs of elder abuse are enormous (Taylor & Mulford, 2015). Protecting victims and holding offenders accountable *is* real police work, regardless of the victim's characteristics or relationship to the offender.

Demographic is the largest contributing factor to shifting policy concerning elder abuse and crime against older adults. No longer is the United States dominated by the youthful. The number of teenagers in the United States was surpassed by the number of seniors in 1983. Seniors are the fastest-growing segment of the population. According to the Federal Interagency Forum on Aging-Related Statistics (2016), the older population in 2030 is estimated to be twice as large as it was in 2000, representing almost 21 percent of the total U.S. population. More than 10,000 people turn 65 every day in the United States.

Along with this population explosion comes the shameful problem of abuse committed against older adults. Every year an estimated 4 million older adults are victims of physical, psychological, or other forms of abuse and neglect in the United States (APA, 2012). These high numbers exist despite the fact that 78 percent of people age 65 and over rate their health as good to excellent (Federal Interagency Forum on Aging-Related Statistics, 2016).

Past practices relied almost exclusively on interviewing elderly victims and dealing with their requests for prosecution of the perpetrator or leniency. This approach leaves the older adult vulnerable to further abuse. When prosecution is considered, the reliability of the victim due to infirmity places extraordinary importance on the victim interview. For these reasons, this chapter is broadened to include a general approach to crimes against older adults in addition to suggestions on interviewing. Legislative changes have amplified the role of the criminal justice community in cases involving crimes against the elderly.

CRIMES TARGETING THE OLDER ADULT

According to the National Institute of Health (2013), older adults are less likely to be victims of crime compared to young people. When targeted, they are victimized by robbery, purse snatching, pick-pocketing, car theft, or home repair scams. During a crime, older adults are more likely to be seriously injured than someone who is younger. While older Americans fear being victimized by strangers, most of the crime committed against them is elder abuse, committed by someone they know or love.

Elder Abuse

Elder abuse can occur in one or two living arrangements, either as domestic violence or institutional abuse. Most people that live in institutional settings have their physical and emotional needs met without experiencing abuse or neglect. On the other hand, approximately 95 percent of older Americans live alone, with a spouse, or with other family members (APA, 2012). The majority of elder abuse is domestic violence. When the perpetrator of elder abuse is a spouse or significant other, it is known as intimate partner violence. It is thought that for every case of elder abuse and neglect reported to authorities, about 23 more cases go unreported (APA, 2012). If that is the case, we have a huge problem!

State laws define **elder** by age, vulnerability-based, or a combination of age and vulnerability. For example, the *Older Americans Act of 1965* refers to any individual who is 60 years of age or older while the *American Medical Association* definition refers to "elderly persons" without reference to age. Age 65 is the more frequent defining characteristic for elder abuse, but this varies by state. New Jersey defines a vulnerable adult without specifically naming elders as a covered population (Jirik & Sanders, 2014). California, on the other hand, specifically names elders as a vulnerable group that is protected by law.

To guide prevention and response efforts, the Centers for Disease Control (CDC) recommends the use of uniform definitions for elder abuse due to the notable differences currently in use (Hall, Karch, & Crosby, 2016). The definition of what constitutes elder abuse also varies by organization and between states. The Department of Justice defines elder abuse as

> physical, sexual, or psychological abuse, as well as neglect, abandonment, and financial exploitation of an older person by another person or entity, that occurs in any setting (e.g., home, community, or facility), either in a relationship where there is an expectation of trust and/or when an older person is targeted based on age or disability.

Legislation and institutional definitions vary. It is important for an investigative interviewer to familiarize oneself with the illegal behaviors in their state, before interviewing with a suspected victim of abuse. There is no single pattern of ill-treatment. Elder **polyvictimization** is defined as an older adult experiencing two or more forms of abuse at the same time. It is not uncommon for multiple forms of abuse to be occurring at the same time. An estimated 30–40% of older adults experience poly-victimization by the same offender. Elder abuse falls into these five common categories:

- *Physical abuse* can range from hitting or slapping to severe beatings and physically restraining with ropes or chains. Look for patterned injuries such as a hand slap or bite marks and marks or scars around wrists, ankles, or neck. When serious medical injuries are suspected, it would be advisable to assist the elder in follow-up with medical evaluations.

- *Emotional/psychological abuse* can be verbal, emotional, or mental. Actions range from name calling to intimidating and threatening the person. Causing emotional distress occurs when a family member or caregiver behaves in a way that causes distress, which may include yelling or swearing. Psychological abuse includes coercive or threatening behaviors. Assure that the person is in a safe environment. Recommendations for counseling may be appropriate. Encourage the older person to accept services from elder abuse services, some of which will deliver to the home of the older adult.

- *Sexual abuse* ranges from sexual exhibition to rape. Sexual abuse includes inappropriate touching, photography, or forcing sexual contact with a third party. Forced sexual contact can occur if the older adult has not given consent or is incapable of giving consent because of physical or mental impairments. Sexual abuse is the most heinous of crimes, but it is also the least reported type of elder abuse. Physical and psychological effects can be traumatic and long-lasting. Shame and embarrassment over the loss of personal control can be devastating for an older person. Trauma-informed intervention is highly suggested in these situations.

- *Financial abuse* includes fraud, taking money under false pretenses, forgery, forced property transfers, buying items with the older persons' money, or denying the person access to his or her funds. Included is the improper use of legal guardianship, powers of attorney, the Internet, or face-to-face scams. Billions of dollars are lost each year to older adults who are unwittingly scammed and deceived. These crimes may be difficult to investigate. Many police departments have organized fiduciary crimes units to mobile responses to financial criminal abuse.

- *Caregiver neglect* can range from withholding the appropriate care unintentionally to intentionally denying care on the physical, medical, social, or emotional needs of the older person. Necessary care includes often needed aids such as eye glasses, dentures, and hearing aids; these are expensive. The day-to-day life of an older person may be improved with social service intervention.

BEEN THERE . . . DONE THAT! 9-1

In response to a call on stolen property, I went to the home of Mr. James, who was 82 years old. He stated that someone had stolen his wallet. He told me that he was in his barn putting blueberries in boxes when he realized the wallet was not in his back pocket. Because he sold blueberries from a street stand, Mr. James claimed any one of the people who bought berries that morning could have been a pickpocket. Before jumping to any conclusions, I asked Mr. James to retrace his steps with me. As we moved from the farm stand to the barn, I noticed a wallet lying on the ground. He said the wallet was in fact his. After checking its contents, he stated that nothing was missing. He was very embarrassed, so I assured him that it was no problem, and we shared a few blueberries. Was Mr. James' fear of being victimized by a pickpocket unrealistic? Had we not found the wallet, what would be the next step?

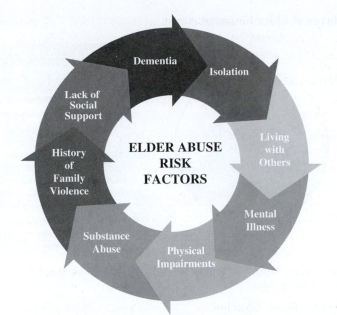

FIGURE 9-1   These eight conditions represent common risk factors for elder abuse.

At times, older adults harm themselves through self-neglect, which is the failure to provide for one's own essential needs. This is the most frequent form of elder abuse. Self-neglect is a noncriminal activity that might require intervention by criminal justice and social services systems on the older person's behalf. The investigator needs to ask questions that will determine whether the condition of the older adult is the result of self-neglect or is the consequence of criminal activity. Procedures that may be helpful in making this determination include the following:

✓ Interview neighbors and other witnesses to identify who might have relevant information and how they might be contacted.

✓ Identify and interview the victim's doctor, conservator, attorney, and social worker and any agencies that provide services to the victim.

✓ Ask the older adult who lives with them or makes visits.

✓ Look to see whether there are any ligature marks on the wrists or legs or around the neck of the victim that would indicate the use of restraints.

✓ Check to see whether the person has food available; ask whether someone prepares meals for him or her and determine who does the shopping.

✓ If the older person seems confused, determine with the aid of medical personnel whether the individual is being overmedicated or is suffering from mental impairment.

✓ If the abuse occurred in a residential care setting, interview the patients and staff to determine if someone witnessed it.

Financial Abuse

Studies suggest that financial abuse is the most commonly reported form of abuse against an older person (Acierno et al., 2010). **Financial abuse** is the financial exploitation or economic abuse of elders; it is the unjust, improper, and/or illegal use of another person's resources, property, and/or assets. Elder financial abuse is committed for profit or benefit of another and involves coercion, enticement, intimidation, or undue influence. Research estimates the loss due to financial abuse is at least 2.9 billion dollars a year, representing a 12 percent increase from 2008 (MetLife, 2011). Financial abuse or exploitation is recognized as a reportable form of elder abuse in all states and the District of Columbia (Hughes, 2003).

Types of Elder Financial Abuse

CRIMES OF OCCASION
Abuse that occurs because the victim is in the way of what the perpetrator wants

CRIMES OF DESPERATION
Family members or friends become so desperate for money they will do anything to get it

CRIMES OF PREDATION
Trust is established for the specific intention of financial abuse later

FIGURE 9-2   The MetLife study (2011) concluded that there are three types of elder financial abuse, illustrated here.

Source: Courtesy of Denise K. Gosselin.

Two categories of financial abuse are fraud committed by strangers and financial exploitation perpetrated by family members or caregivers. From the MetLife study (2011), we know that almost 60 percent of the instances are perpetrated by strangers, which makes this crime different than other forms of elder abuse. Medicare and Medicaid fraud constitutes only 4 percent of the instances but results in the highest average loss to victims (MetLife, 2011). These categories require different approaches by law enforcement and social services due to the different offender/victim relationship. In some states, there is a legal requirement that the older person suffers harm due to the financial abuse or that the perpetrator gain from the financial transaction.

An investigative interview should document how the elder was impacted because of the loss of assets. Women are twice as likely to be victims as men and almost 60 percent of perpetrators are men (MetLife, 2011). Although prosecution of financial elder abuse is rare, multidisciplinary teams may increase prosecution rates (DeLiema, Navarro, Moss, & Wilber, 2016).

LEGAL CONSIDERATIONS

Legal responses to addressing elder abuse vary considerably by state, as each is autonomous in creating its statutes. The autonomy has resulted in a patchwork of individually tailed laws that create difficulties for both elders and those who work to protect them (Jirik & Sanders, 2014). In a recent analysis of elder abuse statutes across the United States, Jirik & Sanders (2014) found that only eight states have laws specifically for seniors, 14 states protect both dependent adults and seniors, and 29 states have statutes for dependent adult abuse (which would include older adults if they meet the criteria). The majority of state statutes were found to honor self-determination; that the older adult could accept or refuse nonemergency protective services in the absence of a court order due to dementia or other specific reason.

Mandatory Elder Abuse Reporting

Crimes of abuse against older adults are acknowledged as underreported, despite the elder abuse reporting mandates. A significant barrier to the identification of elder abuse is the failure to be suspicious unless almost certain evidence is encountered (Fisher, Rudd,

Walker, & Stewart, 2016). **Mandatory reporting** statutes are laws that require certain groups of people to relay reasonable suspicions of elder abuse to designated authorities. In 47 states and the District of Columbia reporting of elder abuse is mandated by statute (Jirik & Sanders, 2014). The majority of states specify the list of professionals required to report and a penalty for those who fail to do so.

There is no consistency in the reporting guidelines and definitions. The majority of the states and territories specifically name health care professionals, such as licensed and registered nurses, physicians, and nurse aides, as mandated reporters of elder/adult abuse. Police officers are among those commonly named as mandated reporters of elder abuse. The Fisher et al. study (2016) highlighted the important fact that professionals rarely identify elder abuse because they do not look for it as an explanation for an older person's injury or discomfort.

Banks are thought of as the first line of defense since they are in the position to observe and report suspicious behaviors. To induce bank officials to fulfill their critical role in preventing the financial abuse of older adults, some states have revised their statutes naming them as mandated reporters. Other jurisdictions have resisted efforts to require personnel to report suspected financial abuse and have opted instead to cooperatively work with law enforcement on "bank reporting projects" (Hughes, 2003). Common indicators of financial abuse include the following:

- Uncharacteristic bank activity.
- Suspicious activity on the person's credit card accounts.
- Frequent or unauthorized use of the person's ATM card.
- Interviewing

THE OLDER PERSON

The priority of the crisis responder is to identify the victim and render first aid if needed. Once an older person is stabilized and safe, everyone at the scene should be separated and interviewed. The interview with the victim should recorded whenever possible. Digital recording serves to document the abuse and the condition of the victim at the time of the offense. The recording serves to preserve the evidence if a prosecution determination is made that does not include the victim testimony. Photographs of injuries and living conditions of the elder should be taken for documentation as necessary.

When investigating complaints of crime committed against the elderly, the interview process is similar to the approach adopted with any other population. Using a trauma-informed interviewing method may be an additional precaution. Experts also suggest the use of the *Cognitive Interviewing Method* (described in previous chapters) to assist older adults with memory retrieval and reduce misinformation effects (Holliday et al., 2012). An assessment of the older person should be made before the actual interview. Go slow and be patient! As you will see, this is a lengthy process. The assessment of an older adult is performed during a preinterview step.

The Preinterview

The initial recommended step is a preinterview to make an assessment. The **conversation-observing evaluation** is an approach to assessing an older adult through direct observation, to identify the limitations of the interviewee as well as the nature of the offense. The evaluation should not be biased by the opinion of individuals who care for the person or those who have a relationship with that person. Except for a police officer or social service worker observer, no one should be present besides the older adult and the interviewer.

Although a determination must be made of the extent of victim participation that can be expected, the mental or physical status of the abused does not dictate the failure or success of any investigation. Medical and physical evidence in addition to witness statements and expert testimony should be considered in all cases, and particularly those that involve vulnerable victims.

- Begin this phase without preconceived ideas on the ability of the victim to testify or about the nature of the offenses. Health concerns need to be identified but are not the primary consideration in the investigation of crimes against the elderly.
- Speak with the person at the place where he or she is most comfortable. For most seniors, this will be the place where they live. The situation may dictate that this preinterview be held in a hospital room or an alternate safe place. The interviewee should be as comfortable as possible.
- Think of this stage as a "friendly visit." Avoid making statements that are judgmental. Have a cup of coffee and talk—at the same time remaining alert to behavioral indicators displayed by the victim. This is not the time to delve into specifics of alleged abuse or neglect.
- Put yourself at the same level as the interviewee, asking the victim where he or she wants you to sit.
- Place yourself face front to the person so that you can observe him or her and where the person can also see your face clearly. It is not unusual for an older person who needs a hearing aid will not be wearing one! Do not chew gum while attempting an interview.
- Refrain from taking notes before asking permission to do so.
- Introduce yourself and state your purpose generally. For example, "My name is Denise Gosselin, I am a police officer. I have been asked to come and talk with you today. Is that okay?"
- Ask the person for his or her full name, even if you already have that information. Refer to the person by her or his title—Miss, Mrs., Mr., Dr., and so on.

At this point it should be obvious whether the interviewee is having difficulty communicating. Evaluate the ability of the person to answer simple questions. Look for signs that she or he is having difficulty hearing or seeing you. Does the person lean forward toward you? Does he or she tend to look at your lips when you speak? If you notice problems, ask the person whether he or she needs an ancillary device such as a hearing aid.

During this stage, you have been gathering information on the living conditions of the victim and his or her personal relationships. You should be gradually coming to an assessment of the individual, the ability of the person to relate information, and his or her overall ability to communicate. If the victim's skills are within the normal to high range, and seemingly accurate information is being related, then using the traditional methods of acquiring the needed information might be the best approach. If the individual appears to be confused or has difficulty remembering events, the *Cognitive Interviewing Method* may be the interviewing choice. When the questioning appears to be difficult due to a mental illness (including Alzheimer's disease), a multidisciplinary team approach might offer the best interviewing alternative. If the person is unable to relate any information that could be considered credible or has died, the investigator must rely on collecting sufficient evidence in the event that prosecution could take place without the victim's testimony.

Encourage the elder person to talk about himself or herself, and comment in ways that promote discussion. During the conversation, the following points should be covered, but the questions are not asked in a traditional interview format:

1. "How are you feeling today?" This question helps to determine what physical conditions and limitations if any exist. If the conversation turns to illness, ask whether the person needs medication for the condition. If the answer is yes, ask

FIGURE 9-3   During the preinterview, an assessment is made using a conversation-observing evaluation approach.

Source: Logoboom/Shutterstock.

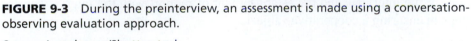

how often it is necessary and whether the person takes it regularly. Does the person take the medication himself or herself, or does someone give it to them to take? Determine how much and how often the interviewee drinks alcoholic beverages on a daily basis, and document the preferred drink.

2. "How old are you?" Encourage the person with positive comments regarding age. Use the information to facilitate conversation about the individual's ability to hear, see, and walk. Determine what forms of aid the individual needs, if any. Although the person's physical condition may seem apparent, the investigator should still talk about the person's strengths and weaknesses.

3. "How long have you lived here?" "Is this your house?" These questions help to determine whether a dependency exists concerning the living arrangements. Listen for indications that "*it used to be my house*, but …." Determine whether the person is financially dependent on another person.

4. "Do you live here by yourself?" Ask this even if it seems apparent. Clarify whether anyone lives temporarily with the person such as a family member or friend. Look for signs of discomfort when an older person is talking about family or friends that spend time with him or her. How isolated is this person? What are their social supports?

5. "Do you live with your husband (or wife)?" "How does your spouse treat you?" Be particularly aware of anxiety or discomfort when discussing a spouse. If the individual begins to offer excuses, such as "I am so difficult to take care of" or "He doesn't mean to take it out on me," listen and be patient. Do not attempt to be friendly by adding to or acknowledging the validity of statements regarding behaviors. Try to learn as much as possible about the dynamics of the relationship. Remember that either or both individuals may be the abuser in the relationships of older adults.

6. "Excuse me for prying, but may I ask if you have a retirement pension or receive Social Security?" "Are you doing okay financially?" "Have you made any financial arrangements with someone to take care of you?" Attempt to get a sense of the anxiety level associated with the financial situation of the person. Is there a fear that his or her money will be depleted? What is the source of that fear?

7. "Is there anyone who helps you out with your daily living?" Identify who the individuals are that occupy a caretaking role and the relationship between the person and the caregiver. "Do you pay this person?" "Do they ask for money or gifts?" Does the older person have reasonable expectations on the extent of care that they receive?

If evidence of abuse is discovered and the perpetrator is defined as having a domestic relationship to the victim, such as a spouse, former spouse, child, parent, or live-in person, then you should proceed according to your department policy for domestic violence. Mandatory and preferred arrest policies do not have exceptions even when the victim is an older person. Financial abuse, physical or sexual abuse, intimidation, and threats are domestic violence offenses when the perpetrator is in a domestic relationship. There are no exclusions for police action in cases of domestic violence that are based on age or infirmity. On the contrary, in many jurisdictions if a victim is an older adult, the crime penalties are enhanced.

CONDUCTING THE INTERVIEW

The steps in interviewing the victim are similar to those with other populations. Preparation for the interview and the establishment of rapport with the interviewee are critical steps in ensuring a cooperative subject.

Step 1: Preparing for the Interview

Prepare for the interview by choosing a quiet location that is free of distractions and noise. Get as much information on the suspect as possible, including prior arrests and commitments. Speak with the victim's neighbors and service providers before the interview

BEEN THERE . . . DONE THAT! 9-2

A female resident of a nursing home in her early eighties was refusing to eat. She had instructed the staff not to be fed intravenously. On investigation, it was determined that she was not physically impaired and had no history or indication of mental illness. There was no history of prior abuse. In conversation, she stated that her only daughter had abandoned her. The daughter had gone on vacation with her husband. I asked the woman if she was aware of the consequences of not eating; she stated, "Yes." She then asked, "Why is it taking so long [to die]?" I told her that she was not sick and only needed food. The woman replied that she knew what she is doing and that she did not want to be fed. This extreme form of manipulation called the "hunger strike" is documented through case examples (Duggal & Lawrence, 2001). In this example, the woman was angry at her daughter for having gone away on a vacation.

with the victim to determine their impression of the medical and cognitive status of the interviewee and the suspect, if one is known.

Step 2: Establishing Rapport

One of the most important ways to establish rapport with an older adult is through respect. Avoid treating the person as if he or she were a child. Explain your role and what the interviewee might expect during the investigation into the allegations.

Step 3: Conducting the Interview

Begin the interview by using nonleading questions. Avoid asking questions that require a yes or no response. Keep questions short and to the point. Use language that is easily understood but not patronizing. Questions should be open-ended to encourage conversation.

If the interviewee is having difficulty remembering when events took place, it may help to relate them to normal daily activities such as eating or watching television. Allow the victim to relate the crime in his or her own words. Avoid the tendency to make suggestions if the person seems slow in responding; some seniors need extra time to collect their thoughts. Encourage the older person to draw pictures to describe abuse or to write down answers if necessary.

Determine whether anyone else was present when the offender arrived. Did anyone witness the abuse? Ask the older person whether she or he knows the person who did "this." Address any fears that the individual has about discussing the incident and reporting it to the police or social service agency. Avoid your natural tendency to react when a victim gives information regarding any crime committed against them. Remain professional and empathetic to any abuse.

Ask the person what they believe the suspect will say about the allegations. The interviewer can anticipate some of the following possible scenarios (Morris, 1999):

- Has the victim been told by the suspect that it was an accident (and apologized), a normal part of aging, or a figment of the confused person's mind? [physical abuse case]
- Has the victim been told by the suspect that what happened is what the elder wanted, that it was an accident, that there was no money for medicine (eyeglasses or food for example), or that the suspect was a stressed caregiver? [neglect elder abuse case]
- The defense will center on consent or on an argument that the event never occurred. [sexual abuse]
- Has the victim been told by the suspect that "it was a gift" (and the elder does not remember it) or that "it was my inheritance" or "you loaned it to me"? [financial/fiduciary abuse]

Look for all of the above possible defenses when discussing the allegations and the victim's perceptions of what the suspect may have relayed to the victim. Such perceptions may be very revealing.

Step 4: Ending the Interview

Address any objections concerning family members. An older adult may be reluctant to permit charges to be brought against a loved one, particularly if he or she is dependent on that person. Explain that decisions regarding the criminal charging of anyone will be left to the district attorney. Advise the person that you are mandated to report suspected abuse or neglect to elder services and that he or she might expect to be contacted by someone who can address his or her needs.

Step 5: Following Up

After the interview, referrals to other agencies should be made, if warranted. Examples of referrals include a report to a state-mandated elder abuse hotline or social services. When an injury to the elder was noted, a future interview should be scheduled to document the abuse. Documentation of an injury may necessitate photographing it days after the initial response, when bruises and marks are more prominently visible.

EMPOWERING THE OLDER VICTIM

Laws specifically protecting vulnerable adults have been enacted across the country. Legislation devised specifically for intervention in cases where in which elderly individuals are unable to protect themselves against fraud, financial abuse, and personal violence should be used wherever possible. Procedures have evolved for investigating cases involving the elderly that center around the empowerment of this population to increase the chances of successful prosecution. When interviewing older victims, respect and deference should always be a consideration.

Advocates suggest providing education and enhancing the level of safety awareness and security planning for the elderly (National Crime Prevention Council, 2017). Fear of crime among some older adults is disproportionate to actual victimization. Even a minor crime, however, can leave older adults feeling vulnerable, leading to isolation and depression. Educate older Americans about the measures they can take to reduce their risk of abuse and the resources that are available to them.

In all cases, victim safety must be the primary consideration, just as it is in all other criminal investigations. Legal provisions and mandated arrest policies that exist for victims of domestic violence must be used regardless of the age of the victim or the alleged perpetrator. If the victim is overly concerned with prosecution, the reasons should be explored and, if possible, discussed with a multidisciplinary team for a final determination. When the objections of the elderly victim involve fear of isolation or loss of a caretaker, then his or her needs for services must be in place before a prosecution.

OLDER ADULTS AS WITNESSES

Sexual predators, drug abusers, and thieves may approach an older adult they view as being vulnerable. Conmen and greedy caretakers target people who are perceived as being needy. Although the likelihood of being afflicted with intellectual deterioration known as dementia or senility increases with age, it is not considered part of the normal aging process. The Office for Victims of Victims of Crime (OVC, 2010) suggests that it is false to assume that older persons have any disability! An interviewer can expect that most older adults are capable of giving accurate and reliable information regarding victimization.

BEEN THERE . . . DONE THAT! 9-3

According to a report from the home health aide who visited Mrs. Jane at her home, the 90-year-old woman claimed that she had been sexually abused by her son. Mrs. Jane was complaining about being hurt "down there." She was believed to have dementia. The aide thought that because the victim could not testify in court, there was no case. Was she right? What were the options?

Physical Limitations

A factor to consider when interviewing the elderly is the extent of substance abuse within this population. Considered an invisible epidemic, substance abuse and prescription drug misuse are common problems among older adults. Research has found that illicit substance abuse among older adults has been incorrectly assumed to end as patients age (Taylor & Grossberg, 2012). An older adult may be overly reliant on drugs or alcohol due to changes that come naturally with aging. Remember that the responsibility for victimization or perpetration does not center on substance abuse, it is only a factor to be identified for appropriate referral and intervention.

Geriatric schizophrenia and bipolar disorder are major causes of disability among older adults (Hahn, Lim, & Lee, 2014). Old age bipolar disease (individuals over 60 years old) represents as much as 25 percent of the population with bipolar disease (Sajatovic et al., 2015). Compared to men, senior women who are socially isolated and have hearing impairments are at greater risk of contracting late-onset schizophrenia. Characterized by hallucinations and delusions, this mental disease was once thought to only affect individuals with onset before age 45. The disease can be treated successfully; therefore, a medical referral is an absolute necessity if this is suspected.

FIGURE 9-4   The majority of older adults can provide accurate statements about victimization.

Source: Arvind Balaraman/Shutterstock.

Normal changes due to aging include visual and hearing loss. Visual acuity may interfere with distant identifications and descriptions of strangers but is not significant when the perpetrator is known to the individual. Older persons commonly lose the ability to hear high frequencies and experience hypersensitivity to loud sounds. In questioning seniors, the Office for Victims of Crime (2012) suggests keeping in mind that it is easier for an older person to understand a man than a woman because the pitch of male voices is usually lower than that of women. Individuals with hearing loss often compensate by lip reading and viewing facial expressions. The individual may have a hearing aid that is not working properly or is not worn at the time of the interview. If the interviewee is having difficulties with understanding, ask if he or she has communication devices that can assist.

The following should be considered when interviewing older persons:

- Schedule the interview for mid-morning, a time when the victim is most likely to be at her or his best.
- Refer persons for medical screening when substance abuse is suspected.
- Ask the interviewee if he or she is having difficulty in hearing, but do not assume that this is the case.
- Many elderly persons elect not to wear their hearing aid at all times; ask the person whether he or she has a hearing aid when it appears that hearing is an issue.
- Avoid speaking loudly to an older adult as a way to compensate for a perceived hearing deficiency.
- Position yourself directly in front of the interviewee because he or she may compensate for hearing loss by concentrating on lip movements and facial expressions.
- Establish eye contact with the interviewee before speaking.
- Avoid covering your mouth, chewing gum, or smoking during the interview.
- Do not speak too quickly.
- Eliminate background noise as much as possible.
- Use visual aids such as drawings and diagrams when possible.
- Male interviewers may be a preferred option.

BEEN THERE . . . DONE THAT! 9-4

The largest investigation that I participated in involved the interviewing of over 100 children suspected to have been raped and sexually abused through a multigenerational sex ring. Working together with the local police department and the department of social services, we identified some of the offenders and obtained evidence against them. The sexual crimes against the children were worst possible you can imagine. Some were crimes of incest, but the men were indiscriminate pedophiles. Young boys and girls were the victims, sometimes having been forced to perform sex acts with the other while the offenders watched. Every child I interviewed provided me with the names of other children who were involved.

The oldest person I arrested in the case was a 72-year-old man. Looking extremely frail and pathetic, he was brought before the court after his arrest. I also arrested his 36-year-old son and 15-year-old grandson as offenders in the sex ring. The charges were dismissed, and the prosecutor admonished me for bringing in an old man. I arrested him again on charges concerning more children whom he had raped. His tools had been hot, sharp objects. The second arrest netted a weekend in jail before an agreement of probation was secured. The man was a monster living among us, just an old one.

Cognitive Impairment

The risk of elder abuse varies significantly according to individual conditions, generally increasing as a persons' cognitive abilities decline (Roberto, 2016). Capacity to learn and remember is expected to change as some people age. This means the elderly may take longer to recall or process information. Memory-jogging techniques may enhance the recall for older victims. Questions such as "Were you eating dinner when he came?" and "What were you watching on television when he came?" are examples. Practice patience by allowing the older adult the time she or he needs to answer a question.

There is a growing amount of contradictory literature looking at the vulnerability of the elderly to source confusion. **Source confusion** is the difficulty in distinguishing what has been personally witnessed from what may have been heard from someone else, or a problem identifying the exact source of information. The introduction of misinformation has been thought to impair the reliability of statements taken from the elderly and cause source confusion. Researchers have concluded that no clear evidence exists to suggest an age-related vulnerability to misinformation (Memon, Gabert, & Hope, 2004). Each being interviewed must be evaluated independently regarding the reliability of the statement, without age bias. These same researchers suggest that the elderly frequently recall fewer correct details of an eyewitness event than younger adults. Also, the elderly are consistently more prone to making false identifications from lineups, and individuals older than 60 years are more likely to raise a "false alarm" to a new face. In other words, they are more likely to recognize a face they had not seen previously falsely. In the eye-witness identification setting, the elderly may be more prone to making false choices and providing fewer descriptions of the perpetrator (physical characteristics, clothing, etc.).

Concerns due to Dependence

A strong reliance on family and friends for assistance may be the reality for senior citizens. In some but not all situations, loneliness, frailty, and medical conditions may cause the older person to view the perpetrator as being nonetheless his or her only hope for an improved lifestyle. Because the most common abusers of the older person are their adult children (Lachs & Pillemer, 2015), a common risk factor exists when the caretaker is financially dependent on the older person. Dysfunctional family interaction before the onset of old age is likely to continue as the members get older unless

FIGURE 9-5 When abuse of an older adult is suspected, the police and other professionals are required by law to make a report to the designated authorities.

Source: Ollyy/Shutterstock.

intervention occurs. Consider the attitude of the elderly person: does he or she have an overly demanding attitude or unrealistic expectations of the caregiver?

When the suspect provides care or services to the older person, the exact nature of the care should be determined. An interview with the suspect should document the following circumstances:

- Based on the condition of the person, does it appear that the caregiver has been reluctant to supply him or her with eyeglasses, dental care, medications, or other needed services?
- When bedsores or incontinence exist, is the care being provided sufficient to meet the needs of the person?
- Are the services or care provided under a contract with specified payments?
- How are these payments made?
- Are cash payments provided by the person or requested by the service provider?
- Has the suspect accepted personal gifts from the victim? If so, what is the approximate value of those gifts?
- Is the caregiver frustrated or angry due to the responsibilities associated with the providing services to the person?

ELDER ABUSE MULTIDISCIPLINARY TEAM APPROACH

The Elder Justice Act (EJA) was passed in 2010 as part of the *Patient Protection and Affordable Care Act.* Among the objectives of the Act are to provide federal support for training, research, and grants that prevent elder abuse and improve agency response when elder abuse is reported. The EJA also calls for the establishment of elder abuse forensic centers, which involve multidisciplinary teams. Multidisciplinary teams (MDT) composed of professionals from law enforcement, adult protective services, mental health agencies, the public guardian's office, and public health agencies represent one example.

The multidisciplinary team approach to investigative elder abuse is only recently gaining widespread acceptance. The *Elder Justice Initiative* is a national government initiative, which provides tools, resource materials, and consultations to facilitate the expansion of elder abuse case review multidisciplinary teams across the United States (EJI, nd). Among the resources offered are a Multidisciplinary Team Technical Assistance Center (MDT TAC) and tool-kit. The *Elder Justice Initiative* (EJI) defines

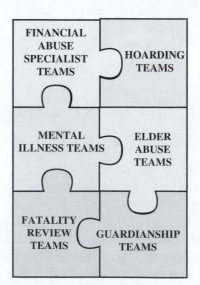

FIGURE 9-6 Types of problems addressed by multidisciplinary teams is illustrated here.

multidisciplinary team as a group of people (made of representatives from three or more disciplines who work collaboratively), bound by a common purpose and characterized by these five elements (Jackson, 2016):

1. Shared decision making—the entire team participates in the decision making
2. Partnership—characterized by a formal Memorandum of Understanding or Interagency Agreement
3. Interdependency—group and individual outcomes are influenced by the team
4. Balanced power—all members have equal input
5. Process—requires the development and use of protocols to introduce predictability and accountability into the case review process

Criminal justice agencies work with a variety of organizations to identify cases of suspected elder abuse and to gather evidence for the prosecution of the perpetrators. Many states require that reports concerning elder abuse be made to adult protective services, not the police. The EJA recommends that investigations should be coordinated with adult protective services personnel or the ombudsman whenever possible to establish cooperative models of intervention. Teams of fiduciary abuse specialists are specially trained to work with bank officials in documenting a paper trail indicative of fiduciary abuse.

Conclusions

This chapter introduced a pre-interview step entitled the *conversation-observing approach*. This initial phase of interviewing an older adult is used to assess the individual and learn as much as possible about the conditions under which he or she lives. The phase also provides sufficient information to determine whether a specific interviewing format should be considered in the future. Some elderly persons will present with physical or mental impairments that hinder investigations. Awareness of the signs and symptoms of common afflictions increases the opportunity for successful evidence gathering. Most seniors are capable of providing the information to needed document the criminal event.

Crimes against the elderly, however, may be complicated by the family relationship between the victim and the perpetrator. Law enforcement should be guided by existing legal responsibilities, mandates, department policy, and procedures in handling domestic violence cases. A multidisciplinary team approach is recommended for cases requiring special investigations.

Questions for Review

Short-Answer Questions

1. How has changing demographics of the elderly population shifted policy?
2. What are the five common categories of elder abuse?
3. Name eight elder abuse risk factors.
4. What are the five steps to interviewing older adults?
5. Describe the multidisciplinary team approach.

Fill-in Questions and Answers

1. An estimated one in _____ older adults report emotional, physical, sexual abuse, or other victimization each year.
2. The majority of elder abuse is _____ violence.
3. It is thought that for every case of elder abuse and neglect reported to authorities, about _____ more cases go unreported.
4. Five common categories of elder abuse are physical, emotional/psychological, sexual, financial, and _____.
5. Studies suggest that _____ abuse is the most commonly reported form of abuse against an older person.
6. _____ statutes are laws that require certain groups of people to relay reasonable suspicions of elder abuse to designated authorities.
7. The _____ evaluation is an approach to assessing an older adult through direct observation, to identify the limitations of the interviewee as well as the nature of the offense.

8. Considered an invisible epidemic, ____ and prescription drug misuse use are common problems among older adults.

9. The risk of elder abuse varies significantly according to individual conditions, generally increasing as a persons' ____ abilities decline.

10. ____ is the difficulty in distinguishing what has been personally witnessed from what may have been heard from someone else, or a problem identifying the exact source of the information.

Exercises

1. Interview a person of age 65 years or older. The person can be a relative, a neighbor, or someone who works on campus. The topic of the interview is whether the person has ever been the victim of a crime. If the subject has never been the victim of a crime, an alternate topic is whether they have been in a car accident or stopped by the police since turning age 60. Using the steps outlined in this chapter on interviewing the elderly, conduct a pre-interview and then follow each of the steps except for the follow-up. Write a report on the assessment and facts.

2. The National Association of Triads is a partnership of three organizations—law enforcement, older adults, and community groups. Learn about the Triad and report to the class! Go to http://www.sheriffs.org/frequent -questions.

References

Acierno, R., Hernandez, M. A., Amstadter, A. B., Resnick, H. S., Steve, K., Muzzy, W., & Kilpatrick, D. G. (2010). Prevalence and correlates of emotional, physical, sexual, and financial abuse and potential neglect in the United States: The National Elder Mistreatment Study. *American Journal of Public Health, 100*(2), 292–297.

APA. (2012). Elder abuse & neglect: In search of solutions. Washington, D.C.: Author.

DeLiema, M., Navarro, A., Moss, M., & Wilber, K. (2016). Prosecutors' perspectives on elder justice using an Elder Abuse Forensic Center. *American Journal of Criminal Justice, 41*(4).

Duggal, A., & Lawrence, R. M. (2001). Aspects of food refusal in the elderly: The "hunger strike." *International Journal of Eating Disorders, 30*, 213–216.

EJI. (nd). *Elder Justice Initiative*. Retrieved from https://www.justice.gov/elderjustice

Federal Interagency Forum on Aging-Related Statistics. (2016). *Older Americans 2016: Key Indicators of Well-Being*. Washington, D.C.: U.S. Government Printing Office.

Fisher, J. M., Rudd, M. P., Walker, R. W., & Stewart, J. (2016). Training tomorrow's doctors to safeguard the patients of today: Using medical student simulation training to explore barriers to recognition of elder abuse. *Journal of the American Geriatrics Society, 64*(1), 168–173.

Hahn, C., Lim, H. K., & Lee, C. U. (2014). Neuroimaging findings in late-onset schizophrenia and bipolar disorder. *Journal of Geriatric Psychiatry and Neurology, 27*(1), 56–62.

Hall, J., Karch, D., & Crosby, A. (2016). *Elder abuse surveillance: Uniform definitions and recommended core data elements*. Atlanta, GA: National Center for Injury Prevention and Control, Centers for Disease Control and Prevention.

Holliday, R. E., Humphries, J. E., Milne, R., Memon, A., Houlder, L., Lyons, A., & Bull, R. (2012). Reducing misinformation effects in older adults with cognitive interview mnemonics. *Psychology and Aging, 27*(4), 1191.

Hughes, S. (2003). Can bank tellers tell? Legal issues related to banks reporting financial abuse of the elderly. *American Bar Association*. Retrieved from https://www.americanbar.org/groups/law_aging/resources/elder_abuse.html#banksreporting.

Jackson, S. (2016). *Developing an Elder Abuse Case Review Multidisciplinary Team in your Community*. Washington, D.C.: U.S. Department of Justice.

Jirik, S., & Sanders, S. (2014). Analysis of Elder Abuse Statutes across the United States, 2011–2012. *Journal of Gerontological Social Work, 57*(5), 478–497.

Lachs, M. S., & Pillemer, K. A. (2015). Elder abuse. *New England Journal of Medicine, 373*(20), 1947–1956.

Memon, A., Gabert, F., & Hope, L. (2004). The aging eyewitness. In J. Adler (Ed.), *Forensic psychology: Concepts, debates, and practice* (pp. 96–112). Portland, OR: Willian Publishing.

MetLife. (2011). *The MetLife study of elder financial abuse: Crimes of occasion, desperation, and predation against America's elder*. Retrieved from https://www.metlife.com/mmi/research/elder-financial-abuse.html#key_findings.

Morris, D. J. (1999). Interviewing cognitively impaired victims. *Prosecutors Brief: The California District Attorneys Association's Quarterly Journal, XXI*(2), 11–12, 41–45.

National Crime Prevention Council. (2017). *Crimes against seniors*. Retrieved from http://www.ncpc.org/topics/crime-against-seniors/

NIH. (2013). *Crime and Older People*. Washington, D.C.: National Institute of Aging.

OVC. (2012). *Elder abuse*. Washington, D.C.: U.S. Department of Justice.

OVC. (2010). *First response to victims of crime*. Washington, D.C.: U.S. Department of Justice.

Roberto, K. A. (2016). The complexities of elder abuse. *American Psychologist, 71*(4), 302–311.

Sajatovic, M., Strejilevich, S. A., Gildengers, A. G., Dols, A., Al Jurdi, R. K., Forester, B. P., … Shulman, K. I. (2015). A report on older-age bipolar disorder from the International Society for Bipolar Disorders Task Force. *Bipolar Disorders, 17*(7), 689–704.

Taylor, M. H., & Grossberg, G. T. (2012). The growing problem of illicit substance abuse in the elderly: A review. *The Primary Care Companion for CNS Disorders, 14*(4), PCC.11r01320.

Taylor, T., & Mulford, C. (2015). Evaluating the Los Angeles County Elder Abuse Forensic Center. *NIJ Journal, 276*, 32–37.

10

Interviewing Persons with Disabilities and Mental Illness

Source: Adam Gregor/Shutterstock.

CHAPTER OBJECTIVES

After completing this chapter, you should be able to:

1. State the six applications of the ADA to policing.

2. Illustrate how the Court interpreted the term *arrest* for cases that allege violations of the ADA.

3. Summarize what effective communication with individuals having disabilities means under the ADA.

4. Explain the term *intellectual disability* and its significance among the prisoner population.

5. Define the term *mental disorder*.

6. Describe the three steps of the interview process.

7. Analyze the considerations for interrogating potentially vulnerable persons.

8. Assess the concern regarding false confessions for individuals with intellectual disability.

KEY TERMS

Anosognosia

Appropriate adult

Bipolar disorder

Cognitive disability

Intellectual disability

Mental disorder

Personality disorders

Schizophrenia

INTRODUCTION

This chapter provides a discussion of issues that affect the practice of interviewing persons with physical, cognitive, and communication impairments and those with mental illness. Changes in legal codes governing patient rights that affirmed the right of individuals with mental illness to live in the community and deinstitutionalization in the 1960s set the stage for increased criminal justice involvement of this population. An estimated 12.6 percent of noninstitutionalized Americans live with a wide variety of physical, cognitive, and emotional disabilities (Erickson, Lee, & Schrader, 2017). This community is more vulnerable to victimization as compared to those without disability or mental disorder.

Impaired individuals are at a higher risk for violent victimization, at a rate that is twice that of individuals without a disability. The number of children from birth to age 14 that experience moderate or severe disability is estimated to be 93 million worldwide by the *World Health Organization* (WHO). WHO cautions that while this estimate is widely used, it is considered an underestimation. Violence against children with disabilities occurs at annual rates at least 1.7 times greater than for their nondisabled peers per the Convention on the Rights of Persons with Disabilities (UN, 2006).

Adding to the newly recognized dilemma of protecting those with disabilities are conflicting studies on the incidence of crime perpetrated by individuals who have a mental illness. Researchers estimate that police encounter a person with mental disorders on average four to six times per month and may be as high as 110 times per month (Cordner, 2006; Kerr, Morabito, & Watson, 2010). Upwards of 7 percent of police contacts in jurisdictions with a population of 100,000 or more involve persons with mental disorders, impacting over 90 percent of patrol officers (Cordner, 2006). Calls to police that are related to mental illness outnumber calls for routine larceny, traffic accidents, and domestic disputes combined (Biasotti, 2011).

The debate regarding the role of the police in dealing with persons having disabilities is intense. Once again, law enforcement is being tasked with policing social problems that often pose often insurmountable challenges. Still, the duty already has been assigned; it is time to meet it head-on. This chapter is intended to aid the criminal justice professional to meet the increased needs of communicating with the impaired community.

THE AMERICANS WITH DISABILITIES ACT

Given the increasing likelihood of police encounters with persons who are disabled, training in effective communications with individuals in this community has taken on greater significance. The *Americans with Disabilities Act* (ADA) is a legislative mandate to provide equal protection and access to government facilities for persons with developmental, physical, and cognitive disabilities or mental disorders. In the years since enactment of the ADA, various courts have settled issues surrounding the extent to which it applies to law enforcement. The courts have expanded the definition of what constitutes police action when applying ADA requirements (*Schorr v. Borough of Lemoyne*, 2003). For example, arrest itself is now broadly interpreted to include prearrest investigations and violent confrontations not technically involving an arrest. According to the U.S. Department of Justice, the ADA applies to every aspect of policing, including the following (U.S. Department of Justice, 2006):

- Receiving citizen complaints
- Interrogating and interviewing witnesses
- Arresting, booking, and holding suspects
- Operating 911 emergency centers
- Enforcing laws
- Incarceration

Title II of the ADA provides that "no qualified individual with a disability shall, by reason of such disability, be excluded from participation in or be denied the benefits of the services, programs, or activities of a public entity, or be subjected to discrimination by any such entity" (ADA, 1994). This mandate of nondiscrimination extends to all state and government services, regardless of whether or not the person receives federal financial assistance.

Accommodations for Interviewing

The ADA requires that public officials attempt effective communication with individuals having disabilities by providing auxiliary devices (U.S. Department of Justice, 2006). To facilitate the reporting of victimization for the disabled community, officers need to make arrangements so that individuals with a disability feel comfortable reporting to the police. This accommodation may involve the use of an interpreter or another third party to assist. The department may not charge the individual with a disability for the utilization of an auxiliary aid. Examples of auxiliary aids and services for those with hearing impairments include qualified interpreters, note takers, transcript services, videotext displays, closed-caption decoders, and telephones compatible with hearing aids. To assist individuals with visual impairments, qualified readers, taped tests, audio recordings, materials in Braille, and large-print materials may be required. Although public entities are required to provide alternative auxiliary aides if available, they are not obliged to alter the nature of the service, program, or activity if it would result in an undue financial or administrative burden (U.S. Department of Justice, 2006).

BEEN THERE . . . DONE THAT! 10-1

While on patrol one winter evening I noted a person walking in the breakdown lane coming toward traffic. From a distance, I noticed that this woman was not wearing a coat or shoes and that there was snow on the ground. The nonverbal assessment was that she required special care; she did not appear to be aware of her surroundings. Pulling the cruiser over and slowing approaching, I yelled out, "Are you okay?" Oblivious to my presence, she kept walking. Calmly and firmly, I kept talking as I approached her, making a determination as to the level of danger that she posed. A missing or wanted check showed no warrants. I arranged for her to be transported to a local mental health clinic that accepted night admissions, where she was evaluated the following day.

Police Liability under the ADA

In light of these changes, communications with persons who may be disabled and are suspected of having committed crimes is a critical skill to develop. Sporadic claims against police departments for failing to train officers on handling persons with disabilities have surfaced in federal court. Under what is referred to as the *wrongful-arrest theory*, courts have been addressing some of the claims arising from Title II of the ADA. The wrongful-arrest situation was dealt with in *Jackson v. Town of Sanford* (1994), a case in which the police had arrested a man for drunk driving when in fact he had been sober, his unsteadiness and slurred speech having resulted from a past stroke. In *Lewis v. Truitt* (1997) police were held accountable for beating and arresting a man for resisting law enforcement when in fact he was deaf and could not understand their commands. In their investigation of these claims, the courts have broadly interpreted the term *arrest* to include arrest, prearrest investigations, and violent confrontations not technically involving an arrest (*Gohier v. Enright*, 1999). Schorr, a case where police officers shot and killed a man who had bipolar disorder, provides an example where the court accepted a claim for "failure to train police" under the ADA requirements (*Schorr v. Borough of Lemoyne*, 2003). The Court concluded that the police department had failed to institute policies to accommodate disabled individuals such as Schorr, by failing to give the officers the tools and resources to properly de-escalate the situation. The message is clear; law enforcement is expected to be prepared to handle these difficult cases by recognizing situations where a person has a disability.

Avoiding these situations requires an increased awareness on the part of the police. Some suggestions include watching for handicapped license plates on cars that are stopped; using hand signals or yelling to people in a crowd to signal that he or she stop running; speaking clearly; and using breathalyzers to obtain accurate results regarding possible cases of driving under the influence. If while attempting to communicate with a motorist it becomes evident that the person cannot speak, he or she should be offered a pen and piece of paper.

There is immense social and legal pressure on law enforcement officers to make the correct decisions and to develop the expertise to de-escalate and safely handle cases involving individuals with mental disorders. Specialized response training is advocated for law enforcement officers so that they may better understand the complexities of mental illness and to debunk myths, reduce fear, and learn methods of defusing potentially difficult situations.

INITIAL CONSIDERATIONS

The first step in investigative interviewing an individual with a disability or mental disorder is self-confrontation. The lack of familiarity with individuals who have a disability may cause you to feel awkward and uncertain on how to proceed. Negative attitudes may be the largest obstacle to successful interviewing of this population. Speak directly to the individual being interviewed, even if they are accompanied by another person. Their condition should not cause repulsion, sympathy, or admiration. Face personal biases through education and awareness.

A common negative attitude exists regarding people whose physical appearance signals to others that they are different. Individuals with a physical or developmental disability are not less of a person but may present with various value systems and behavioral expectations. Persons with a developmental disability tend to obey rules and don't want to get anyone in trouble. They may appear overly compliant and initially deny that they have been victimized, or may not realize that what happened to them was victimization. These individuals are not less credible; interviewers must overcome the tendency to treat people with severe intellectual disabilities as though they were stupid or undeserving of police attention or protection.

Taking the time to become familiar with ways to address individuals with a disability will also help to put you at ease. Take care not to label a person according to his or her disability; he or she is "a person with a disability" and not "a disabled person." Although the distinction may seem trivial, to someone who lives with a physical or developmental disability, it makes a difference. Before any attempt at establishing rapport, the person should feel recognized as an individual, not regarded as an illness. Only ask questions about the disability that pertains to the investigation or to accommodate the individual's needs. Look directly at the person being interviewed, but do not stare at a disfigurement. Treat people with compassion, dignity, and respect.

Research on mental health shows that mental disorders are prevalent throughout the United States. The *National Survey on Drug Use and Health* reports that in 2015 more than 43 million adults aged 18 or older had a mental disorder in the previous year (NSDUH, 2016). Diagnoses made of the same disorder do not necessarily manifest the same way with different people. Diagnosed disorders are also on a continuum; symptoms may lessen or worsen over time—or they may remain the same. There are many variables within each of the disorder categories that people may experience. Having a mental disorder does not predict any specific outcome; so much is dependent on individual pathology and life conditions.

IDENTIFYING WHEN SPECIAL CARE IS NECESSARY

People with a mental disorder or physical disability may require special care. Conduct a background check on the individual just as you would with any other individual. A background check may reveal past convictions and information that would provide investigative leads. It might also provide information if there is a potential threat of violence that the person may pose to the interviewer.

Although they usually can provide reliable evidence, individuals with disabilities may have communication problems that result in misleading statements or inappropriate reactions because of immediate (mis)understanding of the events. The interviewer must observe for signs of disability because the mental or physical impairment may not be immediately obvious.

Recognizing disability is a difficult task because it is not necessarily a stable or static condition. A person who has a disability cannot be identified by a single common characteristic. Some persons will be readily identifiable as having impairment due to physical affect, obvious mechanisms needed for assistance, or inappropriate behaviors. Individuals with impaired sight or hearing are often assisted in ways that are not immediately noticed. Others with less severe impediments or mental illness may not be recognized as requiring special assistance.

Disabilities arise from different causes. Some physical disabilities are caused by brain damage, such as cerebral palsy, but do not necessarily affect intelligence or the ability to communicate. On the other hand, some individuals with cerebral palsy acquired at birth or through traumatic head injury also have speech production impairments and mental illness. Most disabilities do not impair communication or cognition, and impairments that affect speech production may be related to medications and do not necessarily affect intellectual or cognitive abilities.

Some individuals are too sick to understand their mental illness due to anosognosia. **Anosognosia** is a medical condition experienced by someone with an acute mental illness who does not think clearly enough to know that he or she is sick. Approximately half of people with schizophrenia and 40 percent of people with bipolar disorder are affected by anosognosia, placing them at greater risk of homelessness, victimization, or arrest (NAMI, 2015).

Most persons being interviewed by the police will be apprehensive; be aware if it appears that the apprehension is excessive and if an excessive amount of anxiety is evident. A person may require special care if he or she is incoherent and the condition is not drug or alcohol induced. Some individuals with a disability may not be able to understand or answer questions or will show evidence of a mood level that is inconsistent with the situation. Such an individual may have a short attention span, a limited vocabulary, or a speech impediment.

Offenders with severe mental illnesses are more likely to be found incompetent to stand trial than those with an intellectual disability. Between 12.5 and 36 percent of individuals with an intellectual disability who undergo evaluations are determined to be incompetent compared to an estimated 45–65 percent of offenders with schizophrenia or other psychotic diagnoses referred for assessment (Fleischner, 2017).

BEEN THERE . . . DONE THAT! 10-2

Andrew was a 23-year-old man with an intellectual disability who had been victimized sexually by a 72-year-old man. Andrew did not know that it was not right to have oral sex with another man; therefore, it appeared as if he was a willing participant. He was seen having oral sex with the older man and was called "an animal." It was alarming to Andrew to be called that; he did not understand why someone would say bad things about him. He began to have violent outbreaks, which brought this case to the attention of the authorities. Andrew was formally diagnosed as having Down syndrome with a level of understanding of between 7 and 8 years old. Before the incident, Andrew was known to be amiable and to seek to please adults, which is characteristic of individuals with Down syndrome. Andrew was able to give me a detailed statement, although understanding his speech was a challenge.

I arrested the alleged perpetrator and provided his warnings per *Miranda*, which he waived. He stated that he felt guilty about having sex with the young man and was glad that I had found out about it. He further told me that he had been arrested 40 years earlier for "unnatural acts with a child" and had spent 1 year in jail for that.

Your goal as an officer in such a case is to determine, if possible, whether the contact was consensual. If it is unclear, ask for an evaluation of the individual from a trained professional who has expertise with persons having that particular disability. In this case, it was determined that the victim lacked the capacity to consent and that the suspect sought him out as a victim because of his disability. Taking this case to the logical conclusion of making an arrest served to teach Andrew that he was the victim and the act was illegal. It stopped that perpetrator and sent a message to the community that these victimizations would be punished.

FIGURE 10-1   A person having difficulty in problem-solving and academic learning at an early age is now referred to as having an intellectual disability.

Source: ESB Professional/Shutterstock.

Intellectual Disability

A person having difficulty in problem-solving and academic learning at an early age is now referred to as having an **intellectual disability**, a term that replaces mental retardation. Persons with a severe intellectual disability possess significantly less than the average age-appropriate ability to process information. Some persons may not be able to understand or answer questions or will exhibit a mood level that is inconsistent with the situation. Approximately 2–3 percent of the population has an intellectual disability, yet rates as high as 30 percent are documented among prisoners (Griffith & Fedoroff, 2014).

It is thought that individuals with intellectual disability are more vulnerable to being misled due to a strong need to be accepted and an inability to read social cues, which may lead to their being involved in crime (Frank & McGuire, 2010). The primary offenses committed by persons with intellectual disabilities leading to criminal charges are sexual offenses, arson, and violent conduct (Lindsay, Steele, Smith, Quinn, & Allan, 2006).

Attention Deficit-Hyperactivity Disorder

Attention deficit-hyperactivity disorder (ADHD) has been linked to numerous different forms of misconduct in children and as risk factors for adult criminal conduct (Savolainen et al., 2010). Research has suggested that ADHD itself is not the cause of criminal involvement, but rather the symptoms of ADHD that lead to academic failure and behavioral problems at school that predict a risk of future criminality (Watts, 2016). Symptoms include hyperactivity, difficulty in deferring gratification or following instructions, greater risk-taking, and impulsivity. Coupled with lower self-image and poor self-control, these make individuals with ADHD more likely to come to the attention of law enforcement due to their involvement in automobile accidents, underage drinking, and aggressiveness. Disproportionately higher rates of ADHD have been noted among offenders than within the general population (Young, Goodwin, Sedgwick, & Gudjonsson, 2013).

Young et al. (2013) have found that individuals with ADHD tend to give a disproportionate number of "don't know" responses when questioned by the police, which may be misconstrued as being uncooperative. Individuals with ADHD may also be prone to make false confessions during police questioning. Once in a custodial environment, offenders with ADHD may become a management problem as their symptoms are reportedly associated with aggressive behaviors, which may be due to excessive emotional reactions and mood swings.

There are no data to suggest that a specific interviewing or interrogation method is necessary for individuals with ADHD, but recognition of the symptoms is helpful in determining the motivation for criminal behavior. The following questions may help to determine whether an individuals' disorder contributed to their conduct:

- Do you have difficulty paying attention during conversations, in classes, at work, and so on?
- Do you feel excessively stressed or overwhelmed?
- Do you find that your mind drifts off easily?
- Do you become sidetracked easily, leave tasks unfinished, or disrupt tasks in progress to switch to other matters?
- Do you become frustrated easily?
- Do you forget to complete things that you intended to do?
- Do you have sudden outbursts of intense anger?
- Do you easily misunderstand directions?

Autism Spectrum Disorder

Autism spectrum disorder (ASD) is a lifelong neurodevelopmental syndrome characterized by problems communicating in social situations, repetitive behavior patterns, and unusual response to sensory stimuli. Recent research suggests that ASD affects 1 in 68 of 8-year-old children (Christensen, 2016). More than 3.5 million Americans are estimated to live with an ASD at a service cost to U.S. citizens of $236–262 billion annually (Buescher, Cidav, Knapp, & Mandell, 2014). Individuals with autism have a high likelihood of victimization.

During an interrogation, there is the possibility of individuals with ASD producing false confessions or providing misleading statements to the police (Tata, 2017). At high risk during interrogation are individuals with ASD whose condition may present behavioral indicators of guilt such as a lack of eye contact or an apparent aloof and indifferent manner, which may be misinterpreted. Persons with autism may exhibit some of the following traits that could affect an interview:

- They may repeat words or phrases in place of normal responsive language.
- They may laugh (and/or cry) for no apparent reason.
- They may have little or no eye contact and appear aloof.
- They may have no real fear of danger.
- They may be unresponsive to verbal cues and act as if they were deaf.

MENTAL DISORDERS

The most recent version of the Diagnostic and Statistical Manual of Mental Disorders (DSM) is the DSM-5 (APA, 2015). First published in 1952, the Diagnostic and Statistical Manual focuses on clinical aspects of mental disorders. Psychiatrists and psychologists depend on input from patient self-reports, caregivers, parents, and teachers in making an assessment. The American Psychological Association DSM-5 defines a **mental disorder** as

- a behavioral or psychological syndrome or pattern that occurs in an individual;
- reflecting an underlying psychobiological dysfunction;
- the consequences of which are clinically significant distress (e.g., a painful symptom) or disability (i.e., impairment in one or more important areas of functioning);

- must not be merely an expectable response to common stressors and losses (e.g., the loss of a loved one) or a culturally sanctioned response to an event (e.g., trance states in religious rituals);
- not primarily a result of social deviance or conflicts within society.

Several studies concluded that only a weak association between mental disorder and violence exists, suggesting that serious violence is perpetrated by a small fraction of the total number of individuals with mental illness (Steadman et al., 1998). Co-occurring mental disorders, drug, and alcohol use, and noncompliance with medication requirements are among the factors associated with an increase in violent behavior.

Inmates with Mental Illness

Individuals with severe mental disorders are overrepresented in the jail and prison inmate population. There is some evidence that symptoms of specific forms of mental illness, such as bipolar disorder, schizophrenia, and depression, directly account for a small percentage of criminal activity (Peterson, Skeem, Kennealy, Bray, & Zvonkovic, 2014). Of controversy is whether specific types or severity of mental illness have a direct causal link to criminal behavior. Without appropriate medical care, some individuals may be quick to anger, provocative, and dangerous. Serious depression puts people at an increased risk for suicide and self-mutilation and to a lesser degree, with an increased risk of violent crime (Swanson, McGinty, Fazel, & Mays, 2015).

Some experts suggest that only a small proportion of crime can be directly linked to symptoms of mental illness. In one study, researchers examined 429 crimes committed by 143 offenders and found that only 3 percent of those crimes were directly related to symptoms of major depression, 4 percent to symptoms of schizophrenia disorders, and 10 percent to systems of bipolar disorder (Peterson et al., 2014). It is challenging to distinguish between symptoms of mental illness and common risk factors for committing a crime, such as anger and impulsivity, suggesting that intervention would be needed to improve criminal justice outcomes that extend beyond symptoms.

Bipolar disorder, previously known as manic-depressive illness, is a brain disorder that causes unusual shifts in mood, energy, activity levels, and the ability to carry out day-to-day tasks. Rates of violent behavior since age 15 have been found to be greater for bipolar disorder (27.58%) than for other mood disorders (Pulay et al., 2008). Symptoms of bipolar disorder are severe. They are different from the normal ups

FIGURE 10-2 Individuals with certain disabilities and mental disorders are overrepresented among the prison and jail population.

Source: G. Campbell/Shutterstock.

and downs that everyone goes through from time to time. Bipolar disorder symptoms can result in damaged relationships, poor job or school performance, and even suicide. During manic phases some people may be psychotic and experience delusions or hallucinations. Bipolar disorder can be treated, and people with this illness can lead full and productive lives.

Schizophrenia is a chronic, severe, and disabling mental disorder characterized by deficits in thought processes, perceptions, and emotional responsiveness. Its symptoms are typically described as "positive" or "negative." Positive symptoms may include delusions, thought disorders, and hallucinations. Affected individuals may hear voices other people do not hear or believe other people are reading their minds, controlling their thoughts, or plotting to harm them. The negative symptoms may resemble depression such as a lack of desire or motivation to accomplish goals, form social relationships, and blunted affect and emotion. These symptoms make holding a job, forming relationships, and other day-to-day functions are particularly challenging. While there is no cure, the disorder is highly treatable.

While people with schizophrenia are not usually violent, some symptoms are associated with violence, such as delusions of persecution. Substance abuse may also increase the chance a person will become violent. If a person becomes violent, the violence is usually directed at themselves or family members and tends to take place at home. Some psychotic symptoms, such as feeling threatened, may lead directly to criminal conduct (Frank & McGuire, 2010). The risk of violence among people with schizophrenia is small, but individuals with this condition are 50 times more likely to attempt suicide than individuals without the disorder, according to the Treatment Advocacy Center. About 10 percent of those diagnosed with the disease (especially young adult males) die by suicide (Torrey, 2013). It is hard to predict which people will be prone to suicide. Extreme depressio n or psychosis that can result due to lack of treatment are the usual causes of suicide attempts.

Personality disorders are a group of illnesses that involve long-term patterns of thoughts and behaviors that are unhealthy and inflexible, which can lead people to ignore their safety and the safety of others and to be distrustful of others. The most common personality disorders among jail and prison inmates are antisocial personalities and borderline personality disorder (BPD; Fellner, 2003). Persons with antisocial personality disorder, typically men, can be particularly difficult to manage in a correctional setting. They can be manipulative, volatile, disruptive, and likely to engage in aggressive, impulsive acting-out behavior, which can include assaults on others, self-mutilation, and suicide attempts. They are highly represented in the criminal justice system and do not exhibit guilt or remorse.

BPD is a serious mental illness evidenced by unstable moods, behavior, and relationships (APA, 2015). More than 1.5 percent of the adult population in the United States is diagnosed with BPD each year (Lenzenweger, Lane, Loranger, & Kessler, 2007). People with this disorder also have high rates of co-occurring disorders, such as depression, anxiety disorders, substance abuse, and eating disorders, along with self-harm, suicidal behaviors, and completed suicides, which may bring them to the attention of the criminal justice system. While rates of BPD in the community are 1 to 2 percent, rates among inmates have been estimated as high as 45 percent (Conn et al., 2010).

There is overlap between the classifications of mental disability and mental disorders. One example concerns the difference between cognitive disabilities and mental illness. A **cognitive disability** is a comprehensive term used to describe a variety of medical conditions affecting different types of mental tasks (Bronson, Maruschak, & Berzofsky, 2015). Examples of cognitive disabilities, which are prevalent in the criminal justice system, include Down syndrome, ASD, dementia, attention deficit disorder, learning disorders, intellectual disabilities, and traumatic brain injury.

Examples of mental disorders include bipolar disorder, depression, personality disorders, and schizophrenia. A cognitive disability is not the same as a psychiatric disorder, although they often co-occur. A mental disorder can be considered an impairment as well. An estimated 32 percent of prisoners and 40 percent of jail inmates report having at least one disability, the most common of which is a cognitive impairment (Bronson & Berzofsky, 2015).

Violence and Mental Disorders

The question of whether individuals with mental disorders are more violent than the general population has been hotly debated since the 1970s. The *MacArthur Community Violence Study* conducted between 1992 and 1995 made an important contribution to the question of dangerousness among individuals with mental disorders (Steadman et al., 1998). The purpose of the study was to determine the rate of violence by former mental patients and compare it to the rate of violence by other members of the community. The study concluded that drugs and alcohol increase violence in people with mental disorders more than they do in the general population, but otherwise, individuals with mental disorders are not more violent than anyone else. This study is widely cited as proof that individuals with mental illness are not violent due to mental disorders.

Recent shootings have again focused immense national attention on people with mental illnesses. Despite the low risk of violence among people with mental illness, research does substantiate that they carry a modest elevated risk of violent behavior when compared to the general public (Swanson et al., 2015). The occurrence of violence increases the probability that the offender may be arrested at the street level stage. The *National Institute of Mental Health* (NIMH) estimates that especially during an episode of psychosis, people with serious mental illness are three times more likely to be violent than the general public (Insel, 2011). When substance abuse, a previous history of violence or nonadherence to medication is involved, the risk becomes much higher. Swanson et al. (2016) point out that when persons with mental illness do behave violently, it is often for the same reasons that nonmentally ill people engage in violent behavior. Violence is a complex societal problem that is often caused by other things besides mental illness.

BEEN THERE . . . DONE THAT! 10-3

At the scene of a homicide, the female victim was found to have been stabbed about 150 times. An adult son who lived with her was on the scene and was also stabbed more than 100 times but lived. My partner went to the hospital to interview the survivor. The interview was audiotaped, and *Miranda* warnings were issued to the son because he was a suspect in the killing. He appeared to be coherent, and his initial behavior was rational. From time to time during the interview, the suspect would start howling accompanied by blood-curdling screaming and sobbing. He told how the "devil" was present in his TV and was transposed to his mother—he could see it through the redness of her eyes (which is why numerous stabbings were to her eyes). He had to rid her of this devil, whom he also thought had gotten into him, which is why he had stabbed himself in every orifice—ears, eyes, and buttocks. The danger was that he believed what he was doing; this goal-directed behavior was organized and premeditated. The goal of the attack was not to kill his mother but to kill the devil that was in her. Officer safety is a major issue with those who are delusional, suffer from hallucinations, and present with grossly disorganized or catatonic behaviors.

This suspect had a long history of severe mental illness and was under a doctor's care. The defense and the prosecution agreed that he was legally insane and should not be tried for the murder.

FIELD EVALUATION

An important component of policing is observation. The purpose of conducting a field evaluation is to determine an appropriate response to the situation. First responders are often expected to make a quick assessment of the environment with limited information. Two methods of evaluation used to assess the field are categorized based on distance. A distant field evaluation is a nonverbal assessment that is conducted from a distance of greater than 3 feet; this is used when a person attracts interest in the field due to one or more of the following conditions:

- The person may be inappropriately dressed for the weather.
- The person is in a place where he or she does not belong, and personal danger exists.
- The person is stumbling about or appears to be confused.
- The person is engaging in inappropriate actions with peers or people of the opposite sex.
- The individual seems to be gravely disabled either in judgment or because of substance abuse.

A detailed field evaluation is an up-close assessment to determine whether the subject is mentally disordered or physically handicapped. Its purpose is to identify any needs or problems that must be addressed or if a situation of mandated reporting exists. The examination should not be conducted in this manner if there is evidence that the individual is armed or dangerous. The officer's first concern should always be directed toward the safety and protection of persons, both for himself or herself and for others. One should approach the individual in a non-threatening but controlled manner so as not to agitate or cause distress. Speaking firmly and clearly, one should show concern through actions and words. "Are you okay?" and "Do you need help?" are examples of introductory statements used when assessing the situation in the field.

Ask for identifying information to determine the level of stress and cognitive awareness of the person. If an individual is not aware of his or her name or address, this may be indicative of impairment. Do not assume that an individual who fails to answer questions can hear or understand. Failure to respond in itself is not indicative of belligerence or criminal behavior. An indication of alcohol use does not necessarily mean that the individual is drunk; you may be dealing with a person who has a disability who also had an alcoholic beverage.

Most individuals with a disability present no risk to police. To de-escalate a potentially violent situation takes a show of respect and a calm, non-threatening approach to communicating.

Assessing actual risk involves a determination on whether the person is merely threatening.

- *National Alliance on Mental Illness* (NAMI) (2010) suggests that an individual in crisis may find it difficult to understand what others are saying. It is important to empathize with the person, to stay calm and try to de-escalate the crisis. Try to think of the person as he is—someone in need of help. To assist in de-escalation, NAMI suggests that professionals avoid overreacting since the person may be angry, but not necessarily violent. Avoid continuous eye contact and touching the person unless restraint is necessary. Above all, do not argue or try to reason with people in crisis, their thinking is disordered.

VICTIMIZATION OF VULNERABLE INDIVIDUALS

Victims of crime who have a disability may be targeted for criminal activity due to their real or perceived vulnerability; you may be interviewing someone who has repeatedly been victimized. They are targets for abuse and theft from the caregivers who are assigned to care for them. A cycle of victimization and ill-treatment will make it harder to establish rapport and trust with the person being interviewed, another reason to be patient and understanding.

Interviewing a person presenting with a disability involves only a modification of the techniques already discussed throughout this book. Although initially challenging, the interview should be no harder than with any other population. As before, the interviewer must maintain control, elicit responses, and clarify statements. How this is accomplished obviously differs depending on the unique characteristics of the individual being questioned. This takes patience and a willingness to communicate through the most efficient method.

Studies have documented that there is an overlap between victimization and perpetration among individuals with severe mental illness (Silver, Piquero, Jennings, Piquero, & Leiber, 2011).

Victimization rates among homeless adults with serious mental illness are significantly higher than the population as a whole, ranging between 73 percent and 87 percent of homeless (Roy, Crocker, Nicholls, Latimer, & Ayllon, 2014). Among the population of homeless persons, researchers find that lifetime arrest rate range between 62 percent and 90 percent for individuals with severe mental disorders (Roy et al., 2014). These rates are much higher than for the general U.S. population, in which lifetime arrest rates are estimated to be about 15 percent and for community-dwelling adults with mental illness, which ranged between 25 and 33 percent (Roy et al., 2014).

Legal Issues

Before the interview with a person who is physically or mentally impaired, the interviewer must have a good understanding of the statutes that are specific to protecting disabled persons. Typically, the elements of the crime differ for victimized individuals who have limited cognitive and physical abilities, so it is important to be acquainted with the provisions particular to your jurisdiction before the interview. Numerous distinctions have been made in criminal statutes that provide additional protections for persons with a disability from abandonment, financial exploitation, personal victimization, and neglect. Some examples include the following:

- North Carolina provides that second-degree rape [GS 14-27.3(a)(2), Class C felony] includes the vaginal intercourse with a victim whom the perpetrator knows is mentally disabled, incapacitated, or physically helpless. This includes most drug-facilitated sexual assaults, but no force need be established.
- The Illinois Criminal Code includes the Home Repair Fraud Act (815ILCS 515/5). Aggravated home repair fraud occurs if the contractor commits a home repair fraud against a person who has a permanent physically disabling condition. Aggravated home repair fraud is a Class 2 felony if the contractor is to be paid more than $500.
- According to the Indiana Criminal Code of Battery (IC 35-42-2-1), it is a Class D felony if a person who knowingly or intentionally touches another person in a rude, insolent, or angry manner commits battery that results in bodily injury to a person of any age who is mentally or physically disabled and is perpetrated by a person having the care of the mentally or physically handicapped person, whether the care is assumed voluntarily or because of a legal obligation.
- Iowa presents an example in which a crime against an individual with a disability may be construed as a "hate crime" (92 Acts, ch 1157, §9). This category includes one or more of the following public offenses when committed against a person or a person's property because of the individual's race, color, religion, ancestry, national origin, political affiliation, sex, sexual orientation, age, or disability, or

FIGURE 10-3   An "appropriate adult" may sometimes be included in the interview to assist in communication with the police.

Source: Photographee.eu/Shutterstock.

the person's association with a person of a certain race, color, religion, ancestry, national origin, political affiliation, sex, sexual orientation, age, or disability:

1. Assault in violation of individual rights under section 708.2C.
2. Violations of individual rights under section 712.9.
3. Criminal mischief in violation of individual rights under section 716.6A.
4. Trespass in violation of individual rights under section 716.8, subsections 3 and 4.

THE INTERVIEW PROCESS

Trauma-informed victim interviewing protocols should be considered in cases where prior victimization is suspected. The *Office for Victims of Crime* suggests that it may be appropriate for law enforcement to use forensic interviewers in cases where human trafficking is suspected and victims present with cognitive or developmental disabilities. The forensic interviewers conduct nonleading, victim-sensitive, neutral, and developmentally appropriate investigative interviews that help law enforcement determine whether a crime occurred and what happened. For trafficking survivors with disabilities, an investigation may include questioning whether the survivor's disability played a factor in how they were trafficked, and the survivor's mental capacity to be trafficked. These issues can all create hostile interviewing environments, and investigators must take the time to explain the reasons for the questioning.

Step 1: Prepare

Before the interview, determine a location away from the scene that is comfortable and without distractions.

Turn off cell phones. The best scenario is a one-on-one interview. In some cases, it may be advisable to include an appropriate adult. An **appropriate adult** can provide support to the interviewee and to smooth the progress of communication with the police. He or she should have a good understanding or training in dealing with persons who have disabilities or mental disorders or with the needs of a particular group. He or she should be entirely independent of the police and, when possible, the interviewee. As needed, the person should be able to act as an interpreter. It is helpful to have developed a relationship with mental health workers who are willing to be called on in such a case. An alternative is to develop a multidisciplinary team approach for interviewing persons who have a disability. It is not the function of an appropriate adult to advise the person being interviewed whether or how to answer any questions or to object to any questions being asked. It is not proper for the helping adult to tell the police that he or she disapproves of questioning or to lead the witness in any way.

Step 2: Establish Rapport

Introduce yourself and ask the individual what he or she would like to be called. Referring to someone else by a title and then calling the interviewee by a first name implies a lack of respect, so be consistent. Avoid touching a person with a disability because you do not know whether this would be perceived as an invasion of personal space or remind them of an attacker. An individual who is "touch toxic" may become upset and unable to continue the interview; a person with an intellectual disability may not feel able to refuse. Take your cue from the interviewee; if he or she puts out a hand for a handshake, respond. Otherwise, keep your hands to yourself. Don't be afraid to maintain your personal space. Because it is not professional to hug an individual being interviewed, it is appropriate to firmly and gently avoid personal contact of this kind that is initiated by the interviewee. Kindly tell the interviewee that it makes you feel uncomfortable and do not want to hug.

Develop rapport with the interviewee by asking whether he or she requires physical assistance or arrangements to meet his or her needs. Explain the process of the interview; explain that you may need to ask questions more than once to make sure that you understand what is being said. Anticipate an adequate length of time for the interview without the need for excessive time. Arrange for support to be available to the person following the interview, and let the interviewee know that someone will be there for him or her.

For individuals with physical disabilities, do not jump up and assume that the individual needs or wants help. Keep clear of wheelchairs so that the individual can move around and adopt a comfortable position; the wheelchair is part of the individual's space that should not be invaded without specific design. The room should be comfortable without being too large, and absent of children's toys.

Step 3: Conducting the Interview

Use good listening skills; allow the victim to tell the story at first with as few interruptions as possible. Use open-ended questions and avoid overly complicated or technical phrases. Ask the person if he or she knows why he or she is there to speak with you. It may be helpful to explain that you are someone who speaks with people about difficult subjects and give them "permission" to talk with you. Give the individual the opportunity to ask questions.

BEEN THERE . . . DONE THAT! 10-4

I interviewed a woman with an intellectual disability about an allegation of rape. She was clear in stating that she had been raped. Instructing her that I needed to understand her terms, I asked that she name the parts of the body. She did this without a problem using a clothed, anatomically correct doll. Next, I asked if she would tell me how it happened. The woman immediately picked up the doll and rubbed her face on the chest area. "See," she stated, "he raped me like this." What she showed was not rape, but it was a sexual assault. She did not want this to happen and said she told him to stop, over and over. The man was charged with an indecent assault and battery on a disabled person. The interview had been videotaped, and it was shown in the grand jury; the victim also went into the grand jury and with the use of the doll demonstrated what had happened. The fact that her terms were different did not diminish the crime nor the trauma that resulted from it. The perpetrator was indicted, and he pled guilty to the crime in Superior Court.

Questions should not be phrased in legal terms; the victim may not know what an "assault" means, for example. The primary goals of interviewing victims are to

1. Determine whether a crime has been committed.
2. Obtain information to help in the identification of the perpetrator.
3. Gather evidence for a successful prosecution.

The goal of interviewing witnesses is the corroboration of specific events that substantiate criminal activity. With these aims in mind, the purpose of the interview is to acquire the necessary information. Individuals with a disability report violent victimization to the police in roughly similar rates to those who do not have a disability. Do not assume that a person with a physical or cognitive disability is unable to provide creditable information. While reports to the police that involve individuals with a disability are less than 50 percent, of those who do report, 96 percent can identify their perpetrator (Harrell, 2015).

The criminal justice community has already made great strides in interviewing one class of people with cognitive limitations, children. Although care must be taken not to infantilize a person with a disability, we can use the lessons learned from working with children for effective communication. Remember that the person presenting with a disability does not necessarily have limited cognitive abilities along with a physical or neurological limitation. As much as possible, go into the interview without a preconceived notion about the abilities of the interviewee to recount the necessary information.

The cognitive abilities of the individual should be considered when phrasing/asking questions. Be purposeful in your phrasing to avoid miscommunication and misunderstanding. Keep sentences short and to the point. Access the vocabulary of the person being interviewed and attempt consistency in communication. Take extra care not to lead the questioning or to suggest answers. Questions that require a "yes" or "no" response are only helpful for clarification and should be avoided. Encourage the interviewee to express and clarify meanings. All of these considerations must be confined to a relatively short interview period of approximately 0.5 hour. Individuals with a disability may have a short attention span.

Be aware that the vocabulary used by the person being interviewed may have different meanings than you would normally associate with the terms. If the allegation is of sexual abuse, don't just allow the victim to provide the words that he or she uses

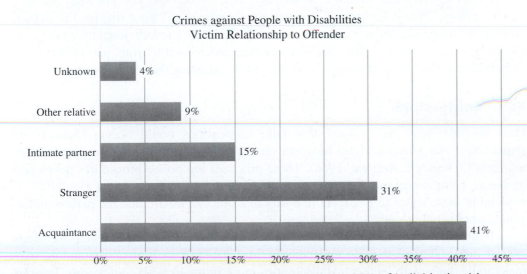

Crimes against People with Disabilities
Victim Relationship to Offender

Relationship	Percentage
Unknown	4%
Other relative	9%
Intimate partner	15%
Stranger	31%
Acquaintance	41%

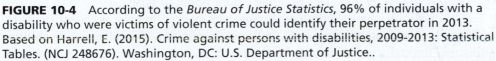

FIGURE 10-4 According to the *Bureau of Justice Statistics*, 96% of individuals with a disability who were victims of violent crime could identify their perpetrator in 2013. Based on Harrell, E. (2015). Crime against persons with disabilities, 2009–2013: Statistical Tables. (NCJ 248676). Washington, DC: U.S. Department of Justice..

to describe his or her body parts, but also have him or her show you on an anatomically correct doll or through drawings what that part of the body is. Encourage the individual to use descriptive terms for what he or she experienced. Avoid asking "Why" questions; they are too complicated and can be confusing.

At the end of the interview thank the interviewee for his or her time and patience. Ask any questions on points that you need to be clarified. Let the victim know that you may need to speak with him or her another time and ask whether that would be all right. Be sure to escort the person outside of the interview room to meet with a counselor or another supportive person.

INTERROGATION CONSIDERATIONS

Persons with disabilities and mental disorders do commit crimes, and accusations must be investigated similar to allegations against any other supposed perpetrator. There are situations in which an officer must interrogate a person suspected of committing a crime where disability or mental disorder is suspected or known. To protect the results of the interrogation, special care must be taken to preserve the integrity of the case. Most important throughout the interrogation is strict adherence to the preservation of all constitutional rights. Taking shortcuts will likely result in a tainted investigation and a statement that is subject to exclusion or worse. Remembering that the purpose of an interrogation is to find the truth if possible; take pains to make sure that it is the truth that is obtained. Follow any department rules and regulations that may exist relative to interrogating potentially vulnerable persons. In all cases, treat the suspect with dignity.

Before conducting an interrogation, determine the level of functioning of the adult suspect. Ask typical questions, such as name, age, and address of the individual. Determine whether the suspect can read; if not, be prepared to read and explain individual rights. Ask questions that are nonleading and straightforward. Avoid questions that require a "yes" or "no" answer. Use language that is simple and easy to understand. Your sentences should be short and to the point.

Follow up any statements suggestive of guilt by asking for details of the event. Answers that typically would be considered "admissions" do not take on the same significance when coming from a person with limited cognitive ability. For example, if a man with a severe intellectual disability is asked, "When did you kill Mrs. Smith?" and he replies, "Was it Thursday?" then absent significant evidence that he did, in fact, commit the homicide, the reply means absolutely nothing. The individual may take your question be about "when" Mrs. Smith was killed and miss the "you" part of the question. Proceed with caution! Justice is not served by arresting the wrong person.

False Confessions

Only recently have we realized that false confessions could occur. There is no requirement that *Miranda* rights be given verbatim or presented to the suspect in written form (*Miranda v. Arizona*, 1966). These practices are police procedures developed to assure compliance and consistency. Officers are therefore given the flexibility of explaining these rights to a suspect in a way that one can assure that the person understands what is being said.

Individuals with an intellectual disability may not understand *Miranda* warnings even if they state that they do understand (Tata, 2017). A lack of understanding may make individuals with intellectual disabilities more prone to false confessions. Persons with mental disabilities may incriminate themselves even if they are innocent to please the police officer or another interviewer. Individuals with severe intellectual disabilities are structured throughout their lives to be compliant and submissive. In an interrogation

FIGURE 10-5   Verify that the suspect fully understands the questions that are being asked. Individuals with intellectual disabilities may be overly compliant and submissive in order to please.

Source: CREATISTA/Shutterstock.

with a suspect who is disabled, do not assume without verification, that he or she understands.

Individuals who have intellectual or mental disorders are more likely to confess to something that they did not do (Leo, 2016). Identifying those with special needs during questioning should be a major focus for the interrogator. Individuals with intellectual or cognitive disorders, those with severe mental illness, and juveniles may be easily confused about the criminal justice process and "confess" even when they are innocent.

The Supreme Court expressed in the *Miranda* decision (id. at 24) some of its concerns regarding persons with low IQ and their subsequent false confessions to police. In pointing out that "Interrogation procedures may even give rise to a false confession," the Court provided a conspicuous example: in New York in 1964 an African American man of limited intelligence confessed to two brutal murders and a rape that he had not committed. The Court in its decision relied on a similar case in which the defendant, a 19-year-old heroin addict described as a "near mental defective," was found guilty of the crime he did not commit; his conviction was subsequently overturned (*Townsend v. Sain*, 1963).

Conclusions

This chapter introduces you to the challenges of interviewing and interrogating persons with disabilities and mental disorders. Victimization of this population is believed to be higher than against the nondisabled or disordered community, yet reporting is much lower. Criminal justice professionals are highly involved with the community through calls for service, decisions on arrest for perpetrating a crime, and within the corrections setting where there is an overrepresentation of individuals with disabilities and mental disorders.

Through the mandates of the Americans with Disabilities Act, professionals are expected to identify and make accommodations as needed for individuals with development, physical, and cognitive disabilities or mental disorders. In every aspect of policing, for example, law enforcement officers are required to assure equal protection and access to government facilities for individuals. The ADA provides the legal impetus to seek justice for this population, but the moral responsibilities exist within every response professional. Responsibilities and police liability extend to every criminal justice activity.

Initial considerations for those who are involved with investigative interviewing are self-confrontation. Facing personal bias and negative attitudes are overcome through education and awareness on disabilities and mental disorders. Understanding that some individuals are too sick to understand that he or she is sick is a condition known as anosognosia, which affects significant numbers of people with severe mental illness. Covered in this chapter are some of the major categories of disability that criminal justice encounters in individuals: intellectual disability, ADHD, ASD. Discussed are some of the more common disorders noted among inmates: bipolar disorder, schizophrenia, and personality disorders. These are not intended to provide an exhaustive list of the challenges, but to introduce you to some common concerns.

Of debate is the level of violence committed by individuals with mental disorders. While the issue is unsettled, there is agreement in the increased dangerousness when co-occurring disorders involve substance abuse. Victims of crime may be targeted because of their disability or perceived vulnerability. Research suggests an overlap between victimization and perpetration among individuals with severe mental illness. There are differences in state statutes, which are specific to protecting disabled individuals. Typically, crimes committed against this population result in additional penalties for the offender. Some state laws address issues involving vulnerable persons as specific offenses.

Skillful interviewing and careful assessments can increase the likelihood of obtaining sufficient information on which to proceed with cases related to a vulnerable community. The three-step process is outlined here, along with options for specific methods of interviewing. It is well established that most individuals with a disability who are victimized by violent crime are able to identify their perpetrator.

Interrogations of persons with disabilities and mental disorders require an informal assessment on the functioning level of the suspect along with frequent validation of information that is provided during the questioning. Investigative interviewers need to be concerned about the possibility of obtaining false confessions, particularly with individuals with intellectual disabilities.

Questions for Review

Short-Answer Questions

1. What does Title II of the ADA refer to, and how does it affect policing in six ways?
2. In *Gohier v. Enright* (1999), how did the Supreme Court interpret the term "arrest"?
3. What are the two significant issues involved in wrongful arrest, and what techniques can prevent mistakes?
4. Explain the term "intellectual disability" and its significance among the prison population.
5. Describe the three steps to an interview with persons who have disability or mental disorders.

Fill-in Questions and Answers

1. Violence against children with _____ occurs at annual rates at least 1.7 times greater than for their nondisabled peers per the Convention on the Rights of Persons with Disabilities.
2. Calls to police, which are related to _____, outnumber calls for routine larceny, traffic accidents, and domestic disputes combined.
3. There is immense social and legal pressure on law enforcement officers to make the correct decisions and to develop the expertise to _____ and safely handle cases involving individuals with mental disorders.

4. _____ provides that "no qualified individual with a disability shall by reason of such disability, be excluded from participation in or be denied the benefits of the services, programs, or activities of a public entity, or be subjected to discrimination by any such entity."

5. The second step in interviewing an individual with disability or mental disorder is _____.

6. _____ is a medical condition experienced by someone with an acute mental illness who does not think clearly enough to know that he or she is sick.

7. A person having difficulty in problem-solving and academic learning at an early age is now referred to as has having an _____.

8. Studies have documented that there is an overlap between victimization and perpetration among individuals with severe _____.

9. Prior to conducting an interrogation, make a determination on the _____ of the adult suspect.

10. At high risk for false confessions during interrogation are individuals with _____ whose condition may present behavioral indicators of guilt such as a lack of eye contact or an apparent aloof and indifferent manner, which may be misinterpreted.

Exercises

1. Explain the two methods for field evaluation of persons with mental illness and persons with intellectual disability and give reasons why the evaluation would be beneficial to potential interviewers. List questions that would be helpful when making a field evaluation of a person suspected of having a disability.

2. Locate "Resources by State" at http://www.thearc.org /NCCJD/resources. Determine which resources for professional training are available in your state. Next, contact your local or state police department and ask if officers are receiving this training. Report your findings to the class.

References

Americans with Disabilities Act. (1994) 42 U.S.C. §12132.

APA. (2015). *Understanding mental disorders: Your guide to DSM-5.* Washington, D.C.: American Psychiatric Publishing.

Biasotti, M. (2011). *The impact of mental illness on law enforcement resources.* Arlington, VA: Treatment Advocacy Center.

Bronson, J., & Berzofsky, M. (2015). *Disabilities among prison and jail inmates, 2011–12* (NCJ 249151). Washington, D.C.: U.S. Department of Justice.

Buescher, A. V., Cidav, Z., Knapp, M., & Mandell, D. S. (2014). Costs of autism spectrum disorders in the United Kingdom and the United States. *JAMA Pediatrics, 168*(8), 721–728.

Christensen, D. L. (2016). Prevalence and characteristics of autism spectrum disorder among children aged 8 years—autism and developmental disabilities monitoring network, 11 sites, United States, 2012. MMWR. *Surveillance Summaries, 65.*

Conn, C., Warden, R., Stuewig, J., Kim, E. H., Harty, L., Hastings, M., & Tangney, J. P. (2010). Borderline personality disorder among jail inmates: How common and how distinct? *Corrections Compendium, 35*(4), 6.

Cordner, G. (2006). *People with mental illness.* Washington, D.C.: U.S. Department of Justice.

Davis, L. (2009). *People with intellectual disabilities in the criminal justice system: Victims & suspects.* Retrieved from http://www.thearc.org/document.doc?id=3664

Erickson, W., Lee, C., & Schrader, S. v. (2017). *Disability statistics from the American Community Survey (ACS).* Ithaca, NY: Cornell University Yang-Tan Institute (YTI) Retrieved from Cornell University Disability Statistics website: www.disabilitystatistics.org.

Fellner, J. (2003). *Ill-equipped: U.S. prisons and offenders with mental illness.* New York: Human Rights Watch.

Fleischner, R. (2017). Competence to stand trial—The experience of defendants with an intellectual disability compared to those with a mental illness. In the Arc's National Center on Criminal Justice and Disability (NCCJD), *Competency of Individuals with Intellectual and Developmental Disabilities in the Criminal Justice System: A Call to Action for the Criminal Justice Community.* Washington, D.C.: The Arc.

Frank, R. G., & McGuire, T. G. (2010). Mental health treatment and criminal justice outcomes *Controlling crime: Strategies and tradeoffs* (pp. 167–207). Chicago, IL: University of Chicago Press.

Gohier v. Enright, 186 F.3rd 1216 (10th Cir.) (1999).

Griffiths, D. M., & Fedoroff, P. (2014). Persons with intellectual disabilities and problematic sexual behaviors. *Psychiatric Clinics of North America, 37*(2), 195–206.

Hansen, S. N., Schendel, D. E., & Parner, E. T. (2015). Explaining the increase in the prevalence of autism spectrum disorders: The proportion attributable to changes in reporting practices. *JAMA Pediatrics, 169*(1), 56–62.

Harrell, E. (2015). *Crime against persons with disabilities, 2009–2013: Statistical Tables.* (NCJ 248676). Washington, D.C.: U.S. Department of Justice.

Insel, T. (2011). Post by Former NIMH Director Thomas Insel: *Understanding severe mental illness.* Retrieved from https://www.nimh.nih.gov/about/directors/thomas-insel/blog/2011/understanding-severe-mental-illness.shtml

Jackson v. Town of Sanford, 63 U.S.L.W. 2351 (1994).

Kerr, A., Morabito, M., & Watson, A. (2010). Police encounters, mental illness and injury: An exploratory investigation. *Journal of Police Crisis Negotiation, 1*(10), 116–132.

Lenzenweger, M., Lane, M., Loranger, A., & Kessler, R. (2007). DSM-IV personality disorders in the National Comorbidity Survey Replication. *Biological Psychiatry, 62*(6), 553–564.

Leo, R. A., & Cutler, B. L. (2016). *False Confessions in the Twenty-First Century*. The Champion Magazine (May 2016).

Lewis v. Truitt, 960 F. Supp. 175 (S.D. Ind.) (1997).

Lindsay, W. R., Steele, L., Smith, A. H., Quinn, K., & Allan, R. (2006). A community forensic intellectual disability service: Twelve year follow up of referrals, analysis of referral patterns and assessment of harm reduction. *Legal and Criminological Psychology, 11*(1), 113–130.

Miranda v. Arizona, 284 U.S. 436 (1966).

NAMI. (2010). *Mental Health Crisis Planning*. Retrieved from http://www.namihelps.org/Crisis-Booklet-Adults.pdf

NAMI. (2015). *Anosognosia*. Retrieved from http://www.nami.org/Find-Support/A-Family-Member-or-Caregiver/Helping-a-Family-Member-Who-Doesn-t-Think-They-re

Peterson, J., Skeem, J., Kennealy, P., Bray, B., & Zvonkovic, A. (2014). How often and how consistently do symptoms directly precede criminal behavior among offenders with mental illness? *Law and Human Behavior, 38*(5), 439–449.

Pulay, A. J., Dawson, D. A., Hasin, D. S., Goldstein, R. B., Ruan, M. M. W. J., Pickering, M. R. P., ... Grant, B. F. (2008). Violent behavior and DSM-IV psychiatric disorders: results from the national epidemiologic survey on alcohol and related conditions. *The Journal of Clinical Psychiatry, 69*(1), 12.

Roy, L., Crocker, A. G., Nicholls, T. L., Latimer, E. A., & Ayllon, A. R. (2014). Criminal behavior and victimization among homeless individuals with severe mental illness: A systematic review. *Psychiatric Services, 65*(6), 739–750.

Savolainen, J., Hurtig, T. M., Ebeling, H. E., Moilanen, I. K., Hughes, L. A., & Taanila, A. M. (2010). Attention deficit hyperactivity disorder (ADHD) and criminal behaviour: The role of adolescent marginalization. *European Journal of Criminology, 7*(6), 442–459.

Schorr v. Borough of Lemoyne, 243 F. Supp. 2d 232 (District Court, MD Pennsylvania 2003).

Silver, E., Piquero, A. R., Jennings, W. G., Piquero, N. L., & Leiber, M. (2011). Assessing the violent offending and violent victimization overlap among discharged psychiatric patients. *Law and Human Behavior, 35*(1), 49–59.

Steadman, H., Mulvey, E., Monahan, J., Robbins, P., Applebaum, P., Grisso, T., ... Silver, E. (1998). Violence by people discharged from acute psychiatric inpatient facilities and by others in the same neighborhoods. *Arch Gen Psychiatry*, 55, 393–401.

Swanson, J. W., Easter, M. M., Robertson, A. G., Swartz, M. S., Alanis-Hirsch, K., Moseley, D., ... Petrila, J. (2016). Gun violence, mental illness, and laws that prohibit gun possession: Evidence from two Florida counties. *Health Affairs*, 35(6), 1067–1075.

Swanson, J. W., McGinty, E. E., Fazel, S., & Mays, V. M. (2015). Mental illness and reduction of gun violence and suicide: Bringing epidemiologic research to policy. *Annals of epidemiology*, 25(5), 366–376.

Tata, V. (2017). Interrogation & interview reform for people with intellectual disabilities: A social marketing approach. In the Arc's National Center on Criminal Justice and Disability (NCCJD), *Competency of Individuals with Intellectual and Developmental Disabilities in the Criminal Justice System: A Call to Action for the Criminal Justice Community*. Washington, D.C.: The Arc.

Torrey, F. (2013). *Surviving schizophrenia: A manual for families, patients, and providers* (6th ed.). New York, NY: HarperCollins.

Townsend v. Sain, 372 U.S. 293 (1963).

UN. (2006). *Convention on the rights of persons with disabilities*. New York, NY: United Nations.

U.S. Department of Justice. (2006). *Commonly asked questions about the Americans with Disabilities Act and law enforcement*. [Online.] Available at https://www.ada.gov/q...a_law.htm.

Watts, S. J. (2016). ADHD symptomatology and criminal behavior during adolescence: Exploring the mediating role of school factors. *International Journal of Offender Therapy and Comparative Criminology*, 0306624X16639970.

Young, S., Goodwin, E. J., Sedgwick, O., & Gudjonsson, G. H. (2013). The effectiveness of police custody assessments in identifying suspects with intellectual disabilities and attention deficit hyperactivity disorder. *BMC Medicine, 11*(1), 248.

PART IV

Interrogation

In this section, each chapter presents a different view of the interrogation process. Chapter 11 discusses the legal guidelines for criminal justice interrogations. Although each state may establish procedures and laws that are more restrictive than the federal guidelines, the final authority rests with the U.S. Supreme Court. These rules are categorized under the constitutional provisions that the courts have identified as applicable to the interrogation process. The four-prong test for lawful interrogations is based on the Fourth, Fifth, Sixth, and Fourteenth Amendments. The *Miranda* standard is a major focus governing interrogation practices, and its requirements are outlined. The difference between compelling a suspect to give up protected constitutional protections and compelling a suspect to give a statement after those rights have been legally relinquished is addressed. Also, the difference between the Sixth Amendment right to counsel and the *Miranda* standard is discussed.

Chapter 12 examines the goal of the interrogation and pitfalls to avoid when conducting interrogations or related procedures. Studies suggest that interrogations should be conducted more frequently than they are. This view is bolstered by the fact that when police officers do conduct interrogations, they are very successful. Current knowledge of the psychology and suggestibility can be as important to include in techniques for increasing the number of successful interrogations. Ways to avoid false confessions and methods for some case-specific criminal interrogations are suggested.

Chapter 13 covers techniques for questioning. The goal of an interrogation is what differentiates it from an interview. The place and timing are critical but do not define the interrogation. Strategies for conducting interrogations in custodial and noncustodial situations are differentiated. Success in interrogation is achieved by using a three-phase approach to preparing, assessing, and getting the confession. Steps for accomplishing each phase are outlined. Evaluating the suspect and determining the barriers that inhibit a suspect from confessing are covered. Numerous confession-eliciting models are described; no one method determines how interrogations must take place. Of note are the PEACE and HUMINT methods.

Chapter 14 addresses challenges and legal obligations concerning juvenile interrogations. The criminal justice system treats a minor in a different way than an adult. The distinction is important for the criminal justice professionals who may be engaged in conducting interrogations. A juvenile can be prosecuted under a civil system that closely resembles the adult penal system. Defining a juvenile can be difficult, and states vary on when a child can be prosecuted as a minor or an adult. The situation is further complicated because some state statutes mandate that juvenile offenders be tried in adult court if they commit specific serious crimes. Juvenile rights are outlined in this chapter within the context of police responsibility. Specific crimes in which juvenile perpetration is of serious concern are addressed along with suggestions for interrogation in these cases.

11

The Interrogation Process and the Law

Source: Sean Nel/123RF.

CHAPTER OBJECTIVES

After completing this chapter, you should be able to:

1. Define the rule of law.
2. Describe the totality-of-the-circumstances test.
3. Explain *Miranda* rights.
4. Compare the constitutional protections deriving from the Fourth, Fifth, and Sixth Amendments.
5. Discuss probable cause.
6. State the protections of the Fourth Amendment and how they apply to interrogation.
7. Restate the exclusionary rule.
8. List the categories in which police officers have the power to make arrests.

KEY TERMS

Custody	Exclusionary rule
Miranda rights	Power to arrest
Probable cause	State action
Totality of the circumstances	Rule of law

INTRODUCTION

The fundamental principle on which the U.S. legal system rests is that law is created to protect citizens against tyranny and lawlessness and to protect freedom. The law that guides the system comes from many sources, with the Constitution of the United States as the supreme law of the land. The Bill of Rights and other amendments to the Constitution developed further protections to the rights and freedoms of individuals. State constitutions expand and define the protections within their jurisdictions, but no state can deprive the individual of the rights established and guaranteed by the U.S. Constitution.

The **rule of law** holds that those who execute the law must rely on the application of known principles or laws and that those principles must be applied uniformly and fairly to all citizens. This concept is also referred to as the *supremacy of law*. General constitutional principles are the result of judicial decisions determining the rights of individuals. According to the rule of stare decisis, judges must make decisions that are guided by previous settled decisions. Many of the decisions that govern interrogation practices by the police are interpretations of the U.S. Constitution that have evolved since the 1960s. These contemporary interpretations of the Constitution illustrate that the law is a fluid entity; it relies on settled principles to form the basis for contemporary legal standards. The courts are settling issues that could not have been anticipated by the framers of the Constitution, such as the legality of wiretapping or the taking of DNA samples. Still, the old concepts must be applied in a way that is consistent with what the Constitution demands and in a manner that is fair to all. The objective application and enforcement of laws concerning interrogations by government officials and their agents are established in the law itself and interpreted by the rulings of judges.

The four-prong test for the admissibility of a confession is based on the Fourth, Fifth, Sixth, and Fourteenth Amendments. In the past, confessions that were considered voluntary were admissible in court and could be used against a suspect if they fulfilled the Fifth Amendment protections against self-incrimination, regardless of any questions of formal legality (*Colombe v. Connecticut*, 1961). Since the Fourteenth Amendment requirement of due process was found to apply to state actions, the Fourth Amendment has joined the list of important legal considerations.

FIFTH AMENDMENT CONSIDERATIONS

The Fifth Amendment of the U.S. Constitution is discussed first in this chapter because it contains the earliest example of protections applied to the admissibility of confessions. It protects the right of a suspect against compelled testimonial communication and self-incrimination. It states:

> *No person shall be held to answer for a capital, or otherwise infamous crime, unless on a presentment or indictment of a Grand Jury, except in cases arising in the land or naval forces, or in the Militia, when in actual service in time of War or public danger; nor shall any person be subject for the same offence to be twice put in jeopardy of life or limb; nor shall be compelled in any criminal case to be a witness against himself, nor be deprived of life, liberty, or property, without due process of law; nor shall private property be taken for public use, without just compensation.*

The Fifth Amendment requires that no person will be incriminated through compelled testimonial communication. *Compel* refers to an official undertaking to induce a witness to provide evidence by the threat of punitive sanctions (Rosenthal, 2017). To be *testimonial*, a "communication must itself, explicitly or implicitly, relate a factual assertion or disclose information" that is the "expression of the contents of an individual's mind" (*Doe v. United States*, 1988). The protection against self-incrimination also permits a person to refuse to testify against himself or herself at a criminal trial in which he or she is a defendant.

The application of the Fifth Amendment to confession has evolved. Under early common law, an admission or confession was allowed to be used in court as evidence of guilt even if it was the product of force or duress. Enforcement officers resorted to torture to extract a confession from the accused during an interrogation rather than conduct an investigation to establish guilt.

Practices of torture as an interrogation method eventually led to the development of rules on the admissibility of confessions in the late eighteenth century. The newer common-law rule excluded coerced confessions from being admitted at trial due to the unreliability of evidence that was the product of torture. During the late 1800s, the Court joined the common-law rule to the Fifth Amendment prohibition of compelling an individual to give witness against himself or herself as the standard for judging the admissibility of confessions (*Bram v. United States*, 1897).

The common-law rule was abandoned for the "free and voluntary" rule during the early twentieth century. This rule required that statements must be freely and voluntarily made without duress, fear, or compulsion and with knowledge of the consequences of the confession (*People v. Fox*, 1925). Involuntary confessions were rejected not because of the illegal or deceitful methods used in obtaining them, but because of their unreliability. Torture as a means of extracting confessions was expressly denounced in 1937 (*Brown v. Mississippi*, 1937). Using a *totality-of-the-circumstances* test, the Court in *Brown* concluded that repeated whippings of the suspect produced a coerced statement that could not be used against him in court. A **totality of the circumstances** test is one in which the court focuses on all of the circumstances surrounding a situation rather than any one factor. In 1966, the *Miranda* standard distinguished between the voluntariness of a statement and its validity (*Miranda v. Arizona*, 1966).

THE *MIRANDA* STANDARD

The Court in *Miranda* said that procedural safeguards must be used to secure the privilege against self-incrimination during custodial interrogations. The Court reasoned that the practices of custodial interrogation were inherently coercive

CASE IN POINT 11-1

CASE IN POINT: MIRANDA V. ARIZONA (1966)

In 1965, the Supreme Court agreed to hear the case of Ernesto Miranda, a poor Mexican immigrant, who had been arrested after a crime victim identified him in a police lineup. At the same time, the Court agreed to hear three similar cases: *Vignera v. New York*, *Westover v. United States*, and *California v. Stewart*. These four cases were combined, and because *Miranda* was the first case listed, the decision came to be known by that name.

Miranda had been charged with rape and kidnapping and interrogated for 2 hours while in police custody. As a result of the interrogation, he had confessed to the crimes with which he was charged. Although his statement included an acknowledgment that he was aware of his right against self-incrimination, he had never been informed of his rights under the Fifth Amendment or of his Sixth Amendment right to the assistance of an attorney. He had been sentenced to 20 to 30 years in prison on each count.

Importance

1. The Supreme Court in *Miranda* set specific guidelines for police officers on how they must advise suspects of their constitutional rights and under what circumstances those warnings must be provided.
2. The Supreme Court combined the Sixth Amendment right to an attorney with the Fifth Amendment right against self-incrimination.

(*Miranda v. Arizona*, 1966). Whether the *Miranda* requirements are complied with requires an analysis using the Fifth Amendment. Known as the *Miranda* **rights**, the following procedural safeguards must be stated before questioning. The person must be told that

1. He or she has a right to remain silent.
2. Any statement he or she does make may be used as evidence against him or her.
3. He or she has a right to the presence of an attorney.
4. If he or she cannot afford an attorney, counsel will be provided at government expense.

When Are the *Miranda* Warnings Required?

Miranda warnings or their equivalent must be given before questioning (direct or indirect) that is initiated by an agent of the state if the suspect has been taken into police custody or otherwise deprived of his or her freedom of action by the police in any significant way.

- **State action:** **State action** is anything done by a government, in particular the intrusion on a person's rights by a government entity (Schmidt, 2016). It occurs in interrogation practices when communication with a suspect is undertaken by federal or state law enforcement officers or their agents. This includes action taken by federal law enforcement officers such as agents of the Federal Bureau of Investigation, the Central Intelligence Agency, and the Drug Enforcement Agency and Postal Inspectors. State and municipal police officers are governed by these federal standards and may also have additional state laws that restrict their action. It does not cover the actions of private citizens who are not acting under police direction or solicitation.

- **Custody:** **Custody** exists when a suspect is either deprived of his or her freedom in any significant way or is in formal detainment such as an arrest. Custody for *Miranda* purposes is more broadly defined than as the traditional arrest. Custody may be subjective, from the point of view of the person being questioned, due

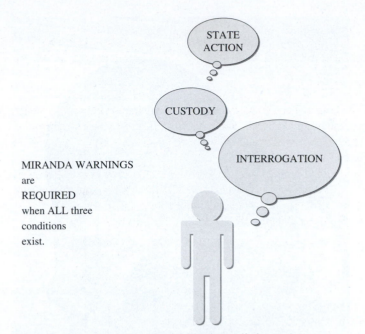

FIGURE 11-1 *Miranda* rights must be provided when all three circumstances exist at the same time.

to a coercive environment. Three factors need to be considered for determining whether a suspect is in a coercive environment:

1. **Nature of the interview.** Is the interview aggressive or informal?
2. **Atmosphere.** Generally the most coercive site is a police station, yet a police station inquiry is not automatically custodial.
3. **Freedom to leave.** At the time that the incriminating statement was made, was the suspect free to end the interview by leaving the place of the interrogation or by asking the interrogator to leave, as evidenced by whether the interview ended with the defendant's arrest?

• **Interrogation:** For a questioning or its functional equivalent by a police officer or his or her agent to be considered an interrogation it must be designed to produce testimonial evidence. The functional equivalent to interrogation includes any words or actions by the police that they should know are reasonably likely to elicit an incriminating response (*Rhode Island v. Innis*, 1980).

When Is a Waiver of *Miranda* Rights Valid?

A defendant may waive *Miranda* rights, provided the waiver is made voluntarily, knowingly, and intelligently. If the suspect waives his or her rights, he or she may refrain from answering questions at any time. The totality-of-the-circumstances test will help the court to determine whether the waiver of rights was valid. This means that all of the factors surrounding the waiver will be considered. Three measures of whether an individual has properly waived his or her right to remain silent are as follows:

• The waiver was made voluntarily: The government must prove that the waiver was not the result of coercion or other factors that adversely influenced the defendant's exercise of free will. Torture, threats, promises of leniency, or other inducements may affect the voluntariness of a waiver. If the person is intoxicated to the point that he or she cannot understand his or her constitutional rights, the waiver is not valid.

FIGURE 11-2   *Miranda* rights must be waived voluntarily, knowingly, and intelligently for the waiver to be considered valid.

Source: MSPhotographic/Shutterstock.

- The waiver was made knowingly: The government must prove that the defendant knew and understood his or her rights. Providing *Miranda* rights to a person who does not speak English, for example, cannot result in a knowing waiver of those rights. If the defendant is suffering from a mental disability that renders him or her incapable of understanding his or her constitutional rights, a wavier may not be valid.
- The waiver was made intelligently: The government must establish that the defendant intelligently relinquished those rights and understood that he or she was agreeing to answer questions. This requires that the suspect be able to understand the consequences of not invoking the *Miranda* rights. This requirement does not suggest that the suspect is intelligent or have any particular IQ to make an intelligent waiver of his or her rights.

VOLUNTARY STATEMENTS.   Statements that are initiated by the defendant are not barred by the *Miranda* decision whether or not the person is in custody. The Court stated that "there is no requirement that police stop a person who enters a police station and states that he wishes to confess to a crime or a person who calls the police to offer a confession or any other statement that he desires to make." Volunteered statements of any kind are not barred by the Fifth Amendment, and their admissibility is not affected by *Miranda*. If a defendant engages in conversation with a police officer and subsequently makes an incriminating statement, he or she does not need to be warned of his or her rights because there was no interrogation.

If a suspect invokes the right to silence and does not provide a statement to the police, he or she has the right to reinitiate a conversation. The waiver of *Miranda* rights may still be valid if it is clear that it was the suspect who reinitiated the conversation without inducement by the police.

PUBLIC SAFETY EXCEPTION.   The Supreme Court did not intend for *Miranda* warnings to govern all police interactions with the members of the public. In fact, the vast majority of police and citizen communications do not fall under *Miranda*'s protective umbrella. In situations in which there is an immediate or impending danger to the public safety, called the public safety exception, the police may arrest a suspect without informing him or her of his or her constitutional rights and ask questions to elicit information in order to remove the threat to the public (*New York v. Quarles*, 1984). Officers must then provide *Miranda* warnings once the threat is over.

Requiring a person in custody to stand or walk in a police lineup, to speak prescribed words, to model special clothing, or to give samples of handwriting, fingerprints, or blood does not fall under self-incrimination within the meaning of the Fifth Amendment (*Schmerber v. California*, 1966). These do not fall under the Fifth Amendment because they are not testimonial in nature.

Right to Counsel under *Miranda*

The *Miranda* standard includes the right to have an attorney present during a custodial interrogation as part of its required procedural process. A suspect is entitled to the assistance of counsel during custodial interrogation even though the Constitution does not provide for such assistance (*Davis v. U.S.*, 2004). *Miranda* went further than previous case analysis of this right by requiring in cases of custodial interrogation that the suspect expressly be told of this right to an attorney and that he or she may voluntarily waive that right under the same standards as govern compelled testimony.

BEEN THERE . . . DONE THAT! 11-1

This case involved a man accused of having burned a covered bridge. The case was investigated, and a warrant was issued for his arrest. He fled the area, which is when I became involved. I located the perpetrator in Louisiana; he was arrested on the Massachusetts warrant. Arrangements were made for his rendition.

He was picked up at the Louisiana jail, and a sergeant and I transported him back to Massachusetts. While he was in a holding cell at the airport I sat outside as his guard, reading a book. I lit up a cigarette, and the suspect asked for one. I gave him the cigarette without responding and continued to read my book. About half an hour later the same thing happened. He asked for a cigarette and I gave it to him. Saying nothing, I went back to reading my book. This time the man settled back in contentment and started to talk to get my attention. He said, "You know ma'am, I am not such a bad guy—now my brother-in-law, he is a bad guy! He cheats on his taxes and steals tools from the place he works. All I did was burn down an old bridge!"

I looked over to the sergeant, who was sitting across the room. He said, "Trooper, give that man another cigarette." While the man was in custody there was no interrogation. His statement of admission was used in evidence against him in court.

FIGURE 11-3 The Sixth Amendment right to an attorney begins at the time of formal processing in the court.

Source: Burlingham/Shutterstock.

In *Edwards v. Arizona* (1981), the Court reiterated and clarified the concerns specified in the *Miranda* decision concerning a suspect's right to counsel. The Court held that the waiver of an attorney during a custodial interrogation must not only be voluntary but also knowing and intelligent. The bright-line *Edwards* rule clearly requires that once a suspect has invoked the right to an attorney per *Miranda*, all questioning must stop. It cannot be reinitiated by the police at any time in the future unless counsel has been made available to the suspect or the suspect initiates further conversation. The request for an attorney must be clearly stated, however, and not be ambiguous. In *Davis v. U.S.* (2004), the Court held that a statement by the suspect, "Maybe I should talk to a lawyer," was not a request for counsel under the requirements of *Miranda*.

If an attorney is made available at the request of the suspect and subsequently leaves, police may not resume interrogation when the attorney is no longer present (*Minnick v. Mississippi*, 1990). The police may not simply avoid the suspect's request for a lawyer by changing the direction of questioning to a nonrelated offense (*Arizona v. Roberson*, 1988).

- **Bright Line:** If a suspect in custody and subjected to interrogation requests an attorney, ALL QUESTIONING MUST CEASE IMMEDIATELY!

SIXTH AMENDMENT CONSIDERATIONS

The Sixth Amendment to the U.S. Constitution protects the rights of persons accused in criminal prosecution. The remedy for violation of a suspect's Sixth Amendment right to counsel is that any evidence obtained through such a violation cannot be used in court. The Sixth Amendment to the U.S. Constitution states:

> *In all criminal prosecutions, the accused shall enjoy the right to a speedy and public trial, by an impartial jury of the State and district wherein the crime shall have been committed, which district shall have been previously ascertained by law, and to be informed of the nature and cause of the accusation; to be confronted with the witnesses against him; to have compulsory process for obtaining witnesses in his favor, and to have the Assistance of Counsel for his defense.*

The right to counsel under the Sixth Amendment prohibits law enforcement officers from deliberately eliciting incriminating information from a defendant in the absence of counsel after a formal (criminal) charge against the defendant has been filed (*Massiah v. U.S.*, 1964). The formal charge refers to the preliminary step in prosecution through a formal accusation of a named suspect (Cassell, Mitchell, & Edwards, 2014). Examples of formal charging include an indictment by a grand jury and an arraignment.

The Sixth Amendment and the due process clause of the Fourteenth Amendment prohibit law enforcement officers from deliberately eliciting incriminating information from a defendant in the absence of counsel after a formal charge against the accused has been filed, regardless of whether or not the defendant is in custody (*Rhode Island v. Innis*, 1980). This means that questioning cannot occur by a police officer in any location at any time, regardless of whether or not the person is in custody. The suspect cannot be questioned about the crime for which he or she was formally charged even if the police officer inadvertently has contact with the suspect. Examples of inadvertent contact are the police officer seeing the suspect on the street or arresting the suspect for an unrelated crime. However, the right to counsel under the Sixth Amendment is offense specific. It holds only for the crimes for which the suspect was formally charged; the suspect can be interrogated about unrelated offenses.

Once the formal process has been initiated against a suspect, his or her Sixth Amendment right to counsel can be violated by less obvious forms of interrogation, such as bugging, eavesdropping, and contact by an informant (*Massiah v. U.S.*, 1964). No form of interrogation of the suspect is permitted, regardless of whether or not the suspect is aware of being questioned by an agent of the government.

FOURTEENTH AMENDMENT CONSIDERATIONS

The Fourteenth Amendment to the U.S. Constitution affirms the rights, privileges, and immunities of citizenship, including due process and equal protection. The Supreme Court has interpreted the amendment as restricting the states from denying any citizen the rights that are guaranteed under the U.S. Constitution. Through the Fourteenth Amendment, all constitutional rules apply equally to federal and state police action. Section 1, which contains the due process clause and equal protection provision, specifically restrict police action. Throughout this chapter, the application of the Fourteenth Amendment to police interrogation procedures will be made evident.

> *Section 1. All persons born or naturalized in the United States and subject to the jurisdiction thereof, are citizens of the United States and of the State wherein they reside. No State shall make or enforce any law which shall abridge the privileges or immunities of citizens of the United States; nor shall any State deprive any person of life, liberty, or property, without due process of law; nor deny to any person within its jurisdiction the equal protection of the laws.*

The Exclusionary Rule

The **exclusionary rule** is a remedy to possible abuse by government officials of the restrictions set by the Constitution. It requires that evidence obtained by police in violation of the Fourteenth Amendment's due process clause, the Sixth Amendment's right to counsel provision, the Fifth Amendment's privilege against self-incrimination, or the Fourth Amendment's protection from illegal search and seizure be excluded from use in a trial against a defendant.

In *Weeks v. U.S.* (1914), the Court first stated that evidence secured through illegal search and seizure and in violation of the Fourth Amendment should be barred from use in federal prosecutions. It was not until 1961 that the rule was made applicable to the states through the Fourteenth Amendment's due process clause (*Mapp v. Ohio*, 1961). There are several alternatives to invoking the exclusionary rule, such as undertaking

CASE IN POINT 11-2

CASE IN POINT: MAPP V. OHIO (1961)

Three Cleveland police officers went to the apartment of Miss Dollree Mapp looking for a person suspected in a bombing. Miss Mapp refused to allow them in without a search warrant. Three hours later, and after four more officers arrived, the police forcibly gained entry. Miss Mapp demanded to see the search warrant. A paper claimed to be a warrant was held up by one of the officers. She grabbed the "warrant" and stuffed it down her blouse. There was a struggle in which the officers recovered the piece of paper. They handcuffed her because she had resisted their official rescue of the paper. She was then forcibly taken upstairs to the second floor, where officers searched her bedroom, a child's bedroom, the living room, the kitchen, and a dinette. In the basement of the building a trunk was found, which was also searched. The obscene materials for possession of which she was ultimately convicted were discovered in the course of that search.

At the trial no search warrant was produced by the prosecution, nor was the failure to produce one explained or accounted for. The State said that even if the search were made without authority, it was not prevented from using the unconstitutionally seized evidence at trial, citing *Wolf v. Colorado* (1949), in which the Court had held that "in a prosecution in a State court for a State crime the Fourteenth Amendment does not forbid the admission of evidence obtained by an unreasonable search and seizure (pg. 33)." The Supreme Court concluded that the Fourth Amendment DOES apply to the states, and evidence obtained in an unreasonable search could not be used against the suspect.

Importance

1. *Mapp* was the first case in which the Supreme Court applied the exclusionary rule to the states.
2. This case is an example of the application of the exclusionary rule in a Fourth Amendment context.

---

criminal prosecutions against officers who violate a suspect's rights, but these are extremely rare. Internal department discipline and prosecutions for civil rights violations in federal courts are other available remedies. Practical considerations render these options fairly ineffective. As a result, the Court has emphasized the exclusionary rule as the most effective way to deter police misconduct.

Exclusion of evidence that is indirectly obtained when a person's rights are violated may also occur under the rule. Sometimes called derivative or secondary evidence, this is evidence resulting from an illegal search or illegal interrogation. The fruit-of-the-poisonous-tree doctrine holds that an illegal search or interrogation taints the evidence obtained as well as facts discovered by the processes initiated by the unlawful procedure and that that evidence must be suppressed (*Wong Sun v. U.S.*, 1963).

The due process clause of the Fourteenth Amendment protects against the admission into evidence of involuntary confessions. For example, a suspect may make a valid waiver of *Miranda* rights, but his or her statement may be in violation of the Fourteenth Amendment because the police used coercive tactics to obtain it. Statements that are the product of coercion, either physical or psychological, cannot be used as evidence, not because of their unlikely truth, but because the methods used to extract them offend the underlying principle in the enforcement of criminal law: that ours is accusatorial and not an inquisitorial system (*Rogers v. Richmond*, 1961). Confessions are an important component in law enforcement, and any statement given freely and voluntarily without any compelling influences is admissible in evidence (*Rhode Island v. Innis*, 1980). A statement is inadmissible in court if the accused was coerced into making it. A statement is compelled if it is

1. The product of either physical or psychological coercion.
2. Extracted by any sort of threat or violence.

3. The product of direct or implied promises.

4. Made as the result of the exertion of any improper influence.

WHEN IS A CONFESSION CONSIDERED TO HAVE BEEN COERCED?   A statement may not be used in court if it was made in an environment that is so coercive as to support the conclusion that it was not freely and voluntarily given (*Colorado v. Connelly*, 1986). Typically, all of the factors surrounding the incident, or the totality of the circumstances, will determine whether physical or psychological pressures unduly influenced the accused to make a statement.

- Generally a promise of leniency will nullify a confession; certain kinds of promises are acceptable, however.
- In *United States v. Guerrero* (1988), the U.S. Court of Appeals ruled that "it is well settled that police may use small deceptions while interrogating witnesses."
- In *United States v. Mendoza-Cecelia* (1992), the U.S. Court of Appeals ruled that "isolated incidents of deception … are usually insufficient to preclude free choice," and acknowledged that "police may use some psychological tactics in interrogating a suspect."
- Threats to arrest members of a suspect's family may cause a confession to be considered involuntary (*Rogers v. Richmond*, 1961).

The following factors are among those that the court will look at in determining if an interrogation process was coercive:

AGE OF THE SUSPECT.   The circumstances surrounding statements from juveniles are more carefully scrutinized because they are more susceptible than adults to coercive forces or intimidation. Courts demand that police officers use caution when questioning juveniles to make sure that they do not confess out of fear. The questioning by several officers at the same time or the absence of a parent may be coercive if the juvenile is young.

EXPERIENCE OF THE SUSPECT.   A child's or adult's history of contact with the police and the criminal justice system may be a significant factor is determining whether his or her statements were voluntary. A person with a history of criminal activity and familiarity with police practice is less likely to feel threatened to the point of being coerced into speaking.

INTELLIGENCE OR MENTAL ILLNESS.   Someone with a low IQ or mental illness may be overly suggestible and subject to intimidation. Persons having mental illness or low intelligence need to be questioned in the same noncoercive atmosphere as a juvenile. Extra care must be taken to assure that the person understands the situation in addition to his or her rights per *Miranda*. A lower educational level of the suspect should alert the police officer to the possibility that there is a greater susceptibility to coercion.

ALCOHOL OR DRUG INTOXICATION.   Although intoxication alone is not enough to negate an otherwise voluntary act, the fact that a statement is given while a suspect is under the influence of alcohol or drugs is relevant to an evaluation of its voluntariness. If a suspect is unduly susceptible to the coercive forces of police questioning due to intoxication, this may impact the voluntariness of any statement he or she gives.

PHYSICAL CONDITION OF THE SUSPECT.   An injured or ill suspect or someone who has had little sleep before interrogation may be more susceptible to coercive forces.

LENGTH OF THE INTERROGATION.   The federal courts have stated a preference that a person under arrest be brought to court for arraignment "without unnecessary delay" for a confession to be admissible (*McNabb v. U.S.*, 1943). This requirement, aimed at addressing incommunicado interrogation and coerced confessions, is known as the McNabb-Mallory doctrine. The Court has never imposed the rule on the states, nor has it set a specific time after which a confession is invalid. Congress set a 6-hour period for interrogation following arrest before the suspect must be presented to the court (Omnibus Crime Control and Safe Streets Act, 1968). Some states have adopted the rule voluntarily. Under the *Rosario* rule, Massachusetts requires that a defendant who has been arrested be brought before a court if it is then in session, and if it is not, at its next session (*Commonwealth v. Rosario*, 1996).

The exclusionary rule has been controversial and criticized since it was established. Numerous decisions have narrowed its application, most notably the "good faith exception." In 1984 the Court held that evidence secured by police officers who rely on a warrant should not be excluded even if the warrant is later found to be defective (*United States v. Leon*, 1984).

FOURTH AMENDMENT CONSIDERATIONS

The Fourth Amendment to the U.S. Constitution protects against unreasonable searches and seizures. It states:

> *The right of the people to be secure in their persons, houses, papers, and effects, against unreasonable searches and seizures, shall not be violated, and no warrants shall issue, but upon probable cause, supported by oath or affirmation, and particularly describing the place to be searched, and the persons or things to be seized.*

Since the application of the exclusionary rule to the states, a confession, statement, or admission that is made by a person who is illegally in custody may be excluded as evidence obtained as a result of an unlawful seizure. The application of the Fourth Amendment as a protection against arbitrary arrests has become established law (*Steagald v. U.S.*, 1981). Under the Fourth Amendment a "seizure" does not necessarily mean a formal arrest to bring the warrant requirement to bear. An objective justification must validate all seizures of a person, including those that only involve a brief detention.

To protect statements and physical evidence that may be acquired from a suspect, attention must be given to the legality of the detention or arrest prior to the interrogation. Under the Fourth Amendment, a seizure is made reasonable by the application for a warrant that is based on probable cause. Probable cause itself may be sufficient to justify detention or arrest in some situations.

The criminal justice process typically begins when a person is placed under arrest. An arrest occurs when a person is taken into police custody and deprived of his or her liberty by legal authority and is no longer free to leave. An arrest may occur when a police officer states that someone is under arrest. The suspect does not have to be placed in handcuffs or restraints, nor do the words need to be stated for an arrest to have been made. When a person submits to the authority of the police either voluntarily or involuntarily, he or she is under arrest. Police have the **power to arrest** in the following circumstances:

- **When the police officer sees someone commit a crime.** For example, if a police officer is patrolling and sees a man hit another man outside of a bar. The police officer may stop the cruiser and arrest the man for having committed an assault and battery against the other.
- **When an arrest warrant has been issued.** The arrest warrant contains information on the crime, the identity of the person to be arrested, a location where the person might be found, and the command that the police officer make that arrest.

CASE IN POINT 11-3

CASE IN POINT: CARROLL V. U.S. (1925)

Federal prohibition agents developed information that the Carroll brothers were regularly transporting whiskey from Detroit to Grand Rapids, Michigan, a distance of 152 miles. The boys outran the law once, and they could not be caught in the act, although they had once agreed to sell three cases of whiskey to an undercover agent. On December 15, 1921, agents saw their Fleet Oldsmobile Roadster and gave chase. The vehicle was stopped, and the agents did not see any contraband in the car. Without consent or a warrant, one agent concluded that the upholstery was harder than normal and cut open the leather seat. The agents removed 69 quarts of illegal gin and whiskey that had been hidden. George Carroll handed the agent several 10 dollar bills and told him to take the liquor and give them one more chance. The defense later said that the bribe offer was a misunderstanding.

Importance

1. The Supreme Court held that a warrantless search of an automobile stopped by police officers who had probable cause to believe the vehicle contained contraband was not unreasonable under the Fourth Amendment. This became known as the "automobile exception," by which the warrant requirement of the Fourth Amendment did not apply to searches of an automobile.
2. The Supreme Court defined probable cause as existing where the facts and circumstances within the officers' knowledge and of which they had reasonably trustworthy information are sufficient in themselves to warrant a person of reasonable caution in the belief that an offense has been or is being committed.

- **When a police officer has a reasonable belief, based on facts and circumstances, that a person has committed or is about to commit a crime.** This is an arrest based on probable cause without a warrant. For example, if a police officer receives a radio call that a store has just been robbed along with the description of the suspect and the officer sees a person matching that description running away from the area, he or she can make an arrest.

Probable Cause

The court has acknowledged that an exact definition of **probable cause** is difficult because it depends on the totality of the circumstances (*Brinegar v. U.S.*, 1949). The courts determine whether probable cause to arrest a person existed by looking at the

FIGURE 11-4   The police officer must have probable cause to make an arrest.

Source: Sirtravelalot/Shutterstock.

CASE IN POINT 11-4

Robert Kaupp, a 17-year-old man, was suspected of murder. The case turned on the Fourth Amendment rule that a confession "obtained by exploitation of an illegal arrest" may not be used against a criminal defendant (*Brown v. Illinois*, 1975). After a 14-year-old girl disappeared in January 1999, the Harris County Sheriff's Department learned that she had had a sexual relationship with her 19-year-old half-brother, who had been in the company of Robert Kaupp on the day of the girl's disappearance. On January 26, deputy sheriffs questioned the brother and Kaupp at headquarters; Kaupp was cooperative and was permitted to leave, but the brother failed a polygraph examination (his third such failure). Eventually, he confessed that he had fatally stabbed his half-sister and placed her body in a drainage ditch. He implicated Kaupp in the crime. Detectives immediately tried but failed to obtain a warrant to question Kaupp due to a lack of probable cause.

The police came to his home at 3:00 AM and told him they had to talk. He responded, "okay." Kaupp was handcuffed and brought to the police station in his underwear and without shoes. Although he was given his rights per *Miranda* prior to an interrogation, the Supreme Court held that the initial detainment was paramount to an arrest without probable cause, causing the confession to be suppressed. His response of "okay" was determined by the Court to be nothing more than submission to lawful authority in a situation in which he had no choice but to go with the police officers.

The seizure of a person within the meaning of the Fourth and Fourteenth Amendments occurs when "taking into account all of the circumstances surrounding the encounter, the police conduct would 'have communicated to a reasonable person that he was not at liberty to ignore the police presence and go about his business'" (*Florida v. Bostick*, 1991, quoting *Michigan v. Chesternut*, 1988).

events leading up to the arrest or detention. However, probable cause means more than mere suspicion (*Carroll v. U.S.*, 1925).

The court will look at the totality of the circumstances to determine whether the police officer had probable cause to make an arrest. Information that was obtained unlawfully, such as statements from an illegal interrogation, cannot be used to establish probable cause for an arrest. An arrest is valid if the police officer had probable cause to arrest at that time, even if the person turns out to be innocent. In order to detain or pick up and take a suspect to the police station for interrogation, police must have probable cause to make an arrest or a warrant (*Kaupp v. Texas*, 2003). A violation of the Fourth and Fourteenth Amendments cannot be remedied by *Miranda* warnings alone (*Taylor v. Alabama*, 1982). Without probable cause for an arrest, a suspect can be requested to come for questioning with a full understanding that this is voluntary.

Probable cause may be based on personal observations of the officer and through information that is provided from another source:

- **Personal observations.**   If the police officer is legally at the location where he or she observes a criminal act, no further probable cause is needed to make an arrest. This means that the officer cannot make a trespass against the person and use the information to furnish probable cause. For example, a police officer may not go onto someone's property and look through the window to gain information to be used as probable cause.

    A suspect's confession or admission that is obtained legally may be used to establish probable cause.

- **Information provided by others.**   Police officers may use information that is provided by victims, witnesses, other police officers, and informants to establish probable cause to make an arrest. The reliability of the information must be determined prior to its use. When other police officers provide information, it is generally considered reliable and may be used as the basis for probable cause to

FIGURE 11-5 A valid arrest protects future statements that may be made by the suspect.

Source: Lisa F. Young/Fotolia.

arrest. For a full discussion on determining the reliability of information from other sources, refer to Chapter 1.

- **Prior criminal record, furtive conduct, evasive answers, or the nature of the area.**   Although these cannot stand alone in establishing probable cause, they are factors that may be considered in determining whether probable cause exists. For example, prior criminal conduct and furtive conduct are factors when the arresting officer has information that a suspect has committed similar crimes in the past to the one that is under investigation, and the defendant attempts to flee when approached by the police officer. During questioning, a police officer may draw reasonable inferences from the suspect's answers and demeanor.

ENTRY INTO A DWELLING.   Unique challenges to the police officer exist for entry into a dwelling to make an arrest. The Fourth Amendment sometimes forbids an entry into a dwelling to make an arrest without a warrant, regardless of exigent circumstances or how likely it is that evidence may be lost or destroyed. Examples where entry is prohibited include entry into a home without a warrant in pursuit of a drunk driver, an underage driver, to pursue fleeing misdemeanants, or to enforce traffic violations. The courts frown on entering a home without a warrant to arrest a minor or a person on a misdemeanor charge, even when evidence might be destroyed, or exigent circumstances exist. Entering the home to prevent injury may be considered exigent circumstances. The following factors may contribute to a finding of exigent circumstances (*Commonwealth v. Forde*, 1975):

- The crime was violent, and the suspect is believed to be armed and dangerous.
- There is probable cause to believe that a felony has been committed and that the suspect is in the dwelling.
- There is a likelihood that the suspect will escape if not immediately apprehended.
- There is a reasonable basis for believing that the delay necessitated by seeking a warrant would subject the officers or others to physical harm.

Probable cause is always a necessary component to making an arrest in a person's home. To arrest a suspect in his or her home in the absence of consent or exigent circumstances, an arrest warrant or search warrant is sufficient, depending on the circumstances.

To arrest a person believed to be in the dwelling of a third party in the absence of exigent circumstances, both an arrest warrant and a search warrant must be obtained (*Steagald v. U.S.*, 1981). If the owner of the home gives the police officer consent to enter the dwelling, then only the arrest warrant is required.

Entry into a third party's house to make an arrest without a search warrant may be legal under exigent circumstances, including hot pursuit. Hot pursuit is perhaps the best-known example of an exigent circumstance that might justify entry into a dwelling to make an arrest without a warrant. Although police officers may justify entry into a dwelling for the purposes of making an arrest, if exigent circumstances can be foreseen and the officers have time to obtain a warrant, then one should be obtained. A "warm pursuit," such as following distinctive footprints in the snow or following an evidence trail, may be acceptable if the crime is exceptionally serious (*People v. Morrow*, 1982).

Conclusions

This chapter outlines some of the legal restrictions on questioning suspects. The primary source limiting police action and providing rights to the accused is the Constitution. The Court's interpretation of the Constitution has resulted in numerous procedural rules and requirements that define the rights of citizens against actions by government agents, such as police officers or individuals working at their request. It does not protect the rights of citizens from actions taken by other citizens. Because the Constitution is the supreme law of the land, the individual state governments cannot infringe on these rights.

The Fourth, Fifth, and Sixth Amendments of the Constitution provide different protections, although they sometimes appear to overlap. The right to an attorney under the Fifth Amendment *Miranda* rule applies to consultation before the interrogation stage and is concerned with police custody of the person. This is different from the Sixth Amendment right, which applies at the time of any formal court proceeding. The Fourteenth Amendment comes into play for all of these requirements when the consideration is one of due process or fundamental fairness.

Questions for Review

Short-Answer Questions

1. What rights of the accused does the Fifth Amendment protect?
2. What rights of the accused does the Sixth Amendment protect?
3. Describe the circumstances leading to *Mapp v. Ohio*. What significance does this case have regarding the exclusionary rule?
4. Explain a police officer's "power to arrest." Who can be arrested? Where, when, and why?

5. *Miranda* warnings must be issued when custody and interrogation occur simultaneously. For purposes of the *Miranda* ruling, what constitutes custody? What constitutes interrogation?

Fill-in Questions

1. The _____ provides that those who execute the law must rely on the application of known principles or laws, and those principles must be applied _____ to all citizens.

2. _____, _____, and _____ protect citizens from actions of government officials and their agents and not from other citizens.

3. The exclusionary rule is a remedy that was _____ to limit the power and authority of government officials and to assist in the enforcement of the _____.

4. The court has acknowledged that an exact definition of _____ is difficult to express because it depends on the _____.

5. Police officers may be justified in making a(n) _____ of a person based on probable cause that he or she has committed a felony, a misdemeanor that amounts to a breach of the peace in the presence of the officer, or in circumstances in which the power to do so is specifically given to police officers _____.

6. The Fifth Amendment of the Constitution contains many protections; of concern in the area of interrogation is that it protects the right against _____ and _____.

7. A defendant may waive *Miranda* rights, provided the waiver is made _____, _____ and _____.

8. The circumstances surrounding the statements from _____ are more carefully scrutinized because they are more susceptible than adults to _____ or _____.

9. The _____ under the Sixth Amendment and the _____ of the Fourteenth Amendment prohibit law enforcement officers from deliberately eliciting incriminating information from a defendant in the absence of counsel after a formal charge against the defendant has been filed, regardless of whether or not the defendant is in custody.

10. The right to an attorney under the Fifth Amendment *Miranda* rule attaches the right to consultation _____ and is concerned with _____ _____ of the person.

Exercises

1. **You be the judge!** Using the cases in this chapter, write the opinion for the court relative to the admissibility of the following confession. Cite your cases and explain your reasoning as if this were a real case.

    John and Jimmy Jones were suspected of a robbery in a liquor store on Fifth Avenue during which the owner was shot and killed. They were brought into the police station for questioning and placed in separate rooms. Officer Smith sat in the room with John and said nothing to him. After 15 minutes Officer Fitzpatrick opened the door to the interrogation room and said to Officer Smith, "Jimmy told me everything," which was a lie, and then left. Officer Smith turned to Jimmy and said, "We do not need anything from you now. Talk to me if you want because we got the goods on you. It sounds like your brother put the whole thing on you." John gave a full confession. A motion to suppress was brought in court by his attorney.

2. **You be the judge!** Using the cases in this chapter, write the opinion for the court relative to the admissibility of the following confession. Cite your cases and explain your reasoning as if this were a real case.

    Cheryl Esposito was arrested for the murder of her boyfriend, Jeffrey Tang. Officer Book advised of her rights per *Miranda,* which she waived. During the interrogation Cheryl would not tell who had disposed of the body or why Jeffrey had been killed. Officer Book told her that Cheryl's son was seen leaving the house on the night of the murder (a lie) and that he would be arrested for the murder if Cheryl did not talk. Cheryl gave a full confession implicating her new lover, Bruce.

References

Arizona v. Roberson, 486 U.S. 675 (1988).

Bram v. United States, 168 U.S. 532 (1897).

Brinegar v. U.S., 338 U.S. 160 (1949).

Brown v. Illinois, 422 U.S. 590, 603 (1975).

Brown v. Mississippi, 297 U.S. 278 (1937).

Carroll v. U.S., 267 U.S. 132 (1925).

Cassell, P. G., Mitchell, N. J., & Edwards, B. J. (2014). Crime Victims' Rights during criminal investigations: Applying the Crime Victims' Rights Act before criminal charges are filed. *Journal of Criminal Law & Criminology, 104*, 59.

Colombe v. Connecticut, 367 U.S. 568 (1961).

Colorado v. Connelly, 479 U.S. 157 (1986).

Commonwealth v. Forde, 367 Mass. 798 (1975).

Commonwealth v. Rosario, 422 Mass. 48 (1996).

Davis v. U.S., 114 S.Ct. 2350 (2004).

Doe v. United States, 487 U.S. 201 (1988).

Edwards v. Arizona, 451 U.S. 477 (1981).

Florida v. Bostick, 501 U.S. 429, 437 (1991).

Kaupp v. Texas, 538 U.S. 626 (2003).

Mapp v. Ohio, 367 U.S. 643 (1961).

Massiah v. U.S., 377 U.S. 201 (1964).

McNabb v. U.S., 318 U.S. 332 (1943).

Michigan v. Chesternut, 486 U.S. 567, 569 (1988).

Minnick v. Mississippi, 498 U.S. 146 (1990).

Miranda v. Arizona, 384 U.S. 436 (1966).

New York v. Quarles, 467 U.S. 649 (1984).

Omnibus Crime Control and Safe Streets Act (1968). 82 Stat. 210, 18 U.S.C. Sec. 3501(c).

People v. Fox, 319 Ill. 606 (1925).

People v. Morrow, 104 Ill. App. 3d 995 (1982).

Rhode Island v. Innis, 446 U.S. 291 (1980).

Rogers v. Richmond, 365 U.S. 534 (1961).

Rosenthal, Lawrence, Compulsion (April 12, 2017). *University of Pennsylvania Journal of Constitutional Law*, Forthcoming; Chapman University, Fowler Law Research Paper No. 16-04. Retrieved from SSRN: https://ssrn.com/abstract=2761681

Schmerber v. California, 384 U.S. 757 (1966).

Schmidt, C. W. (2016). On doctrinal confusion: The case of the State Action Doctrine. *BYU Law Review*, 575.

Steagald v. U.S., 451 U.S. 204 (1981).

Taylor v. Alabama, 457 U.S. 587 (1982).

United States v. Guerrero, 847 F.2d 1363 (1988).

United States v. Leon, 468 U.S. 897 (1984).

United States v. Mendoza-Cecelia, 963 F.2d 1467 (1992).

Weeks v. U.S., 232 U.S. 383 (1914).

Wolf v. Colorado, 338 U.S. 25 (1949).

Wong Sun v. U.S., 371 U.S. 471 (1963).

12

Confessions in a Justice Context

Source: fresnel6/Fotolia.

CHAPTER OBJECTIVES

After completing this chapter, you should be able to:

1. Define *interrogation* according to the Supreme Court.
2. Summarize the concept of the interrogation environment.
3. State the three conditions for legally valid confession.
4. Illustrate the question-first technique and why it is unlawful.
5. Analyze the shortcomings of *Miranda* warnings.
6. Examine the factors that contribute to false convictions.
7. Describe the three categories of false confessions.
8. Assess the promising practices that relate to false convictions.

KEY TERMS

Conviction integrity units   False confession
False conviction   Frisk
Interrogation   Interrogator confidence
Promising practices   Question-first technique

INTRODUCTION

The focus of this chapter is on placing confessions within the larger context of justice. The roles of justice professionals are exceedingly broad. Individuals that are involved in the criminal justice process include anyone who questions victims and suspects, collects or analyzes evidence, engages in the court system, or works in corrections. All have an important place in the criminal justice system. Whether the investigator is employed in the military, law enforcement, security, as a defense or private investigator, the concepts in this chapter are applicable. We all have a duty to examine and protect our system to ensure that justice is done.

The chapter covers a lot of information, pays close attention to the material that goes beyond the definition, and examines the framework. Knowing what interrogation means is the first step to an examination of the interrogation environment. Scholars have long been concerned about policies that fail to protect the accused. On the other hand, the responsibility of protecting the public and enforcing the law is a heavy burden. False confessions are at the forefront of the criminal justice examination, and no one wants to be responsible for having contributed to the false conviction of a person for a crime he or she did not commit. We need to look at what is going on in the context of miscarriages of justice in order to improve. Well-meaning is just not good enough—we need to know what we are doing. But, what are the rules? Are they properly stated and well respected by everyone? It is good to change when informed of better ways to do things!

There are two distinct perspectives concerning interrogations. One view is that false confessions constitute a major problem, despite *Miranda* reforms intended to curtail coercive police interrogation practices. The other view is that interrogation has become a lost art since *Miranda*. When fewer interrogations are attempted, many believe, the innocent are left vulnerable.

A balancing act exists between providing protections to the guilty and the responsibilities of a criminal investigation. Studies show that the police have become compliant with the *Miranda* rules. Studies on the efficacy of interrogation suggest that interrogations leading to confessions are common and that police officers are good at it. This is a logical but misleading conclusion because the majority of these studies do not take into account those cases in which the police do not attempt to elicit confessions.

This chapter provides some major pitfalls and problems associated with miscarriages of justice and case-specific practices for assessing guilt as part of an investigative interview.

WHAT IS AN INTERROGATION?

An interrogation is a process conducted by law enforcement officers and military personnel. Laws on interrogation do not protect citizens from a process initiated by nongovernment civilians. The U.S. Supreme Court has defined an **interrogation** as a questioning initiated by law enforcement officers after a person has been taken into custody or otherwise deprived of his or her freedom of action in any significant way (*Miranda v. Arizona*, 1966). Interest in interrogation practices is widespread, and because practices that government officials use during interrogations are scrutinized by the public, it is useful to study current controversies surrounding the process.

Since *Miranda,* the Court has revisited that opinion to prevent a too narrow interpretation of the case and to address the "interrogation environment." Concern has centered on police practices that would subjugate the individual to the will of the examiner (*Rhode Island v. Innis*, 1980). It is evident therefore that the special procedural safeguards outlined in *Miranda* are required not only when a suspect is taken into custody but also when a suspect in custody is subjected to interrogation. Interrogation, as conceptualized in *Miranda,* must reflect a measure of compulsion above and beyond that inherent in custody itself (*Rhode Island v. Innis*, 1980). The *Miranda* safeguards come into play whenever a person in custody is subjected to either express questioning or its functional equivalent. That is, the term "interrogation" under *Miranda* refers not only to explicit questioning but also to any words or actions on the part of the police (other than those normally attendant to arrest and custody) that the police should know are reasonably likely to elicit an incriminating response from the suspect.

For an interrogation to be conducted lawfully, the following three conditions must be met:

1. The opportunity to interrogate a suspect must be lawfully obtained.
2. There must be an absence of force, the threat of force, or promise of leniency.
3. There must be compliance with requirements for warnings of constitutional rights to a custodial suspect.

Compliance with the warnings per *Miranda* must be taken seriously. The Supreme Court has firmly denounced the **question-first technique** sometimes used by police to avoid the requirements of providing *Miranda* warnings (*Missouri v. Seibert*, 2004). The *question-first* technique is a deliberate attempt by a police officer to avoid providing a suspect with his or her rights per *Miranda*. It occurs when the suspect is interrogated first, a short period is allowed to elapse, and then the warnings are given and the suspect re-interrogated. The second interrogation is made to document the previous confession made without legal warnings.

SINCE *MIRANDA*

Early studies on the impact of the *Miranda* warnings were mixed: A Yale study concluded that the warnings were largely ignored by police and wholly ineffective; some studies concluded that its application did not decrease the percentage of felony complaints; others claimed a large decrease in felony cases that reached the grand jury following *Miranda*. Leo (1996) summed up the literature on *Miranda* up to 1996 with five important findings:

1. After an initial adjustment period, police began to comply regularly with the letter of the *Miranda* requirements.
2. Suspects frequently waived their constitutional rights and chose to speak to detectives.

CASE IN POINT 12-1

CASE IN POINT: MISSOURI V. SEIBERT (2004)

Patrice Seibert's 12-year-old son, Jonathan, had cerebral palsy, and when he died in his sleep, she feared charges of neglect because of bedsores on his body. In her presence, two of her teenage sons and two of their friends devised a plan to conceal the facts surrounding Jonathan's death by setting fire to the family's mobile home, in which they planned to leave Donald Rector, a mentally ill teenager living with the family, to avoid any appearance that Jonathan had been unattended. Seibert's son, Darian, and a friend set the fire, and Donald died.

When a police officer questioned Seibert about Rector's death, the officer intentionally did not read Seibert her *Miranda* rights, hoping to get a confession. During the interrogation, Seibert admitted that she knew that Rector was supposed to die in the fire. After this admission, Seibert was given a 20-minute break from the interrogation; when it resumed, the officer advised Seibert of her *Miranda* rights, which she waived. This is referred to as the question-first technique. Seibert then repeated statements she had made before receiving a *Miranda* warning. Patrice Seibert was convicted of second-degree murder and sentenced to life in prison for her role in the death of Donald Rector. This midstream reading of warnings after interrogation and unwarned confession did not effectively comply with *Miranda*'s constitutional requirement. The U.S. Supreme Court held that this interrogation technique rendered both confessions inadmissible.

Importance

1. In *Seibert,* the Court said that the police could not purposefully avoid providing warnings per *Miranda* to get a confession. In some cases, questioning of a suspect may be the equivalent of custody for the purposes of *Miranda* warnings. Obtaining a confession without the warnings and then giving the warnings a short time later is not acceptable.

3. Once the waiver was obtained, police interrogation techniques did not change as a result of *Miranda*.
4. Suspects continued to provide detectives with confessions and incriminating statements, although in some instances at a lower rate than prior to *Miranda*.
5. The clearance and conviction rate did not appear to be significantly affected by *Miranda*, although in some cases it too had dropped.

Initial evidence suggests that fewer police officers attempted to interrogate post-*Miranda*. Early impact studies indicated that from 1966 to 1969, detectives chose to interrogate fewer suspects (Leo, 1996). Some believed that confessions lost due to procedural handcuffing became a major concern (Cassell, 1999), and clearance rates in some cities dropped significantly after *Miranda* (Leo, 1996). In almost half of felony cases, there may be no attempt by police officers to gain a confession or gather intelligence information (Colaprete, 2002), although police officers are very successful at interrogation when they attempt it (Thomas, 2004).

Whether police officers follow up with an interrogation or not, they do comply with the mandate to provide warnings to suspects. One study found that the police recite *Miranda* warnings to suspects most of the time, with a compliance rate of 95 percent (Thomas, 2004). In only 6 percent of cases did defendants complain that they did not receive their rights.

Shortcomings of *Miranda*

More than 50 years have passed since that controversial ruling in *Miranda v. Arizona* required police officers to inform suspects of their rights when in custody and before questioning. Indications are that police have been compliant in meeting the legal requirements for interrogation, although it appeared that interrogation attempts were reduced. The current question is whether *Miranda* requirements have been diluted or merely proved to be insufficient to protect vulnerable individuals from police interrogation practices. The question is important to ask since we now know that some police interrogations result in false confessions.

This is not the first time in history that police interrogation protocols involving criminal suspects have been challenged. More sophisticated methods gradually replaced widespread use of physical coercion to extract confessions during the 1920s and 1930s. In fact, *Miranda* is credited with having led to the professionalization of interrogation methods and contributed to the declining use of coercion in police practices (Leo, 1996). From the 1990s to the present, police interrogation practices have again become controversial (Leo, 2017). What has changed?

The Supreme Court has destroyed the foundation of *Miranda*, de-constitutionalized its warnings, and rendered the waiver meaningless, according to some experts (Leo, 2017). Over the years, subsequent Supreme Court rulings have watered down its protections. During the 1970s and 1980s, the Burger and Rehnquist Courts declared that *Miranda* warnings were not rights protected by the Constitution. The standard of custody was lowered since an instruction may be issued to the suspect that he is not under arrest and free to leave, instead of providing *Miranda* warnings. Finally, the Supreme Court has held that waivers to Miranda can be implicit, as police officers are not required to obtain a waiver of a defendant's right to remain silent before beginning an interrogation (*Berghuis v. Thompkins*, 2010).

From another perspective, researchers propose that the problem with *Miranda* is the wrong assumption that people can understand what *Miranda* rights mean (knowing), appreciate the consequences of a waiver (intelligently), or are able to withstand the interrogation process (voluntarily) (Smalarz, Scherr, & Kassin, 2016). Studies, they suggest, have exposed limits of comprehension in adults with intellectual disabilities, severe psychological disorders, and among adolescents. Further confounding the issue is that approximately 70 percent of inmates read at or below a sixth-grade level, while most warnings are written at or above that level.

BEEN THERE . . . DONE THAT! 12-1

There are two things that an interrogator can do to give validity to the voluntariness of a confession. First, when the statement is being typed, make a clear error on it, something that the perpetrator will notice. Examples are the name of his or her mother or child or time of day. Second, allow the suspect to express his or her feelings in his or her handwriting.

Purposefully make the error and then ask the perpetrator to read the statement after it has been printed (or handwritten) and to make corrections. If he or she does not read it carefully and misses the error, call his or her attention to it and ask whether the information is correct. Once the error is noticed, ask the suspect to make the correction and initial the change. Having the offender make changes to the confession demonstrates to others who are trying to determine whether the confession was forced that you DID give the suspect the opportunity to read it and object to anything that is contained in it. Next, ask how the suspect feels, and suggest that they write that at the bottom of the page. Most people will simply write, "I am sorry" or "I did not mean to do it." Others may write more. It is the only opportunity that the interrogator has to document the feelings of the perpetrator *at the time of the interrogation*, which may be disputed at a later date. I believe that doing this is why none of the confessions that I took were ever suppressed in court. It is hard to maintain that one was forced when the evidence says otherwise.

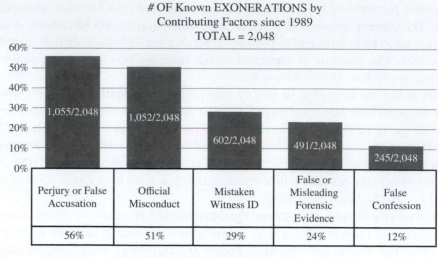

FIGURE 12-1 Factors Contributing to False Conviction.

Note that the total percentage is more than 100 percent, since more than one factor may contribute to the false conviction.

Source: National Registry of Exonerations. (2017). % Exonerations by Contributing Factor. Retrieved from http://www.law.umich.edu/special/exoneration/Pages/ExonerationsContribFactorsByCrime.aspx.

FACTORS IN FALSE CONVICTIONS

The concern over false confessions is part of a larger problem within the criminal justice system—miscarriages of justice. A **false conviction** occurs when a person is wrongfully convicted of a crime. It can result from a false accusation, an erroneous eyewitness identification, nondisclosure of evidence by police or prosecution, false or misleading forensic evidence, overestimation of the evidential value of expert testimony, unreliable confessions, ineffective counsel, and misdirection by a judge during the trial.

According to the National Registry of Exonerations (2017), perjury or false accusation and/or erroneous eyewitness identification were contributing factors in 85 percent of cases (refer to Figure 12-1). Additionally, untrue or misleading forensic evidence was a factor in 29 percent of cases. Undocumented is the extent to which the wrong information influenced police interrogations, which contributed in 12 percent of the false conviction cases. In total, the National Registry of Exonerations has recorded 2,048 known exonerations in the United States since 1989 (as of June 20, 2017). Official misconduct refers to police, prosecutors, or other government officials (examples are social workers, defense attorneys, and probation officers) significantly abusing their authority or the judicial process in a way that contributes to the exoneree's conviction.

What Have We Learned?

What can be learned from the National Registry of Exonerations and the tragic miscarriages of justice which have been uncovered? The most frequent contributing factor to false convictions is the perjury or false accusation from witnesses and victims of crime. Investigative interviewers need to place statements within the context of the entire forensic investigation. Statements should be evaluated alongside factual evidence, and in comparison to multiple statements, when possible. Investigators must be leery of narrowing their focus to one suspect early on in an investigation; it can be dangerous in the absence of fact finding. Witness bias may influence information that is provided to the investigator. Assessment of the credibility and reliability of the reporter statements is an important aspect of interviewing. Interviewing is the backbone of investigation; most law enforcement officers and first responders will never conduct an interrogation.

An atmosphere of accountability and high ethical standards must be established within the forensic professions and court personnel to address the various contributing factors of official misconduct and false or misleading forensic evidence. Prosecutors, defense attorneys, expert witnesses, and all others must be held responsible for ethical misconduct, which ranges from overstating credentials for pay to mishandling evidence, or worse. Failure to admit shortcomings during the trial stage can grow to miscarriages of justice if not handled properly. Not every error is born of evil intent! Human mistakes do happen. Admitting to those errors, mistakes, and unintended consequences are the first step to righting the wrongs which may occur.

FACTORS IN FALSE CONFESSIONS

False confessions do occur, in rare circumstances, without police inducement. Hundreds of people usually come forward to confess to the crime whenever a celebrity, a public official, or a well-known person in the public eye is victimized. They cannot all be the perpetrator. Most, if not all, of the confessions must be false. For example, more than 200 people confessed to kidnapping the Lindbergh baby in 1932, dozens say they murdered Elizabeth Short in the 1947 Black Dahlia murder in Los Angeles, and in 2006 John Mark Karr falsely claimed to have killed JonBenet Ramsay (Geoghegan, 2009). We do not know exactly why or how many people willingly confess to crimes that they did not commit.

> A *false confession* is a written or oral statement acknowledging guilt made by a person who did not commit the crime.

False confessions do occur in police custody; these are also rare occurrences when considering that millions of confessions occur every year. Although there is no precise estimate of the number of persons who have provided a false confession, in 12 percent of wrongful convictions identified nationwide, coercive police interrogations are identified as a factor in the conviction (National Registry of Exonerations, 2017). It has been found that in cases of proven false confession, a common factor is a lengthy interrogation of the suspect, on average 16.3 hours. Young suspects and individuals with learning disabilities are at risk. Psychologists categorize false confessions into three groups (Gudjonsson, 2017):

1. **Voluntary False Confessions.** People may voluntarily give a false confession due to a pathological desire for notoriety, a conscious or unconscious need to relieve guilt over prior wrongdoings, an inability to distinguish fact from fantasy, or a desire to aid and protect the real criminal. Individuals offer voluntary false confessions without any external pressure from the police. These people simply turn themselves into the authorities, claiming they have committed a crime.

2. **Pressured-Compliant False Confessions.** Some suspects will confess falsely to escape an aversive situation, avoid an explicit or implied threat, or gain a promised or implied reward. Examples of this exist in cases of physical or psychological torture. Coerced-compliant false confessions may result from the pressures during the interrogation process. Because such a suspect perceives immediate gains that outweigh the long-term consequences, this person will confess despite knowing that he or she did not commit the crime.

3. **Pressured-Internalized False Confessions.** Some suspects are susceptible to believing during interrogation that they committed the crime, even though they did not. Persons who are particularly vulnerable are those who are young, tired, confused, suggestible, and exposed to false information.

False confessions are confirmed as contributing factors to false convictions. The influences which produce false confessions are complex. Overconfidence or the lack of evidence of the guilt of a suspect may lead to excessive pressure to obtain a confession. Also, some people can be very malleable; mere suggestions and approval of statements made during eyewitness identifications are known to influence the memory of the witness and need to be avoided (Steblay, Wells, & Douglass, 2014). Scholars have long asserted that a person's youthful age and mental impairment are the two most common risk factors for false confessions (Gutierrez, 2011). Long interrogations are also associated with the risk of false confessions (Leo, 2017).

The suggestibility of young age is often associated with heightened obedience to authority figures and decreased decision-making abilities. Concern over the vulnerability of youth has led some states to require that police electronically record interrogations of minors (National Association of Criminal Defense Lawyers, 2014). In a study examining 124 cases of proven interrogation-induced false confessions, authors Drizin and Leo (2004) found that the mean interrogation time was 16.3 hours, which is substantially longer than the 4-hour interrogation time suggested by the Reid Technique.

Experts suggest that there are three investigator errors when combined with misleading specialized knowledge, tunnel vision, and confirmation bias which pave the way to produce a false confession: Misclassification Error, the Coercion Error, and the Contamination Error (Leo & Drizin, 2010):

Error #1 = Misclassification.   **Misclassification** occurs when an investigative interviewer wrongly determines that an innocent man is guilty. Belief in the human lie detector myth is the primary reason for this mistake which can cause the overconfident police officer to interrogate for confirmation instead of further investigation.

Error #2 = Coercion.   Next, subjecting the suspect to an accusatorial interrogation takes on a high priority since there is little to no evidence on which to make an arrest.

Error #3 = Contamination.   Moving the individual from proclaiming innocence to guilt with the introduction of evidence. Being fed with information known only to the perpetrator and investigator introduces to the innocent man knowledge that is then weaved into the statement as if it were his original thought.

PROMISING PRACTICES

Wrongful convictions impact not only the police departments that are involved, but they can also erode the community's confidence in the law enforcement agency (Brooks, 2014). Programs and strategies that have some scientific research or data

---

BEEN THERE . . . DONE THAT! 12-2

For over 23 years of teaching at the college level I began day one of each freshman class with this message: You are now in a criminal justice class. Any person who is involved in a forensic profession must hold themselves to the highest ethical standard possible, and it starts now. There will be zero tolerance for plagiarism or cheating in my courses. Suspected cases will be investigated and any student found to have engaged in plagiarism or cheating of any sort by a preponderance of the evidence will be dismissed with a zero for the course. I personally will report to the administration and recommend dismissal from the criminal justice program.

If this sounds harsh, consider the alternatives. Liars, cheaters, and thieves are cut from the same cloth. We want honest and ethical individuals involved in the future of criminal justice. Anything less will not be tolerated; somebody's life may depend on the integrity of one individual.

showing positive outcomes in delaying an inappropriate or incorrect outcome but do not have enough evidence to support generalizable conclusions fall within the category of **promising practices**. Examples of promising practices which are directly related to justice are included in this section since they relate to false convictions.

Conviction Integrity Units

Conviction integrity units (CIU), also known as conviction review programs, are entities located within prosecutorial offices, which aim to prevent, identify, and reverse wrongful convictions. Case referrals which constitute a large source of cases come from internal audits by the office itself based on previous findings of error or misconduct by prosecutors or police and referrals concerning forensic science errors (Scheck, 2017).

One goal of the integrity units is to identify policies, practices, or individuals which are factors in wrongful convictions and to make a positive change to correct possible problems in the past. An example of recent reviews, according to Scheck (2017), involved scientific errors made by FBI analysts in Composite Bullet Lead Analysis and microscopic hair comparison. Free DNA testing of hairs was made on cases that spanned decades and notifications sent to all stakeholders of the errors. Many of these units have also developed policies designed to reduce future false convictions that are based on false confessions. Conviction integrity units find law enforcement personnel initiating or cooperating in a substantial portion of all exonerations (The National Registry of Exonerations, 2017).

Electronic Recording of Suspect Interviews

Electronic recording of interrogations by audio or video is a highly recommended practice to improve suspect interviewing methods. In a recent podcast by COPs, Chief William Brooks III of Norwood Police Department (MA) talked about what it was like when his department began recording interrogations (Brooks, 2014). While he was initially not in favor of the changes, he said that recording occurs most of the time now in his department and that it has worked very well! Recording of suspect interviews in major felony cases came about in Massachusetts over 15 years ago due to the *DiGiambattista* decision. Massachusetts is an example of a state where recording is not compelled, but there are consequences when they are not. A defendant is entitled (on request) to a jury instruction advising that the state's highest court has expressed a preference that such interrogations be recorded whenever practicable, and cautioning the jury that, because of the absence of any recording of the interrogation in the case before them, they should weigh evidence of the defendant's alleged statement with great caution and care.

Law enforcement officers are required to electronically record their custodial interrogations in some or all felony cases 22 states and the District of Columbia, or a rebuttable presumption is created that the confession should not be admitted into evidence against a criminal defendant (Arledge, nd; Innocence Project, 2017; National Association of Criminal Defense Lawyers, 2014). As you will note on the map (Figure 12-2), Rhode Island is the only state where recording is mandatory through the Police Accreditation Commission agreement.

The recording is not mandated for every interrogation, even in the states where it is compelled. Some states require recording for felony cases, others for homicides or juvenile cases only. Lots of variation exists between the states. In each state where recording is not mandated, there are multiple police departments who do it voluntarily. Courts generally recognize that there are situations when a recording is not feasible and will excuse the requirement if sufficient legal proof is offered to explain the absence. Suspects can also insist that their statements not be recorded.

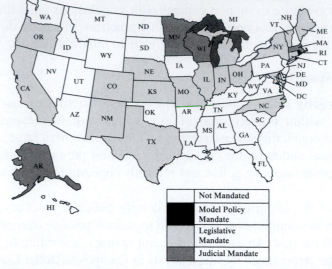

Mandated Recording of Custodial Interrogation

	Not Mandated
	Model Policy Mandate
	Legislative Mandate
	Judicial Mandate

FIGURE 12-2 Only 22 states mandate recording, but voluntary policies exist in every state. Mandates come from Court decisions, State Statues, and one from a Police Accreditation Commission agreement.

CASE IN POINT 12-2

CASE IN POINT: COMMONWEALTH V. DIGIAMBATTISTA (2004)

DiGiambattista was an arson case involving the burning of an unoccupied house at 109 Adams Street in Newton. The defendant had rented the house, moving out three days before the fire. He changed the locks when he left so that he and his mother were the only people with keys to the front door. A neighbor discovered the fire around midnight, and firefighters found the building locked. The investigation revealed the fire had been set between 11:25 p.m. and 11:55 p.m., using gasoline near a stair closet and paper in a kitchen sink.

One month later, DiGiambattista was interviewed by the police, and this questioning became the principal issue in the case. A state trooper and a Newton police officer accompanied him to a Revere fire station, where he was told that he was free to leave, was given *Miranda* warnings, and executed a written rights waiver. DiGiambattista repeatedly denied involvement and agreed to a polygraph. False evidence was presented to DiGiambattista on his involvement. He claimed that the police had violated multiple constitutional safeguards. On appeal to the Supreme Judicial Court (SJC) the Court did not find the claims to be credible but stated:

1. Falling short of requiring that interrogations be recorded, in *DiGiambattista* the Massachusetts Supreme Judicial Court held that whenever the prosecution offers in evidence a defendant's statement that was NOT electronically recorded, and the statement was produced either by custodial interrogation or interrogation in a detention facility, the defendant is entitled to a jury instruction that casts significant doubt on the statement's credibility.

Science-Based Eyewitness Identification

The *Lawson* decision highlighted the pliability of witness certainty and the problems for eyewitness evidence (*State v. Lawson*, 2012). The Court recognized eight different ways in which eyewitness recollection can be impacted by the eyewitness identification method that police use. After the witness memory has been contaminated by faulty procedures, the subsequent trial testimony of the witness will show a misleading level of certainty and distorted reports of the witness's actual experience (Steblay et al., 2014). Refer to Chapter 3 for a full discussion on eyewitness evidence best practices.

IMPROVING INTERROGATIONS

Interrogation techniques are considered coercive by critics who claim they result in false confessions. The criminal justice system is evaluating how to improve procedures to minimize miscarriages of justice. Critics denounce police procedures that involve observing the behavior of suspects as a way of selecting someone for more intensive interrogation tactics. Excessive focus on an individual because of a hunch or because he or she avoids eye contact narrows the investigator's vision. Overcome this by following the facts of the case, investigating all possible leads, and interviewing all suspects, particularly in a major case. To avoid the problems and pitfalls associated with interrogation techniques, some challenges for police officers and ways to overcome them are as follows (Lassiter & Meissner, 2010):

Follow the Facts   Misread the Suspect's Behavior

Misclassification is the first mistake that investigators make when targeting an innocent person as guilty. Poor training and reliance on the presumption of guilt can lead investigators to narrow their focus on one suspect. Misreading body posture, gaze aversion, or uncooperative persons as deceptive and therefore guilty can lead to an accusatorial interrogation. There is no magic cue to detection. Behavioral interviewing is unpredictable because it leads investigators to develop the mistaken belief that they can tell a liar based on a person's reaction. A person who is sweaty may be guilty or may be concerned about being accused of a crime. In other words, the reaction of a person may be real, but there is no magic way to determine what it means.

Protect Vulnerable Persons   Overlook Personal Vulnerabilities

Some individuals are particularly susceptible to police interrogation techniques that may lead to a false confession. Examples are youthfulness, low or borderline IQ, mental disorder, recent bereavement, language barrier, alcohol or other drug withdrawal, illiteracy, fatigue, or inexperience with the criminal justice system. Overcome this by doing a thorough background investigation on potentially questionable suspects before attempting an interrogation. Place the vulnerability in context at the beginning of the interrogation to get an understanding of whether the suspect understands. Document all efforts to show that a fair investigative interview was conducted.

Preserve the Evidence   Contaminate Confessions

Police officers may inadvertently contaminate confessions by using questions that contain crime scene information. Use of crime scene photos may amplify this flaw and educate the suspect about the offense. If the suspect is innocent, the investigator is inadvertently educating him on the crime details. Avoid contaminating any admissions by asking the suspect to describe and explain instead. Use open-ended questions and encourage narrative responses from the suspect.

CASE-SPECIFIC METHODS OF INTERROGATION

The approach to an interrogation will differ based on the offense that was committed as well as the confidence of the interrogator. **Interrogator confidence** is not case-specific; it is gained through education and understanding of the law, empathy for vulnerable populations, and knowledge of crime motivations. Confidence is often demonstrated to others through the posture of an officer, as seen in Figure 12-3. Perpetrators often respond with admissions to their involvement in an offense when a humane interrogation approach is used. Humane does not mean friendly or oversolicitous. A suspect's perceptions are critical; in particular, a suspect's perceptions on the strength of the evidence will affect his or her willingness to confess (Kassin & Gudjosson, 2004). With this in mind, use all available evidence collection methods that are unique to the crime being investigated to increase the perception of a strong case.

Have questions ready regarding the things that you want to know; don't just listen passively. Ask for details and explanations of whatever the suspect admits. Be genuinely interested in what the suspect is saying. Credibility that a suspect is telling the truth will be gained from his or her answers to questions concerning what was smelled, tasted, saw, or heard. Ask why a particular victim was chosen; the perpetrator is rarely indiscriminate. Even a person who chooses randomly will provide that as their method of choosing. Why did the suspect steal from *that* car? Assault *that* person? Break into *that* particular house? Kill *that* person? What happened before the event?

In a seminal study on police interviewing, universal problems were identified that have still have relevance for modern interrogations (Fisher, Geiselman, & Raymond, 1987). Interrogators should be aware of the following:

- Do not excessively interrupt a suspect's description. Interruptions will cause the suspect to experience a considerable loss in concentration.
- When a suspect describes a recollection of the crime, the follow-up questions should be appropriate. For example, unless it is relevant, do not interrupt the suspect to ask about weight, height, age, and so on.

Alleged sexual offenders and child molesters are among the suspects who may be challenging to the investigator; be prepared to ask the difficult questions. It can be appalling or disgusting to hear details about sexual crimes against children or the elderly. Admissions may cause the investigator to feel anger toward the suspect. Never show emotion or react if the details become disturbing. Any show of emotions from the investigator must be purposeful and self-driven. Examples of case-specific approaches follow.

FIGURE 12-3   Interrogator confidence is not case-specific; it is gained through education and understanding of the law, empathy for vulnerable populations, and knowledge of crime motivations.

Source: Ftwitty/E+/Getty Images.

Child Pornography Cases

Interrogators must respond with compassion and understanding during the interrogation of a suspect in a child pornography case (Bowling & Resch, 2005). A two-step interrogation process is useful:

Step 1 Make a direct accusation statement that is convincing in its delivery to the suspect; interrupt and dismiss denials.

Step 2 Avoid using judgmental terms, and use interrogation themes. Theme development offers the suspect a logical reason why he or she committed the crime by excusing the behavior.

- **Rationalize the Crime.** Example: "I understand your situation; you love kids so much; you never meant to hurt anyone."
- **Project Blame onto Others.** Example: "The problem is that parents don't spend enough time with their children."
- **Minimize the Offense.** Example: "We're not talking about hurting children here. We're only talking about a few photographs."

BEEN THERE . . . DONE THAT! 12-3

When Janet was two years old she began to have many medical problems, including severe urinary tract infections and high fevers. Although the child was taken each time to see a doctor, no reason was found for the urinary tract infections, so she was treated for six months on antibiotics. Coincidentally, a new babysitter was found for her after a year and a half with the old one. Within a short time the new babysitter noticed that Janet, now 4 years old, was rubbing herself on a stuffed animal as if masturbating. When asked about it, the child said, "Hank rugs me." Her mother, Susan, reported that soon after she learned of this, Janet told her that she and Hank had a secret. The secret was that Hank used to put his "sickoo" on her "gina." Hank was identified as the husband of the woman who had been babysitting Janet during the time that the urinary tract infections were occurring. The infections had stopped after the child had been sent to a different home for babysitting.

I conducted an interview with Janet. She told me her secret with Hank and drew a picture of him for me. She pointed out on a picture what the "sickoo" and "gina" meant so that I was sure what she was saying. The stick figure of Hank was basically a face with a penis.

Knowing that a trial with a 4-year-old victim would be extremely difficult, I attempted to obtain a confession from Hank. Something clearly had happened to the child, but was it rape or indecent assault and battery? During the interview with Hank, he did admit to fondling Janet over her underwear but denied any penetration. To explain why she drew him naked, Hank said that she had seen him coming out of the shower one day. I was sure that he minimized his assaults on her. There is no doubt that Hank was thinking the whole time that his wife and four kids were going to hear about what he had been doing with this little girl. A 4-year-old against a 35-year-old was not good odds, so I sought to strengthen the confession to make sure that there would not be a fight in court. At the end of the statement, he wrote that he was really sorry for bringing such hardship on the mother and child and understood why they would be angry. He asked for forgiveness. He thanked me for bringing it forward so that he could get help.

In an investigation by the department of social services, Hank told the investigator that he had never touched the child in a sexual way. He said that he was told by me that if he didn't make a statement he'd be arrested and pulled out of his house in handcuffs. When pressed on that claim, he withdrew it and said that "Denise was quite nice during the interview." Funny how things can get turned around when faced with punishment. He further minimized the touching that he had done, saying that he was just kidding around with the child and had accidentally touched her on the inner thigh.

I went with the evidence and the perpetrator pled guilty.

Child Sexual Assault

In a comparison of violent offenders, rapists, and child molesters, the internal need to confess was greatest among child molesters (Kassin & Gudjonsson, 2004). They are more likely to respond to a sensitive approach to overcome their inhibition to confess; most of them will talk to the police. One of the greatest challenges for police officers interrogating a suspect for child sexual assault is in controlling their own emotions. Any expression of anger, disgust, or distain toward the suspect will result in his or her refusal to continue constructively in the interrogation. In many cases the statement from the perpetrator is the strongest evidence available.

1. Give the suspect permission to talk. Start by explaining the investigation. Tell the suspect that you realize that he or she is in a difficult position and are willing to give him or her the opportunity to talk and give his or her side of the story. The interview may be difficult. Assure the suspect that you want to hear the reasons for what happened.
2. Don't share any embarrassing secrets to establish rapport. The suspect who realizes that you are manipulating him or her will become resentful and you will lose any credibility that you have established.
3. Be prepared to listen. During the interview with the suspect, the investigator should (Pence & Wilson, 1992):

   • Display an attitude of confidence in the subject's guilt.
   • Point out some, but by no means all, of the circumstantial evidence indicative of the subject's guilt.
   • Sympathize with the subject by telling him or her that anyone else might have done the same thing under similar circumstances.
   • Reduce the subject's guilt feelings by minimizing the seriousness of the offense. It is also helpful to tell the subject that the interrogator has heard many people tell about sexual activities far worse than any the subject can relate. The conduct itself should be discussed as though it were actually normal.
   • Suggest a less revolting and more acceptable motivation or reason for the offense than that which is known or presumed. An offender should always be offered an opportunity to save face by letting him or her base the initial admission of guilt on a motivation or reason for the act. To secure the initial admission of guilt, the interrogator should suggest such possible reasons, motives, or excuses. The important point is to have the subject place himself or herself at the scene or to connect himself or herself with the event in some way. Following a partial admission, the interrogator can then point out that the circumstantial evidence negates certain explanations. The inconsistency between the subject's original denial of the crime and his or her present admission will deprive him or her of a possible defense.
   • Remember, the main objective of the interview in many instances is to have the subject place himself or herself at the scene or in contact with the victim.
   • Display understanding and sympathy because it may help to get the subject to tell the truth. Urge the subject to tell the truth for the sake of his or her conscience, mental relief, or moral well-being as well as for the sake of everybody concerned, and also because it is the only decent, honorable thing to do.
   • Seek an admission of lying about some incidental aspect of the occurrence. Once a subject has been caught in a lie about some incidental detail, he or she loses a great deal of ground. As the subject tries to convince the interrogator that he or she is telling the truth, the subject can always be politely reminded that he or she was not telling the truth just a short while ago.

- Ask the subject a question regarding some detail of the offense rather than seek a general admission of guilt; getting an admission on seemingly insignificant details will sometimes lead the accused into a confession.

Offenders will not come right out and state that they sexually assaulted the victim. There may be claims of temptation, accidental touching, or an innocent bathing incident. Let the subject talk. Document the incriminating statements and ask for clarification where needed.

Hate Crimes

The National Center for Hate Crime Prevention suggests that some suspects may assume that officers share their biased opinions. Armed with this knowledge, interrogators can encourage suspects to talk about their feelings toward a particular minority group. Without using hate language, the officer should ask the suspect to express his or her bias motivations. The Model Hate Crime Protocol suggests that the following specific questions be asked during an interrogation:

1. How would you like it if someone like the victim moved next door?
2. How do you feel about this victim?
3. What did this person say or do to make you mad?
4. How did the victim provoke you?
5. How do you feel about this person or group?
6. Was this your idea?
7. Has the victim's group hurt you or your friends?

Homicide

If the suspect of the homicide is in custody, the first decision that must be made is whether the subject should be interrogated at the scene of the crime or at the police department. The decision requires flexibility based on the background information available to the investigator. If the suspect is talkative or wants to tell the story at the scene, do not delay. Advise the suspect of his or her *Miranda* rights and let him or her talk. Some important observations that should be noted include the following:

- Does the suspect speak rationally or irrationally?
- Is the response to questioning intelligent or confused?
- Is there any evidence of intoxication, or does the suspect appear to be under the influence of any drugs?
- Does the suspect give any reasons for his or her actions?

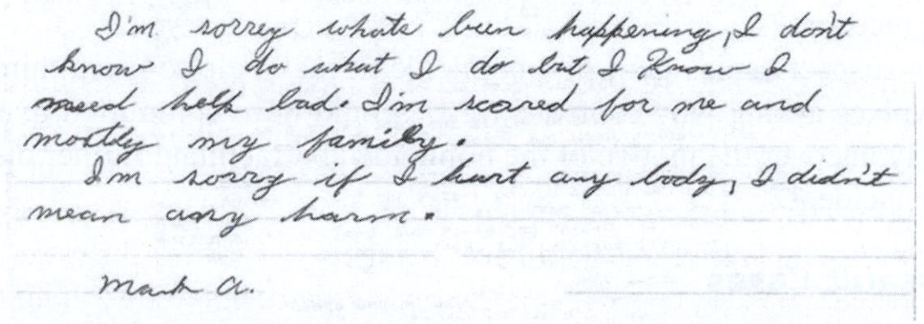

FIGURE 12-4 Perpetrator should always be given the opportunity to read and make corrections to their statement. Ask the person if they have anything else to say. The majority will apologize. Have them put it in their own writing at the bottom of the confession.

Source: Courtesy of Denise K. Gosselin.

Transporting the suspect is a critical point in the investigation. If the suspect's attitude hardens against the victim or the police, this could result in an unwillingness to cooperate with the investigating officer. It can also be the period when the suspect develops remorse for the crime. It is imperative that the transporting officers do nothing that would cause the suspect to resist subsequent investigative efforts. The following are recommended during the transportation of a homicide suspect (Naramore, 1988):

1. If the suspect becomes talkative, officers should listen, remember, and later make notes of statements. It is not the duty of the transporting officers to provide *Miranda* rights or attempt to elicit information from the suspect.
2. Do not discuss the case with the suspect.
3. Do not engage the suspect in friendly conversation.
4. Do not use gestures or language that could be interpreted as hostile by the suspect.
5. Do not insult or berate the suspect.

Questions concerning a homicide are generally organized around four phases of the murder: the pre-crime phase, the murder event, the disposal of the body, and the post-crime phase. In addition to obtaining information about the crime, questions in these categories establish the suspect's motive and opportunity to have committed the act.

PRE-CRIME PHASE.   Determine whether the alleged murderer had a conscious or unconscious intent for the act. Murderers with conscious intent are able to describe what triggered the murder. Those without conscious motive typically do not remember why they killed, but are able to describe their feelings prior to the murder. Ask what the offender did the day prior to the murder and his or her thoughts and feelings prior to encountering the victim.

THE MURDER EVENT.   Questions should concentrate on important aspects of the crime, such as how the suspect gained access to the victim. Conversation and behavior involving the victim, transporting the victim from one location to another, and specifics on methods of torture before or after the victim's death are central to the interrogation. If there is any indication of sexual contact, the interrogator should focus on what was done prior to and after the victim's death.

DISPOSAL OF THE BODY.   Determine through questioning what was done with the body, how the offender left the scene, and whether anything was taken from the body. The interrogator should explore the thoughts and feelings of the murderer during this phase.

POST-CRIME PHASE.   The behaviors that occur after the murder are extremely important to the interrogator. What did the offender do right after the murder? Did he or she wash, go out with friends, go to sleep, or eat? Did he or she return to the crime scene or attend the funeral? Include questions about the recovery of the body. Did the offender assist police in the recovery?

When a suspect denies guilt of a homicide, it may help to use a third-party strategy. This involves asking why someone (else) would have committed that crime. This technique may uncover the motive of the homicide and facilitate further discussion surrounding the incident.

Sexual Assault Cases

Sex offenders generally tend to confess more frequently than other suspects because of a strong internal need to confess, despite their feelings of shame (Kassin & Gudjonsson, 2004). Offer the suspect a viable alternative by suggesting that the victim may have said that he or she was older than he or she really was, or ask whether the victim wanted to do it or did the suspect make the victim do it.

FIGURE 12-5   The suspect should always be given the opportunity to speak, even when statements have not been solicited.

Source: BMP/Shutterstock.

When the identification of the alleged offender is made within a reasonable period of time, the collection of evidence from the suspect's body and clothing contributes to a successful interrogation and aids in solving the cases. Evidence such as pubic and head hair samples, body fluids (dried and wet), and articles of clothing can be used as comparative or reference samples with hair, fibers, and fluids found on the victim. Photographing scratches or bruises on the alleged perpetrator may be indicative of victim resistance in addition to notifying the suspect of your knowledge. Proper collection, conducted under all legal requirements, aids in the establishment of status for the interrogator. Furthermore, it provides possible physical evidence. Accurately record any alibi statements or utterances made by the suspect before the actual interrogation during the process of collection. As illustrated in Figure 12-5, it is advisable to let the suspect talk when unsolicited statements are offered.

Evidence of sexual assault may be collected from the body of the suspect without a warrant if the suspect has been arrested and probable cause exists for the seizure of the suspect's clothing and documenting of injuries as a search incident to arrest due to exigent circumstances. A standard "rape kit" may be used to gather evidence from the suspect and maintain the chain of custody.

WHAT IS NOT AN INTERROGATION?

As stated in *Rhode Island v. Innis* (1980), police words or actions "normally attendant to arrest and custody" do not constitute interrogation. Volunteered statements of any kind, including excited utterances, made to police are not barred by the Fifth Amendment privilege against self-incrimination and are admissible in evidence. An excited utterance is a statement made spontaneously by someone while under the stress of excitement caused by an event or condition. It is an exception to the hearsay rule.

A Stop and Frisk

A police officer may stop a person to question him or her if the officer has a reasonable suspicion that the individual is engaged in criminal activity. For self-protection, the officer can at the same time carry out a limited pat-down search for weapons, which is called a **frisk**. The frisk is not a custody situation nor is this considered a search, although the person being frisked may be asked to show their hands, as illustrated in Figure 12-6. No *Miranda* rights are required.

In two cases decided in the 2000 term, the U.S. Supreme Court interpreted the "stop and frisk" rule. In one instance, the Court held that running away from the police is enough of a reason for the police to stop and frisk the defendant (*Illinois v. Wardlow*, 2000). In another case, the Court ruled that an anonymous tip that a suspect might be armed was insufficient justification for the police to conduct a stop and frisk, absent other facts demonstrating the reliability of the tip (*Florida v. J.L.*, 2000).

Although a frisk may not turn up a weapon, it may turn up a suspicious package of a type that the officer knows is commonly used to carry illegal drugs or some other illegal substance. This suspicion may turn into sufficient cause for a more intensive search of the person's clothing. A frisk often leads to a search. If a search produces an illegal substance, it may result in arrests, which then require *Miranda* warnings before interrogation.

FIGURE 12-6   There are many citizen–police contacts that do not require the *Miranda* warnings be given, including frisk. Properly conducted, under conditions laid out by law, frisk is for the protection of the police officer.

Source: Ronald Bloom/Getty Images.

Traffic Stop

The roadside questioning of a motorist detained during a routine traffic stop does not constitute "custodial interrogation" for the purposes of the *Miranda* rule (*Rhode Island v. Innis*, 1980). Although an ordinary traffic stop curtails the "freedom of action" of the detained motorist and imposes some pressures on the detainee to answer questions, such pressures do not sufficiently impair the detainee's exercise of his or her privilege against self-incrimination to require that he be warned of his constitutional rights. A traffic stop is usually brief, and the motorist expects that, although he or she may be given a citation, in the end he or she most likely will be allowed to continue on the way. Moreover, a typical traffic stop is conducted in public, and the atmosphere surrounding it is substantially less "police dominated" than that surrounding the kinds of interrogation at issue in *Miranda* and subsequent cases in which *Miranda* has been applied.

However, if a motorist who has been detained for a traffic stop is then subjected to treatment that causes him or her "in custody" for practical purposes, he or she is entitled to the protections prescribed by *Miranda* if questioning occurs. A policeman's unspoken plan has no bearing on the question of whether a suspect was "in custody" at a particular time; the only relevant inquiry is how a reasonable person in the suspect's position would have understood the situation.

Sobriety Testing

An individual suspected of driving under the influence may be compelled to submit to sobriety tests of a nontestimonial nature, including physical tests and a breath analysis, in a driving while intoxicated investigation without implicating the right against self-incrimination (*United States v. Hubbell*, 2000). The privilege against self-incrimination protects an accused person from being forced to give evidence of a "testimonial or communicative nature," but not from being compelled to produce "real or physical evidence" (*Pennsylvania v. Muniz*, 1990).

TRUTH AND CONSEQUENCES

Many people have erroneous ideas on what a police officer can or cannot legally do. In examining the following statements, consider them in terms of their consequences. Here are some of the most common examples:

1. What really happens if the police fail to read a suspect his or her rights or use coercion to extract information from a suspect? Many people believe that if they are arrested and not "read their rights," they can escape punishment. Not true. However, if the police fail to read a suspect his or her rights, they cannot use anything the suspect says as evidence against him or her at trial. The prosecution may use the statements to impeach the defendant if he or she decides to take the stand in court. The individual may still be tried if sufficient evidence exists that is not related to the illegally gained evidence. All other evidence not acquired in connection with the statement may be used.

2. Police officers interrogate suspects in most felony arrests. Wrong. Officers do not even attempt interrogations in almost half of all felony arrests (Colaprete, 2002). Why? The variables are experience, motivation, training, and, most important, the randomness of case assignment. Heavy caseload and time are other important facts that influence whether an interrogation takes place.

3. Does an undercover police officer have to admit who they are if a person asks? Many people believe that if they ask someone whether he or she is an undercover police officer and the person denies being a police officer, they are safe to sell or share drugs with that person. Not true. Police officers are not required to reveal their undercover identity.

There is no entrapment because the officer is not forcing someone to buy or use drugs. If the person has shown a willingness to buy or sell drugs, the courts call it predisposition.

4. If you have not been arrested and a police officer wants to question you about a crime, you must answer the questions. Refusing to respond to a policeman's questions is not a crime. Of course, people often voluntarily assist law enforcement officers by supplying information that might help them make an arrest. A police officer generally cannot arrest a person simply for failure to respond to questions. Unless a police officer has "probable cause" to make an arrest or a "reasonable suspicion" to conduct a stop and frisk, the person approached by the police officer has the legal right to walk away. The fact that there may be a legal right to walk away doesn't mean that this is a wise move, however, because there is no way to know what information the officer is using as a basis for his or her actions. In fact, the officer may have information that gives him or her valid legal basis to make an arrest or to conduct a stop and frisk, even if the individual is, in truth, innocent of any wrongdoing.

5. There is no law against lying to the police. Wrong. It is a felony offense punishable by 5-years' imprisonment to lie to a federal police officer (U.S. Code, Title 18, Part I, Chapter 47, Sec. 1001). Remember Martha Stewart. Some, but not all, states have similar laws.

Conclusions

This chapter sought to place confessions within the larger context of justice. Examining the way confessions are obtained through interrogation is an appropriate endeavor for criminal justice interested scholars. We now know that false confessions do occur, even without police intervention. We know that despite the well-intentioned *Miranda* warnings, false confessions do occur. Some assert that *Miranda* has been rendered meaningless through subsequent court action. Others suggest that *Miranda* warnings are not well understood by certain populations, particularly those who are vulnerable due to age or mental disorder. False confessions lead to miscarriages of justice and are a significant factor in false convictions.

A third critical component contributing to false confessions are lengthy interrogations. The suggested period for a confession is four hours. Studies have confirmed that interrogations where false confessions were confirmed typically were conducted over 16 hours.

The purpose of laws restricting interrogation practices is to protect the suspect, whether that individual is innocent or guilty. We also know that confessions are an important aspect of criminal justice evidence. There are no shortcuts or magic words to induce a confession. It takes hard work and self-control. The confession is only part of the investigation process, however, and should never by itself be the basis for a prosecution.

It is not surprising that investigative interviewers use different approaches which are crime-specific. Understanding human behaviors and reasoning why people commit crime are valuable insights for criminal investigators. Remember that criminology class you took in school? Interrogator confidence in conducting proper, legal, and productive interrogations really does involve a vast amount of knowledge and education. Enhanced professionalism translates into the reduced possibility of false confessions; use of the appropriate techniques is the hallmark of a proper interrogation.

Questions for Review

Short-Answer Questions

1. Explain what is meant by the interrogation environment.

2. What are the three major categories of false confessions? Explain each.

3. Explain the three errors which pave the way to produce a false confession.

4. Traffic stops, sobriety testing, and use of stop and frisk are not considered interrogation. Why not?

5. Outline the proper approach for interrogating suspects in cases of child pornography. How does this differ from other interrogation styles?

Fill-in Questions

1. The U.S. Supreme Court has defined an ____ as a questioning initiated by law enforcement officers after a person has been taken into custody or otherwise deprived of his or her freedom of action in any significant way.

2. ____ of interrogations is by audio or video is a highly recommended practice to improve suspect interviewing methods.

3. Experts suggest that there are three investigator errors when combined with misleading specialized knowledge, tunnel vision, and confirmation bias which pave the way to produce a false confession: ____ Error, the Coercion Error, and the Contamination Error

4. Psychologists categorize false confessions into three groups: Voluntary, Pressured-Compliant, and Pressured-____.

5. ____ are entities located within prosecutorial offices' which aim to prevent, identify, and reverse wrongful convictions.

6. Four known contributing factors to wrongful convictions are perjury or false accusation, official misconduct, mistaken witness ID, false or misleading forensic evidence, and ____.

7. Although there is no concrete estimates of the number of persons who have provided a false confession, in ____ percent of wrongful convictions identified nationwide, coercive police interrogations are identified as a factor in the conviction.

8. Programs and strategies that have some scientific research or data showing positive outcomes in delaying an inappropriate or incorrect outcome but do not have enough evidence to support generalizable conclusions fall within the category of ____.

9. ____ of the interrogator is not case-specific, it is gained through education and understanding of the law, empathy for vulnerable populations, and knowledge of crime motivations.

10. For ____, the officer can at the same time carry out a limited pat-down search for weapons, which is called a frisk.

Exercises

1. **National Registry of Exonerations**

   Go to the National Registry of Exonerations and update the information in Figure 1. The site is maintained at the University of Michigan, go to law .umich.edu. The numbers and percentages are exact as of the writing of this text; keep in mind that as new exonerations occur this information may also change. Report to your class what changes are occurring over time.

2. **Innocence Project**

   In cases involving DNA-proven false convictions, the greatest contributing factor is eyewitness identification. Visit the Innocence Project and look for the reforms and solutions that they suggest.

References

Berghuis v. Thompkins, No. No. 08-1470, 130 2250 (Supreme Court 2010).

Bowling, R., & Resch, D. (2005). Child pornography cases: Obtaining confessions with an effective interview strategy. *FBI Law Enforcement Bulletin, 74,* 1–7.

Brooks, W. (2014) *Police reform to prevent wrongful convictions*/Interviewer: N. Comrie. The Beat (Podcast 09-2014), COPS Office. Retrieved from https://cops.usdoj.gov/html/podcasts/the_beat/09-2014/TheBeat-092014_SmathersBrooks.txt.

Cassell, P. G. (1999). The guilty and the "innocent": An examination of alleged cases of wrongful conviction from false confessions. *Harvard Journal of Law and Public Policy, 22,* 523–597. Retrieved from http://www.prodeathpenalty.com/guilt.htm.

Colaprete, F. A. (2002). Managing change in the investigative process: A process-centered approach to professional development and change management. *Police Chief, 69*(10), 121–126.

Drizin, S., & Leo, R. (2004). The problem of false confessions in the post-DNA world. *NC Law Rev,* (82)3, 891–1008.

Fisher, R., Geiselman, E., & Raymond, D. (1987). Critical analysis of police interview techniques. *Journal of Police Science and Administration, 15*(3), 177–185.

Florida v. J.L., 529 U.S. 266 (2000).

Geoghegan, T. (2009). Why do innocent people make false confessions? *BBC News Magazine.*

Gudjonsson, G. (2017). Memory distrust syndrome, confabulation and false confession. *Cortex, 87,* 156–165.

Gutierrez, P. S. (2011). *You have the right to plead guilty: How we can stop police interrogators from inducing false confessions. S. Cal. Rev. L. & Soc. Just.,* 20, 317.

Illinois v. Wardlow, 528 U.S. 119 (2000).

Kassin, S. M., & Gudjonsson, G. H. (2004). The psychology of confessions: A review of the literature and issues. *Psychological Science in the Public Interest, 5,* 67. Retrieved from http://www.psychologicalscience.org/pdf/pspi/pspi5_2.pdf.

Lassiter, D., & Meissner, C. (2010). *Police interrogations and false confessions: Current research, practice, and policy recommendations.* Washington, D.C.: American Psychological Association.

Leo, R., & Drizin, S. (2010). The three errors: Pathways to false confession and wrongful conviction. In D. Lassiter & C. Meissner (Eds.), *Police interrogations and false confessions* (pp. 9–30). Washington, D.C.: American Psychological Association.

Leo, R., & Cutler, B. L. (2016). *False confessions in the twenty-first century*. The Champion magazine (May 2016).

Leo, R. (1996). The impact of *Miranda* revisited. *Journal of Criminal Law and Criminology, 86*, 621.

Miranda v. Arizona, 384 U.S. 436 (1966).

Missouri v. Seibert, 542 U.S. 600 (2004).

Naramore, D. (1988). *Psychology of interviewing,* Unpublished, NESPAC: Homicide School.

National Association of Criminal Defense Lawyers. (2014). *Custodial Interrogation Recording Compendium by State*. Retrieved from nacdl.org/recordingsmap

National Registry of Exonerations. (2017). *% Exonerations by Contributing Factor*. Retrieved from http://www.law.umich.edu/special/exoneration/Pages/ExonerationsContribFactorsByCrime.aspx

Pence, D., & Wilson, C. (1992). *The role of law enforcement in the response to child abuse and neglect*. Washington, D.C.: National Center on Child Abuse and Neglect.

Pennsylvania v. Muniz, 496 U.S. 582 (1990).

Redlich, A. D., Kelly, C. E., & Miller, J. C. (2014). The who, what, and why of human intelligence gathering: Self-reported measures of interrogation methods. *Applied Cognitive Psychology*, 28(6), 817–828.

Rhode Island v. Innis, 446 U.S. 291 (1980).

Scheck, B. (2017). Conviction Integrity Units Revisited. *Ohio State Journal of Criminal Law*, 14(2), 705–752.

Smalarz, L., Scherr, K. C., & Kassin, S. M. (2016). Miranda at 50: A psychological analysis. *Current Directions in Psychological Science*, 25(6), 455–460.

State v. Lawson, 291 P. 3d 673 (Oregon Supreme Court 2012).

Steblay, N. (2013). Lineup instructions. In B. Cutler (Ed.), *Reform of eyewitness identification* Procedures (pp. 65–86). Washington, D.C.: American Psychological Association.

Steblay, N., Wells, G., & Douglass, A. (2014). The eyewitness post identification feedback effect 15 years later: Theoretical and policy implications. *Psychology, Public Policy, and Law*, 20(1), 1–18.

Thomas III, G. (2004). Stories about *Miranda. Michigan Law Review, 102*, 1959–2001.

United States v. Hubbell, 530 U.S. 27 (2000).

Vrij, A., & Granhag, P. (2014). Eliciting information and detecting lies in intelligence interviewing: An overview of recent research. *Applied Cognitive Psychology*, 28(6), 936–944.

13

Techniques for Interrogation

Source: Zsolt Biczo/Shutterstock.

CHAPTER OBJECTIVES

After completing this chapter, you should be able to:

1. Restate the complementarity principle.
2. Explain the purpose of conducting an interrogation.
3. Describe the two interrogation situations.
4. Discuss the Reid technique.
5. Explain the PEACE model.
6. Describe the concept of Human Intelligence Gathering.
7. List three phases of the general confession model.
8. Analyze the steps of each phase of the general confession model.

KEY TERMS

Admission

Confession

Human Intelligence Gathering

Noncustodial interrogation

Complementarity principle

Custodial interrogation

Inculpatory evidence

Scharff technique

INTRODUCTION

Interest in interrogation methods has increased exponentially within the last 25 years (Kelly, Miller, Redlich, & Kleinman, 2013). The term *interrogation* is commonly being referred to as investigative interviewing by scholars. The distinction between investigative interviewing and interrogation is ideological; to some, it means a departure from antiquated methods of a one-sided suspect grilling. Practically speaking, the terms are being used interchangeably in the United States and are less so internationally. One reason to distinguish the two terms is that investigative interviewing is not limited to suspects but is an approach to fact gathering that is used by any person during an investigation of victims, witnesses, and offenders.

The term interrogation is specific to suspect inquiry, and does not imply coercion but may include confrontation. Many of the psychological principles outlined in previous chapters have had a significant international impact on investigative interviewing. Examples of approaches used to determine deceit that is used with suspect interrogations include Cognitive Interviewing (CI), Increasing the Cognitive Load, NICHD protocol, Tactical interviewing, and Strategic Use of Evidence (SUE). Three common confession-eliciting models are covered in this chapter, including the Reid technique, which is the most common interrogating method in America. Other key models include the PEACE method, which is frequently used in the United Kingdom and Australia, and the HUMINT approach, which was developed by the military and is used for interrogation practices in human intelligence contexts.

Many of the techniques for questioning described in this chapter rely on an attempt by the interrogator to understand the behavior of the suspect and his or her resistance to the interrogation process. The interactions between the interrogator and the suspect are critical themes throughout this text. Understanding the interpersonal relations between the interrogator and the suspect provides a good starting point for using interrogation techniques.

COMPLEMENTARITY PRINCIPLE

A useful approach to understanding interpersonal relations is based on the **complementarity principle**, according to which two or more different things improve or emphasize each other's qualities that come from a predictable set of reactions in response to certain actions (Imoedemhe, 2016). The principle involves two major assumptions: first, that interpersonal behaviors invite reciprocal behaviors; and second, that over time these lead to a repetitive pattern of relating. The principle also refers to the foundation of the International Criminal Court, which gives national authorities priority to investigate and prosecute international crimes and exists to complement and remedy the deficiencies of the country/state. The principle of law stipulates that jurisdictions will not overlap in legislation, administration, or prosecution of crime; instead, they coexist and complete the functions of the other.

What does this mean to the investigator? First, the complementarity principle suggests that the interpersonal style of one individual can influence the reaction of another and bring about an expected set of responses. Potentially, an astute interrogator can persuade an offender through knowledge of the expected pairings that occur during human interactions.

Second, the primary interactions between humans are friendliness and dominance (Sadler, Ethier, & Woody, 2011). The interrogator can determine which relationship pairing will work best with a particular person. When a relationship or connection develops, the suspect will respond to the interrogator in a way that is similar. This pairing is seen when rapport is established between the interviewer and interviewee. A connection between two people brings about corresponding levels of friendliness. This connection may be achieved if the suspect feels that the interrogator understands him or her and treats him or her with respect. A friendly relationship encourages a friendly response; a cooperative relationship is likely to have a corresponding cooperative effect.

Pairings of expected behaviors to specific responses are somewhat predictable when the suspect grants status to the interrogator. Status may be achieved when the offender respects the interrogator due to his or her status as a police officer or acknowledges inwardly that the interrogator has sufficient evidence to prove his guilt. When granting of status occurs, what results is an opposite or negative complementarity response. A negative complementarity response is dominant to submissive behavior. For example, the suspect may take the role of being submissive in response to a dominant interrogator. The suspect may become cooperative to overcome a distrustful interrogator. Another possibility is that the individual becomes friendly to the hostile interrogator to please him or her. The investigator should determine if the approach to questioning is best made by establishing a status role or connecting through a rapport relationship.

PURPOSE OF CONDUCTING AN INTERROGATION

The interrogation is an important part of a criminal investigation or intelligence gathering process. The Supreme Court has recognized that a suspect's confession may be the most damaging evidence that can be admitted (*Bruton v. U.S.*, 1968). The only acceptable statement is one that provides the interrogator with the truth. Both confession and admission are valuable pieces of evidence, when attainable.

- A **confession** is a statement in which a person admits to his or her role in committing a crime in a way that excludes the possibility that the offense was committed by someone else.
- An **admission** is any statement that ties the suspect to the crime, the victim, or the place of the offense, which may be used to infer guilt.

Both confessions and admissions are known as inculpatory evidence. **Inculpatory evidence** tends to show a person's involvement in a crime or evidence that can establish guilt (Laudan, 2015). A confession or an admission can be valuable for the investigative interviewer. In criminal cases, the prosecution must prove the case beyond a reasonable doubt, and juries may have difficulty in reaching guilty verdicts when a case is based on circumstantial evidence or on witness testimony that has been impeached by defense counsel.

Although the interrogation is an important part of an investigation, it should not be considered a method of gathering evidence. As stated earlier, interviews of the victim and other witnesses are critical to obtaining evidence. A medical examination when warranted and properly executed search warrants are other methods of gathering essential information. Conducting a background check on an individual is another useful aspect of the investigative process.

The investigation process becomes compromised when the investigator puts all of his or her energy into obtaining a confession rather than collecting evidence. This single-mindedness may mean that evidence exonerating the person is overlooked or that extreme measures are taken to get the confession. Neither is an acceptable alternative to a full and fair investigation. Another reason to be concerned about a strong reliance on interrogations is that in the absence of corroborating evidence, the case is lost if the confession is not admitted (for any number of reasons). A third reason to avoid strong reliance on interrogations is the common view that a confession alone is not enough to prove a person guilty (*Commonwealth v. Forde*, 1984).

Deslauriers-Varin et al. (2011) conducted a study that looked at the factors which were thought to be more likely than not to be involved when someone decides to confess. They found that the number of prior convictions, the seriousness of the crime, the perception of evidence, use of legal advice, and feelings of guilt were all significantly related to the offenders' decisions to confess. Offenders who had multiple prior convictions and had consulted a lawyer were less likely to confess. By contrast, offenders who perceived that there was strong evidence against them and who had feelings of guilt were more likely to confess. Contrary to earlier reports, offenders who committed serious crimes were more rather than less likely to confess their crimes.

INTERROGATION APPROACH

A novel interrogation approach involves assessing the suspect, strategizing the relationship between the individual and interrogator, and documenting the proof obtained through the confession (Rutledge, 1994). An assessment is a process of finding the subject's strengths and weaknesses to help to convince him or her to provide a confession. Guilt, remorse, and entitlement are examples of emotions that the interrogator can exploit. The relationship between the subject and the victim is an important

BEEN THERE . . . DONE THAT! 13-1

In this case, three children told their mother that their grandfather had been touching them. The interviews with these children were particularly difficult. The allegation was indecent touching, a situation in which little physical evidence could be expected. I decided to speak with the alleged perpetrator in his home rather than at the police station since the person was an older man who was neither a flight risk or dangerous. This proved to be the best move I could have made. There was no custody of the subject during this investigative interview. He confirmed that he had been the only person with access to each of the children in the incidents that they had described to me as being sexual. He also tried to convince me that these events were not sexual, and gave some reasons why the children might be saying that he had touched them. In all cases, he had admitted to taking down their underpants. These admissions were not a confession, but they were the information on which the jury based their belief of the children's explanation over his for what had happened. He was found guilty and spent ten years in jail for the assaults. Why was this an interrogation rather than an interview?

FIGURE 13-1 An interrogation is not defined by where it is taking place, but by why it is being conducted.

Source: Courtesy of Denise K. Gosselin.

consideration. Because it is in a person's best interest not to give information against himself or herself, he or she will most likely waive his or her rights if there is the perception that it *is* in his or her best interest to talk. If the individual believes that the interrogator can be convinced of his or her innocence, then he or she is also likely to talk. Understating the position and rank of the interrogator is better than demanding the respect due to status. Offenders are more interested in themselves than with the police officer, so don't bother trying to impress them as a way to obtain a confession.

Kelly and colleagues (2013) have identified six unique domains that are typically used during an interrogation:

#1 Rapport

#2 Context manipulation

#3 Emotion provocation

#4 Confrontation/competition

#5 Collaboration

#6 Presentation of evidence

Another approach to interrogation requires a person to focus on the purpose of the interrogation rather than the place. Typically, the interrogation is conducted as a room designed for that purpose in a police station. The goal of an interrogation is to obtain a statement from the person on whether he or she is guilty of a crime. An admission will provide information that may suggest guilt. Most examples of interrogation involve major offenses such as homicide or rape. The value of confessions and admissions should not be overlooked as part of the investigatory process for all crimes, even minor ones. It is limiting to think of statements taken in the interrogation room as an interrogation and all other encounters as interviews. An interrogation may take place at home, at some neutral setting, or at any other place where privacy can be assured. The suspect can be called on the phone and asked questions. An interrogation can be conducted whether the individual is in custody or not.

One major advantage to carrying out a noncustodial interrogation is that it typically introduces a strong element of surprise. Getting the person to talk is a critical element in obtaining a confession. Rapport may be developed in a place where the individual feels comfortable. Remember that an interrogation is not an option after the individual has been arraigned in court or asks to speak to an attorney, regardless of whether the offender is in custody. Both noncustodial and custodial interrogation situations are described in the next section.

Noncustodial Interrogation Situation

Before an interrogation, the approach must be chosen based on whether the questioning will be in a custodial or noncustodial context. A **noncustodial interrogation** situation is one in which the interviewee is not in police custody or under arrest. The person must be acutely aware that he or she is free to leave at any time. This awareness may be based in part on the location of the interrogation, the attitude of the interrogator, and lack of follow-up arrest of the suspect at that time. Remember that *Miranda* warnings are required when the person is in custody. If the situation changes to a custodial one from a noncustodial interview during the interrogation, warnings must be given. The decision not to arrest unless it is necessary should be determined in advance of the interview. This decision to delay an arrest allows the investigator to probe for information in a non-threatening place such as an individual's home.

A noncustodial interrogation is not as threatening to the individual. A noncustodial interrogation is less formal, allowing the interrogator to understate his or her position as well as giving the impression that statements are less damning. Conduct a noncustodial interrogation by introducing yourself as a police officer investigating the crime. When the individual is willing to voluntarily go to the investigators' office for an interview, ask if he or she would like to follow in his or her car or have a friend accompany him or her in the cruiser. Allowing the interviewee to come to office reinforces the notion that the subject is voluntarily involving himself in the process. If the investigator is invited into a person's home to talk, it is appropriate to accept any offer for coffee or tea to keep the interview informal. After the interrogation is completed, thank the person for cooperating and suggest that you may want to speak to him or her again in the future.

Custodial Interrogation Situation

In a **custodial interrogation**, the subject is under arrest or is not free to leave because the arrest is impending. The *Miranda* warnings are necessary prior to questioning a person in custody. The offender must understand his or her rights and voluntarily waive them. A knowing waiver of rights is compromised if the individual has a mental disability, cannot read or write, or is under the influence of alcohol or drugs. It is the responsibility of the investigator to assess the ability of the individual to understand his or her rights in order for them to provide a knowing and voluntary waiver. An individual cannot be coerced or forced to give up any of his or her rights. The spirit, as well as the letter of the law, must be followed.

Once an individual has made a knowing and voluntary waiver of his or her *Miranda* rights, it is not necessary to repeat them over and over until the person wonders why he or she ever agreed to speak in the first place. Department policy dictates whether the individual must waive his or her rights in writing. *Miranda* does not require this. Neither does *Miranda* require that a person is given his or her rights verbatim. The Court has determined that a suspect who is silent to the question of whether they waive their right to the protection against self-incrimination is in fact agreeing to the interrogation. A person must affirmatively invoke his right to remain silent.

If the individual asks for an attorney, the interrogation *must* stop immediately. The request for a lawyer does not require an explicit mention of an attorney, or a question asked of the interrogator about the need for one. The interrogator should not give legal advice to an individual. However, it is good practice to follow up even a vague mention of a lawyer.

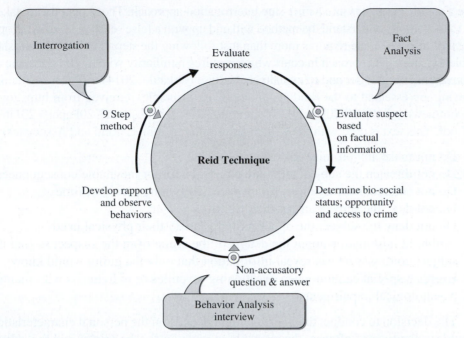

FIGURE 13-2   The Reid technique is a common method of investigative interviewing used in the United States and Canada.

Source: Adapted from John E. Reid & Associates, 2014.

The waiver of right against self-incrimination can be withdrawn at any time. Even when the person agrees to speak with an investigator, the right to stop speaking can be applied at any stage during the questioning. The right against self-incrimination belongs to the individual. No one can take it from him or her, nor can one insist on it for another. For example, an attorney may ask to speak with his or her client, and the person must be informed that a lawyer is available and would like to talk with them. If the subject wants to continue to talk with the police without that attorney, the right is his or hers. Do not interpret this as providing a way to deny individual rights. Inform the person that he or she has the right to continue speaking with authorities and let him or her make the decision.

Common custodial interrogation models include the Reid technique, the PEACE model, and HUMINT. The Reid technique is often referred to as the accusatorial approach, and the PEACE model exemplifies the information gathering method (Kelly et al., 2013). Experts note that actual interrogations do not consist of only one technique, however; therefore, scholars' assessment of any one technique is likely to be different from its use in reality (Kelly et al., 2013).

REID TECHNIQUE

Research shows mixed results about the best way to conduct an interrogation. Awareness of the differences among offenders is incorporated into the Reid technique, which classifies offenders as emotional or nonemotional (Inbau, Reid, Buckley, & Jayne, 2013). Offenders differ considerably based on the level of guilt they experience, so the interrogator must change tactics to be successful in moving a subject to confess. Researchers have found that the suspect's perception of the strength of the police evidence is one of the most important factors influencing a decision to confess to the police (Deslauriers-Varin, Lussier, & St-Yves, 2011).

The Reid technique is a highly structured method which begins with a fact analysis step, moves into a behavior analysis stage, and, if the interrogator is reasonably certain of the suspect's guilt, continues into a nine-step interrogation approach. Those who do not take the time to thoroughly understand the method will end up with a false sense of security. Properly using the Reid technique requires more than just following the steps. An investigator should be able to justify the approach in court which requires familiarity with all the steps, the ability to recite them in order and to explain each phase (Orlando, 2014). Authors maintain the following are essential to the Reid technique (Core Principle, retrieved from https://www.reid.com/newmedia/The%20Reid%20Technique%20A%20Position%20Paper%20Jan%202017.pdf. This text is used with the written permission of John E. Reid and Associates):

- Do not make any promises of leniency
- Do not threaten the subject with any physical harm or inevitable consequences
- Do not conduct interrogations for an excessively long period of time
- Do not deny the subject any of their rights
- Do not deny the subject the opportunity to satisfy their physical needs
- Withhold information about the details of the crime from the suspect so that if the subject confesses he can reveal information that only the guilty would know
- Exercise special caution when questioning juveniles or individuals with mental or psychological impairments

The decision to conduct the interrogation depends on the personal characteristics of the subject, the type of offense, the probable motivation for the crime, and the subject's initial responses to questioning. The nine-step interrogation stage is not as simple as the mere statement provided below might appear. The brief steps of the interrogation stage. (© John E. Reid and Associates. This text is used with the written permission of John E. Reid and Associates).

Step 1—The positive confrontation. The investigator informs the subject that the evidence shows the person's guilt. If the guilt seems clear to the investigator, the statement should be unequivocal.

Step 2—Theme development. A presumption about the reason for the crime's commission with a moral justification (theme) for the offense is proposed.

Step 3—Handling denials. This step involves procedures for handling the initial denials of guilt. An innocent person will not allow such denials to be cut off and he will attempt to take over the situation. A guilty person usually will cease to offer a denial, or they will become weaker.

Step 4—Overcoming objections. When attempts at denial do not succeed, a guilty person often makes objections to support a claim of innocence, or say, why he would never commit such a crime.

Step 5—Procurement and retention of suspect's attention. The investigator will clearly display sincerity in what he says.

Step 6—Handling the suspect's passive mood. The investigator should continue to display an understanding and sympathetic demeanor in urging the subject to tell the truth.

Step 7—Presenting an alternative question. This is the utilization of an alternative suggestion of a choice to be made by the subject concerning some aspect of the crime.

Step 8—Having the suspect orally relate various details of the offense. After the subject accepts one side of the alternative (thus admitting guilt), there should be a statement of reinforcement acknowledging that admission. Obtain a brief oral review of the event before asking more detailed questions.

Step 9—Converting an oral confession to a written or recorded confession. The suspect is encouraged to give a narrative of his participation in the crime.

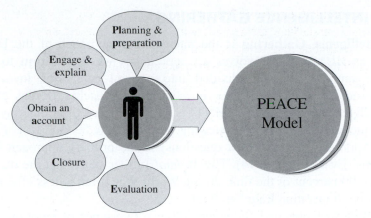

FIGURE 13-3 PEACE is a common method of investigative interviewing used in the United Kingdom and Australia.

PEACE MODEL

In 1993, the Royal Commission on Criminal Justice in England reformed the practice of interrogation (Kassin, Appleby, & Perillo, 2010). This method is called Preparation and Planning, Engage and Explain, Account, Closure and Evaluate (PEACE). Under the PEACE method, investigators allow a subject to tell his or her story without interruption, before presenting the suspect with any inconsistencies or contradictions between the story and other evidence. Interviewers are encouraged to be fair and open-minded. The use of trickery or deception by interviewers is prohibited (Vrij, Meissner, & Kassin, 2015. The PEACE approach is primarily used in the United Kingdom and Australia and is gaining worldwide attention as an approach that can also lead subjects to produce more verbal and nonverbal cues to detection as compared to more confrontational methods of interrogation (Kassin et al., 2010).

1. **Preparation and Planning.** Unlike other models, investigators do not presume that the subject is guilty and obtaining a confession is not the most important goal. A written interview plan should first be made with a focus on the objectives of the questioning and the order of interviews. Among other things, the plan should document the time a person has been detained and the topics to be covered during the interview. Before starting an interview, the investigator should review the points of law necessary to prove the offense and which will provide a defense. Interviewers should consider the characteristics of the interviewee that could be relevant to the plan, such as cultural background, age, and vulnerability. Investigators may also need to consider practical arrangements, such as visiting the scene or the location of the interview.

2. **Engage and Explain.** The interviewer should engage the individual through the establishment of rapport and active listening. The *explain* part of the method requires that the interviewer tell the reasons for the interview as well as reasons for taking notes or recording.

3. **Account.** The interviewers should encourage a free-flowing narrative and listen without interrupting the individual. Questions should be simple and short, used merely to clarify and expand the account. Multi-part questions should typically be avoided due to possible confusion, and leading questions should be used only as a last resort.

4. **Closure.** The closure should be planned to avoid an abrupt end to the interview. Among other things, the interviewers should summarize the person's account of events, allowing the person to make clarifications and ask questions.

5. **Evaluate.** The investigator should evaluate the interview to determine how the interviewee's account fits with the investigation as a whole and to decide if further action is needed. It is also the time to reflect on their performance during the questioning, what worked and what did not work.

HUMAN INTELLIGENCE GATHERING

Human Intelligence Gathering is the interrogation approach of the U.S. military; referred to as HUMINT, it involves 18 approaches which conform to the Geneva Convention standards and are divided into general categories involving Direct, Incentive-based, Emotion, and other questioning approaches (Evans et al., 2014). Human intelligence gathering (HUMINT) is an intelligence discipline involving many techniques, including cognitive interviewing. According to the *U.S. Army Field Manual*, the Direct Approach (asking direct questions) is the primary approach in HUMINT interrogations (Evans et al., 2014). The *Manual* further states that the direct approach was effective 90 percent of the time during World War II but is less effective in recent conflicts such as Operation Iraqi Freedom.

According to Evans and colleagues (2014), two types of emotional approaches appear in the *Manual*, a positive versus a negative emotional reaction, which are illustrated in Figure 13-4. In the "fear-up" and "fear-down" approaches interrogators seek to elicit an emotional outburst, or conversely, softly compassionate to encourage the person to reveal useful information inadvertently. A similar dynamic occurs with the techniques of flattering or insulting the person which is the "ego-up" and "ego-down" approach. Alternately, the interrogator creates a sense of hopelessness and helplessness where the suspect perceives that resistance to questioning is futile.

The Scharff technique is named after Hans Joachim Scharff who is thought to be among the most effective World War II interrogators (Kristoffersen, 2012). The **Scharff technique** (HUMINT) is the collection of information through an interaction between two or more people, with the specific goal of gathering information in a way that the source is oblivious to the actual purpose of the meeting (Granhag, Kleinman, & Oleszkiewicz, 2016). After observing the threat-based techniques used with limited success by his predecessor, Scharff wanted to create an environment that might make the Prisoner of War (POW) forget that he was being questioned. In addition to being interviewed in an office environment, for example, Scharff might take the POW for a walk or drinks at the officer's club. According to Granhag and colleagues (2016), Scharff's approach is similar to the psychological concept of perspective taking, the ability to consider the world from another's viewpoint. Taking another's view, sometimes called empathy, facilitates the anticipation of other people's behavior and reactions.

In a study to compare the differences between the Direct Approach in HUMINT and the Scharff technique in HUMINT, the only difference found was in the confirmation/disconfirmation tactic (May, Granhag, & Oleszkiewicz, 2014). In the Scharff technique, the confirmation tactic was considered more efficient than the disconfirmation

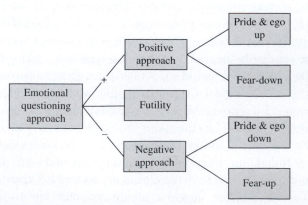

FIGURE 13-4   HUMINT commonly uses the Emotion Provocation domain, illustrated here as being positive or negative.

Source: Adapted from Evans et al., 2014.

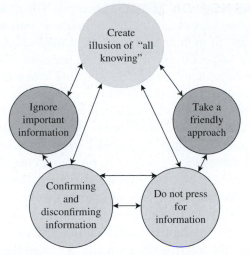

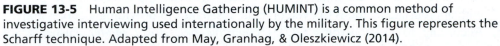

FIGURE 13-5 Human Intelligence Gathering (HUMINT) is a common method of investigative interviewing used internationally by the military. This figure represents the Scharff technique. Adapted from May, Granhag, & Oleszkiewicz (2014).

tactic since the interviewer masked his information objections best in the former. View Figure 13-5 for an illustration. Researchers noted the Scharff technique results in more new information than the Direct Approach, while the sources interviewed thought that they had revealed less new information than they did.

General Confession-Eliciting Models

Scholars have developed a variety of theoretical perspectives that explain why people choose to confess when interrogated. Recently, 71 unique techniques have been identified (Kelly et al., 2013). Each method forwards an approach to interrogation from a different perspective. In their taxonomy study, Kelly et al. (2013) looked at the six domains within interrogation techniques and chose to place rapport in the center of a Theoretical Interactive Process Model of interrogation which includes all six.

Gudjonsson (2003) suggested that custodial interrogation approaches fall into five theoretical confession-producing models: the Reid model, the decision-making model, the psychoanalytic model, the interaction process model, and the cognitive-behavioral model. Each method is broadly based on theory incorporated into the phases of the interrogation:

1. The *Reid model* relies on decreasing the subject's perception of the consequences of confession. The interrogator uses rationalization to help the offender to avoid full responsibility and projection to distort the account of what happened. At the same time, the person's internal anxiety associated with his or her deception is increased by the interrogator, prompting a confession. Manipulating an individual's anxiety is achieved by exaggerating normal feelings of guilt and shame.
2. The *decision-making model* uses a hedonistic calculation by the perpetrator of the options available and the consequences of choosing each one (Yang, Guyll, & Madon, 2017). In this pain versus pleasure analysis, the subject will decide to confess or not based on the factors that pressure him or her in different directions. The pressures include social, psychological, and environmental considerations that make giving a confession the better choice. The interrogator facilitates the process by reinforcing the pressures to confess.
3. The *psychoanalytic model* rests on the assumption that there is a psychological need to confess based on guilt and the desire for self-punishment. Highly controversial,

this approach relies heavily on Freudian concepts. The model tends to emphasize the role of the unconscious as the key determinant of confessions and proposes, for example, that feeling of guilt and remorse drive individuals to confess. Only after confessing will the suspect begin to release the pressure of guilt. According to this model, the two driving forces are the fear of losing love and fear of retaliation. The anxiety that the person endures due to guilt is exploited to elicit the confession.

4. The *interaction process model* views the interrogation as a three-prong process: the characteristics of the offender and his or her offense, the strength of the evidence, and the interrogator's technique. The model stresses the interplay of these influences during the interrogation process. To prompt a confession from the suspect, the interrogator considers the background characteristics of the suspect, such as age and gender in addition to the type of offense that was committed (Beauregard & Mieczkowski, 2012). The strength of the evidence and the technique used by the interrogator are the additional consideration. The success of the interrogation depends on whether the interrogator correctly accessed the subject and responded with appropriate methods to overcome the resistance to providing a confession.

5. According to Gudjonsson's (2003) *cognitive–behavioral model,* suspects are motivated to confess by the social, emotional, and cognitive pressures of isolation, police pressure, personal distress, and the belief that the police know that he or she did it. Additional factors that influence the likelihood of a confession are situational, such as the presence of an attorney or familiarity with police procedures.

INTERROGATION PHASE I: PREPARING

Regardless of the method of interrogation used by the investigator, each approach requires formal and systematic preparation and planning. The subject can be interrogated while in custody or not; it depends on the type of case and goals of the interrogation. The precise nature of the interrogation is important throughout the process. Success is enhanced when the interrogator is well rested and confident about the case. It takes tremendous energy to conduct an interrogation. The interrogator must be one step ahead of the person in every way, from anticipating excuses to confronting denials. The interrogation may be as short as 1 hour or may take several hours. The preparation for an interrogation begins in roughly the same manner as the interview. The interrogator who starts the interrogation must be prepared to follow through to the end.

The five steps in this preparation phase are (1) know the case, (2) determine the prior record, (3) view the scene, (4) establish the timing, and (5) decide who will conduct the interrogation.

Step One: Know the Case

The interrogator should be thoroughly familiar with the case. Statements of victims should be reviewed, particularly if the interrogator did not interview victims or witnesses. If the investigation involves a major felony, there may be more than one person involved in the investigation. The interrogator should speak with each investigator, in a group meeting if possible. It is not unusual for facts of the case to be known to one investigator and unknown to others. Take the time to contact the individuals who have been involved with the case or similar cases that may be linked.

Before conducting an interrogation, review the statutes concerning the crimes that may have already been charged and those that may be considered in the future. Be familiar with the elements of each law that must be satisfied to obtain a court conviction. During the interrogation, it is imperative that evidence concerning the violation of the specific elements be addressed. For example, if the charge is "rape," then the proof of penetration by an object must be established. A lesser crime would be an attempted rape or sexual assault. Did the suspect undress or unzip the fly on his pants? Undressing alone could be used to substantiate the intent to rape in some circumstances. As another example, the crime of "breaking and entering with the intent to commit a felony" requires proof of both the "break" and the "intent" of committing a crime.

Reviewing the offense to determine an interrogation approach includes having an understanding of the case that includes the numerous ways in which the person could be charged. Knowing the legal options provides leverage throughout the interrogation. Reviewing the case goes beyond merely knowing the category of crime that has been committed. Examine how the perpetrator was identified. Examples could include the suspect's voice inflections or the types of words that were stated during the crime. Identification of a suspect might include an identifying mark on them or the way the person smells. Information on the specific words or gestures employed by the alleged perpetrator provides tools that the interrogator will be able to use. Ideally, the interrogator should be the person in the case who has also interviewed the victims and witnesses.

Step Two: Determine the Prior Record

A background check on each suspect should be done before questioning. Determine whether the suspect has been prosecuted and found guilty of crimes in the past. An individual may be concerned if he or she has a violent felony record from prior convictions. In jurisdictions with three strikes or mandatory sentencing laws, the subject may have an additional fear that will impact the interrogation. Under three strikes and mandatory sentencing, a felon will face extended periods of mandated imprisonment for a third conviction.

Check to see whether any outstanding warrants may be used to hold the person in custody if necessary. It is also of value to find out whether the subject has any suspended sentences.

Step Three: View the Scene

Searching for evidence is as important as conducting the interrogation. Viewing the scene may produce indisputable facts for use in the interrogation. Faced with physical evidence that points to his or her guilt, the alleged perpetrator may be less likely to deny the charges.

To determine whether the person is linked to other, similar offenses, it is necessary to find out how the individual committed the crime. Referred to as the *modus operandi* or methods of operation, these are the usual things that the offender does during the commission of a particular crime. In a house break-in, for example, what type of neighborhood did the person invade? Was entry gained through the front door or the back door? Was a tool used or glass broken? Was there a significant difference in the type of items stolen, such as jewelry, electronics, or guns and ammunition? These particulars can later be compared to crimes of a similar nature to determine similarities in another house break-in.

Step Four: Establish the Timing

The suspect should be confronted as soon as is practical, ideally before he or she learns about the investigation. This provides an opportunity to lock the person into a story or alibi. The less time that he or she has to make up an alibi or justify the offense, the better. In cases in which evidence may be found on the body of the individual, speed is of the essence. Whatever timing is chosen, it is the prerogative of the interrogator to determine the best opportunity. The officer must then assess whether it is safe to proceed.

BEEN THERE . . . DONE THAT! 13-2

An officer from the Vermont Sheriff's Office contacted the Massachusetts State Police. He had arrested a man who was passing phony drug prescriptions. A search of the subject revealed evidence of scrips being passed in Northampton, Massachusetts. I was assigned the investigation and learned that the suspect, Mr. T, had gone on a 4-day spree during which he obtained narcotics fraudulently. His *modus operandi* was to phone a pharmacy and order a prescription for a Schedule II narcotic while his wife waited inside the pharmacy to see whether the police were called. In this case, Mrs. T would then come outside and warn her husband if the police were called so that they could flee. Mr. T had also gone to a local doctor complaining of pain, requesting Dilaudid (a Schedule II narcotic). At the time of his arrest, he had numerous labels from prescriptions for codeine issued by a pharmacy in Massachusetts. He had used the prescribing doctor's name for the phony scrips.

Subsequently, I recovered nine prescriptions for Mr. T that had been filled for Schedule II and III narcotics. These supposedly had been phoned in by a "doctor" but were found to be fraudulent. Mr. T and his wife had also stolen scrip pads from legitimate doctors and had written fraudulent prescriptions. The doctors were interviewed and gave statements that they had not issued the medication prescriptions. Mr. T had used at least two aliases in the scheme. An arrest warrant was issued.

Although speed and surprise are general principles for an interrogation, there are times when the purposeful delay is the best approach. Situations that may cause delay to the interrogation include the following:

- Passage of time since the crime
- Existence of multiple victims
- Previous relationship between the alleged offender and the officer
- Need to execute a search warrant

The passage of time makes it more difficult to solve a crime. Leads dry up and evidence can be difficult to generate. The investigation that continues after the case is cold requires an approach that is slow and steady.

The possibility that there were multiple victims can generate a sense of urgency in solving the case. It is an impulse that is best held back. When multiple victims are linked to a single possible suspect, the investigator has the additional responsibility of learning the details of each case. Failure to take the time can result in overlooking details. There may be only one opportunity to conduct an interrogation, so be careful not to go too fast and miss the chance to be thorough.

A previous relationship or newly cultivated relationship with the alleged offender can be used to the benefit of the investigation process. If the subject is accustomed to seeing the officer and some respect has been established, a major barrier against disclosing has been broken down before the interrogation. It can be a sense of relief for the person when the time comes for the case to be discussed. It is possible to have the individual anticipate the day of the interrogation.

Step Five: Determine Who Will Conduct the Interrogation

Many officers have conducted one-on-one interrogations. The primary consideration is whether there might be a threat to the safety of the officer. The seriousness of the case is not necessarily the determining factor; the decision to delay an interrogation should be based on whether the officer will be outnumbered and whether the individual has a mental disorder, is a member of the opposite gender, or has a violent history. It is dangerous and unnecessary to assume that the size or strength of the interrogator determines the place or timing. The bottom line is that the interrogator needs to have

BEEN THERE . . . DONE THAT! 13-3

This investigation started with a phone call from the Department of Social Services. The social worker told me that she had investigated the death of an infant a few days earlier. She had originally thought that the child had died from fractures due to brittle bone disease (osteogenesis imperfecta), a genetic disorder that is characterized by bones that break easily for no apparent reason. The disorder is present at birth, but the individual may not show symptoms for years. In this case, the child had been diagnosed with the disease at the time of birth and had suffered fractures before her death.

The social worker was having second thoughts about the cause of death because a second child of the same parent had just been taken to the hospital with severe injuries that were indicative of abuse. It was unknown at that time whether the second child was going to live. When the social worker gave me the name of the child's mother, I immediately knew who it was. The family was known to be very violent. I had arrested her brother a year prior for homicide. There was no evidence that the mother had killed her sick baby, but I had a sinking feeling that that was exactly what had happened.

I went to her apartment and introduced myself, and explained that I was investigating what had happened to her two children. The mother allowed me into the apartment to look at the room while she described what had happened. Her explanation of the situation did not fit the scene. For example, she said that she had picked up the sick baby, who was crying and had awakened her sleeping boyfriend. She brought the child into the kitchen and had tripped on a toy that was on the floor. The child fell. At my request, she drew a picture of the place she had "tripped" and where the baby had fallen. I took pictures of the apartment. However, there were no toys. Not one. It was a two-room, one-bedroom apartment. The two children slept in the same room with the mother and her boyfriend. The child did not fall straight down (as falling objects tend to do) but came to rest on the opposite side of the kitchen. From the position of the objects in the kitchen, it appeared as though the child had been forcibly thrown against the side of the stove and had landed far to the left of it.

After reviewing the case, I decided to interrogate the mother during a noncustodial interrogation. I asked if she was willing for me to write down her statement at my office and whether there was anyone she would like to accompany her. She asked if I could pick up her mother on the way. I did. Her mother stayed outside of the room during the actual statement. The preceding facts were incorporated into the statement, along with the fact that her boyfriend was furious when the baby started crying. She, in turn, became angry at the children and had "probably thrown" them both. The second child did not die but would be brain damaged for the rest of his life. This was no accident. This was not an interview; persuasion was needed to extract the statement. The goal was to have her admit to causing the death and injury to her children. She did admit it and signed the confession before I brought her and her mother home. She was later indicted and pled guilty.

complete control over the questioning and should not be forced into interrogating in a time or place that is not desirable.

Ideally, two individuals should be in the room during the interrogation, but one should do most of the questioning. There are several reasons for this arrangement. The primary reason is for officer safety. Second, having two persons in the room allows for flexibility in the interrogation. If the suspect is not responding to the first questioning officer, the officers can switch roles. It is not uncommon for a subject to express anger toward one of the officers without reason; having an alternative person available makes it possible to continue the questioning. It is the responsibility of the interrogator to determine when his or her effectiveness is fading and being willing to step back and allow another person to continue the interrogation. Another reason for a second interrogator is that he or she can take detailed notes, freeing the primary interrogator from that responsibility. The note-taker should be seated behind the suspect and slightly to one side, within sight of the primary interrogator but outside the line of vision of the subject. This is done so as not to cause a distraction during the interrogation. An alternative arrangement has the second interrogator monitor the interrogation from behind a two-way mirror. Many jurisdictions have moved to digital recording felony interrogations, which may eliminate the need for a second officer.

When preparing for an interrogation, the most important aspect of the case is the preservation of the constitutional protections of the accused. Know the federal and state mandates before attempting to conduct an interrogation. For this reason, typically a seasoned investigator is the best choice to conducting the interrogation. Denial of the suspect's rights will jeopardize the case. Evidence may later be excluded from the trial if an improper interrogation takes place. A confession is only worthwhile if it is obtained correctly. Confession admissibility is guided by the Fourth, Fifth, Sixth, and Fourteenth Amendments of the Constitution, case law, federal law, and state law. It must be established that a person's incriminating response was not the result of words or actions on the part of the police that violated these provisions.

The place chosen for the interrogation should be quiet and free of distractions. There should be no telephone, radio, clock, or other electronic devices. The officers in the room should turn off their cell phones. Ideally, the room should have a two-way mirror for observation.

Remember that individuals may also be questioned in their own home or any other place where privacy can be assured. The location should encourage them to release their burden of guilt in an atmosphere that is private and safe. An absence of judgment from the interrogator adds to the feeling that the subject has nothing to fear about opening up.

INTERROGATION PHASE II: DEVELOPING OUTCOME-BASED TACTICS

Before beginning the interrogation, the investigator should develop outcome-based tactics. The characteristics of the subject such as age, level of education, addiction issues, mental disorders, and marital status should be considered in determining which interrogation approach is likely to be successful. Employment, community status, and lifestyle also impact the approach used for persuasion.

To be successful, the investigator must consider the many reasons the subject might not want to confess. Fear may cause resistance to the interrogation and inhibit someone from admitting guilt. Identifying these concerns is an important part of developing persuasive arguments. Fear for his or her safety or the safety of a family member can be difficult to overcome.

The most frequent interrogation tactic involves an appeal to the subject's self-interest, which can also be considered as a call to the hope for a better outcome to the case. A common impulse is to suggest that the subject would be "better off" if he or she confessed. A promise of leniency violates the individual's right to due process and may cause legal challenges to any resulting confession.

The investigator should act in a manner that is nonjudgmental. The perpetrator may have committed the crime because it seemed like the only alternative at the time. Afterwards, the fear sets in and the individual may be torn on what to do. Faced with evidence that he stole money or property, consider that there may be reasons that justified the theft at the time but the person now may feel remorseful. Attempt to engage the person about why he or she committed the crime.

If the individual has status in the community or a well-paying job, he or she may be afraid to lose that employment as the result of being arrested. Fear that admitting guilt will have financial repercussions is a real concern. Fear may be related to the category of crime that he or she is accused of committing. The person may be afraid that once the details of the offense are made public, he or she will lose respect, shock family or friends, or suffer embarrassment. Use empathy to counteract shame. Ask why the individual did what he or she did. Abusers of children often speak about their love for the child and how the relationship benefited the child. Remember that these tactics are goal-oriented. They are considered before the interrogation and planned to meet its goals. Failure to consider a plan is like appearing in a play without having rehearsed your lines.

INTERROGATION PHASE III: OBTAINING THE CONFESSION

Don't be overly solicitous or friendly; establish yourself as a professional. Do not use legal terminology or police jargon. Speak with the person firmly but with respect. While maintaining control over the interrogation, don't psychologically back someone into a corner. If the person feels that there is no way out, he or she will stop talking, so give the suspect an out from the very beginning. Instead of focusing on the offense, start with what motivated the commission of the crime. Don't invite a denial, ask for an explanation.

Step One: Make the Claim

Suspects should feel that the interrogator will listen. To begin the interrogation, an accusation must be raised by the interrogator. There are some ways to do this. It is my experience that honesty works best. The interrogator's sincerity will be apparent to all but the hardest of criminals. Use his or her first name and do not shout. Never express anger; it indicates weakness. At all times, the interrogator must be in complete control of her or his emotions and reactions.

> *There is one thing that an innocent man has in common with a guilty man: they will both deny having committed the crime.*

When the moment arrives that the claim is to be made, the interrogator should be sitting near the suspect. There should be no tables or furniture between them. Lean toward them slightly and firmly tell him or her that you know that he or she is guilty. Say that there is no doubt in your mind, based on the investigation, that he or she did it. An innocent person is more likely to have a quick and vigorous denial along with anger at having been accused. He or she may jump right out of the chair and begin yelling. A guilty person is also likely to deny the claim but will be slower or protest more weakly.

Step Two: Lock It In

Once the claim is made, there can be no further discussion on innocence. Having already considered the available outcome-based tactics, this is the time to use persuasion. Tell the subject that he or she needs to move on, understand why the events happened, or tell their version of the story. Present an excuse for the individual, minimize his or her culpability in the crime, or suggest that he or she was tormented and that there was no other choice. No one likes to be caught with his or her hand in the cookie jar. People do not like being confronted with something they did wrong. Allow the person to express their good intentions; suggest that you understand that he or she did not mean to hurt the person, intended to return the money, or whatever fits the events. Giving the suspect a way out will allow the person to maintain face.

The more a person denies something, the more he or she begins to believe in his or her innocence. Prevent this from happening by interrupting them. Encourage the person to continue in a way that is going to move forward and allow him or her to figure out what to do next. Suggest that the situation is not going to go away and that he or she has an opportunity to have his or her side of the story included when it does come out. Allow the person to maintain his or her dignity.

BEEN THERE . . . DONE THAT! 13-4

Jane Doe was 23 years old. She told me during an interview that she had left her home around 6:30 A.M. to go jogging. She was wearing a pair of running shorts, a shirt, and sneakers with socks. As she began running, she noticed a commercial truck with faded red letters on the side and back parked by the side of the road. It later drove past her. As she continued running down the country road, a man came running toward her. He was screaming "ARAHAHH." He tackled her to the ground, and she fell into a cornfield. She hit him in the groin and stomach. He got on top of her and forced her onto her back. She asked what he was doing, and he replied, "I do not know." He grabbed her on the left side of her shirt and touched her left breast. She told me that she was very much in fear and kept trying to hit him. She thought that her life was in danger and she kept swearing and hitting him. Finally, she was able to roll him off of her, and she ran to a house nearby.

She described the assailant as having a high voice for a man. He was a white man in his 20s and was wearing a bright red shirt (pullover type) with a round neck and tight black biker pants that came to his mid-thigh. He had blonde, curly hair (not tight curls) with bangs that half covered his ears.

With what crimes (if any) would you charge this suspect? What approach would you use to interrogate him?

There will be times when the interrogator senses anger or disrespect from the alleged perpetrator that is hard to overcome. It is perfectly acceptable to recognize that the likelihood of your obtaining a confession is low under the circumstances. If there is another individual who can continue the interrogation with better chances at being successful, step back and allow that individual to take over.

Conclusions

By considering the complementarity principle, an interrogator might influence a subject's responses. Further persuasion can occur through the primary interactions of friendliness and dominance. This sets the stage for the interrogator to take charge of the interrogation. The interrogation is an important piece of a criminal investigation or intelligence gathering process. Both a confession and an admission are forms of inculpatory evidence, which tends to illustrate a person's involvement in a crime or to establish guilt. While obtaining either is a successful conclusion to the interrogation process, it never should substitute for a full investigation or be used as a method of obtaining evidence. The same legal standards that were explained in earlier chapters governing the admissibility of a confession pertain to an admission.

The chapter covered different interrogation situations as custodial or noncustodial interrogations. Note that there have been over 70 interrogation approaches identified through research; this should impress on you that there is no one way to conduct an interrogation. The Reid technique is introduced in this chapter, which is often referred to having an accusatorial approach. The PEACE model is an example of the *information gathering method*.

The Reid technique is a three-part process consisting of fact analysis, a behavior analysis interview,

and a nine-step interrogation stage. The PEACE model consists of five steps designed to encourage full narrative accounts of the incident under investigation. Human Intelligence Gathering (HUMINT) consists of 18 different approaches to interrogation. Two that were illustrated are the Emotional Questioning Approach and the Scharff technique. These illustrate the vast difference between the interrogation approaches used by the military.

General confession-eliciting models in this chapter center on the five-theoretical confession-producing models identified by Gudjonsson. The process is complicated. Three phases were suggested as an outline of the interrogation process. The first step is a preparation that should look very familiar. The first three steps are the same as the preparation for an interview. Because the guilt of the suspect should be fairly certain at the time the interrogation takes place, additional preparation involves its timing and the choice of the interrogator. Phase II is a major step in persuading the suspect to confess. The interrogator should go into the process after having already considered the possible tactics to use to overcome resistance to providing a confession. Central to the development of outcome-based tactics is understanding of the suspect's fears. Suggestions were made on how to understand fears, but by no means is this an exhaustive list of possibilities.

Questions for Review

Short-Answer Questions

1. Explain what the complementarity principle can mean to the potential interrogator.
2. Explain the difference between a confession and an admission.
3. What are the primary issues covered in the Reid technique?
4. What is the PEACE method?
5. What do we know about Human Intelligence Gathering?

Fill-in Questions

1. A useful approach to understanding interpersonal relations is based on the ____ principle, according to which two or more different things improve or emphasize each other's qualities that come from a predictable set of reactions in response to certain actions.
2. The two interrogation situations described in this chapter are ____ and noncustodial.
3. The ____ technique is a highly structured method which begins with a fact analysis step, moves into a behavior analysis stage, and, if the interrogator is fairly certain of the suspect's guilt, continues into a nine-step interrogation approach.
4. Under the ____ method, investigators allow a suspect to tell his or her story without interruption, before presenting the suspect with any inconsistencies or contradictions between the story and other evidence.
5. Unlike other models, investigators do not presume that the suspect is guilty and obtaining a confession is not the most important goal of the ____.

6. Human Intelligence Gathering is the interrogation approach of the U.S. military; referred to as ____, it involves 18 approaches which conform to the Geneva Convention standards and are divided into general categories involving Direct, Incentive-based, Emotion, and other questioning approaches.
7. The ____ Technique (HUMINT) is the collection of information through an interaction between two or more people, with the specific goal of gathering information in a way that the source is unaware of the true purpose of the interrogation.
8. Gudjonsson (2003) suggested that custodial interrogation approaches fall into five general ____ models: the Reid model, the decision-making model, the psychoanalytic model, the interaction process model, and the cognitive-behavioral model.
9. Regardless of the method of interrogation used by the investigator, each approach requires formal and systematic preparation and ____.
10. The characteristics of the suspect such as ____, level of education, addiction issues, mental disorders, and marital status should be considered in determining which interrogation approach is likely to be successful.

Exercises

1. Find the statute from your state that defines a crime of your choice. Compare that statute to another state for the same offense. Go to https://www.law.cornell.edu/wex/table_criminal_code
2. Watch a TV program where a crime is committed. Determine the approach you would take to interrogation. Explain your reasoning.

References

Beauregard, E., & Mieczkowski, T. (2012). From police interrogation to prison: Which sex offender characteristics predict confession? *Police Quarterly*, 15(2), 197–214.

Bruton v. U.S., 391 US 123, 139 (1968).

Commonwealth v. Forde, 392 Mass. 453 (1984).

Dando, C., Bull, R., Ormerod, T., & Sandham, A. (2015). Helping to sort the liars from the truth-tellers: The gradual revelation of information during investigative interviews. *Legal and criminological psychology*, 20(1), 114–128.

Deslauriers-Varin, N., Lussier, P., & St-Yves, M. (2011). Confessing their crime: Factors influencing the offender's decision to confess to the police. *Justice Quarterly*, 28(1), 113–145.

Evans, J. R., Houston, K. A., Meissner, C. A., Ross, A. B., LaBianca, J. R., Woestehoff, S. A., & Kleinman, S. M. (2014). An empirical evaluation of intelligence-gathering interrogation techniques from the United States Army field manual. *Applied Cognitive Psychology*, 28(6), 867–875.

Granhag, P. A., Kleinman, S. M., & Oleszkiewicz, S. (2016). The Scharff technique: On how to effectively elicit intelligence from human sources. *International Journal of Intelligence and Counter Intelligence*, 29(1), 132–150.

Gudjonsson, G. H. (2003). *The psychology of interrogations and confessions: A handbook*. Hoboken, NJ: Wiley.

Imoedemhe, O. C. (2016). *The Complementarity Regime of the International Criminal Court: National Implementation in Africa*. New York, NY: Springer.

Inbau, F. E., Reid, J. E., Buckley, J. P., & Jayne, B. C. (2013). *Criminal interrogation and confessions* (5th ed.). Chicago, IL: Jones & Bartlett.

John E. Reid & Associates, I. (2014). *Critics corner*. Retrieved from http://www.reid.com/educational_info/r_ccorner.html

Kassin, S. M., Appleby, S. C., & Perillo, J. T. (2010). Interviewing suspects: Practice, science, and future directions. *Legal and criminological psychology*, 15(1), 39–55.

Kelly, C. E., Miller, J. C., Redlich, A. D., & Kleinman, S. M. (2013). A taxonomy of interrogation methods. *Psychology, Public Policy, and Law*, 19(2), 165–178.

Kristoffersen, R. (2012). Learning from history: What is successful interrogation? *Combating Terrorism Exchange*, 2(3), 29–39.

Laudan, L. (2015). *Why asymmetric rules of procedure make it impossible to calculate a rationally warranted standard of proof.*

May, L., Granhag, P. A., & Oleszkiewicz, S. (2014). Eliciting intelligence using the Scharff-technique: Closing in on the confirmation/disconfirmation-tactic. *Journal of Investigative Psychology and Offender Profiling*, 11(2), 136–150.

Orlando, J. (2014). *Interrogation techniques*. Retrieved from online: https://www.cga.ct.gov/2014/rpt/2014-R-0071.htm

Rutledge, D. (1994). *Criminal interrogation: Law and tactics* (3rd ed.). Placerville, CA: Copperhouse Publishing.

Sadler, P., Ethier, N., & Woody, E. (2011). Interpersonal complementarity. In L. M. Horowitz & S. Strack (Eds.), *Handbook of interpersonal psychology: Theory, research, assessment, and therapeutic interventions* (pp.123–142). New York, NY: Wiley.

Vrij, A., Meissner, C. A., & Kassin, S. M. (2015). Problems in expert deception detection and the risk of false confessions: No proof to the contrary in Levine et al. (2014). *Psychology, Crime & Law, 21*(9), 901–909.

Yang, Y., Guyll, M., & Madon, S. (2017). The interrogation decision-making model: A general theoretical framework for confessions. *Law and Human Behavior*, 41(1), 80.

14

Juvenile Rights and Interviewer Responsibilities

Source: Gina Buliga/Shutterstock.

CHAPTER OBJECTIVES

After completing this chapter, you should be able to:

1. Compare the relationship between AGE and ACT in the juvenile justice system.
2. Describe the difference between delinquency and status offense and juvenile delinquency.
3. Examine the significance of the three Supreme Court juvenile decisions decided between 2005 and 2012.
4. Analyze the 10 basic principles known as the *Institute of Judicial Administration-American Bar Association* (IJA-ABA) *Juvenile Justice Standards*.
5. Explain the recommendations of Todd Warner on how law enforcement can reduce the likelihood of juvenile false confessions.
6. Discuss the *reasonable juvenile* standard.
7. Briefly describe the projections afforded juveniles under the Fifth and the Sixth Amendments.
8. Distinguish between juvenile fireplay and intentional fire setting.

KEY TERMS

Delinquency	Fireplay
Infancy rule	Intentional fire setting
Juvenile	*Parens patriae*
Protective custody	Status offense

INTRODUCTION

This chapter is entitled "Juvenile Rights and Interviewer Responsibilities" since it is not just about getting the statement when it comes to interviews and interrogations of a young person. There is a dual responsibility for an investigator when a minor is suspected of criminal behavior. Simply put, the responsibilities are split between protecting the public and a moral responsibility to protect a vulnerable person. Due to scientific advances, we now know that adolescents really are different from adults. The human brain does not fully develop functioning that controls impulses, calms emotions, and provides an understanding of the consequences of behavior until the mid to late twenties. Younger people may seek short-term rewards and do not consider long-term consequences; they often lack long-term planning and are less oriented toward the future. The absence of long-term planning may lead minors to place more value on the present than the future. Because of these and other differences, a juvenile may be more prone to making a false confession as compared to adults (Arndorfer, Malloy, & Cauffman, 2015).

The treatment of juveniles by society has varied over time. Some cultures stress their innocence, whereas others view children as potential little devils. The English feudal system established the notion of **parens patriae**, which is the power of the state to act on behalf of a child and provide care and protection equivalent to that of a parent, sometimes over the objection of the parent. In other contexts, children were considered an important part of economic life as sources of labor.

Children were treated as adults in criminal matters but lacked the due process rights enjoyed by adults. They were sentenced in adult courts and taken to adult jails. Handling of juveniles in the criminal justice context began to change in the late 1800s.

It was not until 1889 that Illinois enacted the first law to regulate the treatment and control of dependent, neglected, and delinquent children. Under the concept of *parens patriae* the power of the state over children is absolute; therefore, the courts began to make law and determine policies believed to be in the best interests of the child. A distinction was made between the child in need of services and those who committed criminal acts. Juveniles do not automatically have constitutional protection. The rights that apply to minors today have been expressly granted by the courts and through legislative action over the years since.

WHO IS A JUVENILE?

A **juvenile** is defined under federal law as a person who has not attained his or her 18th birthday (U.S. Code 18 U.S.C. §5031, 1994). A person older than 18 years but less than 21 years is also accorded juvenile treatment if the act of juvenile delinquency occurred before his or her 18th birthday. All states specify by statute the maximum age for an individual to be considered a minor, typically 17 years old. Some states specify a younger age. In Georgia, for example, a child is a juvenile until 16 years old, whereas in New York and North Carolina a minor is a person of age 15 years and younger (Zang, 2016).

The distinction between juvenile and adult is becoming more complex as states move toward trying juveniles as adults in court for major crimes and yet law enforcement officers are expected to afford greater protections to young offenders. The dual responsibility imposes a need for the investigator to ensure greater personal protections equivalent to those afforded to adults in addition to special considerations afforded to a minor.

Age of Criminal Responsibility

Criminal responsibility begins by specifying age boundaries in law. Age criteria can be found in various areas of law, which are organized by subject into statutes, also known as codes. Statutes specify which court has original jurisdiction, or initial authority, to rule on a particular matter within certain areas of law. Young people in conflict with the law may be subject to municipal court, criminal court, or juvenile court jurisdiction.

The **infancy rule** is the common law recognition that a child under the age of 7 years is generally presumed to be without the ability to form criminal intent and therefore cannot be charged with a crime. Many states have statutes that specify the age of criminal responsibility, which varies from state to state. Some states do not specify a minimum age for responsibility. Massachusetts, for example, relies on the infancy rule to determine juvenile court jurisdiction; the Colorado delinquency age is 10 years; and Arizona specifies no minimum age for responsibility (Zang, 2016). As illustrated in Figure 14-1, an adolescent may appear younger than their age, neither maturity nor appearance can be the determining factor when deciding the rights of an adolescent.

JUVENILE OFFENDING

Two different categories of wrongdoing apply to juveniles: the status offense and the delinquent offense.

A **status offense** is an act that would not be a crime if an adult committed it; it is illegal only because the child is underage. Examples include truancy, running away, and curfew violations. Some states treat status offenders differently than delinquents. In some jurisdictions, classification as a status offender has relatively little effect on the child's treatment. Many places view status offending behaviors as indicators that the child is in need of services, in which case the matter is handled through social service agencies rather than within the criminal justice system. Many states retain juvenile court jurisdiction for status offenses or abuse, neglect, or dependency through age 21 years (Zang, 2016). Refer to Figure 14-2 for illustration. A status offender is a juvenile that has been found responsible for having committed a status offense.

FIGURE 14-1 At what age can we hold children criminally responsible for their actions? The age of responsibility is found in the state statutes, and it varies from state to state. Do not determine rights based on maturity or appearance.

Source: Lisa F. Young/Shutterstock.

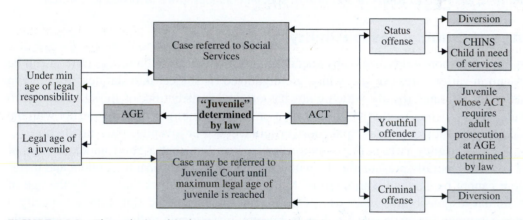

FIGURE 14-2 The relationship between AGE and ACT is one that is used to determine the processing of a juvenile in the juvenile justice system.

Between 2005 and 2014, police officers were the primary source of referrals each year for delinquency, curfew, and liquor law violation cases (Hockenberry & Puzzanchera, 2017). The reporting statistics underscore the vital role that law enforcement officers have as gatekeepers of the justice system.

Juvenile Delinquency

Juvenile **delinquency** is the violation of a law of the United States committed by a person prior to his or her 18th birthday that would have been a crime if it had been committed by an adult (U.S. Code 18 U.S.C. §5031, 1994) (or other age as designated by state law). The age for a minor to be adjudicated under the jurisdiction of the juvenile court varies from state to state depending on its definition of a juvenile. The juvenile court's authority may extend to as late as age 24 years as in California, Montana, Oregon, and Wisconsin, although most states end jurisdiction in delinquency cases at age 21 years (Zang, 2016).

As if it could not get any more complicated, age and offense together provide another way of determining juvenile delinquency versus criminal conduct. Some state statutes exclude types of offenses from juvenile court jurisdiction, mandating that the case is tried in adult criminal court. These are the youthful offender category. For example, in Massachusetts, the Youthful Offender Statute provides:

> .... that all juveniles aged 14 and older charged with murder are automatically treated as adults. It further established the new category of "youthful offender" allowing those juveniles aged 14 or older accused of serious offenses, to be charged as youthful offenders at the prosecutor's discretion and subjected to a juvenile, adult, or combination sentence.

The youth arrest rate grew substantially during the late 1980s and 1990s. Every state toughened its laws for young offenders and expanded transfer legislation to allow or mandate the prosecution of juveniles in adult criminal courts (Cohen, Bonnie, Taylor-Thompson, & Casey, 2015). The changed conception of the young offender would undo an almost century-long tradition of differentiated treatment for juvenile delinquents. Although young adults still commit a disproportionate amount of the nation's crime, arrests in 2011 were down 11 percent from 2010 and down 31 percent since 2002 (Puzzanchera & Adams, 2013). Female offenders represent an increasing proportion of juvenile arrests.

DUE PROCESS AND THE JUVENILE

In 1966, the Supreme Court responded to the problem of nonstandardized procedures and a general lack of juvenile protection in one of its first decisions concerning juvenile rights. Although the *Kent* decision was confined solely to the issue of waiver proceedings in juvenile courts, its expression of disenchantment with juvenile justice has had a wide effect on the entire juvenile justice system (*Kent v. United States*, 1966).

The most famous case in the history of juvenile justice is the *Gault* decision, an attack on the *parens patriae* doctrine. This case is almost solely responsible for changing the juvenile justice system into an adversarial process, bringing it closer to the adult system. The Supreme

---

CASE IN POINT 14-1

CASE IN POINT: IN RE GAULT (1967)

The case of *In re Gault* involved 15-year-old Gerald Gault and his friend, who made lewd telephone calls to a neighbor. After a complaint by that neighbor, Gault was arrested and detained by the police. His parents, worried that their son was not at home, were never notified of his arrest and only found out later through a friend of his. The complainant, Mrs. Cook, never testified about the phone calls. No one was sworn in, and the trial was not recorded. After proceedings before a juvenile court judge, Gault was committed to the State Industrial School for 6 years, until he reached the age of 21. An adult charged with the same crime would have received a maximum of a 50 dollar fine and 2 months in jail.

The Supreme Court decided that the proceedings for juveniles have to comply with the requirements of the Fourteenth Amendment, including adequate notice of charges, notification of both the parents and the child of the minor's right to counsel, the opportunity for confrontation and cross-examination at the hearings, and adequate safeguards against self-incrimination. The Court found that the procedures used in this case met none of these requirements.

Importance

1. *In re Gault* is the most significant case in juvenile justice history. The Court established that minors do have certain due process rights. *In re Gault* changed the adjudication procedure into an adversarial process and opened the door for youth to be treated more formally and increasingly more like adults within the criminal justice system.

Court stated that due process and the Fourteenth Amendment of the U.S. Constitution apply to juveniles when the individual faces possible commitment to a justice facility.

The Juvenile Justice Standards Project developed a set of standards for juvenile justice after the Gault decision (Sobie & Elliott, 2014). Rejecting the conventional medical model based on a need for treatment as the reason for the court's involvement, it adopted a due process model governed by equity and fairness. Several principles were developed, including a greater accountability of the juvenile justice system and clearly stated and enforced rights and responsibilities of the appropriate agencies. Ten core principles emerged, known as the *Institute of Judicial Administration-American Bar Association* (IJA-ABA) *Juvenile Justice Standards* (Sobie & Elliott, 2014):

1. Sanctions should be proportionated to the seriousness of the offense.
2. Sentences should be fixed by the court and there should be no indeterminate sentencing by correctional authorities.
3. The least restrictive alternative should be required at every stage of the proceedings.
4. Status offenses should be removed from juvenile court jurisdiction.
5. Limitations should be imposed on interventions before adjudication.
6. Public hearing proceedings should replace closed sessions.
7. The juvenile should have part in the decision-making process.
8. The parental role in the process should be defined.
9. There should be a right to counsel at all crucial stages and a right to counsel for juveniles which cannot be waived.
10. Strict criteria should be established for waiving juvenile court jurisdiction to regulate the transfer of juveniles to adult court.

This due process approach dominates the justice system for youth. Rather than consistency, however, we now have a different juvenile justice system in every state in the nation. The system increasingly resembles the adult justice system, but no uniform approach has been adopted. The due process model favors accountability and punishment, with much less focus on juvenile rehabilitation.

The legal trend toward the punishment of juveniles as adults for felony crimes is still dominant; the extent varies from state to state. All jurisdictions specify circumstances in which juveniles may be prosecuted as adults. There is no national database to track the number of juvenile cases waived to adult criminal courts. In 45 states there is some form of judicial waiver law in which certain categories of cases may be considered for a waiver, generally at the discretion of the prosecutor (Griffin, Addie, Adams, & Firestine, 2011). In 34 states, once a juvenile has been tried as an adult, they are always considered an adult for additional future offenses (Griffin et al., 2011). Over the last 20 years emerging knowledge about adolescent brain development is slowly swinging policy back toward differential treatment and protection of young people who commit a crime.

BEEN THERE . . . DONE THAT! 14-1

Like other typical 7-year-old boys, Michael and Stephen frequently took turns spending the night at each other's house. The boys, I learned, performed anal and oral sex on each other. The sex had occurred on at least a dozen occasions. I interviewed them to determine who had been victimized by whom.

It was Michael who had initiated the sex; he had been doing it with his stepbrother, Jerry, every night for about a year. Jerry was 16 years old and had come to live with Michael and his parents. They shared a room with bunk beds, and Jerry would come down from his bunk bed at night to have sex with Michael. Jerry was a special education student who had both physical and learning disabilities.

Who is the perpetrator here? Is there more than one? Is the perpetrator a juvenile or an adult?

In 2005, the Supreme Court recognized the evolving information about the adolescent development and banned the death sentence for youth who were under the age of 18 at the time of the crime (*Roper v. Simmons*). The growing influence of research on the Supreme Court was again evidenced in 2010 in *Graham v. Florida* when the Court limited the use of life without parole for juveniles in nonhomicide cases. The issue of life in prison without parole was revisited in *Miller v. Alabama* (2012) when the Court held that a minor convicted of a homicide offense could not be sentenced to life in prison without parole absent consideration of the youth's juvenile's particular circumstances. After the *Miller* decision, the question was raised on whether its holding is retroactive to young offenders whose convictions and sentences were final prior to 2012. In *Montgomery v. Louisiana* (2016), the Court underscored the importance of the principle at the heart of the earlier opinions, that "children are different." It announced that *Miller* created a substantive rule of constitutional law, announcing that the *Miller* decision was retroactive. Adolescents, the Court said, deserve to have a meaningful opportunity for reform and a chance to demonstrate that they have matured and changed.

At the same time, there is an increasing concern over the vulnerability of juveniles interrogated when suspected of criminal conduct. Studies indicate that youthful offenders are among those particularly susceptible to police interrogation techniques that may lead to false confessions (Arndorfer et al., 2015). Examples of at-risk persons include the young, people with low or borderline IQ, some mental disabilities, illiteracy, or fatigue or who lack experience with the criminal justice system. The questioning approach for juveniles requires both attention to due process issues and the recognition that they need special protections because of their age.

QUESTIONING A JUVENILE NOT IN CUSTODY

Juveniles can be approached informally and asked questions without a parent present or *Miranda* warnings (*Miranda v. Arizona*, 1966). It should not be overlooked that every police encounter is not adversarial or accusatory. As illustrated in Figure 14-3, young people may also need protection. It should be standard procedure that when a police officer responds to a home, particularly for domestic disputes, each child in the home be interviewed separately at the scene. The reason is to assess the safety of the child and to obtain information on the crime under investigation. In the investigation of crime, it is legitimate to seek witnesses of any age.

FIGURE 14-3 Young people can be approached informally since every police encounter is not adversarial or accusatory.

Source: Threerocksimages/Shutterstock.

Juveniles may also be questioned about a complaint. There is a significant amount of police discretion on how a matter will be resolved. To settle a complaint, a police officer will likely speak to the juvenile during an encounter. The *National Training and Technical Assistance Center* offers the following 10 strategies to improve law enforcement interactions with youth (IACP & OJJDP, 2015). (Reprinted from The Effects of Adolescent Development on Policing Copyright held by the International Association of Chiefs of Police, Inc, 44 Canal Center Plaza, Suite 200, Alexandria, VA 22314):

1. Approach youth with a calm demeanor, conveying that you are there to help them.
2. Establish rapport.
3. Be patient.
4. Model the respect you expect in return.
5. Use age-appropriate language.
6. Repeat or paraphrase their statements. Affirm their emotions.
7. Take caution with nonverbal communication.
8. Model and praise calm confidence.
9. Empower them through choices.
10. Serve as a positive adult role model.

For nuisance behavior complaints there are usually people who can provide information about what happened. Examples include situations in which a child is accused of stealing, a fight broke out, or a school called to report a student who did not attend. The police officer asks people what happened, including the juvenile who was involved, and the matter quickly may be resolved if it is a minor violation or a status offense. Possible resolutions include calling a parent or guardian to pick up the child along with a warning or a school sanction. If the event is serious or the juvenile is a repeat offender, then a minor probation officer might also be contacted. A summons to juvenile court is requested by the police officer or school official if court involvement is warranted.

Avoid interviewing the juvenile in a public place where he or she can be seen, which would make them more liable to be embarrassed or angered. A minor interviewed on the street is mindful that someone may be watching, which may cause the young person to

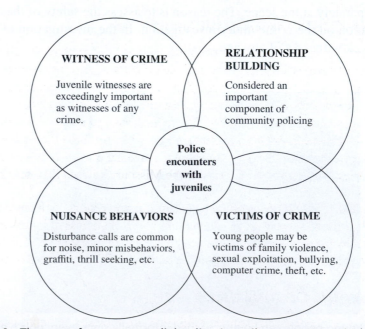

FIGURE 14-4   There are four noncustodial police–juvenile encounters which occur frequently and that are handled informally. *Miranda* warnings are not needed for informal encounters.

BEEN THERE . . . DONE THAT! 14-2

Fifteen-year-old Alice vanished from her home one afternoon. No one knew what happened to her until her body washed up on the bank of the river a week later with something tied around her neck. A canvas of the neighborhood brought no information until two 12-year-old boys claimed that they knew what had happened. I was called in to interview the boys before their statements could be contaminated.

Each boy claimed that he had seen Alice get into a really "hot car" with two boys. She was not forced into the car but got into the front seat between the driver and the passenger. The youngsters had seen the boys around, but neither boy knew who they were. The boys did not look at the two boys in the car and could not describe them in any detail. What they did notice was the car. Armed with my drawing equipment, I asked each boy to draw me a picture of the car and explain to me why it was so hot. What came out of that was a particular car with custom dual tailpipes. From their description, we found the car and identified the driver.

The driver of the car was a 17-year-old, and his passenger was a 16-year-old. They confessed to me and two other interrogators that they had taken their friend Alice for a ride. At the riverbank, they demanded sex. She said no. Angry, the 17-year-old took off his sock and tied it around her neck. She was kicking and scratching as they took her by the arms and legs and threw her into the river alive. They also told me that they were her friends. Concerned that Alice would tell on them they had thrown her into the river.

be overly cautious of what he or she says. Give the juvenile some privacy; even stepping inside a store or around a corner may be of benefit. A sign that this is a problem is evident when the juvenile keeps looking around rather than focusing on the police officer. Further investigation occurs if the offense is serious or the juvenile does not give information about his or her involvement and does not help in the resolution of the complaint. The juvenile may be detained for a short period until the matter is resolved or a legal guardian is available to come to the station to pick him or her up. The investigation allows the officer the opportunity to get background information on the young person and collect evidence if warranted. The officer should have experience in dealing with juvenile offenders and be aware of the possible dispositions available in that jurisdiction.

PROTECTIVE CUSTODY OF JUVENILES

A police officer may take a child into **protective custody**, typically for 24 to 48 hours without a warrant if there is an emergency or if the officer has reason to believe that leaving the child in the present situation would subject the child to further abuse or harm. The right to take a child into protective custody without the consent of the parents or legal guardian without a hearing is allowed under state welfare regulations and codes. Child maltreatment, abandonment, the child's inability to protect himself or herself, and the parental refusal of needed medical care are reasons police might take a juvenile into custody that would not be considered an arrest. An example comes from the Missouri Revised Statutes (2016):

§211 sec. 210.125. 1. A police officer, law enforcement official, or a physician who has reasonable cause to suspect that a child is suffering from illness or injury or is in danger of personal harm by reason of his surroundings and that a case of child abuse or neglect exists, may request that the juvenile officer take the child into protective custody.

INTERROGATION OF JUVENILES

Youth have a lower capacity for self-regulation in emotionally charged contexts, such as interviews or interrogations. They are more susceptible to manipulation and coercion than adults. Law enforcement can reduce the likelihood of juvenile false confessions using a variety of age-appropriate techniques. Results of a 2013 University of Virginia study by Todd Warner suggest limiting lengthy and manipulative techniques and exploring alternative methods of questioning juveniles. In a 2014 interview, Warner makes several recommendations for improving juvenile interrogations (Warner, 2014). Officers should receive training in adolescent brain development to gain a better understanding of how they think and rationalize differently from adults. He further suggests that interrogations should not include fabricated evidence or other forms of deceit to exploit the vulnerabilities of the developing brain. All interrogations should be videotaped to protect the integrity of the evidence. Current lie-detection techniques should not be used because many studies show that attempts to determine whether someone is lying based on eye contact and body language are wrong half the time. "Other methods work better," Warner said, "such as using techniques that increase cognitive load, including having a suspect tell what happened in reverse order." Warner also recommends that social scientists work more closely with police departments and officers to improve the interrogation process rather than simply being critical of current methods.

Questioning a juvenile at his or her home should be avoided if he or she is suspected of wrongdoing. It is not unusual for a minor to be fearful of how a parent will react to bad behavior or criminal involvement. Avoid contacting the juvenile at school and only remove the child from school as a last resort. Be sure that the parents are notified if the child is withdrawn from school. Involving the school tends to stigmatize the juvenile, regardless of the outcome of an interview.

The officer conducting the questioning should have a general understanding of the developmental stages of children. More important, the police officer should feel comfortable with young people, and be willing to speak to whatever level is necessary to put the child at ease. Be mindful that an interrogation without custody means NO custody. The suspect must be acutely aware that he or she is free to go and is not under arrest. The atmosphere should not be adversarial or lead the suspect to believe that he or she is not free to stop the questioning. Factors that affect the issue of custody includes the following:

- Early-morning or late-evening demands to report to the police station
- An interrogation in which the juvenile is not appropriately clothed or is denied food or water
- The absence of any offer to take a break
- Promises to let the suspect go only if a confession is provided

If possible, a parent or guardian should be contacted and requested to bring the young person to the place of questioning. The situation should not be discussed on the telephone, necessitating a personal interview with the child and parent or guardian. Providing the juvenile his or her rights per *Miranda* occurs under the same conditions as with adults; custody and interrogation remain the controlling factors. To obtain a complete and accurate report from the juvenile, avoid alienating him or her. Do not lose your temper, and stay away from a tough-guy attitude. Coercive practices may push an innocent but frightened or emotionally troubled child to confess.

If a juvenile has been arrested on probable cause, the parent or guardian must be contacted along with any other person required by statute. The questioning of juvenile suspects raises legal issues that could have a bearing on the admissibility of any confession made by the juvenile in custody. In addition to federal doctrine, each state has standards for a youth waiver to be considered valid. A legal determination of voluntariness does not depend on youthfulness alone, but it is a major factor. When questioning a minor a substantial break should occur in about 1 hour, and an interrogation should never last more than 4 hours (IACP & OJJDP, 2012).

Experts tell us that the rate of juvenile false confessions is unknown and there is no evidence to indicate that they occur anywhere near the majority of police interrogations

(Cleary, 2017). Instead, according to Cleary, evidence suggests that a small but significant minority of innocent people confess under interrogation. The probability that any particular interrogation, among the numerous interrogations conducted daily among 18,000 law enforcement agencies across the United States, will result in a false confession is quite low.

There is a national movement toward the requirement of recording confessions for both adult and juvenile offenders (refer to Chapter 12). While the practice of police recording of interrogations is mandated in 22 states, some states specifically require the recording of all interrogations involving juvenile offenders according to the National Association of Criminal Defense Lawyers (2014).

Custody Determination

The determination of whether a juvenile is "in custody" for *Miranda* warnings changed significantly in 2011. In *J.D.B. v. North Carolina*, the U.S. Supreme Court considered the case of a 13-year-old middle-school student who was removed from class and interrogated about burglaries by four adults. The interrogators included a police investigator and a uniformed school resource officer and took place in a closed-door conference room. The Court in 2011 held that the test for determining whether or not a juvenile suspect would have felt free to terminate a police interrogation, which is the test for determining "custody" for *Miranda* purposes, must be evaluated through the lens of a *reasonable juvenile*, rather than a reasonable adult.

> The Supreme Court saw no need to "blind themselves to the common-sense reality" that children "will often feel bound to submit to police questioning" when an adult would not, ultimately holding that a police officer must consider a suspect's age when weighing whether he is in custody and entitled to *Miranda* warnings. (*Id.* at 2399–400)

Miranda warnings are specifically designed to protect the individual against the coercive nature of custodial interrogation. As such, they are required when a person is "in custody." To assess whether a person is in custody, courts look at two points: First, what were the circumstances surrounding the interrogation; and second, given those circumstances, would a reasonable person have felt he or she was at liberty to terminate the interrogation and leave. Now, under the totality of the circumstances, a reasonable juvenile in defendant's position would have believed he was under formal arrest or was restrained in his movement to the degree associated with a formal arrest.

Miranda Warnings

The International Association of Chiefs of Police (IACP), in conjunction with the Office of Juvenile Justice and Delinquency Prevention (OJJDP), published a best practice guide to juvenile interviewing and interrogating (IACP & OJJDP, 2012) (Reprinted from IACP's Model Policy on Interview and Interrogation of Juveniles Copyright held by the International Association of Chiefs of Police, Inc, 44 Canal Center Plaza, Suite 200, Alexandria, VA 22314). On *Miranda* warnings, the guide offers proposed language in administering the rights, including a requirement to inform young suspects of the possible adult criminal consequences of the crime (pg. 33):

IACP's Model Policy on Interview and Interrogation of Juveniles

1. You have the right to remain silent. That means you do not have to say anything.
2. Anything you say can be used against you in court.
3. You have the right to get help from a lawyer right now.
4. If you cannot pay a lawyer, we will get you one here for free.
5. You have the right to stop this interview at any time.

6. Do you want to talk to me?

7. Do you want to have a lawyer with you while you talk to me?

Prompt Presentation

In addition to voluntariness, the courts have considered the statutory requirement of a prompt presentment (taking the juvenile before the judge or magistrate) in connection with the admissibility of confessions. State codes provide similar requirements to the following federal provision (Title 18 U.S.C. §5033):

> The juvenile shall be taken before a magistrate forthwith. In no event shall the juvenile be detained for longer than a reasonable period before being brought before a judge.

Similar to the McNabb-Mallory rule for adults, some courts have held confessions obtained during a delay in presenting the juvenile before the court to be inadmissible. Factors used in deciding when the federal provision has been violated include a focus on the "forthwith" language, and some courts rely on the phrase "a reasonable period."

What is considered a reasonable time in which to bring a juvenile before the court for arraignment after an arrest? The Second Circuit held that a delay between a 10:15 A.M. arrest and a 3:00 P.M. presentment was reasonable under the circumstances (*U.S. v. Smith*, 1978). The Ninth Circuit held that a valid waiver of *Miranda* rights also constitutes a waiver of prompt presentment rights (*U.S. v. Indian Boy X*, 1978). Because of the different approaches to this issue, it is essential to consult the law in your jurisdiction and the requirements under your state law.

FOURTH AMENDMENT CONSIDERATIONS

The Fourth Amendment to the Constitution protects citizens from unreasonable search and seizure. The exclusionary rule that prohibits the use in court of any evidence seized illegally was applied to the states in 1961 (*Mapp v. Ohio*, 1961). These same protections against unreasonable search and seizure as well as the remedy of exclusion apply to police action involving juveniles.

The landmark Supreme Court cases that focused on unreasonable search and seizure issues regarding juveniles referred to disputes on the actions of school officials but expressly included police conduct. For example, in *New Jersey v. T.L.O.* (1985) the Court stated as follows:

> The Fourth Amendment's prohibition on unreasonable searches and seizures applies to searches conducted by public school officials and is not limited to searches carried out by law enforcement officers. Nor are school officials exempt from the Amendment's dictates by virtue of the special nature of their authority over students. In carrying out searches and other functions under disciplinary policies mandated by state statutes, school officials act as representatives of the State, not merely as surrogates for the parents of students, and they cannot claim the parents' immunity from the Fourth Amendment's strictures.

The language in state courts has made the specific application of Fourth Amendment protections to juvenile cases a bit clearer. In New Jersey, a Superior Court held as follows in *State v. Lowry* (1967):

> Is it not more outrageous for the police to treat children more harshly than adult offenders, especially when such is violative of due process and fair treatment? Can a court countenance a system, where, as here, an adult may suppress evidence with the usual effect of having the charges dropped for lack of

proof, and on the other hand, a juvenile can be institutionalized for "rehabili-tative" purposes because the Fourth Amendment right is unavailable to him?

FIFTH AMENDMENT CONSIDERATIONS

A juvenile suspected of committing a crime has a privilege against self-incrimination (In re Gault, 1967). A juvenile may waive his or her Fifth Amendment rights and con-sent to interrogation (*Fare v. Michael C.*, 1979). The relinquishment of a right is vol-untary when it is the product of a free and deliberate choice rather than intimidation, coercion, or deception (*Moran v. Burbine*, 1986). A determination on whether the juvenile's waiver is voluntary and knowing needs to be resolved based on the totality of the circumstances surrounding the interrogation.

The court must determine not only that the statements were not coerced or sug-gested but also that they were not the products of ignorance of these rights of fantasy, fright, or despair. A juvenile's waiver of *Miranda* rights will always be suspect if given without the advice of a parent or adult guardian. The presence of a parent or guardian is not required for a voluntary waiver under the federal standard, although it is a factor to be considered. Some states do require that a waiver is made by an interested adult for the juvenile waiver to be valid. Among the factors to be considered are the following:

- The minor's age
- His or her experience with the criminal justice system
- His or her level of education
- His or her background
- His or her level of intelligence
- Whether he or she has the capacity to understand the warning
- The nature of the juvenile's Fifth Amendment rights
- The consequences of waiving those rights

THE RIGHT TO COUNSEL

The difference between the Fifth and Sixth Amendment rights to counsel deserves emphasis. The Fifth Amendment right applies during all custodial interrogations. The Sixth Amendment right is not triggered by custody but by the initiation of adversary judi-cial proceedings. These begin when a formal charge is filed (*Rhode Island v. Innis*, 1980).

BEEN THERE . . . DONE THAT! 14-3

A homicide occurred in an otherwise quiet neighborhood. A 15-year-old girl was bludgeoned to death in the woods on her way to school. There was no apparent sexual offense, although her skirt had been raised up to her waist.

The investigation pointed toward a 15-year-old boy who had recently fallen for the girl but had been rebuked. At the home of the boy, his mother admitted the police into the house. She permitted a search of her son's bedroom. In most situations, a parent can give consent to a search of his or her home and the space that is occupied by a minor in it. Only when the child has a heightened expectation of privacy due to his or her age, the fact that he or she pays rent, or the presence of a lock on the door that does not allow access by other fam-ily members do the parents lose their standing to consent to a search. These conditions vary from state to state. A sneaker was found that appeared to have a blood stain, and it was confiscated.

At the time the law specified that a child in this state could not be tried as an adult unless it could be shown that he or she was not "amenable to treatment." In other words, the prosecution had to prove that the minor had been in treatment before the offense and could not be rehabilitated. This juvenile had never been arrested before, not even for shoplifting. He was tried as a minor and found to be delinquent. At age 18 years he would be released.

The landmark case *In re Gault* (1967) firmly established the right to counsel for juveniles during custodial interrogation. That right does not refer to a probation officer, parent, or another interested adult. A waiver of the assistance of counsel in a majority of states is required by both the juvenile and a parent when the suspect under interrogation is younger than age 14 years. States may require consultation with an adult for a waiver of counsel to be valid. Other states require the "opportunity" for consultation with an adult after age 14 years, and whether that consultation actually occurs is immaterial. Several states prohibit or limit waiver of counsel by juveniles; those that permit it require proof that the juvenile understands the meaning and consequences of a waiver or that the waiver was granted only after a minor consulted with parents or guardians.

The Sixth Amendment protects the right to the assistance of a defense counsel (*Gideon v. Wainwright*, 1963), and applies only "at or after the initiation of adversary judicial criminal proceedings" (*Kirby v. Illinois*, 1972). Once adversary proceedings have begun, a defendant may not be interrogated in the absence of counsel nor be induced into making incriminating statements unless he or she initiates further interrogation and freely waives the Fifth and Sixth Amendment rights. After the Sixth Amendment right to counsel applies and is invoked, any statements obtained from the accused during subsequent *police-initiated* custodial questioning regarding the charge (even if the defendant waives his or her rights) are inadmissible. Police officers are not prohibited from interrogating a juvenile about uncharged crimes following his or her valid waiver under *Miranda* of his right to counsel just because he or she previously appeared with an attorney at a judicial proceeding on an unrelated offense.

The right to effective assistance of counsel has been acknowledged to apply to juveniles (*Stickland v. Washington*, 1984). Some but not all states require appointment of a lawyer at all stages of the juvenile proceedings (Jones, 2004).

DELINQUENT BEHAVIORS

The majority of victims of violence committed by juveniles are also juveniles, as depicted in Figure 14-5. Almost half of the victims of nonfatal violent crimes know the offender. From the *Juvenile Court Statistics 2014* compendium, recent statistics on cases involving young people are available (Hockenberry & Puzzanchera, 2017). Between 1960 and 2014, juvenile court delinquency caseloads more than doubled (141%). Over 31 million youth were under juvenile court jurisdiction in 2014; of these youth, 79 percent were between the ages of 10 and 15, 12 percent were age 16, and 9 percent were age 17. The small ratio of 16- and 17-year-olds among the juvenile court population is related to the upper age of juvenile court jurisdiction, which varies by state. In 2014, youth age 16 were under the original jurisdiction of the criminal court in 2 states, as were youth age 17 in an additional 8 states. Additionally, across all age groups and offense categories, case rates for males exceed rates for females; however, rates for both has declined substantially in the past 10 years.

Juvenile Fire Setting

Arson is the crime most frequently committed by juveniles. In 2014, juveniles younger than 16 accounted for three-quarters (77%) of juvenile arson cases (Hockenberry & Puzzanchera, 2017). If the child is untreated, the probability that he or she will set another fire is greater than 80 percent (Liscio, 1999). The problem of juvenile arson is staggering. In 2011, juveniles accounted for 41 percent of all arson arrests (Campbell, 2014a). The Uniform Crime Reporting Program defines arson as "any willful or malicious burning

FIGURE 14-5   Youthful victims of violence have often been targets of other juveniles.
Source: Twin Design/Shutterstock.

or attempt to burn, with or without intent to defraud, a dwelling house, public building, motor vehicle or aircraft, personal property of another."

A distinction is made between fireplay and intentional fire setting, behaviors with different degrees of damage and intent. **Fireplay** results from curiosity about and fascination with fire, and is most common among children and adolescents; the damage caused is not maliciously inspired. Expressive fireplay suggests unresolved trauma or psychopathology. For example, a young victim of sexual abuse may intentionally set her bed on fire as an expressive means of controlling a situation in which she feels powerless. Between 2007 and 2011, an average of 49,300 fires per year involving play was reported to U.S. municipal fire departments (Campbell, 2014a). These fires resulting from play each year claimed the lives of approximately 80 civilians, caused 860 civilian injuries, and $235 million in property damage each year (Campbell, 2014a).

Intentional fire setting is voluntary action with a higher level of intent to use fire as a weapon and an instrument of power; it is intended to achieve a goal. During 2007–2011, an estimated 282,600 intentional fires were reported to U.S. fire departments each year, with associated annual losses of 420 civilian deaths, 1,360 civilian injuries, and $1.3 billion in direct property damage (Campbell, 2014b). Intentional fire setting specifically includes a deliberate misuse of heat source or a fire of an incendiary nature. Figure 14-6 illustrates the horror of intentional firesetting.

An effective interview of the suspected juvenile may make the difference between an unsolved fire and one with the cause clearly established and the offender arrested (Zipper & Wilcox, 2005). There is give and take between the juvenile and the investigator in which the suspect tests to find out whether the real cause has been determined. The interrogator must go into the interview fully prepared with information from early witness interviews. Similar to other interview techniques, the investigator must first introduce himself or herself and describe the purpose of the interview. Rapport is then established, during which time an analysis of the suspect's living conditions can be determined. Allow the juvenile to give a complete narrative without interruption, using the information to determine follow-up questions. Closure occurs with a statement that there may be a need for a future interview. FEMA has suggested the following format be used when interrogating juveniles suspected of arson (IACP & OJJDP, 2012, pg. 33).

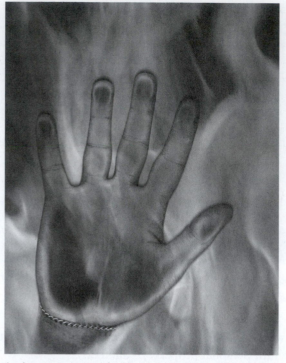

FIGURE 14-6   Arson is the crime most frequently committed by juveniles.
Source: rdegrie/iStock/Thinkstock/Getty Images.

FEMA's Juvenile Fire Setter Intervention Handbook

1. You do not have to talk with us or answer our questions if you do not want to.
2. If you decide to talk with us, you have to understand that anything you say can be used against you. We can tell the Probation Officer and the Judge what you tell us.
3. You can talk to a lawyer now if you want to and you can have him with you when we ask our questions.
4. If you want to have a lawyer, but you do not have enough money to hire your own, then we will get the judge to get one for you and it will not cost you anything.

Questions to consider during an interrogation of the juvenile firesetter include the following:

- What did you use to start this fire?
- Where did you get these lighters or matches?
- What did you set on fire?
- What did you do after you used the lighter or matches to get the fire started?
- How many others were involved? Who were they?
- How did you feel after you started the fire?
- Has anything happened lately that really bothers you?
- What have you set on fire in the past?

Sexual Offending

Sexual offenses committed by juveniles represent a serious problem. Almost one-fifth of rapes and one-half of all cases of child molestation involve youths under the age of 18 years (IACP, 2009). Studies indicate that male perpetrators are the most frequent sexual offenders; however, the rate of female sex offenders is believed to be highly underreported (ICCP, 2009). The Adam Walsh Child Protection and Safety Act of 2006 requires that law enforcement create, collect, and maintain separate registration and notification databases for juveniles convicted of sex crimes.

Significant challenges to the juvenile justice system, particularly law enforcement, are evidenced by the increasing number of cases involving juveniles who commit sex offenses. Information and research on juvenile sex offenders is hard to find. What is known is that the number of cases involving juvenile sex offenders has dramatically increased in recent years. Approximately 500,000 juveniles commit sex crimes each year (Jennings, Piquero, Zimring, & Reingle, 2015). The frequency of sexual offending among juveniles varies by community context (e.g., urban center, suburban, rural), ranging from 0.1 to 1 percent among females, and approximately 1.5–2 percent among males (Tracy, Wolfgang, & Figlio, 2013; Zimring, Piquero, & Jennings, 2007). Preadolescent children as young as 3 and 4 years old have been identified as being sexually aggressive, although the common age of onset appears to be between ages 6 and 9 years (Righthand & Welch, 2001). Early intervention is suggested as the most successful approach to rehabilitation for sexual offenders.

Polygraph tests may be an appropriate method for facilitating a complete disclosure of sexually abusive behavior by juveniles (Righthand & Welch, 2001). Juvenile sexual offenders are often victims as well, and structuring the interview or interrogation requires extreme sensitivity to that possibility. The process of getting ready for the interview is similar whether the juvenile is a victim or a known sexual abuse offender. Preparation includes the following:

- Obtain background information on the offense.
- Obtain a thorough background on the juvenile being questioned. For example, determine whether the child has ever been arrested or accused of a similar offense.
- Determine the living arrangements of the young person. Where and with whom does he or she live? Who is the legal or custodial guardian?
- Determine the age and grade level of the minor. Does he or she have a learning disability or a low functioning level?
- If the child is suspected of committing a sexual offense, is he or she a known victim?

If any of these preparation questions cannot be answered before the interview, the child should be asked about them directly. In some states, the interview of the juvenile will be conducted by social service workers as part of the criminal investigation and sometimes prior to police involvement. Sit with the parent or guardian and explain the juvenile's *Miranda* rights and ask for a waiver of these rights. It is not advisable to interview or interrogate an adolescent suspected of a sexual offense in the presence of a parent or guardian. If a voluntary waiver is obtained, then ask the adult to allow the questioning to proceed in private, if the youth is willing. Explain that it is difficult to speak about these issues and that they would benefit from the privacy. The six stages to interviewing a suspected juvenile sexual offender are as follows.

Step 1 **Introduction.** Explain who you are and why you are speaking with him or her. Establish credibility by telling the child that you frequently talk with people about things that have happened to children.

Step 2 **Rapport building.** This is an important step in the juvenile interrogation as well as an interview. Provide the juvenile with reasons that he or she should speak with you. Include the statement that the purpose of the interview is to learn the truth.

Step 3 **Background.** Explore information about the juvenile, including family composition, criminal history, and employment history. During this phase, you can obtain information about the functioning level of the juvenile. Determine his or her general educational level, linguistic comprehension, understanding of the process, and possible mental health issues. Verify the relationship of the victim to the offender and the circumstances under which access to the victim was gained. Obtain an understanding of the usual eye contact and body language behavior of the juvenile when discussing general topics.

Step 4 **Allegation.** Explain the allegation in very general terms. Do not use legal language or speak above the juvenile's level of understanding.

Puzzanchera, C., & Adams, B. (2013). *Juvenile Arrests 2010. Juvenile offenders and victims: National reports series.* Washington, D.C.: Office of Juvenile Justice & Delinquency Prevention.

Rhode Island v. Innis, 446 U.S. 291 (1980).

Righthand, S., & Welch, C. (2001). *Juveniles who have sexually offended* (Report No. NCJ 184739). Washington, D.C.: Office of Juvenile Justice and Delinquency Prevention.

Roper v. Simmons, 543 U.S. 551 (2005).

Sobie, M., & Elliott, J. D. (2014). The IJA-ABA Juvenile Justice Standards: Why full implementation is long overdue. *Crim. Just., 29*, 23.

State v. Lowry, 230 A.2d 907 (1967).

Stickland v. Washington, 466 U.S. 668 (1984).

Tracy, P. E., Wolfgang, M. E., & Figlio, R. M. (2013). Delinquency careers in two birth cohorts: *Springer Science & Business Media*.

U.S. Code 18 U.S.C. §5031 (1994).

U.S. v. Indian Boy X, 656 F.2d 585, 9th Cir. (1978).

U.S. v. Smith, 574 F.2d 707, 2d Cir. (1978).

Warner, T. (2014) Law and order for juveniles: U.VA. study urges altering police interrogation/Interviewer: F. Samarrai. *UVA Today*, University of Virginia.

Zang, A. (2016). *U.S. age boundaries of delinquency 2015*. Pittsburgh, PA: National Center for Juvenile Justice.

Zimring, F. E., Piquero, A. R., & Jennings, W. G. (2007). Sexual delinquency in Racine: Does early sex offending predict later sex offending in youth and young adulthood? *Criminology & Public Policy, 6*(3), 507–534.

Zipper, P., & Wilcox, D. (2005). Juvenile arson: The importance of early intervention. *FBI Law Enforcement Bulletin, 74* (4), 1–9.

INDEX